10 -

semiotext(e)

canadas

ba P

EDITOR: Jordan Zinovich
ASSOCIATE EDITORS: Carole Beaulieu
and Christof Mignone

semiotext(e) Canadas collective: Carole Beaulieu,
Herménégilde Chiasson, Leslie Dawn, Lorraine Gilbert,
Ron Hall, Brian Massumi, Christof Mignone,
Gail Valiskakis, Jordan Zinovich

translation editors: Carole Beaulieu,
Sylvère Lotringer, Christof Mignone,
Héléne Potter, Daniel Sloate

translators: Philip Beitchman, Ron Cawthorn,
Linda Dawe, Marc Drouin, Donald McGrath,
Daniel Sloate, Brigitte Ouvry-Vial

bp

canadas

semiotext(e) / marginal editions

Semiotext(e)
Editorial Offices:
522 Philosophy Hall, Columbia University, New York, NY 10027 USA
55 South Eleventh Street, Brooklyn, NY 11211-0568 USA
phone (718) 387-6471   fax (718) 963-2603

canadas bₐP

is Semiotext(e) #17
(Volume VI, Issue 2)
ISSN 0-093-95779
US ISBN 1-57027-013-9
Canadian ISBN 0-9698433-0-5

Semiotext(e) is a not-for-profit publication. The semiotext(e) CANADAs collective
gratefully acknowledges assistance from the Canada Council Explorations Program
juries for Ontario, the Northwest Territories, and Québec.

Special thanks to Jim Fleming, Adele Haft, Sylvère Lotringer, Benjamin Meyers, the
Bulldozer Collective, Sylvie Côté Chew and Avataq Cultural Institute—Tumivut Magazine, and all you folks who responded to the Pogo Poll. Also, the collective especially
wants to thank Lorraine Gilbert for her extraordinary treeplanting photo-essay,
only a small part of which we were able to use.

Layout and design by Jordan Zinovich

co-published with
Marginal Editions
277 George Street North
Peterborough, Ontario
CANADA K9J 3G9
phone/fax (705) 745-2326

Printed in USA, the Evil Empire

canadas bœp contents

1 STATIONS

2 TRACKS

3 SWITCHES

4 MONITORS

5 SIGNALS

GRAPHICS

The pieces listed below originally appeared in the following publications. All of them have been used with permission.

Milton Born With A Tooth, "Messenger of the River." From *Nativebeat*, June 1991, Volume 1, Number 10.

Jim Campbell, "The Litton Bombing: 10 Years Later." From *Prison News Service*, September / October 1992, Number 37.

Jim Campbell, "Riot Rocks Toronto." From *Prison News Service*, September / October 1991.

Joe David, "How to Become an Activist in One Easy Lesson." From *This Magazine*, Twenty-Fifth Anniversary Double Issue, Volume 25, Numbers 5 & 6.

Lorne Falk, "L is for Letting Go." Excerpted from the catalogue essay *Barcelone*, Calgary: Nickle Arts Museum, 1989.

William Gibson, "Machine Age Navigator." From *Illusions*, Winter 1992, Number 19.

Roy Glaremin, "Word From the Prisons, 1992." Originally appeared as "The state of things in Canadian Federal Prisons," *Prison News Service*, May / June 1992, Number 35.

Susanne de Lotbinière-Harwood, "The Body Bilingual." Adapted from *Re-Belle et Infidèle / The Body Bilingual*, Toronto: Women's Press, 1991.

Christof Mignone, "Sound Government: A Longitudinal Story of a Canada You Can't Touch." From *Ear Magazine*.

Miles Morriseau, "The Great Canadian Myth." From *Nativebeat*, June 1991, Volume 1, Number 10.

Bharati Mukherjee, "Mosaic? Why Not Fusion?" Excerpted from the transcript of *Bill Moyers World of Ideas*, air date June 3, 1990; show #218.

Ludger Müller-Wille (ed.), "Places and Names in Nunavik." From ᑐᕐᒃ / TUMIVUT, 3, 1992.

Joyce Nelson, "Speaking the Unspeakable: Understanding Ecofeminism." Originally appeared in *La Parole Métèque*.

Catherine Richards, "The Bioapparatus Membrane." From *Virtual Seminar on the Bioapparatus*, Banff: The Banff Centre, 1991.

Michel Serres, "Northwest Passage." From *Oasis*, Semiotext(e) Volume IV, Number 3, 1984.

Anthony Wilden, "Imaginary Canada: Stereotypes and Scapegoating." Adapted and extended from *The Imaginary Canadian: An Examination for Discovery (Authorized Pirate Edition)*, Vancouver: Pulp Press, 1984.

STATIONS

"There is never a single frontier between one nation-state and another, but always TWO. The frontier belonging to ... is at the ... customs post, and that belonging to ... is down the street a bit, at the ... customs post. The peculiarity of it all is that when you are between one customs post and the other, you are nowhere at all. And, having left one structure of conventions and sanctions in which your passport describes you as such and such a person, without yet having entered another similar structure, you are not only nowhere, you are also nobody. Because of the double frontier (opposition) which replaces the single one (distinction), for a few minutes you are really or potentially stateless, that is, STRUCTURELESS. In actual fact, of course, provided you bear suitable markers, you glide across a single boundary like a bit of information moving from one subsystem in the ecosystem to another."

– Anthony Wilden

NORTHWEST PASSAGE

The Northwest passage allows the Atlantic and Pacific oceans to communicate within the frigid environs of the Grand Canadian North. It opens and closes, twists itself throughout the huge archipelago along an incredibly complex labyrinth of gulfs and channels, pools and sounds, between Baffin and Banks. Aleatory distribution and strong regular constraints, disorder and laws. You enter through the Davis Strait, ending in the Beaufort Sea. From there, run over northern Alaska towards the Aleutians, Deliverance, you end up on the name of peace. For thirty years I have been navigating among these waters. They are almost deserted, forgotten as if forbidden. Two cultures are juxtaposed, two families, two collectivities speaking two different tongues. Those who have received a scientific formation have ever since childhood a tendency to exclude from their life, their thought, their everyday actions anything resembling history or art, works of language, works of time. Being educated but uncultivated, they are trained to forget humans, their relationships, their sufferings, trained to forget mortality. Those formed by letters are in turn thrown into what one conventionally calls the Human Sciences, where they lose the natural world forever: works without trees or sea, without clouds or earth except in dreams or dictionaries. Being cultivated but ignorant, they devote themselves to pointless squabble. All they have ever known takes the shape of bets, fetishes or goods. I fear these two groups may be contesting for belongings that have long ago been carried away by a third group; parasites, uncultivated and ignorant, this third group ordinates and administers the others, enjoying their division, nourishing their split.

I have been very lucky to remain alone for thirty years, working in the passage amidst indifference and silence. I stand in the empty intersection between the two groups whose cartography I try to narrate. I am not sure to be at the outlet. The passage is rarified and narrow. From the human to the exact sciences, or vice versa, the path does not lead through homogeneous open space. The metaphor of this extraordinarily complex archipelago designated within the Grand Canadian North is exact. Most of the time, the passage is closed either by lands or by ice, or also because one does get lost.

One usually simplifies by means of a forced choice: continued or discontinued, analysis or synthesis, God or the Devil, yes or no, with me or against me, from two things only one. Yet complexity signals itself in reality, while philosophical dualism calls for a final battle in which new thought dies and the object disappears. The misfortune comes from a simplification by arms. It is this social artifact that one must destroy if one wants to think. The other prejudices are weightless compared to this monstrous animal, stupidity. Yes, struggle is our first habit; it annihilates our intellectual awakening. Yes, thought has no other obstacle than hatred. The misfortune of thought always comes from thought itself.

– translated by Brigitte Ouvry-Vial.

LORNE FALK

THE BORDER PRISM

Visualize the border as a colossal, two-sided, mirror-like screen on which the endless spectacle of cultural differences is played.

A game-site for the aggressive linear movement, the border line inspects the spectator as a radical object and a cultural receptacle, and simultaneously stamps her/him as the figure of its xenophobic closure. But with the accelerated transmigration of peoples in contemporary society, it is becoming more difficult for the border spectator to be satisfied by a simple, unique act of identification with these subject positions. Not unlike the woman spectator watching a classic Hollywood film, the border spectator feels forced, but does not wish to associate with one of the two positions: the (male) cultural-racial-hero subject or the (female) obstacle-matrix-frontier Other.[1] The border spectator's identification therefore swings between the terms put into play by the border apparatus: the look of two cultures and their affirmations on the border, the subject and the object of the border gaze.[2]

The border spectator experiences a state of dislocation as s/he oscillates between activity and passivity—identifying simultaneously with the cultural subject and the political context of the border, as well as with the confrontational structure of the border line and its xenophobia. This double figural identification is an interactive, perceptual process that formalizes the border as a mental object in the mind of the border spectator. Thus, the edge of the border percept is widening; the old mirror is mutating into a many-sided prism...a border prism which diffracts the mental image of the border into a rainbow of many realities. Though the border apparatus continues to act like a two-sided mirror, cultural identification no longer behaves like a reflection. Here the theory of feminism offers insight into this behavior: "This manner of identification would uphold both the possibilities of desire, both active and passive aims; desire for the other, and desire to be desired by the other."[3]

For the people *who live in* border culture, this "manner of identification" is effervescent:

"There are many borders, too many. Some are mythical and others are too real. They exist in history, politics, language, and art, as well as in sexuality, geography, and dreams. Some are visible—barbed wire, pilgrimages of dogs and helicopters; others are invisible, between fear and fiction, between desire and reality.

Border culture is a project of 'redefinition' that conceives of the border not only as the limits of two countries, but also as a cardinal intersection of many realities. In this sense, the border is not an abyss that will have to save us from threatening otherness, but a place where the so-called otherness yields, becomes us, and therefore comprehensible."[4]

"Border culture includes a deep fear, the fear of being seen/caught/asked for identification. It also creates a space for resistance to this fear, a place from which to say, '*Soy indocumentado ...y que?*' Border culture can provide a '*cura*'. The fear of being seen is a fear so deep that many border dwellers choose to look away while police and 'good citizens' are on the look out for their 'undocumented' neighbours. Border culture is a strategy, a strategy for facing the fear, a will to deconstruct the language of representation, stereotypes, imitation and violence. The gaze that can look back at 'the *Migra*', the media, and the official cultures of both countries without fear is the multi-dimensional perspective. The '*espectador activo*' of border writing is the new deterritorialized Orpheus, who can look across the border into the Hell of the double, '*el otro lado*', and the 'horrifying vision', recognize it as her or himself, and stare back at it."[5]

If a new definition of the border would have cultures "on edge", constantly forming and dissolving one into the *other*, it is because the desire for cultural identity is shifting and unstable at the game-site of the old border narrative. And if the border spectator is searching there for an expression of cultural difference, then aspects of this shifting identity cannot be explained solely by what is stored in her/his racial memory. The presence of the multiple-other in the border prism provokes a recognition that it is possible to describe cultural differences differently. The border prism does not confront and polarize; more like the cognitive processes of memory or imagination, it is agnostic, participatory and paradoxical. In other words, the border prism represents the symbolic vision of a deterritorialized world.

Every day, this vision is explored on the border between Tijuana, Mexico and San Diego, California by Guillermo Gomez-Pena, Emily Hicks and their creative brothers and sisters at the Border Arts Workshop, through events such as performances, installations, videos, radio pieces, articles and poems in *La Linea Quebrada*,...through possible models that define a new cultural topography. Contrary to the two sided border narrative, these events describe the potential to transform not only the perception of cultural differences, but their place of storage as well. The border spectator thereby begins the painful process of transfiguration into a multicultural participant.

And then, considering that the text is another such (storage) place, the question arises: How can this transformative potential be represented in discursive formations?

One possibility is to have a circle of friends, each from a different country, decide to play a border event with rules of interactivity that are subject to eventual cancellation. The structure of their play is a game which children use to make decisions: "1-potato, 2-potato, 3-potato, 4; 5-potato, 6-potato, 7-potato, more." The event describes the possible moments of the border's transformation from a xenophobic prison to a living-culture prism.

1-Post-Modo

"For many artists, the great dilemma continues to be the continual loss of 'cultural identity', understood as a monolithic block of values, attitudes, and idiosyncrasies (national culture). For others this identity, when one has it, becomes an inconvenience. We who leave and do not question this identity become, ipso facto, escaped convicts of the 'national culture' (monoreality), migratory intellectuals, smugglers of ideas and cultural 'polleros'; and the journey, full of dangers and uncertainty, has been and continues to be our only certainty. Today we make art and literature in order to clarify the journey."⁶

This morning I woke up thinking I was back then. I wanted to visit you both and then I remembered the border that separated us, even if it wasn't true. I lay there, in a slipstream of border thoughts, wondering.

Words and images are given ingenious ways to cross borders: satellite transmissions, diplomatic immunity, Macdonald's restaurants, free trade agreements, and smuggling, to name a few. How is it that they so willfully cross borders, while bodies, the physical bodies, suffer such complex rites of passage for the right to cross? Detained, interrogated, stopped, turned back, harassed, poked and probed; the incessant, automated questions...there is a long lexicon of actions and interventions, most of them unpleasant, that stalk the border for bodies. The bodies put up with a lot at the border that many words and images never do.

I remember sitting in the back seat of the car, jammed between two stacks of *La Linea Quebrada*, listening to *"la Migra"* patronize you, Guillermo, for your Chicanization and you, Emily, for your Latin Americanization. When he turned his attention to me, I blocked his line of sight with my Canadian passport. He waved it off, as if to say, "Canadian...extra time for my coffee break." Only then, as an afterthought, did he query the silver boxes. You described their content but it meant nothing to him.

"What do Halloween and the Day of the Dead have in common? Superficially, a lot. Children in the U.S. and Tijuana dress up in costumes. Anthropologically, absolutely nothing. The first belongs to the domain of mass-entertainment, a pseudomacabre masquerade that since the sixties has been increasingly spiced with rock & roll, drugs, and hyper-realistic monster costumes. The latter is a centuries-old Indian pilgrimage devoted to the celebration of our dead beloved ones who come back to eat, dance, and talk with us. Images from the celebrations on one side of the border— eating a candy skull with one's own name on it—may appear macabre to a monocultural person on the other side of the border. Citizens of Mexico are horrified by reports of the poisoning of children in the U.S. during Halloween."⁷

"Mexico is sinking
California is on fire

& we are all getting burned
aren't we? we're just
a bunch of burning myths!"
- he begins to yell at the gringos
"but what if suddenly
the continent turned upside down?
what if the U.S. was Mexico?
what if 200,000 Anglo-Saxons
were to cross the border
each month
to work as gardeners, waiters,
3rd chair musicians, movie extras,
bouncers, babysitters, chauffers,
syndicated cartoons, feather-weight
boxers, fruit-pickers & anonymous poets?
what if they were called waspanos,
waspitos, wasperos or waspbacks?
what if we were the top dogs?
what if literature was life?
what if *yo* were you
& *tu fueras* I, Mister?"[8]

Your desire crossed to interact with mine and their mingling nurtured the awareness of my own deterritorialization. Suddenly, my journey took a new form and the mental image of this form was as clear as a prism: Guillermo, Emily, and I first crossed the Mexican-Canadian border together in Arlington, Texas.

It was as if we had crossed into a world of words and images without borders, or perhaps more honestly, into the symbolic maelstrom of border culture. Even so, here was a freedom more indelible than the one encoded in hamburgers and coca-cola, tortillas and tequila. Surely I could discriminate between these codes and the new ones that reside now, side by side, in the border of my memory.

E: When I was 6, I began my journey to the South. I was Mother Bear in *Los Tres Osos*. When you were 5, you began your journey to the North.

G: *¿A que te refieres?*

E: Your sister went to Canada. You loved her, so part of you went with her to another country.

G: Right.

E: What connotations did Canada, the North, have for you?

G: Many. Snow, Indians, prosperity, multi-coloured gardens and other visions conveyed by her postcards. Something similar happened to you. In California, as far as I know, you began listening at the dinner table to conversations about the house that your grandfather was building in Baja, somewhere between Loreto and Muleje. And you were fascinated by "the South." Which connotations did *"Baja"* have for you?

E: Beautiful, exciting and dangerous. The house was never finished because the floods kept washing away the adobe bricks. I never understood why the "house of the South" could be so unprotected.

G: How long did the "house in the South" exist in your mind?

E: It still exists. I must want to finish it.

G: Have you compared it with reality?

E: There is a real gap here. The reason I liked Mexico City (1972) was because it was like San Francisco."[9]

How long can we continue like this?

"*Si queremos sobrevivir el gran debate, necesitamos redisenar nuestro continente, proveerlo de nuevas arterias y pulmones, y reubicarnos dentro de el.* (If we want to survive the great debate, we need to redesign our continent, provide it with new arteries and lungs, and relocate ourselves within it.)"[10]

2-Post-Modo

This revolution was truly different. It was not about to be replaced quickly, in terms of social time, by another one. Its effects were truly long lasting: human life expectancy was extended.

What they did was turn the virulent AIDS virus into a life-sustaining, saprophytic agent. Instead of killing, it fed on the dead and pathologic organic matter that crossed its path—without discrimination.

Actually, "they" didn't do it at all. An accident with a plant was the catalyst. A carrier cosmonaut unwittingly exposed the virus to organic derivatives of the *mescale* button during an experiment concerning the effects of free fall conditions on hallucination. And "they" were the space-med people who later put the cosmonaut through standard reentry examination. Their tests found...nothing. She had no signs of disease; no pathological symptoms whatsoever; not one. Her AIDS virus had disappeared. Later, when they looked more carefully, they discovered that the virus had been genetically transfigured by *mescale* and had crossed the border into every cell in her body. It had become a new organelle, sandwiched in the cell's cytoplasm between the mitochondria and Golgi apparatus.

Then the Russians astonished everyone by sharing this discovery with the rest of the world. Yes. We had the potential to surprise ourselves that way, even then. That gesture was enough to change the way we think of each other—and much more. That year, a lot of borders were crossed for the first time.

The dramatic chain of events began in 1993. First, the plague was eliminated. Then the impact of indeterminate life expectancy hit home. A double-barrelled euphoria swept the world. Soon after, however, a rather odd depression set in: what were people going to do with all the new time? Religious leaders tried to regroup. Except for the United Nations, which experienced a renaissance, political bureaucracies disintegrated into chaos. Others worried about feeding a world population that would grow inexorably, with no aging-to-death cycle and no available means to colonize outer space to relieve the pressure. The revolution affected everyone. For a while, the world seemed suddenly, unbearably, claustrophobic.

Culture changed, too. Before the revolution, for example, art was a bizarre ontological exploration strung out between a rapidly expanding computer class, who were exploiting the potentials of electronic visualization events and inter-active life-styles, and a recalcitrant, neoconservative and historicist academy, largely controlled by the marketplace. The art world swam uncertainly in a theory soup and not a small part of it seemed poised to drown in nihilistic decadence. The promise of extended life expectancy swept all this cacophony aside. It was like stepping from a relentless heat, across an invisible line, into a cave's shaded calm.

People no longer needed imaginary signifiers to perma-press experience. The exhilaration of longevity quite literally replaced that beleaguered function of art. Many suffered severe cultural trauma—what was called "Artists in Deterritori-alized Shock" (with its then still-bitter acronym, AIDS). Art may have been liberated from itself and its vicious societal hegemonies, but it took time to adjust to the different game.

Of course we know now that it was not so traumatic for everyone. Prior to 1993, a provisional climate of receptivity was taking root and its makers crossed the border to the new world community with the celebratory spirit of the carnevalesque. These border artists were posing questions that would set the stage for the post-plague culture from which our own inter-racial culture-web was to form. Their ideas and questions, called post-critical discourse, seem archaic now; yet in them was a latent form of critique-mexique. Take these examples:

"In 1987, 'cultural identity' is a myth, and 'post-modernity' is nothing more than the proof that our traditions have fallen in ruins. What does exist is 'meta-multi-cultural identity', a perpetual displacement and continual deconstruction of values, images, and traditions. 'Cultural identity' is a changing hologram.

We 'awakened' artists of the world share certain fundamental interests, such as the desire to culturally decolonize our countries of origin and to contribute to the creation of new models of understanding the future. The collaborators of this second 'visual-linguistic object' share certain thematic interests: the exploration of concepts such as 'la partida', the encounter with cultural and political other-ness; the loss of identity, or better said, the access to what is transcultural; destruction of borders and therefore the creation of alternative cartographies; the instigation of strident criticism of the dominant culture, and finally, the proposition of new creative languages capable of broadening human liberties."[11]

"Several features distinguish border dwellers and their culture, that is, those who live within the border 'machine': 1) deterritorialization (physical, linguistic, cultural, political); 2) the connection of the individual to political immediacy (the inhabitant of the border does not have a self-determined 'subjectivity' in the traditional European sense but rather is asked for I.D./ refused medical service/ threatened with deportation and directly affected economically and politically by Mexico-U.S. relations); 3) the collective assemblage of enunciation: everything takes on a collective value. When one leaves her or his country or place of origin, everyday life changes. The objects which continually remind one of the past are gone. Nostalgia, or reterritorialization, begins."[12]

"Place yourself
in the lungs of the future
& from there, *bien afliado*
re-invent the entire continent
if necessary
turn it upside down
recuerda
contra cultura no hay antidoto"[13]

(Author's note: The practice of critique-mexique was widely adopted after 1993. It coincided with the sudden worldwide demand for the life-giving *mescale* buttons that proliferated in Mexico. The renewed interest in Mexican culture was just one of the revolution's many side effects that benefitted culture as a whole.)

3-Post-Modo

We are living in a social haze and it has a poor memory.

The stratosphere has been punctured by runaway pollution and things are leaking in and out. An imbalance in the whole system is evident. The Earth suffers amnesia; its metabolism rides the brink of irreversible shock. Soon, very soon, the planet will affect us in every way. But in the meantime, people seem totally bogged down in the social haze. Their memory is leaking away; their cultures are mutating. Cultural identity is characterized by a kind of insipid transience and people seem dislocated, like travellers on a journey of naive self-realization.

"we were born on the pavement
we were nursed on milk and Pepsi
we grew up dislocated
between Merida and New York
linked by cables and coconut palm trees
We admired the Mayans and the Rolling Stones
we seduced barefoot gringas
in pre-Cortesian stone slabs
we plotted revolutions

in recording studios
we practiced tantra and cinema
we gathered fragments from a thousand traditions
we re-arranged them at will
and from so much travelling
from north to south
from past to future
we lost the much-touted sense of time."[14]

To inhabit is to move constantly. In a fixed position, we are particularly vulnerable to the social haze. And constant movement is not avoiding the situation; it's a mental state in which working and living are inseparable. The citizen is a nomad; the artist is a nomad. When the citizen-artist becomes a nomad who has the confidence to go from one site to another, every resting place is home. Then we will begin to create new borders, borders that keep moving, like the nomad.

For now, culture has to be condensed to a form the individual can handle—a knapsack of meta-culture each of us can carry on our back. We have to decide whether we want to be light or heavy when we are on the move like this. Right now, this meta-culture needs to be quite light.

> "The Spanish-speaking agent asked to see my purse. I was carrying a portable altar. As soon as he opened it, he hesitated. He was unnerved by the handmade doll, photographs, chilis, 'milagros', stones, dice, gold chains, white plastic doll's shoe, currency from several countries, beads, and the business card from Botanica Ochun in Los Angeles. He spent less than thirty seconds looking at the altar and shut it very respectfully. He then proceeded to allow me into the country."[15]

4

Dear metainvestigador canadiense.

Flying back from Frisco to the border, a little drunk and overworked.

Art lost its philosophical meaning when my troubled country entered the second Circle of Deterrence. That was in 1988, I believe, and I became a partisan of the Border Resistance League (BRL).

The psychotropic empathy between me and my audience has long been broken. My biconsciousness is fractured and all I can do is recall a series of impressions. Fragments of memories and issues. Disjointed symbols of sorts. I see myself performing on the ruins of our continental postmodernity. Québec and Tijuana are, for the moment, the only margins of my uncertainty. A saber:

- recapitulate the relation between the artist and critic/institution and space/metiers and media/sexuality and politics.
- the Québécois experience vs. the Chicano experience. A film.

- the need to come to terms with cultural otherness—the number one priority for contemporary U.S. intellectuals.
- the *"flaneur flambé"*: a performance piece at *Cambro de tinta nuevamente*...the Tijuana Cathedral.
- shift the east/west axis of thought and dialogue to the north/south one. You go to Venezuela. We go to Québec. The border is not an historical abyss: "to arrive my dear friends, is just an illusion."
- performance art as a "living border archaeology".
- the importance of being trilingual. Spanish. French. English. Political praxis in the nineties.

I have information that the INS are setting up detention camps for bilingual people, but I'm still learning French via cybervision. Tomorrow in Philadelphia. My job is to remind them that there are other ways to socialize/humanize the artistic process.[16]

5-Post-Modo

Dear Emily & Guillermo,

Responses to your performance:

/Mother of Spain fanning/ Chevy/
/A bride gestures with her foot/ Avant-garde/
/The first resurrection/ Earthquake victims/
/Black cloth genital trick/ Wrestler/
/Mask Peel/ Diablo/
/The second chair/ Indian image/
/"Sit down, General"/ Bloody hamburger/
/Washing feet/ Midget/
/Shoot/ Madonna/
Blank
Blank
Blank
/The third chair/ *La frontera*/
/Drunk/ CRAK!/
/Low rider/ Topographic arrow/
/Dress up rap/ Clint/
/Freeze/ INS/
/Cool rap/ Chopper/
/Freeze/ Scorpion/
/English/ Reagan mask/
/Knife dance/ Three Chicano boys/
/Fast rap/ Black out/
Rock & roll
/Ascendent bride with a wrestler's mask/ Third world chopper/
Documented/ *Incomuentado*/

The punked out Mother of Spain, the suave Colombian drug smuggler, the Latin American General, the waitress in an artists' cafe, the low rider, the wrestler bride, the aligned intellectual...laughing, weeping, dancing, smoking, dreaming, loving, dying, a carnival of *espectadores activos* who have come to watch us cross the border. Everything else is historical foreplay; a cultural activism decapitated. The performers are the question marks, the death masks that scratch the surface of the border, looking for eyes that see the Hell of the double.

> are you looking for the camera?
> or the fast forward button?
> and who indoctrinated that one?
> and what kind of freedom
> has this one lost?
> look
> on the border
> a *flaneur flambé*
> stinking of modern perfume
> burns
> and look
> there's a floating white boy
> confronted by a language cornucopia
> crossing the border
> with eyes turned back
> as if he has walked
> backward
> all his life
> when he turns
> around
> will he recognize
> what it is
> the other sees?

I asked, "You live in the border. How far is it across?"
You said, "My heart is broken, my consciousness is ruptured, my wounds are open."

6-Post-Modo

"From cultural anthropology we have learned that meaning is culturally specific. For example, 'Mexican' does not have universal connotative meanings. This term, linked to 'undocumented workers' in the U.S.-Mexico border region, might be linked to 'exotic' in the context of a literary salon in Paris. Border semiotics is the study of codes in a border region."

The cultural codes of a person living in Tijuana and working in San Diego may actually be overdetermined by U.S. cultural codes, Tijuana cultural codes, and the cultural codes of that person's village in Oaxaca. For example, at the same time that a maid is learning to shop in a U.S. supermarket, she may be remembering with nostalgia the marketplace in the town where she was raised, and, during the same day, when she returns to Tijuana after work, she will cross the border to shop in Cali-max, a hybrid of the two.

Certain oppositions are more important on one side of the border than the other. For example, the female-male is important for Anglo feminists, while documented-undocumented is of greater importance for both men and women crossing the border. The decoding of a border image depends on knowledge of conflicting codes.[17]

"We are almost at the intersection of Border Field Park & *Playas de Tijuana,* northernmost point of Latin America/ westernmost point of *La Frontera.* Soon this place might become the very end of western civilization & the epicenter of a new cultural spiral.

> Today, October 12, 1986, we face the Pacific with eyes filled with doubt.
> Will Christopher Columbus come back to rediscover us?
> Will Quetzalcoatl return instead to head a human rights commission?
> Will the '*migra*' & the marines intervene?
> Will art prove once more the artificiality of the border?
> Will the media understand what we are doing?"[18]

"The U.S. wrestlers were big, nasty, flamboyant and comically hyper. They appeared unmasked and their costumes emphasized the size of their breasts in the tradition of 'bosom bruising' pornography. They had done Las Vegas, the program stated. However, their gestures underlined their physical strength and challenge to male dominance. In contrast, the Mexican wrestlers seemed more concerned with the sport of wrestling and with telling a story than with redefining the role of women or displaying super strength. U.S. wrestlers were fighting an invisible battle against U.S. sexism. The enemy they were trying to defeat (U.S. Males) wasn't there. On the other hand, the Mexican wrestlers were fighting the U.S. as a political monster. They were there as Mexicans, not as women, and the real enemy wasn't present, but implied: the Simpson-Rodino Bill, Reagan, the Marines, *la Migra,* cultural imperialism, the dollar, etc."[19]

7-Post-Modo

More[20]

1. The first part of this essay owes much to the essay, "When Medusa Smiles" by the artist, Mireille Perron. Her essay explores the potential for a new symbolic visualization of the world as it is expressed in feminist theory and the theories of interactive simulation in computer technology.

    Perron, Mireille, "*Quand Meduse sourit,*" (French with English translation), *Parallélogramme,* ANNPAC/RACA, Toronto, Winter 1988-89, Volume 14, Number 4.

2. De Lauretis, Teresa, *Alice Doesn't*. Bloomington: Indiana Press, 1984, (paraphrased), p. 142.
3. *Ibid.*, p. 143.
4. Gomez-Peña, Guillermo, "Border Culture: A Process of Negotiation Toward Utopia," *The Broken Line/ La Linea Quebrada*, a Border Arts publication, San Diego-Tijuana, Year 1, Number 1, May, 1986.
5. Hicks, Emily, "What The Broken Line Is Not," *The Broken Line/ La Linea Quebrada*, a Border Arts publication, San Diego-Tijuana, Year 2, Number 2, March, 1987.
6. Gomez-Peña, Guillermo, "Border Culture and Deterritorialization," *The Broken Line/ La Linea Quebrada*, a Border Arts publication, San Diego-Tijuana, Year 2, Number 2, March, 1987.
7. Hicks, Emily, "What is Border Semiotics?" catalogue essay for the exhibition, Border Realities, Part Two, 1986.
8. Gomez-Peña, Guillermo, "CALIFAS," excerpt, *The Broken Line/ La Linea Quebrada*, a Border Arts publication, San Diego-Tijuana, Year 2, Number 2, March, 1987.

CALIFAS speaks of a world in crisis, of cultures undergoing a process of rupture, and of art forms undergoing a process of hybridization. In CALIFAS, language shifts from Spanish to English to Spanglish to Indian dialects in order to express the linguistic complexities of the border paradigm.

CALIFAS is a bilingual performance poem with modular structure. There are two levels: the narrative, describing "impossible situations" which subvert historical, political, and cultural facts (in cursive), and the poetical level, operating as memory or inner monologue. The second level has been put in the mouths of several mythical characters. The modular structure makes it possible to recycle parts of it into other formats such as performance, radio-art and book art.

9. Hicks, Emily and Guillermo Gomez-Peña, excerpt from a transcript for "Border Dialogue No. 2."
10. Gomez-Peña, Guillermo, "Border Culture: A Process of Negotiation Toward Utopia," Op. cit.
11. Gomez-Peña, Guillermo, "Border Culture and Deterritorialization," Op. cit.
12. Hicks, Emily, "What The Broken Line Is Not," Op. cit.
13. Gomez-Peña, Guillermo, "CALIFAS," Op. cit.
14. Gomez-Peña, Guillermo, "Dislocated," postcard poem.
15. Hicks, Emily, "I Couldn't Reveal My Identity," excerpt from a video tape of the same name.

"I Couldn't Reveal My Identity" recounts the experience of the Wrestler-Bride crossing the border from Mexico to the United States at San Ysidro. Her crossing was one of many performance pilgrimages that occurred on the weekend of Halloween/The Day of the Dead in 1988.

16. A letter from Emily Hicks and Guillermo Gomez-Peña, 1988.
17. Gomez-Peña, Guillermo, "Border Meta-Reportaje," a multi-dimensional poem, excerpt.
18. Hicks, Emily, "What is Border Semiotics?" Op. cit.
19. Hicks, Emily and Guillermo Gomez-Peña, "Mexico vs. the U.S.—First Binational Female Wrestling Event in Tijuana," High Performance, Los Angeles, 1987.
20. As I wrote, Emily, Guillermo and I first crossed the border together in 1987, but that was just one of many crossings. All any of us can do is cross it again and again—the shifting nature of the game-site involves the players, too. Something different always happens.

The rules of the game are always changing, too. Take the North American Free Trade Agreement (NAFTA) between Mexico, the United States, and Canada. If the border prism represents the symbolic vision of a deterritorialized world, NAFTA is a geopolitical drama representing one of the political processes of deterritorialization that is paradoxical to the vision of the border prism. The politicians and capitalists say the prize is economic well being for their respective countries. But isn't the passage of NAFTA bodies across the border another sign that we are living through the beginning of the end of (our) nation states?

KEVIN COOK
DETROIT: APPROPRIATELY CANADIAN

The stomach curdles as the eyes focus on urban tundra swishing by too rapidly, staring out the side window of a slum blender, whizzing along from somewhere to somewhere else. Many suffer a similar nausea when they direct their thoughts toward the city of Detroit, the city of my dreams. For these people, Detroit is highly symbolic. Another bridge collapses, another airplane crashes. Cities become vulnerable as the walls built around them crumble. Man-made inventions vindictively poison man himself. The condolences that these people so sincerely extend to themselves break through their skin, forming social acne, reducing their civil vanity at this time when virtually no one can find totally positive things to celebrate about Detroit.

Standing on the Canadian side of the river, I see a foreign country, slightly exotic (is it really?), with a different history and a different attitude. All this is contained in my view. All those television shows I used to watch came from over there; one of the great skylines, which I had probably seen many times on the TV screen, is before me and I, still a starry-eyed small town boy, just gape, no longer aware that I am my former self. Despite my years in Montréal, a city with a memorable skyline of its own, one significant enough for me to have declared more than once my place of residence with typical Montréal haughtiness, I just stand here. I pore over this image of excitement.

High above the city, privileged people revolve ever so gently atop the Renaissance Center (in the heart of what paid city publicists have called the Renaissance City), sheltered from the despicable deadness down below, enjoying the view of that deadness. Trees and houses blur across the mid-Western ooze of flat land which discontinues alarmingly close to the high-rise district, as if dammed but gathering force to tip the tall buildings into the river. Humankind has apparently not yet adjusted to the phenomenon of being suspended in the air. Everything looks wonderful from above. The dirty plate-glass windows miraculously become crystal clear, and the insipid weather casts not its usual gloom over the city. Glass-walled elevators being dragged up the side[s] of skyscrapers still succeed in thrilling their occupants.

Choice. Sometimes it matters. A 180-degree turn brings Canada into the field of vision. The pretty little city of Windsor, Ontario welcomes Americans into the country and invites them to travel northward into the rural landscape. If they drive far enough they will penetrate two of Canada's three metropolises: Toronto, and then Montréal. Are the windows really cleaner on this side of the building?

Je me souviens. I have vanished from all possible bird's-eye views. I am inside the American immigration office at the Detroit-Windsor tunnel. I am stoned on apathy. I watch every human being in front of me undergo the questioning routine. I hear the same words pronounced by the same voice, over and over again.

I notice when someone is asked the same question more than once. I am afraid that I might forget my birth date again. I wonder if, maybe, I might not be able to enter the United States due to some circumstance beyond my control. Such nonsense will be entirely unacceptable to me—all I want to do is to cross the river and set foot on that land over there, in that city. I understand my cognitive faculties better than government policies—I can see the river and I know how to cross it, but I can not see the border.

Je me souviens. Welcome to the United States. Travellers exiting Canada funnel continuously into the American immigration office. If "Detroit" is your answer to the "Where are you going?" question, and you replied "Pleasure" when asked "Business or pleasure?" you may merit special attention. "Have you ever BEEN to Detroit?" "Where do you plan to stay?" "What are you going to DO there?"

The presence of waste in the idyllic living environment that North Americans have strived to create for themselves remains a constant source of embarrassment, as if it represented some sort of failure on society's part, or some unfortunately unconcealable human imperfectibility. The fact that this attitude lives on must rely heavily on certain widely held conceptions about what constitutes social refinement, perpetuated by the population's ingrained avoidance of all that might be seen as unpleasant. The acceptability, even desirability of us distancing ourselves from our normal biological functions—after all, our bodies constantly excrete waste matter—marks a turning point in our evolution, though colloquial but bizarrely impolite expressions like "Even the Queen wipes her ass" serve as acknowledgements of our recent history, a time when people still shit in outhouses.

I am reminded of the weeks that I spent in the Canadian High Arctic a few years ago, during which I primarily devoted myself to walking around and filming the environment that surrounded me. The lack of trees, shrubs, and even grass in and around the village of Resolute Bay (1981 population, 168) meant that every individual piece of litter was exposed to view. The cold temperatures in that region result in a very slow rate of organic decomposition, and coupled with the area's general uninhabitedness the litter seems less arbitrary than it might be in a more populated southern area. Scattered, it seemed to be the wind-blown pages of a nearly completed diary that detailed the consumption habits of each inhabitant of this accessible-only-by-airplane village. Perhaps the disgust that people frequently feel upon seeing garbage isn't related to distastefulness as often as we think. Are we simply embarrassed because we possess information about other consumers, because we've caught ourselves infringing on others' self-styled right to white-plastic-bag privacy? This hypothesis is especially pertinent in this era, because we no longer recognize products according to their actual physical characteristics. Instead, we rely on their flamboyant and seductive packaging to perform the identification process for us.

About a year after my return to the south (to Montréal), a Resolute Bay resident was in town to visit her hospitalized son, so I arranged to show her some of the film footage that I had shot. She was horrified to see that my films were pervaded by images of garbage, and she claimed they were defamatory toward her village. I tried to explain my point of view to her—that I see waste as a normal part of life, without any negative connotation, and that I consider waste production to be one of those great phenomena that unites all factions of humanity, it being a common characteristic of every culture in the world. She wanted to hear nothing of the sort.

After my first day of driving around Detroit, still feeling delirious from my immersion in constantly unfamiliar surroundings, I notice that I have slipped into a chimerical world of personal fantasy. I have long had a dream of purchasing my own house—an inexpensive one, probably a very dilapidated one that I can never afford to rebuild. Never again would my rent increase at a higher rate than that of the minimum wage. In 1984, I decided against buying the slum rowhouse in which I lived in Halifax, Nova Scotia for $15,000.00, primarily because I knew that I would definitively leave that city within the following twelve months. Little did I know then that I would never have such an opportunity again. Until I discovered Detroit.

"All immigrants are daring and ambitious—the unambitious stay home."[1] One way of spurring activity in Detroit would be to relax the international boundary—the Canadian-American border—and create a special free-admission zone within its city limits. In doing so, Detroit would no longer be just one of the most northern urban agglomerations in the United States; it would become the southernmost and largest metropolis to which Canadians could have free access. This is indeed a subversive suggestion in this age of omnipresent multiple phobias, when American immigration policies apply stringent criteria to those seeking immigrant status in the country. However, it is clear that the United States and its citizens have all but banned Detroit from any consideration as a great North American city. This mentally-inflicted rejection of Detroit amounts to physical abandonment of the city, from the outside in. Perhaps the time has come to proclaim an International Republic of Detroit.

One could not expect Windsor, Ontario residents to pour into Detroit if the border were softened, as it can safely be assumed that the people there thrive on the town-like atmosphere that envelops them. They would not be attracted to the grittier big-city reality of Detroit. On the other hand, for resolutely urban Canadians the current choice between three major cities—Montréal, Toronto, and Vancouver—is simply too limited to offer the possibility of accumulating a sufficiently varied urban experience during any life span in the home country. Detroit the dejected. Detroit the demonized. A kind of anti-city. A city waiting to become Canada's fourth metropolis. A nervous centre ready to excite the mythically calm emotions of Canadians.

I hang my head and my glassy eyes revel in the familiar image of a slightly weather-beaten Canadian cigarette package, half crumpled, half flattened. With the ease of a smoker I apprehend that this is a relatively recent addition to Detroit's ground cover. I ascertain this fact effortlessly by recognizing the package's new design, the one that due to newly imposed legal obligations incorporates an enlarged health warning. The way it reposes in the gravel on the side of this Detroit street seems to imitate with the utmost authenticity a similar three-dimensional arrangement that I have previously contemplated, on several occasions as a matter of fact, alongside the unpaved roads of the Canadian Arctic. "Yes, yes," I think, as if scientifically deducing something. "This is not a coincidence. Detroit. The Arctic. Canada's final frontiers."

I have not yet purchased a house in Detroit. I pondered the idea extensively and contacted American immigration officials to inform myself on their rules and procedures. I explained that I am a Canadian who will be working in Windsor, on the Canadian side of the river. Not good enough. As a foreigner, I will not be allowed to maintain my residence in the United States without concurrently holding a Green Card (work permit), even if I am not actually employed in the United States. If, in fact, I were working in Windsor while living in Detroit, not only would I require the Green Card, but I would also need a commuter visa permitting me to work outside the U.S.A. I was told, however, that I may purchase a house in Detroit—I just cannot live in it. I occasionally wonder what it is they are protecting Detroit from.

1. Benjamin Playthell, "Showdown in Flatbush," The Village Voice, Vol. XXXV, No. 22 (May 29, 1990), p. 40.

JODY BERLAND

REMOTE SENSORS: CANADA AND SPACE

"For communication purposes a satellite is any heavenly object off which radio signals can be bounced."[1]

When we look at the weather, to find out what's coming we now take the viewpoint of the angels: looking down at the earth, rather than up at the sky. Sadly we do without the celestial music—though on Montréal's MeteoMedia, the cross-Canada cable weather station, one hears a heavenly choir begin to sing as the scenery switches from tossing waves to satellite views of a cloud-covered earth. Our "wisdom from the skies" comes to us (ordinarily with less paradigmatic pluralism than on the weather channel, but with equal assurance of divine knowledge) by virtue of NASA and a host of circling and geostationary satellites, and a plethora of cybernetic and optical innovations. Their products—not photographs, exactly, but colour-enhanced digitally processed atmospheric data—tend to be stunningly beautiful but completely silent, unlike the trees, winds, insects, and animals, whose sounds once taught our forebearers to know what was coming.

Our ancestors looked upward, and saw in the stars what they already knew: the twinkling outlines of goddesses and gods, astrological figures, and mythic animals. Looking downwards, we too see what we already know: the battle between cold and warm fronts and the chaotic coherence of global meteorological systems, filtered through the reassuring vision of a distant but attentive eye, which translates atmospheric movement, change, and sensation onto the legible surface of a screen.

In the northernmost part of the New World, the range of intemperate weather provides Canadians with their only universally shared experience. This bond offers in the place of a common history the ironies, vulnerabilities, and solidarities occasioned by the unpredictability and hazardous shared displeasures of the north's uncommonly difficult weather. Not surprisingly, for Canadians the subject of weather has accumulated over time the mundane profundities of widespread nonpartisan ritual conversation and elaborate metaphorical embellishment. But visual depictions of Canada give little hint of the range and extremes of its weather; or that was the case until they were safely distanced and mediated by post-aeronautic optical technologies. Everyone talked about it, as Mark Twain said, but no one was willing to show it in public.

This absence can be understood symptomatically, as evidence of trauma. The condition is not hard to explain. It is now widely acknowledged that the idealized landscapes of a traumatized European romanticism were colonially embraced and imposed on the Canadian middle class. The emergence of a northern natural-pictorial mythos, the gradual socio-topographic sacralization of landscapes usually rendered empty of humans but nevertheless clearly recognizable as here and nowhere else, has been the dominant trope by which new inhabitants came to possess and define the country as their own. Historically, Canada's most visually and touristically elaborated symbol came to be its landscape—an uncontroversial means for its citizens to imagine and aestheticize a "natural" white (I don't simply mean snow-bound) collectivity otherwise deprived not only of identity, but also of topographic and climatic logic. It was a trope charged with paradox. Implacable weather, implacable logic, and implacable presence: that was the unsaid metonymic in the patriotic landscape. Through elements that could be terrifyingly hostile, the Canadian situation was revealing new truths about what Europeans had learned to believe was a divine and harmonious nature. Were we supposed to be part of this same newly discovered, unforgiving nature? No doubt the need to invent themselves as a civilized (near)northern national community explains why (English) Canada's artistic representations of landscape so rarely did justice to the nation's brutally sublime real winter weather.[2]

An illustrated encyclopedia of sacred places I saw recently leaves Canada blank in its annotated maps. Like the (undoubtedly American) authors of this book, many philosophers and historians speak of the sacred spirit of a place by reference to its past, observing the way such spirit of place is marked and commemorated by architecture. Of course Canada suffers from no absence of sacred sites, which may not derive exclusively from western classical traditions, but which are nonetheless powerful enough to engender mysteries, divinities, and (as recently as two years ago) military conflicts over their use. Yet if you explore contemporary cultural terrain, the national myths connected to the landscape are not usually associated with the past, but rather with the future. Outside of the picturesque tradition of post-European painting, which, so often lacking visible human presence, admits to neither past nor future, Canada's topographic iconography commemorates its past mainly where such past already heralds the country's future—other than at places like the antique port sections of Montréal and Québec now inhabited by tourists.

Besides these originary landscapes, the "sacred" national images depict explorers, discoverers, the canoe, the railway, and, with special intensity, the technical wonders enabling us to surpass both topographical and vertical space: broadcast transmission towers, telephone lines, and above all, satellites, which are widely celebrated on postage stamps, in national exhibitions, government documents, television and computer graphics, political fables in cartoons, and the daily weather reports.

Perhaps these signs celebrate a future that never came? Though the new Biodome is already Montréal's foremost popular attraction, none of the other pan-spatial technical wonders in which our scientists seem ever more invested have vanquished either space or snow. Perhaps this is why Canada now seems so easily to stand in for the world. The future is constantly evoked, but its rewards are strangely evasive. We who live here can only know Canada as a paradoxical concept—it shouldn't be, but it is—and these signs are part of how we come to know ourselves.

> *"Know the enemy, know yourself; your victory will never be endangered. Know the ground, know the weather—your victory will then be total."*[3]

In the 17th century, European science undertook the measurement of climate and temperature at least in part because of new problems and needs created by wider travel. In the 20th century, if we are to believe our technical books, policy-makers, and science writers, the reverse is true: satellite-based research and exploration is setting the technical framework and goals for Canadian science and technology because of our unique climate and topography. Canadians pioneered the use of satellites to observe, map, and communicate with remote, frozen areas that were previously beyond the reach of geological science and/or electronic media. That experience not only provided a new technical and mythical infrastructure for nationhood, but also laid the foundation for Canada's secure niche in current space research.

Mastery over the climate and vast northern territory is frequently cited as the rationale behind Canada's most important contribution to space science: the remote sensing technologies which ride piggy-back on NASA satellites to produce brilliantly enhanced images of the earth's surfaces. These technologies make possible the beautiful, mythically reunifying landscapes of the late 20th century: colour-coded digital images of the earth's surface from space in which forests appear purple, oceans are red and gold, and solar radiation is blue and red. Changes in atmosphere, topography, vegetation, and human settlement can be detected from many miles above our heads. This landscape works as our new metonym for nationhood: it confirms the fusion of a techno-apparatus with a land that is here and nowhere else. But at the same time, threatening to override this sentimental link is the satellite view's status as global analogue, and thus (paradoxically once again) out of our hands—the product of a technical-administrative system imposed from above.

Contemporary weather forecasting is predicated on the near-instantaneous transformation of extremely distant real atmospheric data into two-dimensional images on a monitor. This capability arises from the complex interdependent systems of satellite-based radar, infrared and near-infrared imaging, meteorological software and data processing, telecommunications, computer graphics, and television, and remains one of the more important applications of NASA space-related technological research. The first American satellite was sent up in 1958, the year the Eisenhower administration formed NASA to administer the U.S.'s space race with Russia. The first NASA satellite assigned to conduct practical research carried meteorological instruments. Its genealogy exemplifies what Langdon Winner calls the process of "reverse adaptation": with a complex technological system in place you search for applications, and thus reverse the conventional relationship of means and ends.[4]

Over time, U.S. meteorological science and public services have become relatively autonomous from military administration. Whether for this or other reasons, the U.S. has not been in the forefront of developing economic spinoffs and technical services from "eye-in-the-sky" satellites. The leadership in this area has been assumed by Canada, whose new multi-billion dollar space program is promoting its "enviable world record" in providing such services.[5] Of course, improved knowledge about weather patterns has made weather itself increasingly available to military activity. Though there is no available record of current "weather modification" activities such as occurred in Indo-China in the late 1960s, the U.S. Air Force operates two meteorological satellites that fly over the Persian Gulf twice every 24 hours—and Baghdad is one of the few world cities about which it is impossible to obtain weather information through private, cable, or home-terminal weather services.[6]

(When a Canadian weather station in London, Ontario ventured to show weather maps from the Gulf in 1991, the maps disappeared very fast. If weather imaging technologies are quintessentially Canadian, the increasingly complex technical web that conducts news and images into our living rooms is not.)

In 1962, Canada was the third country in the world—after Russia and the US—to launch a satellite, *Alouette 1*. Communications and aerial photography were already Canada's fields of expertise, and space research quickly focused on these as most suited to Canadian needs. Aerial photography had been a focus for scientific research and both military and commercial activity from the 1920s. By the 1930s, the National Research Council had developed equipment for plotting maps from highly oblique aerial photographs and a stereoscope plotter, and during World War II the Canadian Air Force concentrated on photographic surveying.[7] Early in its development of space research, Canada committed itself to developing and interpreting satellite communications, initially to help communicate across the vast regions of the country's north. In 1972, the launch of *Anik A1* made Canada the first nation to place a domestic satellite in geostationary orbit. During this period, Canadian earth-observation technologies were being tested on US satellites. Currently preparations are being made to launch *Radarsat*, due to begin its working-life in orbit in 1995; and it is the subject of global advance marketing. *Radarsat* will introduce a new generation of remote sensing from space. By employing magnetic waves to "see" the earth's surface, *Radarsat* will surpass *Landsat* and raise earth-surveillance capabilities to a new level.

What is paradoxical here is not so much the implosion of land, landscape, and *Landsat* suggested by this history, as that in *Radarsat's* technical superiority and organizational subservience to NASA's *Landsat* we witness an ironic reiteration of the same structural paradox that previously befell Canadian broadcasting. In the 1930s, as the only viable alternative to the commercial American

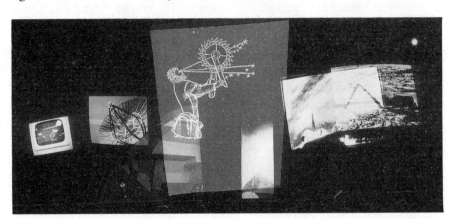

photo by Cheryle Sourkes

stations flooding the Canadian air waves, the federal government established a national public broadcasting system to provide a national public service. Ultimately Canada built one of the most technically sophisticated communication infrastructures in the world, reaching even to remote regions of the north, with the purpose of extending citizenship to those it could not be profitable for the commercial broadcasters to reach. It became, in what communication historians term a "tragic paradox", a superb vehicle for the dissemination of American music and television.

Canada's contributions to space research have grown increasingly specialized. The areas of specialization have a frequently cited originary purpose related to Canadian natural resources: the need to map, survey, and communicate across the mountains, the tundra, and the ice fields. Yet many of the space agency's current projects (in harmony with Conservative policy and international finance) are linked to larger projects funded by NASA or the European Space Agency. Canada's industries are contracted to provide guided robotic instruments (the much celebrated Canadarm flies on every space shuttle flight) and innovative technologies for remote sensing of the earth from space, in which it claims world leadership.

Meanwhile, none of the satellites which now provide weather data to Canadian meteorological services are owned by Canada. The "natural" logic of continental interdependency—the fact that weather systems are, after all, continental, if not global—is variously challenged and confirmed by weather maps in the two countries. US weather maps end precipitously at the 49th Parallel (with arrows signalling the cold fronts coming from the hidden North), while Canadian weather maps are dynamically continental. We are looking at a relationship that is at once geographical, technological, administrative, and cultural. Canadians see themselves as part of a larger natural topography and living system—the weather—and thus appropriately subject to a continental aerial gaze. But the US takes its borders—topographic, technical, even meteorological—as absolutes.

> "In so many fields of endeavor, from business to culture, the postcolonial craves international recognition—only to find that the pursuit of such recognition distances them from their original, albeit compromised, sense of themselves... [As Sylvia Lawson writes] in her introduction to The Archibald Paradox: 'The Archibald Paradox is simply the paradox of being colonial... To know enough of the metropolitan world, colonials must, in limited ways at least, move and think internationally; to resist it strongly enough for the colony to cease to be colonial and become its own place, they must become nationalists.'"[8]

Canada's military advisors on space policy have observed that continuing support and investment in space technologies resolves the fundamental contradiction between the economic progress guaranteed by war and the social well-being which is ostensibly the purpose of government. They call space a "paradox of opportunity."[9] If we continue to develop space technologies, the argument goes, we can simultaneously advance our technological resources, increase our usable knowledge of nature, develop peaceful and profitable spin-offs, and keep our place in the continental military-economic system. (They would approve of my dentist, who tells me he can fill my teeth with non-toxic white matter because of research in space.) Their position is also an indirect acknowledgement that Canada is itself a kind of satellite, a poor relative with higher latitude and moral consciousness whose economic survival depends on remaining useful to the surveillance requirements of continental military defence. Being so conscientious, so marginal, even Canada's military thinking is articulated in terms of paradox: space research earns health and well-being for its citizens by advancing the dangerous militarization of space. Isn't that strange, and yet so true. Canadian artists, notwithstanding shared preoccupations with landscape, technology, and politics, never learned to aestheticize or glamorize military imagery as contemporary American artists and film makers—regardless of their political leanings—did and continue to do. In parallel with this, Canadian military thinking has always emphasized the peace-keeping, life-saving goals of military intervention. Once again Canada volunteers a humanist impulse in its technocratic trajectory. It dreams of a social democratic prescription for an order in which governance regrettably travels from the imperatives of technical systems to the policies of the state, rather than the reverse.

Popular reliance on weather fore-
casts has helped to legitimize huge
expenditures on space and computer technologies with primarily
military genesis and purpose. The
scope and expense of satellite observation far surpasses its demonstrated usefulness to weather
prediction: so far it adds 24 hours to
a 4-day forecast, but predictions are
still wrong over 20% of the time. In
exception to this, there are the
important cases of tracking hurri-
cane movement and other catastro-
phes, and military needs, neither of
which requires or receives daily
exposure on television. What continuous satellite-based weather forecasting   more   definitively
accomplishes is to create a consumer market for satellite surveillance technologies that otherwise
would have to be funded entirely by
government and military agencies.
This consumer market is not con-
fined to national borders: the Cana-

dian Centre for Remote Sensing is marketing *Radarsat* to the new Bangkok
Land Information Project, whose first intended use is tax collection.

Our everyday need and aesthetic appreciation for satellite-based observation
services, much aided by the entertaining sophistication and even gorgeousness
of constantly improving visuals and computer graphics, is therefore both facili-
tator and byproduct of government space and defense policy. Weather fore-
casts rely on a set of technological tools originating in what, in this context, it still
makes sense to call the military-industrial complex (everything from satellites,
radar, and other optical equipment, to software, and television itself), whose
socially beneficial applications are thereby demonstrated—and financially com-
pensated—on a daily basis.

Recently we witnessed the inauguration of a Canadian-designed satellite
instrument to measure ozone levels; as a consequence of government sponsor-
ship, the results can be ascertained daily on the weather channel. Typically
Canadian is the way this innovation ostensibly serves to unite and protect the
nation's citizens, while simultaneously justifying and advancing the necessity for
developing technologies that bear a complicated relationship to the problem
they purportedly protect against (in this instance, damage to the atmosphere),

and which also further circumscribe and rationalize the conduct of the citizenry itself. Our device simultaneously brings the problem to the forefront of our attention, and diverts us from it; one could say that it measures the atmosphere in much the same way as one of our many Royal Commissions does. Both of these instruments address a genuine problem; both speak more honestly than the government that appoints them; both lack the power to force anyone to resolve the issue; both become part of our habitual environment; and significantly, both of them are dependent on the media for their apparent success.

With its clear moral purpose, ozone measurement helps to legitimize our growing reliance on the technological surveillance of the atmosphere. Placed in the midst of ritually repeating reports on local and regional weather, that endlessly changing, endlessly similar visual narrative of cable television, the ozone story has now bravely entered the public map of our "natural" landscape: adding to the increasingly scientific flow of meteorological news to which we northerners so often turn with apprehension and futile ambivalence.

In this sense, as in so many others, the subject of weather inhabits a discourse that seems typically Canadian. This same history of reform, invention and collusion has repeated itself in different guise with each modern innovation in communication and surveillance technologies; in fact, it might be (and has been) said to define the trajectory of Canada itself, so much has it been shaped by our ambivalent and paradoxical love for our natural environment, and by our leaders' capacity to discover ingenious technical solutions to problems arising from the imperial drive towards technological mastery. These innovations reinscribe their administrators' most benign visions of improvement and order, and enrich technology's dual capacities to emancipate and dominate our daily lives.

1. Brian Winston, *Misunderstanding Media*. Cambridge, Mass: Harvard University Press, 1986, p. 245.
2. I have further elaborated this argument, "Weathering the North: Climate, Colonialism and the Mediated Body." *Relocating Cultural Studies*, Valda Blundell, John Shepherd and Ian Taylor (eds.). London: Routledge, 1993.
3. Chinese strategist Sun Tzu, 6th Century B.C. Quoted by Charles Bates and John Fuller, *America's Weather Warriors 1814-1985*. College Station: Texas A&M University Press, 1986.
4. Langdon Winner, *Autonomous Technology: Technics Out-of-Control as a Theme in Political Thought*. Cambridge, Mass: MIT Press, 1986.
5. "Space agency to present astronomical program to Ottawa," Montréal *Gazette*, March 25, 1993, C1 and C4. Cf. "Everyone has been trying to develop this technology, but Canada has made the most progress over the years.... and now *Radarsat* will put us on the map,"Toronto *Globe and Mail*, March 15, 1993, B1.
6. Kris Herbst, "Satellites help US forces control the skies over Iraq." *Network World* 8:3, 1991: 1, 45.
7. Doris H. Jelly, *Canada: 25 years in Space*. Montréal: Polyscience Publications/National Museum of Science and Technology/National Museums of Canada, 1988.
8. Graeme Turner, "Of rocks and hard places: The colonized, the national and the Australian cultural studies," *Cultural Studies* 6/3, 1992: 427.
9. Brian MacDonald, (ed.) *Canada's Strategies for Space: A Paradox of Opportunity*. Toronto: The Canadian Institute of Strategic Studies, 1983.

CHRISTOF MIGNONE

SOUND GOVERNMENT: A LONGITUDINAL STORY OF A CANADA YOU CAN'T TOUCH

The emergence of a concept of "Canada" as a nation was dependent on, and artic-ulated through, the building of the national railway, and subsequently—at first lit-erally in its tracks—the national broadcasting system. The Canadian hypersensitivity to acoustics as a dimension of politics is surely based on the long-standing association of the national political process with sound, which was and probably remains its privileged carrier. Radio was conceived as an auditory means for circumscribing Canada as a nation and for providing that "Canada" with a meaning that transcended (and thus, of course, legitimized) territoriality.

– Jody Berland, *Toward Creative Anachronism:*
An Essay on Radio, the State,and Sound Government

Identifying a nation by prioritizing its communication technologies might seem quite civil, an improvement upon waging war to establish borders. But Canada became a flag and an anthem through an extensive negation of the USA: we can't tell you who (or what) we are, but we know who we are not. This negative formulation of identity locks us into an endless imitative phase. Nevertheless, our territorial border was established, and the 49th Parallel's fluidity and sheer geographical scale makes fencing appropriate only when it is invisible. Thus, we can extend Jody Berland's comment and state unequivocally that Canada employs sound government. The medium of radio is the state's vehicle for con-stituting territory—through an invisible agenda of Canadian content. (The license agreement between each station and the Canadian Radio Television and Telecommunications Commission (CRTC) consists of a "Promise of Perfor-mance," which quantifies each station's programming within a complex system of categories, including mandatory percentages of Canadian content.) The On Air light comes on, demarcating a national territory washed over by modulated transmissions, confirming every second that one frequency is not another because if it were you would be somebody else,...and all that is asked is that you be loyal to your frequency. Don't touch that dial! You are bracketed, guarded by an aural artillery in maneuvers.

Words belong to those who use them, until someone else steals them back. In Canada the word is *sovereignty*: it's in the air, it's about the air, and it has been stolen. The Canadian state is said to be a construct in stereo: an English channel and a French channel. But Canada's stereo model suffers from a recur-ring localized lesion to the left brain hemisphere, which causes a statist language disorder known as aphasia. Symptoms are numerous: an aphasic may be capa-ble of reading a word but unable to identify its referent, or incapable of reading a word but able to point to its referent. Language loses its meaning and becomes sound (government)—an eerie, tranquil zone, the Quiet Revolution. The two "founding peoples" of this nation have learned to swear in each other's tongues so well that neither is comfortable speaking. In radio, the disorder is known as disembodiment, voices without bodies probing your erogenous ears. Touch that dial before it touches you! There is a certain terror in intimacies received technologically: "the spirit of Montréal," CHOM-FM, coming to you with megawatts of power.

The emergence of other nations within the officially constructed nation is based on the promotion of a distinctness among cultures—the mosaic—defining itself through opposition. In this fiction of Canada, this empty metaphor, one becomes a people only through the struggle for autonomy from the anonymous majority. Communications technology is one of the tools that cultures use to flex the rhetorics of their nationalism. Now that the old "Two Solitudes" story finds itself narrated through the barrel of a gun over various barricades around the Montréal area, we can hear it shatter, releasing fragments of other real cultures. The multiplication of solitudes into a lonely crowd brings us back to the radiophonic relationship, the voice and listener together alone. The nationalist language of radio has no A-Z, but might have some parallels elsewhere:

> Traditionally, the Inuktitut language did not parcel out time nor separate it from space. We (whites) speak of time as a solid, as mass—a bit, a span, a segment. As opposed to the English language, Inuktitut makes little distinction between objects and actions. The names of objects sometimes change relative to their movement—their direction and speed—and to their relationship to other objects. Inuktitut evolved among people for whom all senses had equal importance; for whom more than seeing was believing. One's sense of space and objects is very different if it takes into account their sound and smell as well as their visible outline.
>
> – Kevin McMahon, Arctic Twilight

The introduction of northern control of communication technology in the North, therefore, seemed to be of particular interest to radio artists exploring alternative uses of the medium. Radio's temporal and spatial qualities—it, too, does not parcel out time nor separate it from space—those paradoxical essences we in the South find so difficult to grasp, seemed to find a conceptual home in the Inuit matrix of thought. Is radio's slavery to the distribution of music and news, to formatted programming for a formatted audience, inherent to the technology? Or is it misuse that makes radio a mere distributor rather than an intimate communicator? Radio in the North presented an opportunity to observe the theoretical preoccupations of radio artists who feared that their medium had become just one more voice of authority, and hoped that the form of radio could demonstrate greater pluralism and malleability.

Community radio spread like wildfire. The technology seemed to be no barrier whatsoever. People had no sense that they had to be professional broadcasters; they just grabbed the microphone. People knew the impact immediately, they knew it reached their community instantly. There was no other form of accomplishing that, except by calling a meeting. That was a good indication that it was appropriate technology: the radio was completely a part of the framework of community. The definition of radio was instant and quite well developed. I was amazed at that because I came from a tradition where radio was given to me and I had no sense of it being a communication tool, but up there it just seemed to fit into the culture, where communication is important by voice.

– Florence Woolner, Chief,
Aboriginal Broadcasting,
Secretary of State

This sounds too good to be true, doesn't it? Within the context of the systematic genocidal attack on the North, by what Kevin McMahon calls "the rain of metal" (the DEW line, the James Bay hydro projects, Cruise Missile testing, pipelines, etc.), one could hardly celebrate; yet it sounded as if the Inuit may have been able to transcend not only government regulation, but the limits of radio itself: their disembodied voices were made whole in the context of their holistic culture. But this is an idealized scenario. Actually, sanctioned government experts implemented the introduction of communications technologies to the North, with their training at the ready. Primarily, it seems that Northerners could change the content of radio, but not its proscribed form.

I do not propose to participate in the carnage of the metal rain by further translating the Inuit *other.* We can never, however, dismiss challenges to the dominant format. Radio artists explore the nature of their medium, not to understand it but to reappropriate its potentialities, which remain constrained by category minute by minute across the country. The effects of categorical nationalism make radio a visible instrument. I believe that it is more at home in its nebulous, unseen world.

Ultimately, we cannot pretend that radio will ever replace the warmth of touch. It is inherently obtuse and one-sided. Its angle of transmission is ephemeral, deflecting and reflecting the dominant structures of our Statist constructions. Had the Northerners not been pre-formatted as Canadian nationals, they might have offered challenging insights into the relationships that stand.

"OKA GAVE US A VOICE."
– Elijah Harper

TONY HALL

MANY NATIONS, FEW STATES

We live in a world of many nations but of relatively few nation states. Using language as the primary criteria, our crowded planet hosts almost 3000 distinct nationalities. On the other hand even though the number of states recognized by the United Nations has almost quadrupled since the Second World War, there are still less than 200 governments represented in the General Assembly. This numerical gap dramatizes the dangerous reality of a globe carved into geopolitical chunks that correspond poorly with the perceptual outlines of community and motherland held most dear by a huge percentage of the world's population. The decay of old empires has hastened the turmoil arising from the poor fit between governments and the complex ethnic configurations on which many of them sit. As old constraints fall away, many theaters of ethnic tension are exploding into outright war zones.

The rush of escalating tragedy, epitomized now in the apocalypse of Bosnia-Hercegovina, places new responsibilities daily on the United Nations. In some parts of the planet the sociological and political meltdown faced by the UN is marked by the clash of competing nationalist armies. In other parts of the planet the failure of the international system of law and governance is marked in quieter ways, such as in the attempt by the Davis Inlet youths to annihilate themselves.

The Davis Inlet story, which was reported widely throughout the world, has once again drawn Canada's Aboriginal policies to the attention of the UN's Commission on Human Rights. This attention comes partly from a growing recognition in some UN circles that high rates of Native suicide in Canada are but one manifestation of a profoundly inequitable regime, a system that consistently places Indigenous societies under the antagonistic rule of state authorities.

Along with this recognition has come a heightened appreciation that exploitation and subservience characterize the relations of Indigenous societies with many nation states. Thus there are many commonalities in the dilemmas faced, for instance, by the Basques of Europe or by the Sami of the nordic countries or by the Maori of New Zealand or by the Indian nations of the Americas. The issues which arise, therefore, are often global in scope. Likewise the problems to be addressed often transcend the limitations of domestic politics. Only by concerted responses at the international level will many Aboriginal societies on this planet ever move beyond the marginalized, phantom-like role presently assigned them in the world community.

Questions about the relationship between Indigenous societies and states have been discussed at the League of Nations in the 1920s and at the International Labour Organization in the 1950s. Since the early 1980s the UN's main human rights body has been overseeing the endeavours of a working group

whose primary aim is to produce a document outlining basic international principles on the rights of Indigenous peoples. Their efforts may result in a resolution
that will come before the UN General Assembly as early as the end of 1993. (The
United Nations has designated 1993 as the International Year for the World's
Indigenous Peoples.)

Generally the government of Canada has insisted on asserting a major influence on the course of these developments. In the view of some, however, the role
of our representatives has often been less than constructive. Canada's foreign
policies on Aboriginal issues have been more directed at checking the impetus
for change rather than facilitating it, diverting the momentum for reform rather
than helping to consolidate it.

The defensiveness felt by Canadian officials at the UN is not surprising given
the tarnished nature of Canada's reputation with respect to its treatment of
Aboriginal people. The perception of Canada as a human rights delinquent in
this field began to harden internationally even before the pictures of the confrontation at Oka and the Mercier bridge began to be beamed around the planet.
In 1989, for instance, Stephen Lewis made the following comment about his
years as Canada's Ambassador to the United Nations. He said: "The treatment
of Native people was without doubt the Achilles heel for Canada in the human
rights arena. It undermined our influence, our prestige, our reputation. It made
less compelling the human rights arguments we were making. It was very humil-
iating, very embarrassing."

Much of Canada's attention at the UN has been directed at a study of treaties
and other agreements between Indigenous peoples and states. This study has
been underway since 1989 when a Special *Rapporteur* from Cuba, Dr. Miguel
Alfonso Martinez, was charged by a Sub-Commission of the main UN human
rights body to conduct the investigation.

According to Matthew Coon-Come, Grand Chief of the Grand Council of
the Crees of Québec, "in Geneva Canada led the crusade against the Treaty
study." UN diplomats were "lobbied by Canada to stop it." According to a representative of another Aboriginal organization involved in the process, the Canadian government went as far as to threaten to cut the foreign aid of some African
countries if their delegates supported the Martinez treaty study.

The obstructionism of the Canadian delegation was effectively countered
largely through the diplomacy in Geneva of representatives of the Grand Council of the Crees of Québec. The GCCQ conduct their work at the UN with the status of a Non-Governmental Organization. Their successes at the world
organization owe much to the dogged persistence of Ted Moses, a former Grand
Chief who has essentially become the Crees' UN Ambassador. Moses works
closely with Russell Barsh, an incredibly prolific American scholar who is the
international representative of the Grand Council of the Micmac Nation. The
Micmacs share a Non-Governmental Organization with the Lakota Sioux in the
United States. The other UN NGOs that represent Aboriginal people in Canada

are the Inuit Circumpolar Conference and the International Organization for Indigenous Resource Development.

It is not a new phenomenon for Native people from Canada to act as primary proponents of a strengthened regime of international protection for Indigenous societies. The pattern began in the 1920s when Levi General went to the League of Nations in Geneva as a representative of the Six Nations Iroquois. General's major objective in that era was similar to the goals which motivate many of the Aboriginal groups who have pushed for the current treaty study. General tried to persuade League members that the government of Canada was violating many treaties linking his people with the sovereign of the British empire. General spoke on behalf of the traditional Longhouse Confederacy, who maintained that the Six Nations were not subject to the authority of the Canadian parliament. Instead, argued the traditionalists, the Six Nations maintained a constitutional status as allies of the British Imperial Crown rather than as subjects of Canadian law.

The assertions of the Six Nations Iroquois are discussed at some length in the first progress report issued by Dr. Martinez. Although the scope of his study is global, much of his attention has been devoted to Canada because of the fact that treaties with Indigenous groups were made especially frequently in those parts of the world colonized by Britain. The rich variety of Crown treaties covering much of the northern half of North America bears witness to the continuing influence of the British Imperial legacy on the institutional shape of Canada. Treaties between the Six Nations and the British sovereign tended to establish patterns which were later projected towards the Northwest, as Crown officials endeavoured to secure Aboriginal sanction for the territorial claims of Canadian dominion. In return, Aboriginal diplomats secured a number of commitments from Crown officials involving matters such as land rights, education, economic development, health care, and the prohibition of alcohol sales to Indians.

The Martinez report deals squarely with the racist bias of several schools of social science which historically have been used to rationalize the subordination of Indigenous societies under the higher authority of empires and nation states. By anthropologically characterizing many non-European societies as savage or primitive, for instance, social Darwinists seemed to give legitimacy to some of the most aggressive campaigns of racist exploitation and repression. In the same fashion, various theories about hierarchical structures in human relationships have been employed to downgrade the international status of treaties with Indigenous groups.

Nevertheless, the Martinez study indicates that treaties negotiated with Indigenous societies during earlier phases of European or Euro-American colonization tended to be afforded higher international status. In 1789, for instance, George Washington issued a presidential message specifying that "the Executive was particularly keen to give treaties entered into with Indigenous nations, the very same institutional consideration and value as to those formalized with European nations." This position resulted from the weak and untried character of the central government of the United States during the first years of the country's existence. As long as the USA was seen as an unstable new entry into international politics, it remained true that "the first nations were in more of a position to recognize the legitimacy of the United States than the other way around."

MESSIEURS BOURASSA ET MULRONEY, VOUS AVEZ PASSÉ UN BON ÉTÉ?

art by Catherine Everet

MISTER BOURASSA. MISTER MULRONEY. DID YOU HAVE A NICE SUMMER?

Regardless of the international status assigned such treaties when first negotiated, there has been a marked tendency for states to ignore these agreements or to relegate them to the exclusive realm of domestic law and politics as soon as the balance of power shifted to the disadvantage of Aboriginal groups. In the view of most of the Indigenous participants in the study, there can be no honest justification for continuing to deny their treaties international recognition or for relegating their treaties to a lower order of international law.

The author of the report anticipates that the restoration of treaties and other similar agreements with Aboriginal people could play an important role "in the present-day recognition/restitution of Indigenous rights and freedoms." Moreover, he anticipates that the elaboration of new treaties could be a means "to construct and fully implement the rights written into national and international texts and to facilitate, at all levels, conflict resolution of Indigenous issues." This emphasis on treaties as primary instruments of Indigenous-state relations is based on the "consensual, bilateral" manner in which they are made. "The negotiating and consenting process inherent in treaties" is characterized as "the most suitable way" to secure Aboriginal sanction for arrangements that will help identify their place and function in future political processes.

Although the Martinez progress report remains mute on the subject, the sharing of power and the sharing of lands and resources constitute the bottom line that must be considered in any realistic assessment of the success or failure of treaty relations between Indigenous nations and states. In Canada the formulation of the Charlottetown accord constituted the first significant effort in our history to formalize a governmental regime of power sharing with Indian, Inuit, and Metis societies.

As with the population at large, there are complex reasons why the Charlottetown accord was rejected by a majority of voters who cast their referendum ballots on Indian reserves. There can be no doubt, however, that for a significant number of elders and senior diplomats in the elite brain trusts of the First Nations, the accord was interpreted as offering less potential in the way of power and resource sharing than do the treaty provisions already embedded at the base of Canada's constitutional infrastructure. The international community is thought to hold the key that will make it possible to transform treaties from a latent into an active force for the amelioration of First Nations relations with Canada and with the outside world.

Much of the Indian distrust of the accord, then, grew out of the fear that its passage could result in the domestication of their treaties with a corresponding diminishment of Indian access to international forums. The accord's demise, therefore, probably assures the growing involvement of Native people from Canada in efforts to construct a UN regime that includes mechanisms geared to the Aboriginal and treaty rights of Indigenous nations around the globe.

Efforts to achieve this objective will meet tremendous resistance as long as the UN continues to misrepresent itself as an organization of nations rather than as an organization of states. Direct participation in the decision making processes of the UN as presently constituted remains the exclusive preserve of those governments who hold seats in the General Assembly. All other political constituencies, no matter how old or how linguistically or culturally distinct or how cohesive, can only take part in the UN's proceedings on the sufferance of those states who share an exclusive proprietary interest in the world body. The fact that Indigenous peoples are most often represented at the UN by vehicles called Non-Governmental Organizations, speaks eloquently of a powerful bias in the structure of the organization. Some kinds of voices are tremendously amplified at the UN while other kinds of voices are carried at low volume, if at all.

According to Russell Barsh, who represents the Micmac Grand Council at the UN, the Canadian government has sometimes "made itself look ugly" in its effort to hold the Aboriginal agenda to the sidelines of international politics. The Canadian delegation, it seems, has set itself up as "a kind of chief gate keeper," with considerable control over the movement of resolutions and principles between the Aboriginal groups at the margins of the UN and the states at the organization's core. In Barsh's view the basic Canadian objective is to see that "nothing of too much significance gets through."

Canada's external positions *vis-a-vis* Indigenous peoples internationally seem not to be formulated at the Ministry of External Affairs. Rather the primary role in the making of this branch of foreign policy seems presently to belong to officials at the Department of Indian Affairs and Northern Development and at the Ministry of Justice. They have become predominant in an increasingly vital policy area that so far has received little scrutiny from either the domestic media or the opposition parties.

Marilyn Whitaker, Director of International Relations for DIAND, justifies Canada's international assertiveness on Aboriginal issues on the basis of the country's broad experience in the field. She affirms that "in our dealings with treaties, with land claims, and with constitutional and legislative approaches to issues of Aboriginal self-government, the Canadian government has been very involved domestically with many of the questions that just now are beginning to emerge internationally. We take our commitments seriously and we want to make sure that things are not done at the international level without careful consideration."

It would be naive to imagine that Canadian officials have been formulating policies on Aboriginal issues at the UN without careful reference to the interests of the United States. After all, Canada and the USA share a similar identity as New World countries whose territorial base has been imperfectly acquired from scores of Indian nations. In Canada there have been dozens of treaties made to advance this imperfect acquisition of Indian land. In the United States there have been literally hundreds of treaties that have been made and subsequently broken without any regard whatsoever for the principles of international law. Given these historical similarities it does not seem unreasonable to suspect that Canadian and American officials have privately developed a collaborative response to initiatives such as the UN treaty study.

Seen in this light, Canada's actions at the UN can easily be interpreted as those of an obedient client state. The Canadian delegation agrees to take much of the responsibility and heat for a visible role in holding Aboriginal issues to the sidelines of international politics. Meanwhile, the American government stays largely out of the fray and thereby does not directly expose one of its potentially most vulnerable flanks.

The Martinez study on treaties should broaden the debate on some of the most fundamental questions presently facing the United Nations. What is at issue are essentially the international ground rules related to the exercise of sovereignty. From what source do groups of people derive a claim to sovereign existence? What role does history play in determining the capacity of various collectivities to exercise sovereignty? Who can grant sovereignty and who can legitimately deny it? Can different kinds of sovereignty co-exist in relatively harmonious enjoyment of a common territory?

The geopolitical chaos in so many areas of the world offers clear evidence of the failure of the existing international system. A growing constituency simply will no longer accept the simplistic notion that it is possible to treat the globe as a kind of vast real estate development, where the land title is carved up between a relatively small number of states who hold a monopoly on the access to sovereign authority. Nowhere does the inadequacy of this monolithic system become so apparent as when the focus of attention is on Indigenous peoples, especially those whose deep territorial rights have been pre-empted by newcomers intent on imposing their own Eurocentric obsessions on the land.

The fact that many of these Aboriginal collectivities have treaties with sovereign authorities at the very heart of the international system underlines the extent of the lawlessness that has been allowed to prevail in the making of the Old World Order. In the view of most Indigenous groups who hold treaties, these agreements confirmed their recognition as nations with an inherent right of self-determination. It is nations, after all, that make treaties. Treaties do not make nations except in a superficial sense. From what source would Aboriginal groups derive the authority to make treaties, other than from their own sovereignty as Indigenous nationalities?

Present abuses of the international system are nowhere so apparent as in the seizure by corporate interests of the treaty making powers of states. The agenda is aimed ultimately at the further simplification and standardization of the world's geopolitics through the creation of a few trading blocks designed to lower national barriers faced by transnational corporations. An ironic outgrowth of this scheme is that the treaty making powers of states are being manipulated to remake the domestic political and economic landscape of the participating countries. Hence the highly placed operatives of transnational corporations have found a strategy to achieve domestic objectives that probably would have been blocked to them through channels of domestic politics alone. The key is the treaty making powers of sovereign governments.

This vast standardizing scheme, of course, constitutes the next wave of assault on the beautiful diversity of human cultures. Moreover, the sterile technocratic character of this worldwide megaproject represents a fundamental shift of power towards the influence of dollars over democracy. One need only notice the resistance to the Maastrict Treaty in Europe to observe the awakening realization that entry into a global economic block eliminates many levers of self-determination from the grip of those who do not control vast blocks of capital.

Compare the historical context of the Maastrict Treaty to the context of the NAFTA Treaty currently working its way through the governments of Canada, Mexico and the United States. Although there are many stateless nationalities in Europe, the vast majority of the people there are represented by governments that are deeply rooted in their land's Indigenous culture. On the other hand the three largest states in North America, with the possible exception of Mexico, definitely do not reflect the Indigenous identities of the Native people. Moreover, the sovereign authorities of Canada and the United States have entered into hundreds of treaties with the Indigenous nations of their countries.

Only a corrupt international regime would sanction a North American treaty that in no way responds to older treaty arrangements already in place over much of the territory of the trading block. The governments of Canada, the United States, and Mexico, all of which draw most heavily on their European heritage, simply cannot present themselves as friends of law and order in the international arena if they continue to ignore history by acting as if their territories are not subject to various forms of shared jurisdiction with sovereign Aboriginal groups.

There is no reversing the emergence of Indigenous issues as a major subject of international politics. Indigenous rights, for instance, have cast a long shadow over the negotiation of the international treaty on biodiversity. One of the reasons the American government won't sign it is because the treaty acknowledges that Indigenous peoples have some say in controlling access to wild plants and animals in their territories. This provision is resisted by the biotechnology corporations which have their headquarters in the United States.

No other individual has done more to increase the visibility of Indigenous peoples than Rigoberta Menchu, winner of the Nobel Peace Prize in 1992. She and her people have experienced tremendous brutality from the anti-Indian regime in Guatemala that is supported by the United States. The worldwide attention on her story has helped clarify for many that, by and large, decolonization has not been extended to the Indigenous peoples of the planet. The Indian wars never ended. Instead the campaign of genocide was broadened and expanded to global proportions.

In her speech to the United Nations, Menchu declared on behalf of all Indigenous peoples that "We seek to protect our roots, so as to pour all the richness of Indigenous values and original thinking into a new concept of development." She continued by affirming that "the Indigenous peoples require the cooperation of the other sectors of society if their struggle for full respect for their rights and identity is to be crowned with success."

In light of this request, it seems appropriate to conclude by citing her warning: "The International Year for the World's Indigenous Peoples is not receiving the attention it deserves—not even from the countries sponsoring it. It is important to make a special appeal to all countries to ensure that the year does not become a symbolic gesture, but, on the contrary, that its observance marks the beginning of a new era for the Indigenous peoples within the United Nations system."

ANTHONY WILDEN

IMAGINARY CANADA: STEREOTYPES AND SCAPEGOATING

In society today, especially in Canada and other countries with colonial histories, the Imaginary dominates our understanding of social and economic relationships. This means that we do not primarily perceive and understand our relationships to the many different kinds of people in Canadian society on the basis of actual images and actual concepts. Rather we depend on Imaginary images and Imaginary concepts. These are in effect socially defined and accepted fantasies which are commonly assumed to be a reflection of fact.

In the process, society induces us to stereotype other people and to turn different groups of Canadians into scapegoats for our fears and frustrations. "Other people" may thus be turned by dominant social and economic values into "*the others*", that is to say, into Imaginary *others*, or stereotypes, who can conveniently be blamed for practically anything the dominant groups in Canadian society want to blame them for.

Selves and others

Imaginary relationships imposed over real and symbolic social relations are constructed out of images, imaginings, and fantasies—images of the "self", images of the "other". But they are ordinarily constructed in such an unrecognized or unconscious way that we are easily induced by the actual social and economic alienation we experience (in many different ways) to believe these Imaginary relations to be true, and hence to go on treating them as if they actually were. Indeed, alienation as we experience it at work, in school, in the family, in personal relations, and in the madhouse is always dominated by an Imaginary interpretation of our actual relations.

The dominance of the Imaginary over our actual social and economic relations in our kind of society is a collectively experienced and collectively supported system of mirages. This collective experience leads to apparently individual and apparently psychological behavior (behavior seeming to have its main source in individuals or in "human nature"). In fact, this behavior has its primary source in social and economic relations. The reason that it may appear "inherent" in the "individual" is simply that this behavior is characteristic of the social and economic *system* which brings us up to behave as we actually do.

This is not to say that we all behave in precisely the same ways, because we do not. But it is to say that all of us are constrained by society to behave within certain *limits*, and that these limits or *constraints* are defined by society, not by individuals.

In other words: within the general constraints of the dominant values of our society; within the constraints of the socially and economically enforced hierarchies of class, race, and sex; and within the limits of what is believed to be "normal" behavior in our system; we can do what these limits permit us to do (hence the diversity of individual behavior). But we cannot ordinarily do what the limits (the constraints) do *not* permit us to do, without running into social and economic and political sanctions which, at the very least, can make life extremely uncomfortable for us. (Hence the overall similarities of the *patterns* of individual behavior, the patterns which can be detected, at deeper levels, within the diversity of our individual actions.)

If the dominant values and constraints of our socioeconomic system were different, then our range and type of social behavior would be different also, and, within the biological constraints of our physical make-up, we individuals would be different too.

When our dominant social relations induce us to accept the Imaginary as the value system which constrains the type and extent of our "freedom of action" (relative to the social whole), the Imaginary sets the stage for specific kinds of alienated social behavior. This behavior includes the social (and ideological) processes of Imaginary projection, identification, objectification, and opposition.

Imaginary *projection* is a social and ideological process associated with paranoia (personal and/or collective feelings of persecution), as well as with stereotyping and scapegoating. Projection in this sense is the process by which we are induced, by the combination of apparent personal experience and social norms, to select a particular *other* or a group of *others* as scapegoats for our alienated feelings. These *others* are most often groups of people who are defined by society as subordinate in the various socioeconomic hierarchies (non-whites, women, workers, children, and so on). These *others* are people who cannot possibly be responsible for our situation, and yet by Imaginary projection we make them so. We project onto them our unrecognized desires, our unrecognized alienation, and our unrecognized behavior. This kind of projection is an act of violence against other human beings; and in consequence, it has its almost automatic complement: the fear of retaliation. Thus we make the *others* responsible for aspects of our selves and our behavior that we cannot for some reason bear to recognize; and what we fear in them is what we fear about ourselves.

Such paranoid behavior always has its source in violence. We experience our alienation by the social system as various forms of violence against our own persons. We proceed to look for someone or some group that may be "safely" blamed, and then we project the violence we have experienced onto them. By blaming *others* in this way, we participate in the social manipulations of divide-and-rule.

Whatever our supposed intentions, most of us have been induced to believe that if only the *others* would stop whatever it is we have been persuaded to believe that they are doing, then our own alienation would disappear. We would at last be safe and secure in the selves that our social relations have induced us to construct. But those very selves, our Imaginary selves, are dependent for many of their characteristics on the paranoid relationship of opposition to the *others* ("I'm *not* like *them*"); and this is where Imaginary identifications come in to complement Imaginary projections.

Imaginary *identification* is the process by which we identify the image of our "self" with the image of the *other* (positive identification); or else we identify our "self-image" in *opposition* to the *other* (negative identification). In both cases, we are defining the *image* of the *other* (as distinct from the reality of the *other*) as essential to the image of our self. This is true whether the *other* is viewed as positively essential to our image, or as a negative threat to that image. Both of these aspects of the social process of Imaginary identification will ordinarily turn out to involve the same practical effects, because in the Imaginary both will be operating—usually in contradictory ways—at the very same time.

In human terms, *objectification* is a way of closing one's "self" off from the *other*, a way of trying to maintain a radical separation between self and *other*. It is a way of basing a social relation on the attempted denial or rejection of relationship itself. The *other* becomes the *alien*, the thing—"beyond the pale," "outside the Law," "on the wrong side of the tracks," "beyond freedom and dignity." The objectification of the *other* thus serves both personally and collectively as a defense against our actual relation to the *other*; as an (illusory) protection against recognizing our collusion in the oppression of the other; and as a persistent reaffirmation of the "group-self" we, and the individualized "*I*", both defined in opposition to *them*.

The Imaginary *other*, the *other* we exploit and oppress actively (by what we say and do) or passively (by what we do not say and do), may also be translated by our own social and economic alienation into an Imaginary Other, into the worst image of all our strangled hopes and distorted fears.

An Imaginary relationship is thus dependent on the collective and individual projection of image into image, on the identification of image with image, on the opposition of image against image, and on the objectification of images (and therefore other human beings)—and all this pathological behavior takes place as if in a single dimension, at a single level, and without a symbolic and real context whose recognition would bring the whole insane business to an immediate end.

Imaginary Images

An Imaginary image is not the same as a real one. Nor does an Imaginary image have to be communicated in the visual and painted sense of the term "image". Imaginary images are also expressed in speech and print and tone and gesture.

Some of the commonest Imaginary images of other people are those produced by war propaganda. These include images produced and reproduced by the warfare of the dominant groups against the subordinates under modern capitalism. Such propaganda is designed to create hatred, and thence to use this hatred as a deadly weapon against whoever has been defined as "the enemy" in a particular situation. The dominant thus hold a pistol to the head of the *other*, for the "final solution" to the "*other* problem" is always some form of genocide.

Apart from the stereotyping of women, peasants, and workers, probably the commonest stereotype in the Anglo-European tradition is the Imaginary image of the Jew. One version of this images is the Fagin of Dickens' *Oliver Twist* (serialized 1837-39). Along with "lower-class" criminals and prostitutes. Fagin is described as the "vilest evil" by Dickens. A more recent example of this image of Fagin—the alien, non-white, "medieval Jew"—is the Fagin portrayed by Alec Guiness, wearing a grotesquely artificial nose and repeatedly slipping in and out of his "Jewish accent," in the film *Oliver Twist* (1948). This English film by David Lean is a stunning example of the combination of sight, sound, and sense in film. However, one naturally wonders why Lean, a magnificent artist, should have chosen to make this particular film so soon after the Holocaust of 1933-45. I remember the effect of this film on me. The Jews were waging underground warfare against the British in Palestine at that time.

Relatively more common examples of violence of the Imaginary in Canada today—not to mention the television series "Sirens," "Highlander," and their ilk—are images of French Canada, third-world immigrants, and the native Canadians as they are projected by the media, both in and out of school, to the non-Québécois and the non-native majority. These images (e.g. *Riél!* by the CBC and General Motors of Canada, 1979) do not originate in the media as such, however: they originate in society. The various media—in which we have to include the schools, the family, and the history books—simply use for their own and others' purposes, the *expression*, in Imaginary terms, of real social and economic conflicts.

For example, the expression "the battle of the sexes" makes an actual contradiction between levels of power in a hierarchy dominated by males appear to be an Imaginary opposition between presumed equals in society.

Racism and Responsibility

Imaginary relationships extend from images considered valid by the dominant in society as a whole to equally Imaginary images constructed by individuals on the basis of what are believed to be real personal experiences. In such relationships, the Imaginary components of the stereotype, the "other half" of the Imaginary "self"[1], are commonly quite complex, and usually far more difficult to recognize and understand than the Fagin example.

If we, as individuals, have been induced by our "socialization" into participating in the many aspects of the Imaginary—in an Imaginary world more like *Star Trek* than reality—then we will unconsciously develop a *vested interest* in protecting and reproducing our Imaginary images of "self" and "other". These socially-constructed images of ours will come to appear to us to be real relationships that we cannot afford easily to give up—for the simple reason that in accepting the social construction of an Imaginary image of the *other*, we are willy-nilly involved in accepting an equivalently Imaginary image of our *self*.

Along with its other characteristics, our Imaginary self will ordinarily be constructed out of all that we believe the *others* are *not*. The Imaginary other will take on the characteristics of an (absolute) *not-self*—which means that any time when we discover that we, as social beings, are very much like it, then we are likely to feel even more uneasy and insecure (about our "selfness") than we were already. The Imaginary it which our social relations have created in the process of providing each of us with an Imaginary identity as an individual(ist) will return to us from the others as what we perceive to be a threat.

The Imaginary *others* in this Imaginary opposition between "self" and "other" are collectively regarded by the various groups of dominant "selves" as inferior, as alien, as evil, as "uncivilized," and "genetically" or "biologically" unequal, as dangerous to "law and order," as "primitive," as "irrational," as "hysterical," as "promiscuous," and so on. In this way, whole groups of people, including the female majority, are stereotyped to act as scapegoats to be blamed for personal and collective problems.

When one or many *others* are being used in this way to mask the real sources of discontent, dissatisfaction, and distress in our society, then we are not likely to recognize that when we consciously and unconsciously attack the Imaginary *others*—when we blame the victims—it is in reality the other half of our Imaginary selves we are seeing in the *others* we blame or condemn.

This divisive and destructive activity, derived from alienating "social norms," is nowhere more obvious than in the colonies, where one group of the colonized, e.g. the Anglicized Canadian majority, project the violence they experience onto another group, more colonized than they are, e.g. the Québécois.

We may quite sincerely believe that, in expressing our Imagined "superiority" over the *other*, or in blaming the *other*, we are responding to real characteristics of these *others*—having failed to notice that between our "self" and the *other*, our social and economic alienation has erected a mirror, as it were, a mirror in which it is our own Imaginary reflection that we see.

It can easily be shown, for instance, and by means of a host of examples past and present, that every stereotype of supposedly "primitive" behavior which whites attribute collectively to non-whites, partakes in its essence of this Imaginary relation. Some of the commonest adjectives applied with a generous lack of discrimination by whites to non-whites—and by Anglos to Québécois—include their stigmatization as savage, crafty, greedy, untrustworthy, ignorant, backward, superstitious, cowardly, stupid, irrational, reactionary, lazy, given to sharp practice and supposedly childlike emotional gratification, or to too much or to too little concern for their own kind—not to mention racist and violent. They also work like hell when driven.

To make matters worse, some groups already defined by society as *others* will use the very same terms to attack other groups of *others*.

Yet every one of these characterizations is in reality an accurate description, not of the *others*, but of the ordinary pathologies of the collective behavior of WASPs and WASP males towards those they believe to be—or want to make—inferior (Irish or Portuguese Catholics, for example). This white collectivity includes people who actually teach, encourage, and perpetuate violence, physical and otherwise, against those defined as the *others*; people who condone such activities; and people whose ignorance of the reality, or whose refusal to recognize it and its daily violence, can not excuse them of responsibility for it, in both word and deed.

Whites have had plenty of practice in such matters. After all, practically every one of the characterizations mentioned—as well as the statement that "they breed like rabbits"—was commonly applied to the laboring poor in England throughout the nineteenth century by the upper and middle classes, but especially by the upper class, the one that believes in "merit" supposedly attained by "good breeding" (the "eugenics" that they have traditionally applied to cattle, horses, and dogs). Their descendants still do the same in one way or another—as their equivalents in North America also do for those they call the "masses," the "rednecks," the "white trash," the unemployed, the "welfare bums," the workers, the homeless....

So widespread and interconnected are these attitudes and behaviors that one may well wonder where individual responsibility fits into the system.

The "equal" and "individual" responsibility invented by the capitalist revolution on its way through the seventeenth century is mostly Imaginary. In contrast, real responsibility is not an "absolute" or "innate" or "individual" or "either/or" characteristic of members of our society. Responsibility is a function of the *relative power to be responsible* in a given social and historical context. In societies such as ours, where relative power is distributed in a hierarchical fashion at various levels, relative responsibilities will be similarly distributed.

For example, a man at work cannot be held responsible for his exploitation on the job, for it is not within his individual power to change it. But if he brings the resulting alienation home and turns it into oppression in the family, then he is fully responsible for what he does at the family level. He is responsible because in a male dominated society, the male is given power over wife and children. At another level, the mother is not responsible for male domination. But if she, in turn, converts this alienation into oppression of the children, then she is responsible, within the family, in so far as she, being an adult, has the power not to act in such a way. (No adult is entirely powerless in our society.) Similarly, also, with an older child who takes out on brothers and sisters the (verbal and non-verbal) violence of parents and/or teachers.

Subjects and Objects

As we become aware of the role of the Imaginary in capitalist social and economic relationships—relationships in which the dominant use Imaginary excuses to explain away real oppressions—we are faced with understanding how such mirror-like relations become socially and economically articulated as Imaginary *symmetries* between the dominant and the subordinate in modern society.

A dominant-subordinate relationship is a hierarchical relationship of *levels* (levels of oppression, levels of exploitation, and so on). Such relations cannot be properly understood unless the mode of explanation one uses itself includes explicit ways of talking about various levels of relationship which actually occur in real socioeconomic hierarchies. This is the mode of explanation employed throughout this piece.

In contrast, relationships of symmetry are very much like the relation between ourselves and our images as reflected in a mirror. There are of course differences between the self and its mirror-image, but the reflection of the "body-image" in the mirror does not involve differences or distinctions in levels. Reflections are symmetries in which there is but a single level. Each image is identical and opposite to the other.

The Imaginary involves much more than a simple visual relationship, but the metaphor of the mirror-image is a useful one to employ in explaining it. The metaphor of the (single-level) reflection or (symmetrical) image emphasizes that so long as we are perceiving and experiencing the actual context of our lives in an Imaginary way, then the actual relations of "self" and "other", and the actual levels of relationship between people in an oppressive society, become practically impossible to sort out. Not only do we commonly fail to perceive and understand the levels of relationship in which we ourselves are actually involved, but when the Imaginary is dominant in our perceptions, we have no reliable way (no point of reference in the actual context) which enables us to tell the difference between what we perceive (and do and say) and what we think we are perceiving (and doing and saying).

In the world of the Imaginary as it now dominates our understanding and our immediate behavior in this society, actual social and contextual relationships between people become individualized and atomized. The real relationship of communication between you and me (for instance) is often represented in the Imaginary as a relationship between two "independent" atoms floating about in a social void—instead of as a relationship between two communicators dependent on a real social and historical *context* which makes our actual relationship possible. In the Imaginary, in other words, the social relationship between us, full as it actually is with all kinds of information, is represented as an empty space between us, an empty space just like that space that appears at first sight to exist between an object and its image in a mirror.

The Imaginary "flattens out" and obscures the real contexts of relations between people (which are always relations of communication). As a result, many important social relations are *represented* in the Imaginary as being relations between subjects and objects. In the Imaginary, there is only one subject in the world—you (or me!)—and in this "*either/or*" relationship in the Imaginary, everyone else is simply an object floating around your "field of view" (or mine).

Finally, every form of social and economic oppression and exploitation depends at some or several levels on objectification. The exploited person is treated as the equivalent of an object, as a thing, or as an organism considered to be a thing.

Symmetrization and Inversion

There are four basic Imaginary interpretations of inequity and inequality in modern society: the fascist, the pseudo-democratic, the liberal-idealist, and the utterly paranoid.

The fascist version recognizes that inequalities exist, but ascribes their sources to supposedly biological factors outside society as such. This is the pseudo-genetic or "socio-biological" justification of oppression, the "causes" of which will be said to be "lack of ambition," "constitutional laziness," "lack of physical strength," and so on.

The pseudo-democratic version of this Imaginary interpretation implies that while individual inequities and inequalities exist, collective oppression and exploitation do not. Like the fascists, the pseudo-democrats believe that "equal opportunity" (to compete) exists. Thus, they help to maintain real oppressions.

The liberal-idealists recognize that there is "*unequal* opportunity" (to compete) in our society, but also believe that if we could just get the system working properly (without changing it significantly), then all would be well. Since they do not recognize that competition between people as it is required under capitalism is an inherently oppressive relation, nor pay much attention to what it is that people are obliged to compete for, the liberal-idealists also contribute to the maintenance of oppression.

The utterly paranoid take practically any political position you can name, including the three just outlined. They depend on various and shifting definitions of the Imaginary *others* who they believe to be the source of the persecution they experience. In general, these unfortunately misguided people believe that they are threatened by those below them on the various social scales. Their paranoia has specific sources in the oppression and alienation they experience, but they fail to recognize these sources for what they are. Thus they commonly interpret their real oppression by dominating Others (e.g. business) as if it were an attack on their freedom and security by various Imaginary *others* (e.g. labor). In doing so, they come to believe that these are threats from above them in the hierarchies of power. The Imaginary *others* are thus converted ideologically into Imaginary Others.

When these and other Imaginary interpretations are imposed over our actual social and economic relations—when they mediate those relations—the consequence is a denial, a repression, or a rejection of the actual social reality we experience.

In this way, real socioeconomic hierarchies between people and groups (levels of relation, levels of power) become ideologically deprived of the political, economic, and historical context which would allow these relationships to be perceived as they really are. (This "loss of context," or this "substitution of an Imaginary context," can of course take place only in the realm of Imaginary ideas—i.e. at the ideological level— because the actual context and our actual ideas about it are always there.)

The result will ordinarily be *symmetrization* or *inversion*. By symmetrization I mean the ideological and unreal "flattening out" of a hierarchical relationship as it actually exists. Along with the denial, the repression, or the rejection of the actual context, the actual power relations sustaining and enforcing the hierarchy will also be ideologically "neutralized," as if they did not exist. People caught up in this kind of Imaginary behavior and belief will refuse to recognize the socially and economically enforced domination of men over women in our society, for example. Or they will hold that the dominant-subordinate relationship between capital and labor under state and private capitalism is "really" a relationship of "competition in the market." Or they will treat a colony as if it were a nation—which it does indeed appear to be, *if you remove, invert, or symmetrize the real context made up of those who are doing the colonizing.*

As a result of this *symmetrization of levels*, distinct socioeconomic levels which *contradict* each other in society will commonly be perceived and acted on as if the various levels were simply in a single-level *opposition* to each other. (Man opposes woman, capital opposes labor, white opposes non-white, and so on.)

At the same time, however, these Imaginary symmetrizations will usually contain enough of a half-spoken truth about the actual relationship to make the pseudo-symmetry believable. Indeed, all ideological mispunctuations and misrepresentations of real relations in our society do tell some kind of truth about some aspect of our relationships. These misrepresentations of reality are rarely outright lies—and this is part of what makes them so difficult to deal with.

Take the example of the symmetry overtly implied but covertly denied in the phrase: "My wife and I are equals." There is only one first-person subject in the sentence (the "I"). The word "my" is a possessive, which along with the word "wife" (third person), defines the woman being spoken of as an "equal" only in relation to her definition as an adjunct of the "I" in the sentence. This is an "I" which is paternalistically granting an Imaginary equality to the woman who the "I" openly declares—when we examine the sentence in detail—that he possesses. The half-told truth here, of course, is that the commonest way in which men regard their relationship to women in our society is through possession.

The example just given shows us an Imaginary symmetrization of an actual relation of domination in our society. The male speaker fails to recognize his socially-coded domination in any conscious way and yet at the very same time he confirms the domination by the words he uses. It is as if the man involved had a split personality. Each half of this personality makes exactly the same statement, but one half of it understands the message to mean "equality," while the other half knows it means domination.

We all know that oppressive socioeconomic hierarchies exist all around us: whether and how we *recognize* them as they are is another matter. Practically all of us, at some level (or at several levels) are the objects of various forms of alienating domination. Heterosexual men, for example, are not oppressed or exploited on sexual grounds, but the majority of the men in any country are oppressed and exploited by other men, for they are oppressed and exploited by class and by race. In most countries, however, men are provided by society with scapegoats for the anger and frustration they feel: women.

Figure 1: Symmetrization and Inversion

a) Examples of presently existing, short-term power relationships between the dominant and subordinate (contradictions:

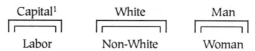

b) Imaginary symmetrization (oppositions) in the present context:

Capital] [Labor   White] [Non-White   Man] [Woman

c) Imaginary inversion of the present power relations:

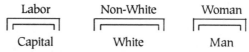

[1]Note that in the long-range, since labor alone can produce true wealth (use values for exchange), labor power or labor potential–human creative capacity–is ultimately dominant over capital, because it is the source of capital. The third level in the relationship between capital and labor is of course the natural environment: the organic and inorganic source of the reproduction of society over time. The socioeconomic and other relations of race and sex are thus distinct from those between labor and capital, in the sense that no one race and no one sex is in recent evolution the source of any other.

This is the world of male paranoia. Once the Imaginary has deprived a real hierarchical relationship of its real context, then the dominant participants in the real relationship are "free" to substitute for it an Imaginary hierarchy. This means that once a relationship of power and control has been symmetrized in the Imaginary, then it can also be *inverted* from "men dominate women," for example, to "women dominate men."

Paranoia is said to involve "delusions of persecution" (a "persecution complex"). What the psychotherapists generally fail to recognize is that the persecution always is (or originally was) entirely real. The "delusions" are not delusions about the fact of being (or having been) injured and terrorized. They are delusions about *who is really responsible* for the persecution.

In other words, when we are behaving in a paranoid way, we are confused about the real source of the oppression we have suffered (and may still be suffering). As a result, we will project a distorted memory or representation of this real source, as an Imaginary image, onto any *other* we feel threatened by, no matter how unjustly. We were relatively powerless to do anything against the original aggressor—we were children—and we are usually powerless to deal with real aggressors later in life. Divide-and-rule, however, provides us with Imaginary aggressors to attack in place of representatives of the original ones. We thus become used to making *indirect* responses to real aggressors (who have the power to hurt us), reserving our *direct* attacks for Imaginary aggressors—the *others* who have much less power and opportunity to protest the tyranny they experience.

As a result, our paranoia—our *misguided* attempts at self-defense—will generally be expressed in a projection through which we not only "flatten out" a real hierarchy, in one breath (thus making the victim the Imaginary equal of the oppressor), but in the next, we turn the hierarchy upside-down. Thus we fall into the further Imaginary fiction that it is the socially and economically subordinate who are "really" dominant after all (Figure 1)— and therefore "really" responsible for the state we are in.

---

1. Note that only in the Imaginary does the "not-I" appear to be the "negative" or the "opposite" of the "I". In the Real, the "not-I" cannot be the "opposite," the "negative," the "negation," the "symmetrical complement," or the "other half" of the "I"—no more than "nature" can be the "opposite" or the "negative" of "society." The reason is so obvious that we rarely recognize it. It is that the "not-I" (which is a *general* relation englobing the rest of the universe) is the *environment* of the "I" (which is a *particular* relation)—or, in a different terminology, the "not-I" is the ground or basis of the "I". As the environment of the "I", the "not-I" is of a level of relation which is distinct from the level of relation of the "I". And the "not" is the boundary between them.

Pierre Vallières

NATIONALISM ISN'T THE SOLUTION TO SOCIAL PROBLEMS!

Carole Beaulieu: Prior to your emprisonment in New York and your writing *Négres blancs d'Amérique*[1] had you ever had any contact with the Situationists?

Pierre Vallières: I had read some of the magazines published by them. The Québécois who were coming back from France in the early sixties brought material back with them. I had read their writing but it didn't strike me any more than anything else. There were also the Anarchists, and the anti-colonialists, Aim Césaire and Franz Fanon.

CB: In what way have your ideas changed since *Négres blancs d'Amérique* and Joyce Wieland's film *Pierre Valliéres*?

PV: My ideas haven't really changed very much. What has changed is the way that I participate in Québec society. This society has changed a great deal, but my intuition and my fundamental beliefs have remained the same. I am against all forms of alienation and the exploitation of one human being by another. I believe in freedom, equality, and solidarity.

The dominant discourse today is economic and focuses on competition, the survival of the fittest, and the elimination of the weak, whether they be weak institutions and industry, or weak individuals. We are becoming a society which in some ways is as harsh as that of the Industrial Revolution of the 19th century, a society which excludes a great many people. We even have a return to forced labour, now that people on welfare are required to work for starvation wages or be penalized. And now they're trying to stop people from quitting their jobs by withdrawing their right to unemployment insurance, as if it weren't workers who pay for the system.

We are becoming a society without pity, a world without pity, especially for young people who haven't experienced the cultural revolution and the rising standards of living of the sixties and seventies. They haven't had the period of hopefulness that we had. Even though those years may have been too full of illusion, the resulting dynamism in society was very interesting for everyone.

CB: There was a motivation...

PV: Yes. Young people today have come into a very harsh world which focuses on gross national product, where everything is classified statistically, and calculated on profitability—including health care. When you consider that more and more people are sick because of pollution and specifically because of the deterioration in the quality of urban life, should sickness turn a profit? It must be as cheap as possible.

People are trained to be useful to today's industry. People are becoming appendages of economic development strategies, which are decided by a few multinationals.

In that respect, my political beliefs about culture and society haven't changed. I continue to fight against a system which traps people in a pattern which has nothing to do with freedom and the pleasure of living.

CB: Can you describe your ideal society?

PV: I have always dreamed of a country—it could be Québec or somewhere else—where the most important values were solidarity, equality, and the eradication of sexism and patriarchy. A self-determined society, something like what the Spanish and Italian Anarchists dreamed of. This is utopian, but life is hard outside of such an ideal. There is no great movement pushing for the emergence of such a society, and that is disappointing. People very quickly become used to functioning in a society that they haven't created, that they accept as a fact of life. I dream of a society where art and creativity and the environment are central. I don't see anything like it in North America or anywhere else.

CB: Your ideas haven't changed, but the way you act on them has.

PV: I used to want to blow up all the bastards in charge. Now I just hope they die as quickly as possible.

CB: You would no longer advocate armed struggle?

PV: Sometimes I'm tempted again when I watch the politicians in power, not just here, but in the United States and Europe, and around the world. We are governed by dangerous people. Many heads of state are torturers. If you can justify using violence to maintain people in power, you must surely be justified in using it to oust them from power. The only thing is that, on an almost metaphysical level, the decision to use systematic, physical violence can have a boomerang effect on those who use it, even if they have the best intentions. Life becomes dull, except during the exhilaration of carrying out a violent action. Terrorist violence can be intoxicating, especially for small groups in an urban setting.

CB: I've noticed that in armed struggles each member of the group has a specific duty, and when the war is won, it is very hard for people to have a national strategy where each person can think and act as an individual.

PV: A military mind-set can easily become totalitarian because clandestine revolutionary action requires very strict security measures. There is no room for error or accident. People who pose a threat, who could derail the process and endanger others, are excluded. Consequently it isn't an environment that encourages critical analysis or concensus-making. You end up with very rigid people in power. However, there isn't often any other way of overthrowing a system or ending foreign occupation. On the other hand, our democracy subjects us to other kinds of pressure, the pressures of multinationals, of communication systems, of media, the pressures of the manufacturers of images, of objects, of needs and of mercenary values. The system gives the illusion of freedom because we can decide whether or not to turn off the television. But it's still drowning us with billboards, newspapers, television. The result is a dictatorship of dominant values. That's why this society generates its own violence.

CB: Racism is on a rapid upswing.

PV: There is both moral and economic confusion. They tried so hard to convince people that without economic growth there could be no future, that now when there is no growth, a "no future" sentiment dominates. In pre-capitalist societies, economic growth was a less important factor in the future of a people. Societies were based on trading and sharing, like the original indigenous societies. Economic growth didn't mean much. Reality was based on the economy, on nature, on work, and social and cultural life taken together as a whole.

CB: It was based on the quality of life.

PV: That's right. Nowadays economic growth can continue while negating any quality of life. When it comes right down to it, you can get a product for the best possible price in a concentration camp. I know that's extreme but we are forcing people to work. It is forced labour. They don't cost anything, but they produce. People have no choice but to produce to survive.

CB: You say that you wouldn't necessarily encourage armed struggle as a way of taking power here, with the democratic system that we have. Would you be tempted to participate in political life here, try to get elected?

PV: No, I've never been tempted, and I don't think I could be now.

CB: Would you allow yourself to be convinced?

PV: I don't believe in profound societal changes that are implemented from above, by proxy. The political parties are made up of too many mediocre individuals. For example, I believe that we should take the Constitution back to the drawing board with committees of citizens, reform power at the base, beginning with the most ordinary, elemental issues. As long as people don't take hold of power where they are, it's a delusion to think that they will take it on higher up, at the national level, for example. And it's an illusion to think that the people they elect will take care of their problems if they don't do so themselves.

I believe very strongly in the development of citizens' committees and of popular movements and associations of every kind. The feminist movement is a good model to follow. A movement grows when it coincides with a widespread need in society. If women hadn't had particular needs when the first feminists began to raise their voices at the beginning of the seventies, we wouldn't have observed the development that we did. The same goes for the environmental movement. I believe in that kind of action.

CB: Tomorrow you will give a lecture on independence and socialism. Can you tell us what you will speak about?

PV: The social discourse must base itself on a new analysis of the economic situation and the economic system. You cannot use a 19th century analysis of the economic system today. From the Industrial Revolution on, you have to take into account the globalization of the dual economy. That is, an economy that uses less and less people, that excludes more and more, and that can take advantage of manpower worldwide, moving from country to country, where people are the poorest, the least demanding, and the most biddable. A work force that is less biddable, that has political and labour experience and which is oppositional, this work force becomes too economically and politically expensive and so it is laid off. It is penalized because it has freed itself more than others. Freedom is frowned on by the business world, more than anything else.

So freedom is the most important virtue to encourage, and freedom always starts with disobedience, with a "no". If there is no freedom, there is only submission and resignation. Whether you obey God or General Motors, it's the same damn thing. There's a lot of talk about freedom and a craving for it. But in the free world, it is the quality that is the least well looked upon by the business world.

I think it's necessary to go through this kind of socialist analysis in order to formulate new demands. I don't think that collective ownership of the means of production is the solution. There's no future for a society in collectivizing Hydro Québec's dams or the paper mills that pollute and destroy the forests, or the aluminum smelters. There's a future there for bureaucrats, but that's why we have to find other ways of living that are less focused on consuming and are more equal. We have to reassess the whole thing. Also, the equality of men and women needs to be set out from the start. Traditionally, until the Marxist-Leninist groups disappeared, the concept was in people's heads but was never carried out. There are still too many instances where the masculine stands for both genders.

Ecology is also central and gives a planetary perspective. The left has always had a universalist perspective. Now universalism is also going to have to be pluralist, inclusive. We are going to have to accept that there are different ways of living, that there are different histories, and accept that the West is not the cutting edge of humanity. That's very important. The future of the world is not necessarily in the West.

The problem for nationalists is that there is no such thing as a pure nation. Nationalism must not be based on ethnicity, but on a national direction. In that sense there are no ethnically based nations. If there were we would be seeing many more situations like that of the former Yugoslavia. That may be the final blow for the West. It's incredible to see Yugoslavians reaching such a level of barbarity so quickly. It hardly makes sense. They were not a backward people, so we need to be just as vigilant here as elsewhere.

CB: In 1990, I often heard you speak at rallies in support of the Mohawks, and you signed a statement of support that I published in *Le Devoir*. It seems that you have always supported indigenous peoples.

PV: We didn't actually think about it very much in the sixties. At one point we talked about red niggers but they were only mentioned along with other groups. It wasn't until the First Nations people organized among themselves that their demands were supported by the left. And I'd have to say that the support isn't very strong in Québec right now.

North and South America, when it comes right down to it, have to admit that their societies are based on genocide. That's a very hard thing for the majority of *"pure laine"* anglophones and francophones to accept. I don't think there has ever been a comparable conquest in the world.

The Europeans colonized the African people but they never intended to eliminate them completely, whereas in America they aimed for the complete elimination of the indigenous peoples, who numbered several million. They were not as successful in Latin America, but on the other hand, the indigenous populations there have no democratic rights. In Bolivia and Guatemala they make up the majority of the population, and yet have no representation. They are worse off than Blacks in the United States, who aren't very well off at all.

That reality must be recognized, first off. But how do you atone for genocide? It's almost impossible. At the very least, I think that priority must be given to Native demands so that the situation doesn't simply deteriorate. The only future right now for most Native people is suicide, destitution, and alcoholism.

I've never understood why in Québec, for example, it has never occurred to Hydro Québec to bring the Inuit and the Cree in on their hydroelectric development plans. If they had at least thought of it, or made some steps in that direction... You can't just say we're going to expropriate you, give you a couple of million bucks and then you're on your own. It's unacceptable, it means the end for them.

Logically, the Cree and the Inuit should have a say in the development of their land. They should have first say about what development they want. That way they'd have a chance to put down the roots that they need to create a stable cultural, social, and economic base for young people. Young people won't stay on the reserves where alcohol is the only defense. The biggest danger for Native communities, once again because of our policies, is the exodus of young people. There are no young people left, like in the Gaspé and Saguenay-Lac-St-Jean. And in Charlevoix and Abitibi. Communities and regions that have no young people haven't got much future. They lack the cultural dynamism which is essential for a society's development.

Native people are haunted by this. It's the biggest danger facing them right now, in my opinion. And young people are leaving for all sorts of reasons. In Québec many young Native women that I know have left their reserves because they can't take the violence anymore.

Giving Native peoples back their freedom and their right to dignity would be the starting point for a society that really wanted to be civilized. A society that isn't able to do that cannot be civilised within itself. As far as I'm concerned all people have equal value. If we consider Native people sub-human, then we'll be ready to do the same to the unemployed, drug addicts, handicapped people, and the mentally ill who we removed from institutions to save money and put out on the street with no support. We tend to use too many words, also.

CB: Have you noticed any change in the opinion of people in this neighbourhood (*centre-sud*), since the summer of 1990?

PV: No, people here haven't changed. They aren't well-informed about the Native situation. They still have the same prejudices. If there was another crisis, they would be even more anti-Native. There is the mainstream analysis that paints Native people as warriors, smugglers, etc., and there is the analysis of Native leaders, which is in English. It would be a big help if the Native leadership spoke the same language as the people here. Because they speak English they are perceived as being part of the majority that has colonized and dominated Québec for a long time. So there is a kind of discrepancy. You hear Mohawks speaking their own language when they pray. It's unusual to hear a speech in Mohawk.

It would be easier for Québécois to understand that Native people are in a conquered and dominated position if Ovide Mercredi spoke Cree and George Erasmus spoke Dene.

CB: If they were asked about that they would probably say that they want to speak to the majority.

PV: I don't know how things will develop provincially or federally, because we've got two governments that aren't likely to do much before the next elections. And it is getting stranger because Canada is fast disintegrating. I think that Québec will become independent once Canada has fallen apart. The former Eastern Block republics gained independence almost despite themselves because of the collapse of the Soviet Union and East Germany. I think Canada is coming apart because it has no national direction. There is no such thing as a Canadian social strategy.

CB: Let's hope Québec has one...

PV: It did have one, it does in a way. There is a difference here. You just have to go to Ontario to see the difference. I hope we will develop an interesting strategy.

CB: I haven't seen one yet.

PV: Nor have I. We had higher hopes twenty years ago.

CB: Can you talk about your work at the Montréal Gay and Lesbian Community Centre?

PV: It's a young community centre that wants to bring together gay and lesbian organizations and individuals. It's one of the few centres which is open seven days a week. People come from other areas too, for information, follow-ups, advice. And for psychological support. There is also outreach, countering anti-gay violence. And promoting gay culture. Many gays are beaten up because of their lifestyle. But gay culture is one of the most dynamic of any grassroots group I know. That encourages me. Things are depressing elsewhere, I don't know why. Nothing is happening, there are no young people. And people wonder why there's no one involved.

CB: They don't know how to draw people in.

PV: Popular organizations are stagnant because they've come to depend on funding, and when the funding dries up, there's no enthusiasm left. Whereas here there's never been any funding. There's still too much homophobia. The Charter of Rights is nice, but governments and the public service are very homophobic. There is also no tradition of patronage in Québec, as there is in the United States, so we make do with what we've got. We have about twenty volunteers, some of them work more than forty hours a week. Some of the people who work here are sick. Others are working here because they can't get jobs, some unemployed sociologists, for example. They come and work here, meet people, put together projects...

I'm in charge of communications, so I started up a community newspaper. I also do administration. The centre is one of the groups that I'm the most involved in.

CB: What's the name of the newspaper?

PV: *La Grand'jaune*. It was a small town expression for a unconventional woman. Then it was used to describe the transvestites on St-Laurent street. La Grand'jaune was the woman who didn't fit the conventional mold, who didn't get married, who stuck to herself. We chose it to symbolize marginality but also the strength to go your own way.

– translation by Sabrina Matthews

---

1. Pierre Valliers, *White Niggers of America*. Montréal and Toronto: McClelland and Stewart Limited, 1971 (translated by Joan Pinkham).

Contact: CDL, P.O. Box 5209, Station C, Montréal, Québec, H2X 3N2

MACDONALD

photo by Carole Beaulieu

DARREN WERSHLER-HENRY
CANADIAN PATAPHYSICS: GEOGNOSTIC INTERROGATIONS OF A DISTANT SOMEWHERE

1 Baffling Philosophy

[T]he curtain rises on a set which is supposed to represent Nowhere, with trees at the foot of beds and white snow in a summer sky; and too, the action takes place in Canada,[1] a country so legendary, so dismembered that it is well quali-fied to be this particular Nowhere, or, in terms of a putative Franco-Greek ety-mology, a distantly interrogative somewhere. (Jarry, "Ubu Roi", 79)

In the world of 'Pataphysics, Canada is Nowhere. Just look at the map. *The Evergreen Review*'s "Planisphere of the Pataphysical World, indicating the pre-sent Cures, Sees, Missions, and Provinces established by the College of 'Pata-physics" (158-59) repeats the gesture of imperial cartography throughout history, determining and detailing a putative European Center at the expense of its alleged peripheries. Accordingly, Canada is Empty, or perhaps blank(eted) under "white snow in a summer sky"...anOther cold Orient(alism).

Edward Said, quoting Bachelard's *The Poetics of Space*, points out that "objec-tive space. . .is far less important than what poetically it is endowed with" (*Ori-entalism*, 55) and in this case, Canada has been endowed with Nothing. What are the stakes involved in allowing that snow-covered map to stand as a repre-sentation of the 'Pataphysical world? After all, Jean Baudrillard has served notice that it is now the map that engenders the territory[2], or at least the other signs that stand in its place. Have hordes of Canadian "Pataphysicists, alarmed at the ongoing prospect of being overwritten, erased, and ignored, mobilized their onto-logical snowblowers in a strategic attempt to unveil their obscured presence? Not at all.

Their response to the situation is baffling.

Along the base of vertical facades "snow baffles" are recommended. These simu-lated plastic or concrete dunes correspond exactly with the past snow accumula-tions of a particular site. When installed they prevent further snow drifts from forming. In this manner entire cities [or countries] could be "snow-proofed."

In general appearance such cities [or countries] would look as though they had been recently hit by a major blizzard; but such as deceives the eye would likewise deceive the flurries which—unable to find suitable structures around which to accumulate—would pass over the city [or country] without leaving behind a single flake of snow. (Fones "A Theory of Snow Prevention," 39-40)

Canadian "Pataphysicians are more than happy to let the map stand as is; what matters is not the thing itself so much as the manner of its interpretation. To a "Pataphysician with a knowledge of Robert Fones' theory of snow baffling, the map no longer appears empty. Instead, it illustrates a country and tradition that is thriving, placed *sous nature* by a series of metaphorical snow baffles. The "Pataphysical field remains perpetually open, "smooth space" that baffles State attempts at philosophical containment.

2 My Definition Is This

What is 'Pataphysics, and what is Canadian "Pataphysics? Alfred Jarry defines the former as follows:

> *Pataphysics is the science of imaginary solutions, which symbolically attributes the properties of objects, described by their virtuality, to their lineaments. (Exploits and Opinions of Doctor Faustroll, Pataphysician, 193)*

'Pataphysics, then, is "the science of the particular, despite the common opinion that the only science is that of the general;" it examines the laws governing exceptions, and describes a universe which can and should be envisioned in place of the traditional one (Jarry, *Exploits*, 192).

As "the science..." (Jarry, *Exploits*, 256), 'Pataphysics is necessarily the science of identity, and it demonstrates that all identity is constituted through difference rather than self-similarity. In *The Anxiety of Influence*, Harold Bloom describes 'Pataphysics as the paradigm (or perhaps the 'Patadigm) of poetic influence, and its mode of operation as a *clinamen* ("swerve"). What the ('Pataphysical) text does, in fact, is to reinterpret its entire context in its own light, paradoxically ('Patadoxically) determining its precursors (Bloom, 42-43). It in turn will be recontextualized by the deliberate misinterpretations of its antecedents; every reading is necessarily a misreading, every identity a mistaken one (Bloom, 43). This is a *productive* rather than a *reductive* relativism—to know a thing by its clinamen is to know it in a way that does not purchase that knowledge by the loss of that thing's power (Bloom, 43).

It should come as no surprise, then, that Canadian "Pataphysics marks its differance from its imperial cousin ('Pataphysics) through a swerve (clinamen) "from elision (') to quotation (") through a superinducement on elision ('+'=")" (TRG, "Introduction to Canadian Pataphysics," 301).[3] Therefore, "If..."Pataphysics (according to Jarry) is 'the science of imaginary solutions' and thereby the source of answers to questions never posed, then "Pataphysics (diacriticized via the open quotation of a double elision) will be 'the literature of all imaginary sciences'" (TRG, "Introduction," 302). "Pataphysics provides the quotation of those givens that we do not understand, and accompanies them with supplementary notes constituting an explanation. Simultaneously, it moves both closer toward and away from the notion of Origin(s).

"Pataphysics has much to say about the subject of Canadian identity; however, what it has to say in any given instance is never exactly the same. And that is exactly the way that Canadian "Pataphysicists want it.

3 The Invisible College

In "A Short History of 'Pataphysics," Karl Jirgens adds a further meaning to the significance of the doubled elide ("Pata-): "[it] stood for the theft of both the speaker's words and his voice" (10). In 1992, it therefore seems appropriate to appropriate and recontextualize the opening sentence of Simon Watson Taylor's 1960 piece, "The College of 'Pataphysics: An Apodiectic Outline": "The [Invisible] College of [Canadian] ["]Pataphysics or Collegium ["]Pataphysicum has been in existence now for more than ten years" (Taylor, "The College of Pataphysics: An Apodeictic Outline," 150).

Exactly *how* much longer is a moot point, for 'Pataphysics is, apostrophically, beyond the notion of a Beginning; "'Pataphysics, I reiterate, has always existed" (Shattuck, "Superliminal Note," 25). Other problems quickly arise in any attempt to define Canadian "Pataphysics with any consistency, because many Canadian "Pataphysicists share the affinity of their European and American colleagues for dissimulation.[4] Pseudonyms and collective appellations (another form of baffling) abound, circulating freely with those of "legitimate" writers and learned institutions: Christopher Dewdney, Lledir NhahNhoj, Prof. Kurt Wurstwagen, Steve McCaffery, Dr. R.W. Sanderson, bp Nichol, Adrian Fortesque, The TRG, The Institute of Linguistic Onto-Genetics, The D.U.C.K. (Deconstructivists' University of Canadian Knowledge), The Institute of Hmmrian Studies, etc. The customarily cavalier attitude of "Pataphysicians regarding publication[5] combined with the scarcity of the material that eventually does become published[6] also creates problems for anyone interested in researching the subject.

Attempting to objectively summarize the history of Canadian "Pataphysics to date would be an extremely un"Pataphysical act. Therefore, the remainder of this article will stubbornly (and perhaps perversely) focus on one particular lexical chain that runs through the strata of Canadian "Pataphysics like a vein of precious metal, linking many disparate elements in intriguing ways.

4 National Geognostic

The third section of the "Pataphysics issue of *Open Letter*, "Towards a Grammatology of the Canadian Unconscious," deals with the possibility that the rock formation known as the Canadian Shield (which comprises most of central Canada, the prime region of "Pataphysical activity) might have some influence on the consciousness of its inhabitants (Jirgens, "A Short History of Pataphysics," 10). Since at least that time (and in some cases, before), much of Canadian "Pataphysics has been explicitly geological in focus.

However, in its speculations regarding the material substrates of Canadian psychotopography, "Pataphysics proceeds not so much according to a geo-logic as to a geognosis:

GEOGNOSIS: [Incorrectly for GEOGNOSY].

GEOGNOSY: 1. A knowledge of the structure of the earth, its strata, their relative position and the probable constitution of the interior. Often used as nearly equivalent to GEOLOGY. (OED I, 1132)

The paleonym[7] "geognosis," an incorrect synonym for the near-equivalent of a hard science, enacts the "Pataphysical notion of quotation as an inverted doubling. As a result, it serves as a useful umbrella term for the textual thread that I wish to discuss here.

4.1 Christopher Dewdney: Concretion Poet

[T]he poet [is] in the same vanguard of research as physics, molecular chemistry, and pure mathematics. (Dewdney, "Parasite Maintenance," 21)

Steve McCaffery first pointed out the similarities between Dewdney's methodology and that of 'Pataphysics in 1976, in "Strata and Strategy: 'Pataphysics in the Poetry of Christopher Dewdney."[8] After re-citing Jarry's definition of 'Pataphysics as "an expressly pseudo-science which provides a solution to a non-existent problem," McCaffery suggests that "Dewdney offers his 'imaginary solution' [geology as an analogy for language] to the pseudo-problem of poetic form itself" ("Strata," 189). However, Dewdney's imaginary solution can also be applied to the pseudo-problem of Canadian identity.

Because any identity is bound up in the process of signification, it is continually shifting and unstable, and can never be pinned down in any final sense. But as McCaffery writes,

That the problem is a pseudo-problem [or the solution a pseudo-science] in no way nullifies the pursuit of a solution, for the pursuit in itself will evince the problematic nature of both "problem" and "solution" as the terms are shaped and defined through the suspect process of language. ("Strata," 189)[9]

The best option for proceeding, then, seems to be an examination of how "Pataphysics and notions of Canadian identity play off against each other.

In poems such as "THE MEMORY TABLE I," Dewdney's geognostic psychotopography does seem to suppose some sort of collective Imaginary: "As there is / a water table / there is also / a memory table" (Predators of the Adoration, 19). And although, as critic Stan Dragland points out, this memory table would be part of "a millennial palimpsest that exists everywhere" (190), it does contain nodes of specificity, which Dewdney dubs "concretions."

The concretions, which "Power Glen II" describes as "sacraments of the memory table" (Dewdney, Predators, 25), are capable of "becom[ing] imprinted with the dreams of isolated individuals even hundreds of miles away" (Dewdney, Predators, 26). Later, they may "begin arbitrarily to transmit previously recorded dreams mutated over the years by stellar and meteoric interference"(Dewdney, *Predators*, 26). Consequently, although they are repositories of something like a collective unconscious, the contents of that unconscious is a constantly mutating non-identity. There is nothing quintessential about the concretions themselves; they remain "unknowns which, however perfectly dissected, never yield their identity" (Dewdney, *Predators*, 25). Their identity is processual and relative, constantly shifting, simultaneously determining and determined. This can be said of the entire memory table, or of other strata in any "dream topography":

> A dream topography
> or such intimate theatre
> as we conceive
> delineate no vision,
> have rather, motion,
> involute
> (Dewdney, *Predators*, 30)

4.2 Steve McCaffery: Rational Geomancer

Steve McCaffery's "Pataphysical exploits are many and varied, but the one most immediately relevant in this context is "The Perseus Project: Paleogorgonization and the Sexual Life of Fossils." This essay, allegedly based on the "unpublished manuscripts and notebooks of the unknown but remarkable Samuel Gatty" (69), presents the "Pataphysical notion that fossils are in fact "paleoglyphs": "the first intelligent attempts at creating a comprehensive system of written significative marks" (70). McCaffery's own remarks on Dewdney's use of the figure of the fossil explain its geognostic "Pataphysicality:

> *[F]ossil operates as a linguistic insertion into a geological fact providing an answer to a question never asked. It is from this precessional answering that paleontology formulates its questions by a system of back-formation. The fossil "sentence" that answers a non-existent question and hence is by nature 'pataphysical. ("Strata," 192)*

The similarity to Dewdney's work does not end here. Like the concretions in "GAS PORT I," paleoglyphs play a role in the formation of human consciousness. "I am proposing language to be a sexual system entirely alien to the human species, a paleozoic conspiracy, a saturated network of fossil sex and paleontic lusts that uses man far more than man uses it" (McCaffery, "Perseus," 75). According to the theory of paleogorgonization, paleontology inserts the proper name of the fossil ("its taxonomic alphabetic chromosomes") into the realm of language through the process of taxonomization. At this point, "the fossil as word disseminates itself as a hidden anagram throughout any number of printed texts" (McCaffery, "Perseus," 75-76). The fossil then completes its reproductive cycle by resedimenting itself on the level of the page, which can be further incorporated into larger units of strata, such as a book, bookcase, bookstore, or library (McCaffery, "Perseus," 77).

The implications of this notion for questions regarding Canadian (or other) identities are startling. Almost all texts, including proper names, can be demonstrated to contain mimetic traces of their geological precursors. McCaffery's example is that the name "John MacPherson" exhibits a total of eight active "alphabetic chromosomes" (i.e. letters) inherited from the Phacops fossil (an Ordovician-Devonian trilobite)—"an amazing example of complete anagrammatic reproduction restricted to a ruthless economy" ("Perseus," 76).

Strange as it initially sounds, paleogorgonization is not all that far removed from the theory of mimetics that Richard Dawkins formulates in *The Selfish Gene*. The book's basic argument is that in the earth's prehistory, certain molecules called replicators (because they have the property of being able to create copies of themselves [Dawkins 15]) were the impetus for the evolution of more complex living systems, like human beings. "Replicators began not merely to exist, but to construct for themselves containers, vehicles for their continued existence" (Dawkins 19). In other words, we are the survival machines constructed by the strain of replicator known as the gene.

As does McCaffery, Dawkins sites genetic replication as the middle stage in a gradual translation of information from geology to language. "A. G. Cairns-Smith has made the intriguing suggestion that our ancestors, the first replicators, may have been not organic molecules at all, but inorganic crystals—minerals, little bits of clay" (Dawkins 21-22). On the other end of the cycle, Dawkins posits the emergence of a new kind of replicator, the meme, a unit of cultural transmission which moves from brain to brain, propagating itself through language (192)[10]. It is therefore possible for the same information to replicate itself (and a multitude of slightly inaccurate copies) through all three stages: mineral, biological, and linguistic.

McCaffery sums up the results of his efforts as follows:

art by Bill E. Burns

If nothing else the Perseus project should open the curtains on a new philo-
sophic theatre in which the Medusa story can be re-staged; where Perseus might
return the same prince as before and stand with face averted from the gorgon. But
this time his shining shield will be the blank pages of a voluminous and obsolete
dictionary and the image reflected there will be his own.

Beyond reason we always find the dialectic and behind the dialectic is always the
laughter. So the final question will be the first question and the first question will
be this:

NOT how the head will be decapitated

BUT whose head it is that must eventually roll? ("Perseus," 78-79)

"Pataphysics is an intellectual game that allows for the rethinking of the myths and assumptions that determine identity. As such, it is one weapon in McCaffery's arsenal of strategies for attempting to demonstrate the limitations of dominant writerly and philosophic conventions, largely determined by "White Anglo-Saxon heterosexual males" (Markus 30). Since McCaffery—and virtually all other currently practicing "Pataphysicists (except for the French "White *Gallic* hetero-sexual males")—belong to this Group, the act becomes one of self-decapitation. "Pataphysics, then, is a tool that might allow patriarchal systems of knowledge to confront themselves, exposing their own constructions as non-sense.

4.3 The Institute of Hmmrian Studies

Strangely enough, outside of the immediate "Pataphysical community, few people are willing to acknowledge the existence of Hmmr, the world's oldest civilization. Allegedly founded in 9300 B.C. by Xrtzh and his nine companions (the Ptntr), the Hmmrian civilization effectively ruled Southwestern Ontario until its destruction ca. 7779 B.C. (Sanderson, "Hmmrian Studies: Some Reports," 135-37). Through their geognostic explorations of and ruminations on the holy island of Hmmr (Pelee Island) and Piccu Carlu (Point Carling), various members of the Institute—especially Dr. R. W. Sanderson, Prof. Kurt Wurstwagen, Richard Truhlar, and Adrian Fortesque—have struggled to bring knowledge of Hmmrian civilization to a resistant twentieth century audience.

The reaction to the discovery of a proto-Mayan pyramid at Piccu Carlu ("the only surviving example of proto-Mayan architecture in all of the Americas" [Wurstwagen "Piccu Carlu: The Muskoka-Maya Connection" 151]) is an excellent example of the adversity facing these dedicated "Pataphysicists. As Prof. Wurstwagen relates, in somewhat embittered fashion:

Modern mythobastardization has nurtured the common belief that the structure
is a Victorian water tower erected to supply the early settlement with a plentiful
water supply from the proximous lakes.... [A] conspiracy has been operative, an
attempt to effect a geomantic pseudicity upon the clear facts of history. (144-45)

Those "clear facts," illuminated by the often blindingly brilliant insights of "Pataphysics, point once again to the influence of geognosis on language, and hence on consciousness.

The Piccu Carlu pyramid is a remarkably austere structure; Wurstwagen, referring to the 1873 Schrodinger translation of the legendary stone Book of Mool, attributes this austerity to a belief in the always-already written nature of stone (148-49). The effect of this belief was the production of a society that placed heavy proscriptions on writing, since it was regarded to be "the extra-human activity *par excellence*" (Wurstwagen 151), and fetishized the act of reading the granitic Ur-text, "the signature of the god(s)" (Wurstwagen 148).

When the (proto-)Mayan culture moved southward to the Yucatan, granite ceased to be the signifier of silent prohibition, and writing emerged through a process of mimesis and an eventual deviation from that mimesis. Professor Wurstwagen follows the speculations of Mrs. Mindermast in this regard:

> *Writing became the self-assertion of the stone, an overinscribing, a rendering into excess and overflow of its own inherent message. The ultimate mimetic practice. And somewhere between 550 B.C. and 300 A.D. [sic] Mayan writing became transgressive, a countermark or anti-script, a strategy of priestly power and control. And granite, once the immutable grammatologic origin becomes the vulnerable surface submitted to the onslaught of logocentric plasticity. (qtd. in Wurstwagen 152)*

Once again, "Pataphysics simultaneously creates and problematizes a link between writing and place. In its mimetic stage, when writing acts as a literal overinscribing of geologic striations, it can be said to act as a re-presentation of what the Hmmrians called tzn, "the invisible grammar or structure which generated, not merely the particular shape and material of the object, but its history as well" (Sanderson, 132) [Cf. Dewdney's concretions]. But writing always transgresses its mimetic function, and becomes a palimpincestuous over-writing—an inverted doubling.

In other words, writing is akin to geomancy as well as geognosis. "Geomancy took the existing elements in nature, aligning and shaping them to augment and focus the yin/yang energy currents that flow over the earth's surface" (TRG, *Rational Geomancy: The Kids of the Book Machine* 33). As a paradoxical "augmentation" of the natural, it is totally excessive: the "Pataphysical solution to an imaginary problem. It is the deployment of geomancy that allows Wurstwagen to decide that the culture of Piccu Carlu had a form of writing after all. By connecting points on aerial photographs representing the Piccu Carlu pyramid and the remains of other such sites[11], he discovers "the Muskokan 'vacuscript' or topographic cipher, the incision without incision that circumvented without transgression the great lithic taboo" (Wurstwagen, 153). This (non)existent writing structured upon its own absence, "hidden for all time in a macrotext inscribed within the land," transliterates as "moo-ul-staa-aat": ancestral home (Wurstwagen, 154).

4.4 bp Nichol: Alphabet Archaeologist

Wurstwagen and his colleagues at the Institute are not the only "Pataphysicists who have speculated on the relationship between language, geology, and ancient Canadian civilizations. bp Nichol, Supremet Satrap of the Canadian "Pataphysical movement, Grand Master of Strategic Eristics and Alphabet Research, and secretary for Writers in Support of Alphabet Archaeology, has done extensive research into the geognostic and geomantic activities of the prehistoric Manitoba alphabet cult.

Most of this work appears in Nichol's *Probable Systems* 36, entitled "Digging Up The Pas T." Through careful examination of maps of Winnipeg and the surrounding area, Nichol presents a case for the existence of messages coded into the environment in two forms: "landuage" and "air say" ("Digging," 26). Since *Probable Systems* 34, which was to expand on his ruminations on air say, remains unpublished[12], I will deal here chiefly with the notion of landuage, which is, in any event, more in line with the geognostic focus of this essay.

"Digging Up The Pas T" expresses a belief in Manitoban place names as encoded transmissions from a (possibly nonhuman) civilization ancestral to the Hmmrian empire (37-38). These messages were "deliberately wrinkled"— written with implicit redundancies and overcodings in the manner of James Joyce and Gertrude Stein—in order to ensure that some of their content survived the inevitable deterioration to be encountered in their transmission through "the noisy channel of history" ("Nichol, "Digging," 33).

For example, Nichol translates the name of Hnausa (an Icelandic-settled community north of Winnipeg) as "Hn(sdnnr) was A (i.e. the beginning)" ("Digging," 36). In other words, Hnausa was at one time the site of Hnsdnnr, one of the Three Cities of Hnsdnnr mentioned in the Lewis and Sanderson translation of the Hmmrian "Royal Cylinder" 2957.345: "As Naked children, O Xrtznqrh, my people fled the Three Cities of Hnsdnnr in ancient time" (Sanderson 137).[13] Aside from demonstrating that, contra Sanderson's claims, the origins of the world's oldest civilization are in Manitoba rather than Wisconsin, this argument dates the inception of that civilization to ca. 12,000 B.C., and makes some tentative efforts to identify the first recruits of the alphabet cult.[14]

Nichol's "Pataphysical work is also important for its challenging of the Wurstwagen/Truhlar thesis re: the proto-Mayan taboo against writing. He rereads the Schrodinger translation of the stone Book of Mool in light of the principles of "wrinkling" (layering & redundancy) discovered in the Manitoban texts, pointing out that the Muskokan vacuscript is not a ground writing, but a tracing of air say, the letters in the sky. "Stone is also 's tone'...& 'speech dies' the 'speeched eyes' thru which eternity, & the gods, are glimpsed. Every stone rimes the sky in some way" (Nichol, "Digging," n. 13, 34).

Nichol, as proprietor of the "Pataphysical Hardware Company, did his best to bring "Pataphysics to the masses with such useful products as inflatable thought balloons, "Jarry Brand" Plaster of Paris (to scatter on books for that fashionably antiquated look), and "Grow Your Own Stein" rose (is a rose is a rose) seeds. The most useful of these devices, though, because it subsumes all of "Pataphysics (in the true fashion of the inverted metonym), is The "PhD Tested & Approved" CRITICAL FRAME OF REFERENCE. The FRAME (Fixed Reference And Meaning Explainer) is a transparent piece of plastic measuring 4" by 5". It can be used to easily win arguments with doubters who ask "what's your frame of reference?" by simply placing it over an area of text.

In addition, the FRAME demonstrates that "any frame of reference is just a window on the world." Such an insight is one of many heralded by the accompanying pamphlet's bold announcement: "you'll reach new levels of philosophical *and* philological awareness and implication thru the daily application of our device." Unlike cheaper FRAMES "from less reputable companies," the one produced by the "PHC lacks "the now obsolete black border whose funereal aspect properly announces the intellectual death of its users." Instead, its clear edges, which are nevertheless tightly defined, blur at a distance and become invisible. As Nichol writes, "at the proper distance the whole world fits inside the frame." "Pataphysics is *the* science....

5 Tentative Conclusion: Beginning Again

What does all this "Pataphysical geognosticism accomplish? Here are a few suggestions. "Pataphysics seems to fall under the aegis of what Brian Massumi (quoting heavily from Deleuze and Guattari) calls "a bastard philosophy."

> Legitimate philosophy is the handiwork of "bureaucrats" of pure reason who speak in "the shadow of the despot" and are in historical complicity with the State. They invent "a properly spiritual...absolute State that...effectively functions in the mind." Theirs is the discourse of sovereign judgement, of stable subjectivity legislated by "good" sense, of rocklike identity, "universal" truth, and (white male) justice. "Thus the exercise of their thought is in comformity with the aims of the real State, with the dominant significations, and with the requirements of the established order." (A User's Guide to Capitalism and Schizophrenia: Deviations From Deleuze and Guattari, 1)

As a form of "nomad thought," "Pataphysics ("a science of the perpetually open" [TRG, "Introduction" 7]) replaces the closed equation of representation (I=I=not you) with an open one (...+y+z+a+...) (Massumi, 6). As such, it allows for the inclusion of traditionally excluded subject positions and ideologies.

"Pataphysics, then, has the possibility to become supplementary to efforts by postcolonial scholars attempting to re-insert the obscured history of indigenous and colonized peoples, by demonstrating the absurdity of the theories and methodologies of the colonizers themselves.

Our hope is a faint one: that others will follow and in following lead to the col-
lection of the neglected and (who knows, as a poetic corollary, the neglect of the
collected) those who we have failed to remember or were forced to ignore, the
already passed or the yet to come. (TRG, "Introduction," 8)

Like Jarry's famous "How To Build A Time Machine," the geognostic texts of
Canadian "Pataphysics simulate the tropes of academicism (professorial titles,
academic writing styles) so well that it it often difficult to tell where they modu-
late into fantasy. Stylistically, they represent what Roger Shattuck calls "sci-
ence-nonfiction" in his Introduction to Jarry's selected works (11)—writing that
satirically and sardonically propels the presumptions of the sciences to their logical and imaginary extremes. "Pataphysics reflects the orientalist mirror of academic discourse back against itself, creating an infinite tunnel of funhouse
mirrors.

But this is not the end of the narrative. As Jarry well knew, each generation
of "Pataphysicians must anticipate its own irrelevance:

We too shall become solemn, fat, and Ubu-like and shall publish extremely
classical books which will probably lead to our becoming mayors of small towns
where, when we become academicians, the blockheads constituting the local
intelligentsia will present us with Sèvres vases, while they present their mous-
taches on velvet cushions to our children. And another lot of young people will
appear, and consider us completely out of date, and they will write ballads to
express their loathing of us, and that is just the way things should always be.
("Theater" 85)

Even as this essay is being written, a new wave of Canadian "Pataphysics is
about to break, and once again the geognostic langscape will be transformed.

After a thoroughly "Pataphysical evening involving an open microphone
poetry reading, too much draft beer, threatening gestures from travelling insurance salesmen, and a holdup man waving "a big shiny gun" at him, poet
Michael Holmes, referring back to Jarry's definition of 'Pataphysics, was inspired
by the possibility of a *virtual* "Pataphysics: a high-tech lowlife screed on society
(how it is and how it might be) as seen through the wizened eyes of suburban
youth, marginalized and mediated by technology. Holmes finds his blueprints in
the secret doctrines of Canadian "Pataphysics, bp Nichol's paragrammar and
Christopher Dewdney's "Parasite Maintenance": "The radio telescope becomes
a model of the *bi-conscious* interface between 'the mind' and signals from the
'outside' which the poet receives" (Dewdney, "Parasite," 20). In the manuscript
for his second book, tentatively titled *Satellite Dishes from the Future Bakery*,
Holmes welds together fragments from the suburban scrapheap ([p]rose tattoos,
Ernie & Bert, HLG Lsker DLGL, the Toronto Maple Leafs, lumberjackets, Ontario
ditchweed, and the streets of Bramalea's "Alphabet City"). The result is a Jarry-
rigged but highly effective parabolic antenna—a pirate TV station of the mind.

Christian Bök (a.k.a. Book) 15, another young Canadian poet, is currently working on a "Pataphysically and geognostically flavoured text entitled *Crystallography: Book One of Information Theory.* The title itself (which translates as "lucid writing") is an ironic pun, for the text uses a difficult and opaque scientific lexicon to address the ambiguities of language and identity. Bök also pushes the tendency of "Pataphysics to delineate the macro within the micro by focusing on the internal structure of individual letters (see, for example, his "Figure 2.5: A photomicrograph of the letter "Y" magnified 25x to reveal its innate crystalline structure" (Bök, 30). In effect, he has gone one step beside and beyond the geognostics of the previous generation of "Pataphysicians.

There is also the matter of the mysterious manitoba alphabet cult. Nichol writes that "I had begun to suspect, further, that the alphabet cult, tho its beginnings were shrouded in pre-history, had continued in an unbroken tradition into, at least, the recent historical past, & that clues to it, & perhaps even the cult itself, might exist in the present" ("Digging," 25). There is growing evidence to support the thesis that that cult may still exist. Texts written in an odd hermetic "proximalphabet signed "manitoba alphabet cult" (always in the lower case) have begun to surface both in Winnipeg and southwestern Ontario, suggesting that the connections to Hnsdnnr and Hmmr are still strong.

The smooth space of Canadian "Pataphysics remains, then, (in)completely open. The only appropriate conclusion regarding what might constitute its next development can be the one drawn by Jarry himself (channeled by Steve McCaffery) on the final line of "The Claim to Shape in a "Patalogmena Towards A Zero Reading (for Ihab Hassan)".

---

1. "Poland" in the original. In *Alfred Jarry: The Man With the Axe*, Nigey Lennon notes that "Poland, as a result of partition and political chaos, was in 1896 virtually absent from the map"(49). Questions of partitioning and political chaos aside, Canada is without question absent from the 'Pataphysical map, so the analogy holds.

2. A field, a heterogenous smooth space, is wedded to a very particular type of multiplicity: nonmetric, acentered, rhizomatic multiplicities that occupy space without "counting" it....They do not meet the visual condition of being observable from a point in space external to them. (Deluze & Guattari, *Mille Plateaux*, 371.)

3. There are two versions of the TRG's "Introduction" to Canadian "Pataphysics: *Open Letter* 4.6 & 7 (Winter 1980-81): 7-8, and a slightly different version, which appears in *Rational Geomancy*. I have chosen to refer to the latter here because of its parenthetical glossing of the more obscure points of the definition, which constitutes the major difference between the two versions.

4. In the concluding notes to her book on Jarry, Nigey Lennon makes the following remarks:

[I]t has proved virtually impossible to deal with the College [de 'Pataphysique] by mail from the United States. They simply do not respond to letters, whether due to understaffing or perhaps because they consider letters requesting specific information to be unpataphysical by nature. Furthermore, the official regents of the Collège de 'Pataphysique based in the united states have been equally unwilling to answer letters from myself and my publisher regarding translations of Jarry's writing. I guess professional pataphysicians are just a gang of rugged individualists (124).

5. "A special number on 'Pataphysics of any review, annual or perennial, evergreen or deciduous, can serve no constructive purpose" (Shattuck, "Superliminal," 30).
6. The last page of the *Papers Delivered at The Symposium of Linguistic Onto-Genetics* reads "100 copies printed. Distributed in the great now-you-see-it-now-you-don't tradition by grOnk."
7. "Paleonym" is Jacques Derrida's term for an "old" signifier that has also become associated with a "new" meaning (see *Dissemination*, 3-5). It too is a kind of 'Pataphysical inverted and doubled quotation. That factor, plus the geo-logical connotations of its prefix, suggests its usage in a discussion of 'Pataphysics.
8. N.B. This was noticeably earlier than the doubling of the 'Pataphysical elide.
9. Even those "Pataphysicists who see the notion of identity and the Imaginary as less problematic come to the same conclusions. Michael Dean, The Director of the Institute of Linguistic Onto-Genetics (another branch of Canadian 'Pataphysics), writes that:

> [I]f "Pataphysics can be described...as "the science of imaginary solutions," then surly [*sic*] Linguistic Onto-Genetics must be described as "the solution to the imaginary, the clarification of the mysteries of Imagination."

> But Imagination can never be known in itself. So, in Linguistic Onto-Genetics we attend to its affects: language and art....("An Introduction From the Chair," 5-6.)

10. In *"THE STRAYTEXT DEVICE*: Pure and Applied Research," "Pataphysicist Lledir Nhah-Nhoj poses the following question: "It is no secret that, as Aldo Breun has said, 'man is the landscape of language.' The question is: does mankind provide a suitable landscape for language, or not?" (109). The answer seems to be that yes, language is propagating like mad...but its propagation may have detrimental effects on humanity similar to those that humanity has on the landscape.
11. "Geomancy is defined as...'usually, divination by means of lines or figures formed by jotting down on paper a number of dots at random' [*OED*]" (qtd. in TRG, *Rational*, 153).
12. In "Digging Up the Pas T," Nichol provides a fragment of PS 34, consisting of what anyone but a "Pataphysician would interpret as a weathermap. Instead, he reads it instead as "track[ing] the movement of giant airborne H's & L's over continental North America & the surrounding oceans." Nichol then concludes that these maps detailing the movement of airborne letters "point to alphabet worship as tied to real phenomena in the atmosphere, [at] a time when the letter (& hence the word) was present in the world as thing, as visible fact in the land & air scapes" (Nichol, "Digging," 24-25).

Sadly, this work was incomplete at the time of Nichol's death in 1988, and will have to remain so until some other member of the College takes up the project. However, given the present economic climate, even the best qualified of "Pataphysicians will likely encounter even more difficulty in procuring funds for this work than did Nichol (see "Digging," 39).
13. Nichol locates the other two cities of Hnsdnnr close by at Gimli (which translates from the Icelandic as "home of the gods"), and Hecla Island, which is remarkably similar in climate to Pelee Island in southwestern Ontario. "Xrtzh chose a site, an island on a large inland lake near extensive marshes, that matched the garbled descriptions in the fragmentary texts of his own history" (Nichol, "Digging," 37).
14. Nichol comments that he uses the term "alphabet cult" rather loosely to refer to both the (nonhuman, godlike) originators of the Manotoba texts and the people with whom they were entrusted ("Digging," 31). In addition, he suggests that the manitoba alphabet cult may still be in existence in some form, a possibility which I will touch on later in this essay.
15. "Christian Bök/Book" is one of the more subtle of "Pataphysical pseudonyms. Jarry had a close friend named Christian Beck, a Belgian writer who himself wrote under the pseudonym of Joseph Bossi (See Simon Watson Taylor's annotations to Chapter 10 in Jarry, *Exploits*, 260-61).
Bök/Book, of course, strenuously denies any such connection.

REVIEW OF DIFFICULT WORDS

our　　eight　　right　　no　　whole　　sum　　tale　　meet

	Place	Chinese	English
⌒ᘔ	Sandon	聖頓	sanitary
⌒ᘔ	Sardis	沙地士	Saxon
⌒ᘔ	Saunders Harbor	山呀士下巴	scabbard
⌒ᘔ	Salmon River	沙面李巴	scavenger
⌒ᘔ	Saanich	山汝治	scenery
⌒ᘔ	Salt Spring Island	所路市丙令埃嵩	schedule
⌒ᘔ	Savanas	蕃市嘩利	sciatica
⌒ᘔ	Sea Island	四埃嵩	science
⌒ᘔ	Semilkameen	士墨架文	scimitar
⌒ᘔ	Shuswap	所市滑	scrutineer
⌒ᘔ	Shapland	澀璧粦	sculler
⌒ᘔ	Sicamous	昔儉塵士	scythe
⌒ᘔ	Sidney Island	雪汝埃嵩	secretary
⌒ᘔ	Skeena	市卷拿	secrete
⌒ᘔ	Skidegate	市結地笨	serial
⌒ᘔ	Snowshoe Creek	士駑數隙	sheriff
⌒ᘔ	Somenos	心文弩士	shrewd
⌒ᘔ	Spallumacheen	市卑路尾申	siege
⌒ᘔ	Spalsum	市卑森	sirloin
⌒ᘔ	Spences Bridge	市片士卑唎治	skye-terrier
⌒ᘔ	Spuzzum	市正砧	slaughter
⌒ᘔ	Stanley	市丹利	sorrel
⌒ᘔ	Steveston	市地厰	Spaniard
⌒ᘔ	St. Mary's Mission	媽利尾善	spectacle
⌒ᘔ	Stony Creek	市蠶汝隙	spectre
⌒ᘔ	Stump Lake	市胆瀝	sprightly
⌒ᘔ	Sumas	所媽	squabble
⌒ᘔ	Surrey Centre	沙利仙呀	steward
⌒ᘔ	Union Mine	天寅米	stirrup
⌒ᘔ	Vancouver	云巧巴（即咸水埠）	stubborn
⌒ᘔ	Vanwinkle	云永路	sumac
⌒ᘔ	Van-Anda	溫晏呀	summons
⌒ᘔ	Vernon	云宵	super

our　　ate　　write　　know　　hole　　some　　tail　　meat

Jacques Boivin

ARE ANDREA DWORKIN'S BOOKS STILL OBSCENE IN CANADA?

On Jan. 15, Andrea Dworkin's *Pornography: Men Possessing Women* and *Woman Hating* were examined, determined to be obscene, and their entry into Canada prohibited by Canada Customs. Ironically, as reported in *Ms.* (May/June 1992, p. 14), Andrea Dworkin coauthored with Catharine MacKinnon the analysis of pornography which formed the basis of the winning intervention in the Supreme Court of Canada's new definition of obscenity (R. vs Butler). When a columnist for the Montréal *Gazette* lampooned the determination, Dworkin's books and other publications seized simultaneously were released with such haste that Canada Customs didn't even wait for a formal appeal. Yet in the 1992 banning of *Heroes, Dreams and Incest* by retired psychologist Robert Lally, Canada Customs took the position that once they determine an item to be obscene, it remains so if no formal appeal is received. Although the Alberta Attorney-General's office ruled that *Heroes, Dreams and Incest* was not obscene, an official with the Prohibited Importations Directorate stated that "it shouldn't change anything from our perspective" and Robert Lally's novel remains on their prohibited list, albeit misspelled. After claiming to derive their power to destroy books from the Criminal Code, Canada Customs places its bureaucracy above the judiciary and then disregards that bureaucracy when damage control requires it. (see page 3 of enclosed letter)

Are Censors Censoring "Censorship"?

Canada Customs' officials also disregard explicit treatments of censorship in books and encyclopedias so that they can deny being "censors." This denial is based on a literal reading of definitions of "censor" in abridged dictionaries that focus on the origin of the word in 443 B.C., when the office of the Roman censor was established, on overt expurgation, and on "prior restraint" as practised until the Age of Enlightenment. The unabridged *Webster's* defines the noun "censor" as "an official empowered to examine printed matter...in order to forbid...circulation" and the verb "censor" as "to...ban completely after examination," applicable descriptions of Canada Customs' activities. The censors' predilection for censorship may explain their censoring the word "censor." (see page 4)

What Does Censorship Promote ?

Selective prior restraint, international style, is Canada Customs' bag. As an optional "service" offered in Memorandum D9-1-1 (their policy and procedure regarding obscenity and hate propaganda) Canada Customs "reviews advance samples of goods, prior to commercial importation (...) and provides the importer or publisher with an opinion regarding its admissibility into Canada," a sugarcoating of prior restraint and covert expurgation. The Prohibited Importations Unit "also provides advice and guidance (...) to encourage and promote voluntary compliance," a service of little appeal to self-respecting creative individuals. Artistic pride or integrity aside, the small presses victimized by Canada Customs can ill afford to produce separate publications "edited for Canada", as profit-motivated disseminators do. Thus censors promote the exploitation and domination of standardized marketplaces with superficial, repetitive material that reflects neither the best in human beings nor their diversity...but rather the moribund values of a good ole bureaucrats' club.

*

Montréal, February 28th 1993
Department of Prohibited Goods
Tariff Programs and Appraisal Division
National Revenue
400 Youville Square 3rd floor
Montréal H2Y 2C2

Dear Canada Customs,

This is in response to your Detailed Adjustment Statement dated Dec. 2 1992 which redetermines that one copy of *Sexy Stories from the World Religions* (Last Gasp Eco-Funnies, 1990), and one copy of *Weird Smut Comics #3* (JAM Press, 1989), which I purchased from Last Gasp of San Francisco are to remain in your possession without compensation, and that any other copies of these two comic books are prohibited entry into Canada until such a time as you will no longer judge them to be "obscene."

On your original Notice of Determination dated July 31 1992, *Weird Smut Comics #3* is referred to as *Weird Smut Comics*, while on your Detailed Adjustment Statement it is called simply *Weird Smut*. Four different issues of *Weird Smut Comics* have been published in the past six years, and you have failed to specify that this is No. 3 even though it is clearly indicated on the comic book's cover and in the indicia. The other "prohibited" comic book is referred to as *Sexy stories from the world religion* (sic) by your Inspector on the Notice of Determination, whereas on the Detailed Adjustment Statement it underwent considerable degradation at the hands of your Tariff and Values Administrator to emerge as *Sexy Story from the Religions*. Again, the correct title is on the cover, elaborately rendered by talented young French artist Pascal Mezzo, and repeated in the indicia. Technically, you have yet to properly identify what you have seized, and have been holding non-existent publications for over six months. It's not as if numerous forms had been filled and truly detailed statements furnished; these are simple forms and filling them should be the specific expertise of your trained inspectors and administrators. In order to engage in book theft, you must violate my Human Rights, and the Butler decision confirmed that such practices also violate the fundamental freedoms of Canadians. Is this something to be done in cavalier fashion? Your inability to correctly perform such an elementary task as referring to a book by its proper title is symptomatic of a blatant disrespect for creative property, a regrettable contempt for human expression and a failure to intellectually grasp what you physically seize.

The same Detailed Adjustment Statement refers to comic books as "livres comiques." When I showed this document to the comics critic of *Le Devoir*, he became enraged and began to lecture me that only an australopithecine who doesn't know the first thing about either comics or "bandes dessinees" would attempt to coin such a term as "livres comiques." Caught off guard by this attack, my spontaneous response (believe it or not) was to defend your Tariff and Values Administrator. However, Pierre was not impressed by my chosen defense (the alienated brainlessness of bureaucracy). He also pointed out that your zany term "livres comiques" is incorrectly followed by the word "importees" in the feminine form, although the remainder of this clumsy sentence correctly reverts to the masculine. If the government of Canada sees fit to hire individuals to snoop around in my mail and tell me what I may or may not read, it might not be a bad idea to select individuals who can write.

NOTHING THREATENS FREEDOM OF THE PERSONAL-ITY AND THE MEANING OF LIFE LIKE WAR, POVERTY, TERROR. BUT THERE ARE ALSO INDIRECT AND ONLY SLIGHTLY MORE REMOTE DANGERS. ONE OF THESE IS THE STUPEFACTION OF MAN BY MASS CULTURE WITH ITS INTENTIONAL OR COMMERCIALLY MOTIVATED LOWERING OF INTELLECTUAL LEVEL AND CONTENT, WITH ITS STRESS ON ENTERTAINMENT OR UTILITARI-ANISM AND WITH ITS CAREFULLY PROTECTIVE CEN-SORSHIP.

– Andrei Sakharov

In an article on adult comics by Richard Gehr in the *Voice Literary Supplement* for December 1992 (New York, No. 111, p. 28), the *Weird Smut* series is referred to as "less turn-ons than put-ons of conventional sexual representation." In other words, the *Weird Smut* comics are satirical rather than exploitative. Apparently you disagree with this and believe not only that *Weird Smut Comics* #3 is exploitative but that it is unduly exploitative and furthermore, that this is its dominant characteristic (00.7%) and that it is not protected by freedom of expression or even by "any doubt in this regard" (R. v. Butler). I regret to announce that the willingness to burn books does not automatically make you better critics than writers published in the *Voice Literary Supplement*.

A review of *Sexy Stories from the World Religions* by comics critic Hal Hargit appeared in *The Comics Fandom Examiner*, No. 15, May 1990, Mu Press, Seattle, p. 26. Strangely enough, this positive review does not even contain a passing reference to "scenes de degradation" so predominantly and exclusively evident in the eyes of your Tariff and Values Administrator. Nor does the review mention "anal penetration" (a minuscule detail in one out of 242 illustrations) or other "acts" referred to on your original Notice of Determination and which your Memorandum D9-1-1 so carefully enumerates. Instead, Mr. Hargit focuses on the impressive roster of artists assembled by editor Erick Gilbert, praises some individual contributions, and appears amused by the tone of irreverent dissent aimed at religious zeal which characterizes the book as a whole. How can this point of view possibly be reconciled with your own? Could it be that *The New Encyclopaedia Britannica* (1990) is correct in its Micropaedia entry for "obscenity" when it unhesitatingly states that "obscenity, like beauty, is in the eye of the beholder"?

In referring to Section 163 of the Criminal Code, the Butler decision specifies that "Materials which have scientific, artistic or literary merit are not caught by the provision." A problem may perhaps arise when such materials are not caught by the provision, but by Canada Customs. In my letter of October 26th 1992 (page 2) I provided you with a brief sampling of the critical attention that the artists represented in these two seized comic books have attracted. Such critical attention is particularly remarkable considering that most of the contributors are still young, struggling artists. But perhaps I took the wrong approach. Perhaps you've never heard of *Artforum*, let alone read it. Perhaps you've never seen an *Encyclopaedia Universalis* in the pulp. Perhaps you believe that the Gale Research Company compiles data on the wind chill factor. And who is this Sotheby's, and why is he or she auctioning the work of pornographers?

LA CENSURE...IMPOSE AUX ÉCRIVAINS LA VOLONTÉ DE GENS LITTÉRAIREMENT ANALPHABÉTES. SURVIVANCE DU MOYEN AGE, LA CENSURE TRAINE JUSQU'AUX ABORDS DU XXIe SIÉCLE DES VESTIGES DE L'AGE ANCESTRAL! ÉTANT MORTELLE PAR NATURE, ELLE A LA PRÉTENTION DE S'ARROGER LA FACULTÉ— PROPRE AU TEMPS IMMORTEL—DE DISCERNER LES LIVRES INDIGNES.

– Alexandre Soljénitsyne

On page 4 of my October 26 letter, I also provided you with background information on Last Gasp of San Francisco. I attempted to succinctly convey Last Gasp's marginal but unique cultural position and implied that you cease targeting packages originating from them. To no avail. By mid-December, a shipment from Last Gasp intended for Montréal's Le Dernier too had become a source of conflict between the two, due to tardiness. On Jan. 15, the probable culprit was revealed when you released part of the shipment and forwarded a Notice of Determination to the effect that the remainder (multiple copies of 2 books by Andrea Dworkin, one by Kathy Acker, and 5 periodicals) had been examined and seized due to a mixture of 6A3 ("depictions or descriptions of bondage, involuntary servitude and the state of human beings subjected to external control, in a sexual context") and 6A4 ("depictions or descriptions which appear to be associating sexual pleasure or gratification with pain and suffering, and with the mutilation of or letting of blood from any part of the human body, involving violence, coercion, and lack of basic dignity and respect for a human being"). As "emphasized" in your Memorandum D9-1-1, the presence of 6A3 and 6A4 was "assessed as an integral part of the entire work and in the context of its theme." Also, "full recognition" (not partial recognition) was "given to freedom of expression." Unlike most of your confused or frightened victims, Stephane Gelinas of Le Dernier Mot hollered and got lucky: on Jan. 22, The Page Two Column of the *Gazette* made jolly good fun of your determination. There's a nice bunch of Montréalers still flabbergasted by the ensuing hot potato speed with which ALL of the prohibited items were sent to Le Dernier Mot without any letter of apology or explanation. Case closed? In your haste, you overlooked a bureaucratic detail which I will point out after the following paragraph.

In early 1992, as reported in the *Globe and Mail* (June 22, pages A1 & A2), you seized a manuscript entitled *Heroes, Dreams and Incest* by retired psychologist Robert Lally and determined that it was child pornography containing degradation, sex with violence, etc. You then contacted the Royal Canadian Mounted Police, who raided Mr. Lally's home, but the Alberta Attorney-General's office took a more enlightened view and ruled that the book did not violate the Criminal Code. Consequently, *Heroes, Dreams and Incest* is now legal in this country—yet Canada Customs maintains that its future entry into Canada is prohibited because Mr. Lally never appealed your unilateral "determination." Mr. Lally did write to you within the 90-day period, informing you of the Alberta Attorney-General's decision but this letter (not being a formal appeal) was apparently given as much consideration as my letter of October 26, in which I suggested you cease seizing shipments from Last Gasp. Your *List of Material Reviewed by the Prohibited Importations Directorate* covering the first four months of 1992 indexes as obscene and prohibited a "booklet" (*sic*) entitled *Heros, Dreams and Incest*. Although some may interpret this Freudian slip as a shadowy preoccupation with "eros," my interpretation is that it means that any manuscript or book entitled *Heroes, Dreams and Incest* by Robert Lally does not appear as such in your Technical Reference System and that its importation is therefore not prohibited. Problem solved! You're very welcome. (Incidentally, are D. H. Lawrence's *Baby Chatterley's Lovers* and James Joyce's *Ulcers* still considered obscene?)

Returning now to your seizure of January 15, note that Le Dernier Mot HAS NOT APPEALED your determination. Their B2 Adjustment Request form remains unfiled. Thus, by the very logic which you exhibited in the Robert Lally case, Andrea Dworkin's two books, Kathy Acker's novel, and the seized issues of five periodicals remain obscene and their entry into Canada is prohibited. Investigating Canada Customs' track record quickly reveals that in the absence of media attention, you rarely release items that submit to your "appeals" process, whereas if media attention either precedes the importation of a controversial item or follows one of your seizures, the rate of release is quite generous. May I remind you that despite your aversion to scrutiny, a media appeal is not a formal appeal. If you wish to properly clear Ms. Dworkin's books and the other seized items, one honest option remains. Since they have been determined to be obscene and not appealed, snatch them again if you can spot them crossing the border, hope that your victim appeals and THEN do a redetermination as you see fit. I'm sure you'll appreciate my fine grasp of bureaucratic etiquette.

LA CENSURE, VIOLATION INSOLENTE DE NOS DROITS, ASSUJETTISSEMENT DE LA PARTIE ÉCLAIRÉE DE LA NATION A SA PARTIE VILE ET STUPIDE

– Benjamin Constant

Interestingly enough, you have made verbal admissions to the effect that the Last Gasp/Dernier Mot seizure was "a mistake." And what kind of mistake would that be? Did all eight publications miraculously and simultaneously become devoid of objectionable elements? If this seizure was a mistake, does that mean that your shameful harassment of gay & lesbian bookstores over the years has not been a mistake? How about the fact that comic books containing work by artists mentioned in the Encyclopaedia Britannica are 217 times more likely than other comic books to be seized by you, is that a mistake or not? Perhaps you are referring to the same kind of mistake that occurred on my Notice of Determination and Detailed Adjustment Statement, which together contain a total of ten (10) errors and omissions? Or do you mean to imply that the violation of human rights, the scapegoating of culture and the witch-hunt for books may be labelled "a mistake" ?

It has been reported to me that officials of the Prohibited Importations Directorate deny being "censors" or that what they perform is "censorship." Since censors have persistently suppressed the truth, appealed to fear and promoted mediocrity, your reticence is understandable. On the other hand, maintaining a state of denial happens to be a cornerstone of the psychology of censorship. In order to help you gain a better knowledge of who you are, here are some key segments from the unabridged Webster's Third New International Dictionary:

1 cen-sor \'*sen(t)se(r)*\ *n -s [L. fr. censere to assess, tax; akin to Skt samsati he recites, praises]*

a: an official empowered to examine written or printed matter (as manuscripts of books or plays) in order to forbid publication, circulation, or representation if it contains anything objectionable

e: one who is lacking official sanction but acting ostensibly in society's interests scrutinizes communications, compositions, and entertainments to discover anything immoral, profane, seditious, heretical, or otherwise offensive

2 censor \'\ *vt censor; censored; censoring\-n(t)s(e)ring\censors: to subject to a censor's examination; often: to alter, delete, or ban completely after examination*

censorship \'*sen(t)se(r),ship*\ *n -s* 1: *the institution, system, or practice of censoring: the actions or practices of censors or censorates;*

3: *the process of excluding from consciousness those ideas and feelings that would be intolerable in other than symbolic form*

I suppose it is second nature for censors to censor definitions of censorship until censorship becomes some other censor's censorship. If you are not censors, what are you? Comedians? "We're not censors, we only ban, burn and/or shred books and stuff." Bear in mind that the censor's power operates only in the present and that the censor's philosophy is limited to constantly shifting self-justification. The history of censors is never written by censors but by the censored. The one scenario open to would-be censors for a graceful entry into history is exemplified in the text for "*Erotisme (Arts et littérature)*" of the *Encyclopaedia Universalis:*

"tenons pour faste le ler juillet 1969, date à laquelle on abolit au Danemark l'article 234 du Code pénal, celui précisément en vertu duquel on avait condamné l'Histoire d'O. Décision d'autant inattendue que prise par un ministre conservateur de la Justice, M. Knud Thestrup...plutôt la solution danoise que la russe, la chrétienne, la confuceenne, la maoïste."

After stating that prohibited goods may be abandoned to Her Majesty, the reverse side of your Notice of Determination ends on this cryptic note: "For your further information, section 142 outlines the manner in which abandoned and forfeited goods will be disposed." My curiosity was aroused by this promise of further information outlining manner of disposal and I searched out the soporific document in question. The Customs Act in the 1991 *Statutes of Canada* indeed fulfilled the stated promise with astonishing flair: prohibited goods will "be disposed of in such a manner, otherwise than by sale, as the Minister may direct." Is this truly what you mean by FURTHER INFORMATION that OUTLINES the MANNER IN WHICH prohibited goods are disposed? So transparent you'd best wash them bricks with Windex. It's such a Sisyphean struggle being book burners in a state of denial, eh?

b_P   7

Good news, sort of! I would like to acknowledge receiving in good condition on December 2nd 1992 the 12 other comic books ordered by me from Last Gasp and which you had been holding in undeclared detainment since sometime between June 6 (shipping date from Last Gasp) and July 31 (date of your Notice of Determination). I enthusiastically paid the $3.22 in GST plus the euphemistic "handling fee" of $5.00, equivalent to a 17.90 assessment. From the point of view of national revenue, this certainly compares favorably to the fees I would have owed in the protectionist days before Free Trade (0%).

When I accuse you of "undeclared detainment," it's only fair that I admit making abstraction of the fact that the Notice of Detention accompanying your Notice of Determination described my comic books as "VHS." Your Notice of Determination stated that the goods were "declared" and Last Gasp's packaging (now in my possession) identifies the contents as "14 magazines." So if we can agree that comic books (or magazines) occasionally bear a striking resemblance to "VHS," then you did in fact notify me of the ongoing detainment on July 31. It is puzzling that an Inspector who stumbles at the distinction between comic books and "VHS" is nevertheless capable of discriminating between due exploitation, undue exploitation, due non-exploitation and overdue exploration.

Although it should not be construed to denote in any way that I condone undue paternalistic interference in cultural activity, I formally request a further re-determination of the two comic books which you have abducted and jailed on death row for artistic crimes against your XXX imagination.

Sincerely yours,

Jacques Boivin
4531 Bordeaux
Montréal, Québec

AS SEEMS POSSIBLE, OUR CHILDREN MAY HAVE TO FIGHT ALL OVER AGAIN THE BATTLE FOR THE FREEDOM OF THE MIND.

– Will and Ariel Durant

MICHAEL WILLIAM
WHEN THE NATIONALIST FRENZY STRIKES...

Are you a victim of the following situations?

More and more, René Lévesque pops up in your dreams; even in your erotic fantasies;

or

Your husband (or wife) complains: "Ginette (or Pierre), you've been wearing that separatist T-shirt for the last four days, and it stinks. We're doing laundry tomorrow. Can't you put something else on?"
But wearing anything else makes you feel naked, and you can't bear the shame.

If you're suffering from experiences similar to these, you may want to seek the help of *Nationalists Anonymous.*

Nationalists Anonymous (NA) is a support group of former nationalists who, together, face up to the problem of nationalism. In a world where the rise of nationalism has spread everywhere, we believe it's more urgent than ever to talk openly about this plague, which is responsible for wreaking such havoc in our personal lives, and to fight it.

At first, in many cases, the nationalist believes that nationalism is good for him. Brandishing flags and other nationalist symbols, being proud to be Québécois (or American or Japanese or whatever), creates a feeling of power, an intense but usually short-lived euphoria. Blending into the crowd, grasping at a false sense of community appears to give him a much-needed identity, the feeling that he's a somebody. At the same time, it enables the nationalist to avoid confronting what he has truly become.

Trying to regain that initial feeling of well-being, the nationalist has the tendency to resort increasingly to nationalism, and at more foolhardy levels. But as nationalism fails to identify and target the real enemies, since it doesn't respond to his genuine underlying needs and desires, the nationalist remains dissatisfied. His daily life, the existence of which can't be denied, stays as banal as ever, while his relationship with "the people" continues to be distant and alienating. Disoriented, frustrated, afflicted by hallucinations, the nationalist holds dear the illusion that everything will be better come independence (even though similar scenarios throughout the world clearly demonstrate that the birth of the Nation doesn't resolve the problems of the average Joe). Habitually placing people into categories of "us" and "them" according to their ethnic or national origins, more and more intoxicated by nationalist fever, in some extreme cases the nationalist ends up wallowing in a blatantly racist state.

As a result of indulging in nationalism on a regular basis, the critical faculties of the nationalist become blurred and dulled. Firm in his belief that "our" culture must be protected at all costs, the nationalist accepts, because he is "of our stripe," all sorts of crap and mediocrities thrown at him by the forces of capital and the media. Smug, self-important, incapable of any honest self-criticism or of envisaging a truly different way of life, he becomes the best champion of the status quo (when it's precisely "our" culture that needs in large part to be dismantled). At the same time, the confused and agitated nationalist succeeds, in many cases, in convincing himself that his culture differs from, and is even superior to that of the Americans, the French, the Ontarians, the Germans, etc., ignoring the simple truth that these societies all share the same fundamental values.

Ironically, he fervently believes in the great equalizers of contemporary culture: mass communication (rare are those who don't have a T.V.) and the fundamental necessity of capital, industrialism, and the State. Having accepted the basis of contemporary domination, he readily submits to its economic demands and hierarchies. Instead of rebelling against the system, against his role as a mere cog in a mega-machine beyond his control, he bows down to the dictates of "his" economy, the national economy. Passive, subjugated, he's an easy target for the slogans of the myriad politicians, corporate leaders, and careerist nationalists, on the right and the left, searching out cannon fodder for their pathetic racketeering.

Unable to recognize and appreciate the unique qualities of people he encounters, the colourful tapestry woven into the fabric of humanity, he judges people solely according to how they fit into the nationalist plan, setting them against the people, the will of the masses. Instead of forming qualitatively different relationships with individuals in his life, enriching his emotional contacts, he mechanically throws in his lot with those who, far from friends, are people he doesn't even know!

Nationalism inspires our pity. But though the nationalist has to be helped through this madness, and is usually in a sorry state, we mustn't pity him too much. These days nationalism is no longer a joke! Throughout the world it is becoming the reigning ideology, perhaps the most formidable obstacle to the birth of a new world democracy.

*

NA is at your disposal for any questions you may have regarding nationalism. Call us today, and become part of the NA group in your area (please consult your local directory). In the final analysis, it is up to each and every nationalist to face his problem head on and to find the will to uproot it at the source.

– translation by Linda Dawe

LISA ROBERTSON
CHRISTINE STEWART
CATRIONA STRANG

BARSCHEIT NATION

A. We Hold These Truths to be Self-Evident:

1. Dissensual language is a machine of enchantments.

2. This machine, with all its archaisms, is a means of locomotion toward polysexual futures.

3. Wrenched history is our machine's frontier.

B. The Machine is the Nation:

Borders: We cannot contain our pleasure.

Language: Stolen without ransom.

Trade Policy: Those whose fantasies condemn them.

Currency: We have no currency.

Constitution: Camped in the hinterland, basking in the rectitude of our intentions, we renounce entropic capital; we renounce the bogus repertoires of gender; we renounce post-historical gloating; we renounce proscribed rebuttal of memory; we renounce boredom. We know that beyond the Fantasy Empire lurks an improbable nation of subjects composed of countless tendrils, each with a new little sensory tissue at its tip. We travel there.

art by Michael William

TRACKS

ᖁᑎᐊᓗᒃ
ᐅᒥᐊᕐᔪᐊᖅ
ᑕᓯᐊᓗᒃ
ᑕᓯᑯᑖᒍᓗᒃ
ᑕᓯᑯᑖᖅ
ᑭᕕᓂᓚᒃ
ᖃᖅᑳᓗᒃ
ᓄᕗᑲᓪᓚᒃ
ᖃᕐᓂᐊᑉ ᓄᕗᐊ
ᓴᕐᕿᓚᐊᖅ
ᓴᕐᕿᓚᐊᑉ ᓄᕗᐊ
ᓂᐊᖁᔅᔪᑉ ᑲᖏᕐᓯᖓ

ᑲᐅᑦᑐᐊᐱᒃ

ᐊᓪᓛᕿᐊᑉ ᑯᖓ
ᐊᓪᓛᕿᐊᖅ
ᖃᕐᒪᐃᑦ
ᐊᕐᐱᐊᕋᐃᑦ
ᑲᖏᕐᓱᔪᐊᖅ
ᑕᓯᐅᔭᖅ
ᐃᒥᕐᑕᕕᐊᓗᒃ
ᕿᑭᕐᑖᔫᒃ
ᐸᐅᑦᓯᐊᖅ
ᐸᐅᑦᓯᐊᑉ ᑕᓯᖓ
ᖃᒡᒋᐊᓗᒃ

ᐃᕿ(ᒃ)
ᐃᕿᐅᑉ ᓄᕗᐊ
ᐅᖃᒻᒪᖅ
ᑭᑦᓰᔭᖅ
ᐃᖃᓪᓚᕕᐅᑉ ᑯᖓ

ᐃᓪᓗᓗᐊᕐᔪᐃᑦ
ᑯᒃ
ᐊᕐᐱᐊᕋᐃᑦ ᑲᖏᕐᓯᖓ
ᖁᕐᔪᖅ
ᐊᒡᒍᓚᐊᓇᐊᖅ
ᕿᓚᓇᐅᑦ (ᕿᓚᓇᐃᑦ)
ᑭᑦᓰᔭᓘᒃ

ᐱᑦᓯᐅᓛᕐᓯᑎᒃ
ᐃᕿᒃ
ᐊᑯᓚᕕᒃ
ᐃᕿᐅᓚᑦᑑᖅ
ᕿᑭᕐᑖᓗᒃ
ᕿᑭᕐᑕᑲᓪᓚᒃ

SCOTT WATSON

RACE, WILDERNESS, TERRITORY AND THE ORIGINS OF MODERN CANADIAN LANDSCAPE PAINTING

In March, 1991, British Columbia Supreme Court Judge Allan McEachern handed down his long awaited decision on the land claims of the Gitskan and Wet'suwet'en. These peoples, who live in the northwest of the Province, have been in court over issues like land and aboriginal rights for over one hundred years. The judge's text revealed the workings of a mind within a white supremacist frame of reference. For Canada, despite the anti-apartheid role its leaders like to play on the international stage, like all the countries of the "New World," is founded on acts of genocide that continue to this day. (South Africa's apartheid system was, in fact, modeled after Canada's reservation system.) The very way Canadians conceive the large territory their nation claims sovereignty over is saturated with a genocidal intent. Canadians are often told that the challenge to visualize this territory, to confront and psychically own the land of Canada has been the highest task of her writers and artists. But few question the relation of this tradition to historical reality.

A key notion in the imagining of Canada is the idea of "wilderness" as empty, uninhabited, unmapped, unnamed territory. The notion is used in the McEachern judgment to metaphorically dispossess the Gitskan and Wet'suwet'en of land that for them is named, fabled, and criss-crossed with an economy of use and knowledge. In dismissing the land claim, McEachern refers to the territory in question as "a vast emptiness." It was as if no one could be said to own this emptiness: instead the territory sort of waited for exploitation and ownership that would fill it or bring it into a reality it could not yet be said to participate in. For McEachern, in noticing how empty the land was, also noted; "There are, unquestionably, immense forestry reserves throughout the territory which are of great economic value."[1]

Wilderness denotes a special kind of imaginary non-economy when thinking of land claims. As McEachern puts it, "It is common when one thinks of Indian land claims, to think of Indians living off the land in pristine wilderness." In other words, McEachern is saying that Indians are a part of nature. In any event, McEachern really thinks pre-contact life must have been so awful that the Gitskan ought to be grateful the white man arrived and rescued them; "it would not be accurate to assume that even pre-contact existence in the territory was in the least bit idyllic. The plaintiff's ancestors had no written language, no horses or wheeled vehicles, slavery and starvation was not uncommon, wars with neighbouring peoples were common, and there is no doubt, to quote Hobbes, that aboriginal life in the territory was, at best, 'nasty, brutish and short.'"

These characterizations serve as the basis for McEachern's denial that the Gitskan and Wet'suwet'en had sufficient social organization or social continuity to conceptualize the territory they claim as property. Representations of the wilderness have been a terrible instrument in law. They are part of a larger pattern of cultural genocide. They have also been central to what one would call the search for an essential-Canadian in the country's national literature and art. These representations are not unlike the representations in McEachern in that they too function to erase First Nations' presence, polity, and, finally, humanity.

One of the greatest architects of an essential Canadianness was the literary critic, Northrop Frye. Like the legal opinions of Judge McEachern, Frye's notions are dependent on an idea of wilderness and are shot through with racism and genocidal intent. Frye's arguments about Canada's colonial mentality are famous. A colony, he wrote, is a place "treated less like a society than a place to look for things."[2] And Canada wasn't just any colony but, "practically the only country left in the world which is a pure colony, colonial in psychology as well as in mercantile economics."[3]

Much ink has been spilled lamenting poor old Canada's lingering colonial state of mind. But Canada, in terms of its relation to First Nations, is also a colonial power. It doesn't usually think of itself that way because the erasure of First Nations territories into grand and sublime concepts of empty wilderness has been so complete. Frye was a master of this act of erasure, even claiming that the "wilderness" is the central problem or irritant that defines the Canadian psyche. From the point of view of Frye's southern Ontario, the territories occupied by Canada both poison and stimulate the Canadian imagination. It is as if their acquisition had been too abrupt, as if the development of Canada had skipped some otherwise "natural" stage in the growth of nations. "The mystique of Canadianism," he wrote, "...came so suddenly after the pioneer period that it was still full of wilderness. To feel Canadian was to feel part of no-man's land with huge rivers, lakes, and islands that very few Canadians have ever seen." For Frye wilderness was "the unknown, the unrealized, the humanly undigested." It is these qualities that instigate an anxiety that can only be overcome by a poetic or artistic possession of the wilderness. As Frye bluntly observed, "the creative instinct has to do with the assertion of territorial rights."

And what of the Indians who inconveniently might claim their territorial rights? Frye, unfortunately like the majority of white Canadians, could not or chose not to think of Indians in terms of history or politics. Instead Frye thought Indians are symbolic of the sinister side of nature. He argued that, "nature makes a direct impression on the artist's mind, an impression of its primeval lawlessness and moral nihilism, its indifference to the supreme value placed on life in human society, its faceless mindless unconsciousness, which fosters life without benevolence and destroys it without malice."[4] In a discussion of E. J. Pratt's poem "Brebeuf," a work he designated "not only the greatest but most complete Canadian narrative," Frye identified an allegory in which "the Indians represent humanity in the state of nature and are agents of its unconscious barbarity." The struggle against the Indians was part of an eternal battle against mindless nature. Writing in 1943, on the eve of the Allied victory in Europe, Frye made an extraordinary analogy. Speaking of the Iroquois in Pratt's poem, he wrote "their way of savagery is doomed; it is doomed in their Nazi descendants; it is doomed even if it lasts to the end of time."[5] The irony, of course, is that the Iroquois who killed Brebeuf did so in a war in which they were allies of England.

Frye maintained that the "uninhabited loneliness" of Canada seemed to inspire "curious guilt feelings." Perhaps these curious feelings have their source in the largely unacknowledged fate of those who have been displaced by conquest. Around such feelings, Frye constructed a demonic or ghost world that erupted through the emptiness of the wilderness, animating it with sinister forces. In a flight of fancy, which is however key to his articulation of the wilderness myth, Frye imagined Canada as the ancient Aegean: "Explorers, tormented by a sense of the unreality of the unseen, are first: pioneers and traders follow. But the land is still not imaginatively absorbed, and the incubus moves on to haunt the artists. It is a very real incubus. It glares through the sirens, gorgons, centaurs, griffins, cyclops, pygmies, and chimeras of the poems which followed the Greek colonies: there the historical defeat which left a world of mystery outside the Greek clearing increased the imaginative triumph."[6] In the process of territorial possession Frye believed to be the particular province of the arts, the conquered became mythic monsters.

This portrayal of First Nations peoples as the agents of dark natural forces is only one part of the assimilationist formula. Another is to appropriate their cultures as part of a Canadian heritage. "The problem," as Margaret Atwood, perhaps ironically, posed it, "is what do you do for a past if you are white, relatively new to the continent, and rootless?"[7] The answer, at least in the examples Atwood provided from John Newlove's poetry, was to take over First Nations history as one's own and to deny specificity to First Nations peoples' experiences. She cited Newlove's "Resources, Certain Earths." Here he refused the grievances of coastal peoples, privileging his own in act of poetic aggression:

> "...These
> paranoid peoples, these coastal Salish,
> Kwakiutl, Nootka, Tsimshian, Haida,
> what do I have to apologize to them for?—
> their fears, legends of malicious tricks,
> colors and maskings, knowledge of
> the wild woman of the woods wearing
> a hummingbird in her hair, deaths
> are mine, because I am a man also
> and hammed in: it is done
> to me."[8]

In another poem of conquest, "The Pride," Newlove concludes with an amazing transformation of the whites into Indians, the dead Indians absorbed as dust until "at last we become them!" and "they/ become our true forebearers, moulded/ by the same wind or rain, / and in this land we/ are their people, come/ back to life again."

This imaginary negotiation with "the dead Indians" depends upon placing them in the past tense. As Atwood noted of Al Purdy's use of First Nations images: "it is natives who are dead or extinct that really say something to him, give him a meaningful reflection of himself; it is these whose 'broken consonants' he can hear."

In his analysis of the essentially Canadian in Canadian literature and art, Northrop Frye emphasized the unvisualized territory, as if picture-making, in poems or oil-paintings, could enact a conquest for the imagination what was already conquered by commerce and the state. The "poets" of this territory were the painters known as the Group of Seven, who, in the early years of this century established a national school of modernist landscape painting. The painters who would become involved with the Group were all children of British immigrants or immigrants themselves. Their nationalism was enfolded in the colonial project. They did not imagine an independent country, but pride of place within the Empire, a bastion of whiteness in a poly-coloured world. The Group liked to think of itself as springing from a natural necessity. But the national school of painting was really commissioned into being by interests who also worked under the banner of a nationalist agenda. Chief among these was Sir Edmund Walker, President of the Canadian Bank of Commerce. In 1913, Sir Edmund became President of the Art Gallery of Toronto, which he had helped found, and a trustee of the National Gallery of Canada (NGC). It was Walker and NGC Director Eric Brown who encouraged the group of young commercial artists by purchasing their work. Walker also knew the painter, Lawren Harris through business and political connections. Walker had a large investment in the Harris family firm, Massey-Harris, and in 1911, joined Lloyd Harris, MP for Brantford and Lawren's cousin, in the "Toronto 18"—eighteen prominent Liberals who defected to the Conservatives in order to bring down the pro-free trade Laurier government. In short, political and financial connections bound Harris and Walker to common interests, interests that shaped their view of the national landscape school they helped to establish.

As legend has it, and this legend is available as history at any major Canadian art museum, the group created a uniquely Canadian art. That they did so using European methods—that is, oil paintings of landscapes—and European models—the modernism of the post-impressionists and art nouveau, but specifically Scandinavian landscape painting—is well known but has not undermined the Group's claim to have made authentic Canadian images. Fred Housser, a close friend of the Group and financial editor for *The Toronto Star*, published his account of the painters in 1926. The book spread the ideas and legends of the Group across the country and established the painters as the fathers of Canadian art. Like Harris, Housser was a theosophist and devotee of Walt Whitman. The language of *A Canadian Art Movement: The Story of the Group of Seven* is flowery and hyperbolic. Generations of Canadians appear to have read it oblivious to its not-so-hidden character as a white supremacist tract.

Housser's intention, as he stated it, was not to write "so much the story of an art movement as of the dawn of a consciousness of a national environment which, today, is taking a most definite form in the life of the nation."[9] He proposed that a distinct Canadian race was emerging and that this race found in the wilderness its spiritual home and succour. "For Canada to find true racial expression of herself through art," he wrote, "a complete break with European traditions was necessary; a new type of artist was required."

Identifying the Canadian race with the wilderness and the north, Housser evoked a mystique of snow and "whiteness". Whiteness represented the northern expanses, but it also had racial connotations. For Lawren Harris the north was a metaphysical environment. "We," he wrote of Canadians, "are in the fringe of the great North and its living whiteness, its loneliness and its replenishment, its resignations and release, its call and answer, its cleansing rhythms. It seems that the top of the continent is a source of spiritual flow that will ever shed clarity on the growing American race, and we Canadians being closest to this source seem destined to produce an art somewhat different from our Southern fellows."[10] He didn't have to spell it out: Canada was to be the white head on America's mixed race body.

The paintings that celebrated the north or the wilderness were intended for the middle-class of Toronto. The paintings would be touchstones of the spiritual experience not just of place, but of race. The specific region the first painters depicted was the "near north" of Ontario. The area between Georgian Bay and the Ottawa Valley was summer vacation territory, and the painters often stayed in the summer homes of their wealthy friends to paint the landscapes of the Pre-Cambrian Shield. For Housser this was "the race's inescapable environment. It is the playground of hundreds of thousands of Canadian people." The group's painting campaigns were rarely in summer, however. Perhaps they wished to avoid other campers. But by painting from late fall to early spring they also wished to extract something quintessential from their landscape subjects. They thought of winter as Canada's season, as if the cold and the snow were metaphors of the nation's whiteness.

Housser imagined the Group's pictures as myth or a proto-literature. Referring to Homer and Hesiod, he claimed that, "The group's Northern Ontario canvases are doing for Canadian painting what the epic poets do for their races." But the transformation into epic or myth depended on the eventual disappearance of the wilderness and its eventual conquest by civilization. Housser noted the threat with little regret, writing, "The wilderness is being reclaimed and the forest is making its last stand. No first class literature has been created to preserve its mood." The forests might disappear, but they were not as important as the paintings of them, for the paintings, not the actual territory, mediated race consciousness. Housser predicted the appearance of "a spirit which as time advances will be capitalized in literature and more recognized in the race than it is at present. While these pictures live we can never forget our cradle environment. The work of the pioneer and explorer and the tenacious love of the red Indian for the land of his ancestors will be understood and the spirit of still unwritten epics will be preserved for us on canvas."

Indians in Housser's book were the dead Indians that Canadians love to lament. They inhabit the wilderness as ghosts. The wilderness itself exists in a permanent past tense, always at the origin of things. As Housser himself wrote, "...this Canadian group drew its inspiration from the past of this country, the wilderness." The wilderness managed to produce an artist who represented the new Canadian type from the concoction of Indian, explorer, and pioneer who called the wilderness home. In Tom Thomson, the Group found a type and martyr.

Thomson was said to have been shaped by the north itself and was therefore a transparent medium for its spirit. Unschooled, virile, a woodsman, "a sort of modern coureur-de-bois," he was the perfect foil to the reviled European type: the artist as dandy or decadent. He was white and there was nothing queer about him. The maintenance of Thomson in type took extreme form. A replica of a northern trapper's shack was built for him in Toronto, so he could stay in role even in the metropolis. His characteristics, but most notably a certain reticence, if not muteness, included a kind of magical absorption of Indianness. "He knew the woods as the red Indian knew them before him," extolled Housser, claiming: "the cries of the wild were in every stroke of his brush." It was his special knowledge of the wilderness that made Thomson's canvases "unique in the annals of all art." For "never before had such knowledge and the feeling for such things been given expression in paint." It was "as though northern nature itself were speaking to you through a perfectly attuned and seasoned medium."

Yet Thomson's experiences and pictures required considerable analogical explanation to approach what Housser called their pure "being". They could be comprehended by imagining that what European painters "felt for their Madonnas, Thomson re-experienced in his contact with northern nature." Or that a single tree in one of his pictures was "to the nature-worshipper Thomson what the symbol of the cross was to a medieval mystic." The single trees came to represent the singularity of Thomson as a type, and through them one can experience "that sweet loneliness which is exaltation." As was suitable to this high spiritual calling, Thomson was imagined as chaste, married to a wilderness which eventually consumed him.

Thomson died in a canoe accident in Algonquin Park in 1917, and the painters who survived him consecrated the park to him by never painting there again. His Algonquin Park pictures would be increasingly described as somber, moody, haunted, as if they themselves contained a premonition of their author's death, as if that death were destined. Northrop Frye described the pictures as disquieting and sinister. Claiming that Thomson's pictures evoke the feeling of something not quite emerging, Frye saw the incubus in their "twisted stumps," "strident colouring," and "scarecrow evergreens." The appearance of the incubus was, according to Frye, the result of an incomplete absorption or possession of the land.

Algonquin Park, now kind of a national shrine to Thomson (and his whiteness), was made a park in 1893, not so many years before Thomson painted there. Many of Thomson's pictures of the "wilderness" show the evidence of logging, past and present. The park had been created as a forest reserve in response to an 1892 Royal Commission that had found the region in serious danger of being over-logged. This park, in which Housser and Frye like to hear the tread of the dead red man, was part of a large territory claimed by Algonquin speaking peoples living in the region. They were not dead at all. In fact they have been in court every few years since the end of the eighteenth century protesting and petitioning the loss of their territory and infringements on their rights. The Group's imagination of the park obliterates all this contentiousness and is itself, as Frye points out, a kind of territorial claim in itself.

When Tom Thomson painted Algonquin park it was part of a territory that was not just contested by the Algonquin. The Group of Seven's pictures look the way they do, extolling a "wilderness" vision, because they are implicated in the politics and finances of land use and exploitation. The area of Ontario that was chosen as the mould for the Canadian racial stamp had a long history before it was discovered as the home of the Canadian soul. It is part of what was once the nation called Huronia and had been inhabited by Algonquin speaking peoples for many thousands of years before conquest. Treaties and court cases in the nineteenth century defined much of what is now northern Ontario's present system of governance and administration. Eighty percent of Ontario is crown land, and from the early nineteenth century on the near north was subject to a conflict between the industrial uses envisioned by people living in the south, between resource extraction and an agrarian dream. Before the Group of Seven cast the near north as wilderness, many Ontarians imagined the territory in the future tense, not the past, as farmland. A plan to colonize the north with farmer-settlers, most of them immigrants, was Ontario policy, implemented with varying degrees of conviction until it was officially abandoned in 1935. The vision of Housser, that the wilderness was disappearing, was that of a succession of governments for whom, in the words of historian Joseph Schull, "the lands of the nearer north with their great forests and infinite maze of waterways would someday yield to the plow."[11]

But the Group was not allied to the vision of the north as farmland. The wilderness they were interested in was more allied to industrial and extractive uses of the territory of the near north. The era in which they painted and developed their myth spans the years from 1912—the year in which Ontario acquired part of Keewatin Territory, nearly doubling its size with, to paraphrase Frye, more unvisualized territory—to 1919, the year the Group officially declared itself and the Farmer's Union Party won an election and formed a new government in Ontario. The First World War brought a renewed effort to pastoralize or colonize the north when plans were made to replace immigrants with returning soldiers as pioneering farmers. These plans resulted in failure. The period of the war also saw increasing conflict between settler-farmers, First Nations communities, and communities of industrial proletariat who worked the mines, mills, and railways that criss-crossed the industrial north, which was becoming dotted with towns named after Ontario industrialists and politicians. During the years the Group of Seven first painted the north, the management of the resources of northern Ontario had become so corrupt, part of the orgy of profiteering that characterized the war years, that it was described as "the rottenest system of forest pilfering that ever existed on the continent." At the end of the war the north was in chaos and unrest. But it was the industrial and rural crisis of southern Ontario that lead to the dramatic election of the Farmer's Union Party as the government in 1919. Mobilized by their protest against conscription in 1918, and aggravated by the precipitous decline in the stability of rural southern Ontario where the population had declined by over 100,000 since the 1880s, the farmers allied with disenchanted urban voters and wrested power from a government that had been dominated by men who had interests in the north. Priorities shifted from funneling money into pockets of northern developers to reconstruction of the war-battered southern economy. It was around this time that the painters who had survived Tom Thomson and the Great War began to paint the north again.

The Farmer's Union Party was pro-free-trade and it may be more than coincidence that the painters that anti-free-trade Sir Edmund Walker promoted as the national school by and large eschewed southern rural Ontario as subject matter. Housser explained this choice in typically racial terms: "Our Canadian pasture lands have not yet the racial stamp given by generations of war and peasantry such as the rural landscape of Europe has. This offered Housser the trope to explain how it was that the wilderness had become the past: "Just as European artists have long gone to Europe's past for inspiration, so this Canadian group drew its inspiration from the past of this country, the wilderness."

The interest in the north as rugged, resource-extraction territory was reinforced by the Group's postwar painting campaigns. Having left Algonquin Park as a shrine to Thomson, the painters looked next to the Algoma district for images of the national landscape. Housser reported that the war was itself a stimulus for the new painting school. Harris in particular hoped that the "swells of national feeling" induced by "the long list of casualties" could be redirected to "a more creative and magnificent communion than the communion of war" through wilderness images. Thus there was a patriotic, memorializing impulse in

art by Jin-me Yoon

우리도 이 땅의 주인 입니다.

這片大地也是我們的家鄉

私達もこの国の一部を構成しています。

the search for red maple leaves in the autumnal Algoma region, a search for what one painter called "the desirable spot of red."

The Algoma district was painted between 1918 and 1922, by which time it was already industrialized, although at the time the group painted it, its industries were in financial crisis. Some have advanced the thesis that the group's excursions into Algoma, in a boxcar especially outfitted for them which traveled on the Algoma Central and Eastern Railways, both insolvent since 1916, were underwritten to create new investment interest in the region.[12] Determined to give a picture of the wilderness as a territory that was just opening up, there were to be no pictures of mines, railways, or even the boxcar they rode in.

With Algoma, the painters who formed the core of the Group of Seven set out to define a quintessential wilderness imagery that could be deployed to galvanize the national psyche. The somberness and disquiet of Thomson's pictures were discarded for a new set of values based on terms that emphasized dynamism. Roaring cataracts and vertiginous vistas replaced the relative serenity of Thomson's Algonquin Park scenes. Thomson's pictures had been painted when pastoralization of the north might have appeared inevitable and they partly served, as Housser thought all the group's paintings did, as a preface to the civilization of the north. After the war, the Group's major patrons found themselves at loggerheads with a populist agrarian government that threatened to dry up the flow of public money into the pockets of northern developers. It is with these later interests that the Group's paintings conspire in presenting a new vision of the north, creating images of landscape fit for industrialization, canyons ideal for hydro-electric dams, navigable waterways, huge tracts of forest and Pre-Cambrian hills waiting for open pit mines. To this new industry-ready wilderness they attached the swells of national feeling. Housser exhorted his readers to "surrender to the rhythm of the North shore of Lake Superior" and to "the tempo of the mood Canadian."

A great deal of the effectiveness of the Algoma paintings appeared to depend on a sense of first-time discovery. Housser claimed, rather rashly, that with the group the Algoma wilderness had been painted by artists for the first time. Frye argued that Lawren Harris's Algoma paintings were "as much of an exploration as the literal or physical explorations of La Vérendrye or Mackenzie." It would be straining credibility to imagine that the construction of the Tom Thomson type out of Indians and coureur-de-bois was some sort of meaningful recognition of First Nations' history, polity, and presence in the north. The construction of Thomson involved forgetfulness. However the post-war painters, perhaps acting as operatives for industrial interests, by investing so much in their myth of discovery, utterly erased any sign of the long term inhabitation of the region along with its prior industrial uses and instead showed us tracts of territory cleared of liens and bankruptcies, waiting to be claimed and exploited anew.

The history of Algoma includes the ceding of the territory to the British Crown by the Salteux people of the Ojibway nation in 1873. In the 1880s a struggle between the governments of Ontario and Canada broke out over timber rights

우리도 이 땅의 주인 입니다.
這片大地也是我們的家鄉
私達もこの国の一部を構成しています。

art by Jin-me Yoon

in West Algoma. Ontario's ownership of the timber and its right to issue licenses to cut it were challenged by the Federal Government on the basis that the Salteaux retained rights over the resources and that as the Salteaux, like all First Nations people, were wards of the Federal Government, those rights accrued to Canada, not Ontario. Ontario won the case in 1889. Not uncoincidently, this case was regarded by Allan McEachern as of "fundamental importance. It is one of the few Canadian appellate cases which makes any comment on the nature of aboriginal rights." In Canada, the case serves as "authority against aboriginal ownership and jurisdiction."[13]

The namelessness of the Canadian landscape is still an instrument to be used in court. Schedule Five of Allan McEachern's judgement against the Gitskan and Wet'suwet'en prints lists of rivers, creeks, lakes, and mountains in the disputed territories. In one column is listed the Gitskan or Wet'suwet'en name, in another the "white" name, but as often as not, "un-named on government maps." Naming is part of possession. Namelessness is a preface to, if not quite permission for, conquest. The assertion of wilderness is also an assertion of namelessness and ownerlessness. It was on this basis that the Group could be said to extend a psychic or spiritual ownership to unvisualized and unnamed regions they depicted in the name of the Canadian race.

Northrop Frye wrote that "Canada with its empty spaces, its largely unknown lakes, rivers, islands...has had this particular problem of an obliterated environment throughout most of its history." I would like to restate this problematic by reversing the terms: The Canadian problem is an obliterated history throughout most of its environment.

---

1. Reasons for judgement of The Honourable Chief Justice Allan McEachern, No. 0843 Smithers Registry in the Supreme Court of British Columbia, Dates of trial: 374 Days between May 11 and June 30, l990, p. 12. It is quite clear that in this legal judgement, territory is empty, must be empty, when the Gitskan and Wet'suwet'en claim it as theirs, but it can become full when thought of in terms of logging leases and mining permits.
2. Northrop Frye, "Conclusion to A Literary History of Canada," in *The Bush Garden: Essays on the Canadian Imagination*. Toronto: House of Anansi Press Ltd., 1971, p. 221.
3. *Ibid.*, "Preface," p. iii.
4. "The Narrative Tradition in English-Canadian Poetry." (1946).
5. "Canada and its Poetry," (1943), p. 142.
6. Northrop Frye, "Canadian and Colonial Painting," (1940) p. 199.
7. Margaret Atwood, *Survival: A Thematic Guide to Canadian Literature*. Toronto: House of Anansi Press Ltd., 1972, p. 104.
8. *Ibid.*, p. 104.
9. F.B. Housser, *A Canadian Art Movement: The Story of the Group of Seven*. Toronto: The MacMillan Company of Canada Ltd., 1926, p. 32.
10. Lawren Harris, "Revelation of Art in Canada," *The Canadian Theosophist*, vol. VII, No. 5 (July 15, 1926) pp. 85-86.
11. Joseph Schull, *Ontario Since 1867*. Toronto: McClelland and Stewart,1978, p. 43.
12. See Allan John Fletcher, "Industrial Algoma and the Myth of Wilderness: Algoma Landscapes and the Emergence of the Group of Seven 1918-1920," MA Thesis for the Department of Fine Arts, The University of British Columbia, 1989.
13. McEachern, "Judgement", p. 193.

MONTY CANTSIN

to the attention of
Shirley Thompson
director
The National Gallery of Canada
OTTAWA

jan 30, 1991

IDEAL GIFT

LETTER OF DONATION

I hereby declare that I donate a blood painting, entitled IDEAL GIFT, to The National Gallery of Canada, Ottawa, on jan 30, 1991. To create IDEAL GIFT I have used six vials of blood, taken from *my* arm. My donation includes an additional interpretation to IDEAL GIFT entitled SWEET BLOOD OF A DEAD PIGEON MANIFEST, as well as supplementary information about *Blood Campaign.*

With great expectations

AMEN

photo by Krista Goddess

LON CAYEWAY

SUNRISE FACES, SUNSET MIST

A distant call; a partial memory of an inaccessible place, of a milieu defined through extremes of geologic occurrence. Glacial ice fields, where uplifted ocean winds freeze, howling of their shrinking emptiness. Ridge after ridge of rough, barren rock scraped together and piled up high on the hard, raw youth of a continent's drifting edge.

Here, the vast scale of the world imparts to sensation an insistence, a charge which persists within memory, as a living thing might. Such memories exceed sense thresholds, imprinting themselves viscerally. These energies leap beyond reason, to trace along the motor reflexes; and then to settle in a physical embodiment which skirts around the edges of the intellect, as might the furtive silence shadowing some forgotten sensory extreme.

And a photograph, a perspective to cast a memory within. The mountains here fall through thousands of vertical feet, and although a strong and proud people lived here once, no one moves through that high country now. Those strange high places are almost forgotten; this photograph remains the image of a place beyond experience. The image exists as an invitation to the imagination, to the point where desire wills its own experience. This is a shared hallucination.

This is a story of those high mountain people. It is a story of fragments, of shattered realities, a story which I do not know, and yet which I must try to remember. I must fill my body's organ cavities with the swirling, thunderous mist of this far, high place, and shift my attention to the animal texture of the energies that then leap within me. I must allow the voices of this story to continue to unfold, and to continuously enfold me in their texture, for this a story in which I am but another glowing thread.

It is also a dream...the dream of a far away waterfall cutting incessantly back into a mountain of living rock. It is the story of a great tear in the side of a mountain, a hidden chasm, and a shuddering column of

photo by John Morton

half-living mist which bursts into a rainbow splendor of swirling spectral shifts whenever the sun shines within this mountain's outstretched arms.

It is a story I tell for an unseen, shapeless people, a shadow people who rest suspended in this waterfall's thunderous rush, at the edge of the sunrise. They are the *kyahlkyofsenuh*, unseen people with fiery eyes, who appear for an instant only. This is a story for the memory of their people; a story told in memory of their land.

In the Archives of Encroachment

"At the period we lived there (spring, 1893-fall, 1897), the Chilcotins came every winter to the coast and what a time it was for us kids. They put up bark wigwams and spent the winter making snowshoes, moccasins, beadwork, etc., and tanning mowitch (deer) skins to take back in the spring with them."

– Dennis G. Walker, in 1941, to W.A. Don Munday.

The area with which my story entwines acquired the interest of the colonial authorities in the mid 1800s. At that time, a final and easy pass was being sought to the Pacific Ocean. This route was to have connected the interior of the continent with the ocean shipping of the colonial capitalists, who lived in the island city of Victoria. No cross-country railway existed yet, and Canada itself would not exist until 1867.

The search for a pass to the interior attracted an opportunist named William Downie, who "was foremost and most persistent of those explorers working with the governor's approval." Contact between Indigenous and colonial cultures had not been great to that point in time. The Coast Indians were such notable sea travellers that few trading posts had been established upon the mainland coast. Downie was the earliest and most persistent white influence in the area.

Of his experiences on the coast in 1858, Downie wrote that the villagers he encountered:

"...had a disagreeably insinuating way of hanging over the gunwale of our canoe with big bowie knives in their hands...on the occasion of my first introduction to these people, their manner of approaching strangers offended my sensibilities."

Another time:

"My eye caught sight of one old dame, who carried a long bag, apparently containing lumps of something. My curiosity was aroused, and, thinking that it was gold, I made up my mind to lay siege to the goodwill of the ancient beauty; but I entirely lost my ambition in that direction, when I saw her opening the bag a few minutes later and take from it a number of musket balls, which she distributed among the young braves, that they might make holes in us..."

Again:

"...passed another Indian village gave them some tobacco and passed on here they had their muskets out ramming the balls down, as if they were going to blow us out of the water...."

There is no misreading the mistrust Downie initially encountered. Soon, though, this changed to an attitude of good, clean fun on the part of Downie's guides:

"Never in my life have I beheld such a scene as presented itself to our wondering gaze in this solitude. We were completely shut in by this wild nature. On either side, lofty mountains reared their precipitous sides far above us, pointing to the leaden overcast sky, and looking like threatening giants guarding the entrance to some land of mystery...Ahead of us lay a field of insurmountable glaciers, forming a barrier to any further progress, and giving the situation additional awe and grandeur...When I asked our Indian guides how they proposed for us to proceed any further, they said we would have to ascend the glaciers in the best way we could, and pull one another up by ropes. "And the wagons?" I asked. "Pull them up after you!" came the reply...We camped here for the night, and spent a wretched time waiting for the dawn to break...Our traps—even our provisions— were carried away, and we had to stand up most of the night holding on to our blankets and utensils, for fear of seeing them carried away by the waters and the violent gusts of wind that came down upon us."

Obviously, these guides had a good sense of humour.

"Saturday 16th the guides have taken us across and recross the river 15 times this forenoon. It is evident they wish to turn back and they think to discourage us by taking us across streams and through Swamps where there is no necessity to for us to go...they are all the time telling about the snow that we will have to cross..."

By the time of his 1861 trip, Downie is resorting to kidnapping guides:

"Our Indian began to get sick and commenced crying and wanted to turn back, but as we could not go on without his assistance in working the Canoe, we would not permit him to return. 17th July 1861. We were now most of the time in the water, pulling the canoe along and cutting away masses of drift timber...Started ahead hauling the Canoe along, came to a bad place for whirls and riffles. The Indian now seemed overjoyed as he supposed we could turn back now...The Indian when he saw us getting rollers, and cutting a trail for the conveyance of the canoe began to look chop fallen indeed...20th July 1861. Found it was impossible to proceed farther with the Canoe and came near loosing it again. Mr. McDonald and I then started on foot leaving the two Indians in Camp."

Munday reports: "Within a few years (of 1858), the power and pride of the coastal tribes was to be broken by smallpox and other epidemics introduced by the white men; some tribes no longer had a separate existence."

In 1861, 3 years after his first coastal expedition, Downie notes on a return trip:

> "I may say that they are as hard a Lot of Indians to get along with as I have seen on the Coast, and it required all my tact to get them to go up the river at all. I used them well before starting and gave them all papers for a Blanket each and sundries when we came back."

In British Columbia, the Indian population was reduced from 70,000 or so in 1835 to around 28,000 in 1885. There are at least two recorded instances of blankets infected with smallpox being sold to Indian bands in this period.

In 1862, a horribly virulent strain of smallpox raged through the province, killing up to one third of B.C.'s remaining First Nations' population. Although crude forms of inoculation were practised in this period, the Hudson's Bay Company's vaccination program of 1835 had not been maintained beyond a sporadic effort.

There is little left of the world that existed here before men like Downie arrived to break it open.

One or Many Durations?

One portal opening toward the people who were here before European contact is a small stone I shall show you. I found it just sitting on a logging road, in the area Downie described exploring almost a century and a half ago.

On this small stone, there is a circular constellation of black marks arranged around a central dot on the rock's top. This pattern caught my eye as I walked down the logging road on which the stone sat. Days passed before I realized this stone had been marked by human hands. Then, months passed before I managed to get another person to agree with me that the stone bore markings placed upon it by an ancient people.

I even showed it to someone at a local university's anthropology museum, and asked if it was an artifact.

"Nope," she said, handing it back. "It's just a nice stone."

Then I asked Ron Barbour, editor of the First Nations paper *KHATOU*, what he thought of it.

"That ring of black marks on the top is a medicine wheel, if I've ever seen one," he said. "Sometimes these things show up. That might be for you to show to other people, or it might be just for you. It depends."

Later, while attending a protest about the way in which Seagrams/DuPont has been ripping

photo by John Morton

holes in the earth's ozone bubble, I was referred to a gentleman named Warchief.

"Oh yes," he said, studying the stone, "this was made by the Snow-On-Rock people. They use to live up the coast, up where the glaciers drop to the sea from the mountains. They used to live up where the streams and rivers start, at the base of the glaciers. Up in the mountains. Of course, there isn't much else up that way except ice and mountain; if you're going to live up there, that's what you've got to live with. So their name comes from the glaciers and the mountains there. It also comes from the stone work they were known for, where they used white rocks like this and uncovered images in the black stone underneath. They were considered to be responsible for the waters that feed the streams, and the streams are the lifeblood of the valleys. You can eventually use this stone for healing, and it can tell you stories from long ago. Time can run in both directions, you know; you can ask this stone to show you things from the past. This stone would have been passed around, and talked over by countless people through a long part of the past. Something of that will always be with this."

photo by John Morton

Forever Changed

Thus, I am left to ponder this small artifact that my hand has chanced upon; to wonder at its peoples' history, and to lament their fate and the fate of their land. I am left to tell a last story for them, that their genius in stonework might be remembered still: a story I do not remember, from a tongue I do not speak. I can only hope that the spirit of those people's dreams will guide me in this.

One of the great benefactors of the Kwakiutl is the Transformer, *Xe'els*. Transformation is at the heart of the medicine wheel. The medicine stone of which I tell is marked all over with shifting images, which change from being one creature, to being another.

Deleuze and Guattari devote a chapter in *Mille Plateaus* to the way dynamics play upon faces. Let us consider:

> *"Since all semiotics are mixed and strata come at least in twos, it should come as no surprise that a very special mechanism is situated at the intersection of significance and subjectification. Oddly enough, it is a face; the white wall/black hole system..."*

Such is the space we are dealing with here: a collection of black marks set against an enveloping whiteness. Here we assemble the creatures which make a world full. Here we struggle to produce changes in our perception, in our understanding. Grouping together seemingly appropriate constellations of marks, we reconstruct a vanished world through an indirect objectivity of intentionally altered material. Tools, weapons, eyes, mouths, silhouettes, all meld and merge to make the faces flow from one perspective to the next. Relations of scale, proportion, placement, and identity stretch, flow, or dissolve as the eye devises a material declension of bioregional images. Narratives are implied, sub-narratives assert themselves. Circles and clusters supplement the primary medicine wheel, with smaller strings found curling nomadically off around the rock's edges.

> *"The black hole is on the white wall. It is not a unit, since the black hole is in constant motion on the wall and operates by binarization. Two black holes, four black holes, n black holes distribute themselves like eyes. Faciality is always a multiplicity. The landscape will be populated with eyes or black holes..."*

Truly a landscape. Identities multiply, with more and more animals peering out from the stone. Implied environments assemble, with each bio-regional niche marked with its characteristic and associated animals. Salmon, whale, and seal point past the otter to the freshwater streams where beaver, bear, and deer browse; mountain lion and lynx present themselves over the steep slope of coastal mountains. Eventually, the animal images that the markings imply begin to present the context of their occurrence: certain areas, shadings, and nuances of rock become specific environmental niches. The animals present their world as co-extensive with their images...as if their identity and their environment were inseparable. As if the animals piece together their world from their experience of existence. The fuzzy aggregate these images create presents us with an indistinct world, which the animals themselves imply.

> *"The face, at least the concrete face, vaguely begins to take shape on the white wall. It vaguely begins to appear in the black hole...A psychologist once said that the face is a visual percept that crystallizes out of "different varieties of vague luminosity without form or dimension." A suggestive whiteness, a hole that captures, a face..."*

This world is traced upon indistinct planes. Shadow and highlight, image and etching; the clarity of crystal and the opaque white of quartz blend with the black of a darker mineral's mottling presence. Images erased by time, through the slow abrasion of uncounted hands, dance fleetingly over the newer and more distinct markings. The black marks present outlines of images; the black marks combine to present faces; individual black marks display both polished (scraped, as well as rotary drilled), and etched surfaces. All of this is interlaced within a shifting, differentially repetitive narrative that creates the place of its becomings from flowing threads of shifting identity. All of this, in minute detail, painstakingly cared for and carried through thousands of years.

> "A multiplicity is defined not by its elements, nor by a centre of unification or comprehension. It is defined by the number of dimensions it has; it is not divisible, it cannot lose or gain a dimension without changing its nature...Since its variations and dimensions are immanent to it...each multiplicity is already composed of heterogeneous terms in symbiosis, and that multiplicity is continually transforming itself into a string of other multiplicities, according to its thresholds and doors."

Many dimensions are already lost from the world that created this small stone. But perhaps the echo spirits remain still, as minute men about four finger-breadths high who roam the night collecting things. These are the *kyahlmuhlitanak* ("dust shaken from a mat upon a floor") and the *munakehl* ("picking up objects in the house"). May they guide us to always gather in peace!

Gather Wild Peace

Here and there, in wilderness areas with a history of human habitation, one can find places to stop a while and rest. To gather thoughts. Invitingly smooth rocks wait beside pools of quiet water, overhung with massive, moss draped trees. The hollowed-out banks of fast running streams hold tree root roofs over the edges of washed gravel beaches. Raw rock seats sit at the edges of high ridges overlooking the web-work interlay of tiny alpine lakes, in which singular trees stand distinctly reflected. It is to a place like this that I would take you, to tell you my story.

In such places, we could let the abstract lines demarcated by the flows of the surrounding environment criss-cross our lives, we could link our sensations of being directly with the environment around us. We could compose our self perceptions anew, using the patterns, processes, and durations that the rocks, trees, animals, and energies of the life around us present. We might tap these essential lines of development, and grasp essential moments of nature's interconnectedness. Thus arrayed, we might sit imperceptibly, with the clandestine elegance of the camouflaged fish.

We would sit into darkness, perhaps by the cold, clear, crystalline blue movement of a very young stream as it spills icily from beneath a glacier's base. We could sit as the stars carved their dizzying arcs between the mountains above. We could listen as the blackness of night resonates with the contained force of the speeding stream; listen for the whistling sound of *hunwalaqi'kilis* spirits, and their riverside magic and quivering reeds...

> *"...movement also 'must' be perceived, it cannot but be perceived, the imperceptible is also the percipiendum. There is no contradiction in this. If movement is imperceptible by nature, it is so always in relation to a given threshold of perception, which is by nature relative and thus plays the role of a mediation on the plane that effects the distribution of thresholds and percepts and makes forms perceivable to perceiving subjects. It is the plane of organization and development, the plane of transcendence, that renders perceptible without itself being perceived, without being capable of being perceived."* (Mille Plateaus, p. 281)

In the morning, we could try and find the greatest trees of the surrounding forest. We could look for ancient hemlock trees, where the *nawalakwus* spirits reside with their ground magic. We could walk through the living, breathing forest and wonder at the lichen-wisp life hung in living suspension from hundreds of vertical feet of trees flowing with an airstream alive as some moist, tactile entity come swirling down from the low, laden clouds caught in dripping tatters on the tree needle tips at the topmost forest edge set hugging the high, steep hill sides; we would wander through sea-weed pale curtains of green lace-work lichen, awash in every seawater shade of soaking green intensity seen beyond the ocean; and wonder if the sea hadn't indeed suddenly receded, leaving the trees free to weave deep water dreams and undersea memories into on land grottos of moss cushioned softness and subtle green silence. Perhaps, with the wet assent of coastal winds, we could coax the *nahnawalaqa*, the magic rock spirits whose whistling, guttural grinding can be heard on the turning tide, up out of the ocean and into the forest for a visit.

photo by John Morton

Except that, there aren't any forests here to visit any more. It's all gone. Now, there is only the hard empty tilt of the barren, burnt hills. Now, there is just brittle black ash sifting with the wind across the dry, broken slopes. Oh, a few tattered fragments of this ecosystem remain clinging to the raw rock cliffs at either edge of the valley; but there isn't much point in fighting your way up to those, since the mountains rise straight into glacier there.

Below that point, clear-cut logging has obliterated the forest entirely. The slash burning which follows clear-cut logging sterilizes the ground, and consumes the mesh of interwoven roots that holds the thin soils in place on the mountains. Hundreds of thousands of years of slowly accumulated soil is washed down into the streams, and out into the sea. At current rates of cutting, there won't be ANY watersheds left in B.C. that haven't been compromised by logging (apart from parkland) by 2007.

All that is left of this particular area's natural ecosystem is the rock, the ice, and the weather. The global business economy swept the rest of it away: centuries of it, millennia of evolutionary adaptations. Now, no matter how well we might meld with the world around us, no matter what zones of indiscernibility we might camouflage our becomings with, the fragmented bio-diversity from which we would have to garner the proximities of our molecular interconnectedness would give back to us only broken pieces, and emptied realities.

So stands the land where I would tell you my story; so lies the land where this story is from. Such is the stuff which I am left to tell you a story of. I would love to tell you this story right there, in front of the fiery eyed *kyahlkyofsenuh*, who are said to resemble humans, but who appear for the merest fraction of an instant...the instant of a green sunrise or, a glancing flash of crystal. These "unseen people", the shadow people, must look out over this destruction every day. From the hard sky shadows of high mountain edges, and from alongside the mist of the high glacial gorges where waterfalls plunge into rainbow spray sunshine, they must look down and lament.

Maybe they are the ones who should tell this story to you. I am sure they can tell it as well as I since they, too, do not exist...

"It is not the gods who are encountered; even hidden, the gods are only forms for recognition. What is encountered are the demons, the powers of jumping, of the interval, of the intensive or the instant, which fills in difference only with the different; they are the sign bearers."

– G. Deleuze

JORDAN ZINOVICH AND RAMI ROTHKOP

BUSHCAMP NOTES

Lucier River. The fires of 1986 stripped a 15-kilometer length of this valley to the ridge crests on either side. Ten years ago we planted here. At Coyote Creek I passed a small plot of trees R and I planted. They're slightly less than a meter high. Bob was still alive then.

It's cool. The clouds drift east, up Ram Creek Pass and over us. A fingernail crescent hangs above me (Munchausen must be up there somewhere, talking to disembodied heads).

5/11/89

I've gotten through my first day on the slopes, and don't feel too bad. I'm switching from a mattock to a long-handled shovel. The new planting style seems to punish my upper body, but I'm almost certain that I won't ache as much as I would if I were "maggoting" it.

D and F both appeared this morning with the same reefer-loony smile on their faces. "Identical grins," I called them.

During the day it snowed, and beyond the fire's edges white still drapes the Rockies. A cold moon glimmers in the sky, with woolly white clouds clinging to the western peaks like strange, shy animals.

5/12/89

Until someone mentioned it, I couldn't even hear the wind whistling through the stands of snags. I actually thought it was traffic noise. L claims it's "the screaming spirits of dead trees." Tonight I came home, showered, ate, then laid down for a brief nap. It is now 11:30 p.m. I slept right through. Outside the tent the sky is absolutely clear. Stars glitter at me, frosting the air.

5/15/89

Today is our day off. Aside from a bit of water on the knee, I've gotten through this week unscathed. The water must have come from stepping too hard on my shovel; or perhaps from the last run I made yesterday, when I planted twice as many trees as I should when starting out.

Our campsite is in the only patch of green that survived the fire. It's quite nice, and I love the isolation. My forearms are getting enormous—like the Lunar King's.

5/17/89

I just had the most extraordinary experience. L (the sculptor) and I have amused ourselves by trying to establish personal definitions of Art over the preceding few days, and yesterday his friend L arrived in camp. I had heard her described as "the photographer," and she's for real. She arrived with a portable studio and all the paraphernalia. She's photographed treeplanting and treeplanters for the past five years.

Tonight she stunned me with an exhibition in the yellow cooktent. Her documentary photos capture all the levels of pain and intensity we inhabit every day. They give us dignity, and a certain magic.

5/18/89

I had my best planting day in a long time, so that's something. However, it has started snowing. Hail began falling as we laboured through the afternoon. Not hard little pellets, but soft little snowballs tumbling and rolling over our trees. For a very short time we almost lost sight of the ones we had planted, then things got milder and now we have snowflakes.

5/21/89

Today we had to change our long-set planting attitudes. The Forest Service and Compo are forcing hardhats on us. Nobody seems very pleased. The damn slopes are so bare that snow, birdshit, and forestry propaganda are the only things that can possibly fall from the sky.

5/22/89

I guess there should be more for me to say. Mostly, this whole camp is geared to driving tired minds and battered bodies on. Laughter is more frequent here than anger, at least this early in the season, although frustration can eat up whole chunks of days. We joke, and develop strategies, and D and E feed us heaps of glorious food.

D has a travelling kitchen in an old schoolbus, with an attached yellow cooktent tent for us. She is blimp pregnant; fat and sassy. E says she gets up mornings and screams at her stomach to get out of her way so she can work.

We spend each day with our noses in the dirt, our peripheral visions searching out *naturals* (naturally reseeded trees). If I can't get started in the morning, then each bend warps my agonized perceptions. If I do get started, my partner and I sail into a punishing routine designed to bury a thousand little trees up to their photosynthetic bits.

Breaking bodies distress me most. We needn't be smashed. Too often the *greedometers* kick in, overwhelming the fact that we are performing a useful service in an awesomely beautiful part of the world.

Lately I've tried taking a moment each day to sit and gaze around me. Gibralter fire-lookout sits atop a mountain about 15 kilometers north of where I work. (I believe it was unmanned the year this fire started.) From it to us the peaks are torn and folded.

How to describe this fire to you? It ran from the western mountain crests across to the valley's eastern peaks, licking into every peripheral valley. It leapt the fire guards and ate: animals, trees, even rocks—which simply exploded in the heat. Its enormity pressed itself upon me the other day. As we planted the Lucier floodplain we came upon the remains of a bunch of at least five Bighorn Sheep. When the fire overtook them they clustered nose to nose, and burned to piles of crumbling bone. Even their horns crumbled. The valley has all the stark apocalyptic beauty of an industrial site: where unremitting shapes crown the blasted earth.

5/23/89

What a day! We awoke to pissing rain, and stumbled half-deflated to our breakfasts in the glowing tent. It is the third week of this contract. All day long flurries and squalls have battered us. What a relief it was to realize why I am here. I'm trying to prove I'm still a male animal. Today I proved it. Tonight we settle down to recoup.

It has always seemed extraordinarily difficult to explain to you what treeplanting is all about. L, the photographer, has taken some shots that might help convey it to you. The image with the trees on the right and the coastline in the distance could be any cut-block when we first set foot upon it. The one with three jumbled stumps on a rocky background shows a planted block. Those strange little sticks are planted trees. For them we sweat away, secure in the conviction that we are making an impact on the future.

The image of the barren block is, however, the truest view of our world. The clear-cutting rapists slash the forests down, dwarfing our pitiful efforts to replace them. They flay these mountains. I suppose that if even one of the trees I plant reaches cone-bearing age it could *regenerate* a forest. But what if none of them do?

5/25/89

We woke up to snow yesterday morning. This is the time when everyone begins wondering if there's life beyond the nylon walls. My knees ache. I creak when I move. My hands are so swollen that I can hardly write. The attrition has begun. Everyone is in the same condition. Now it's simply a constant search for easier ways to do things well: Attempts to save wrists, elbows, and knees. Anger bubbles over, and hysteria. Humour has a cutting edge. I keep my trouser bottoms rolled.

5/26/89

It occurs to me that you might like to learn a little of our argot. People are more interesting to write about, of course, but the characters around me have gathered together for just one purpose: to *reforest* the planet. Before I can talk much about them, I guess I'd better build something of the universe within which we exist.

photos by Lorraine Gilbert

Mornings are our chaos. We stumble from our warm beds trying to look and act intelligent. We seldom succeed, which doesn't prevent us from trying. We're responsible for taking our own food and warm drinks to the slopes, so sometime during breakfast each one of us packs some sort of lunch. Then we pile into the *crummies* and *crew cabs* to ride to the *tree stashes* on the *blocks* where we will work that day.

Although we used to work as *line crews*—that is to say, in small groups strung out across the slopes—now most of us *area plant* with one or two other planters. And it's astonishing how much ground a good crew can cover.

Once we're on the block, there are several ways to plant. Before anything else, however, a planter has to *bag up* for the first *run*. Right now we're planting various *stocks*: pine, spruce, and larch mostly, but some fir too. The *seedlings* come in *bundles*, and the type of tree largely determines how many a planter can carry. Pine are the lightest (today I carried 600 on one run) and spruce the heaviest (no more than 400). Most of the seedlings are raised with a small soil, vermiculite, and fertilizer *plug* containing their roots. Last week, though, we got some jumbo *bare roots*. They were enormous, some of them almost a meter high, with unmanageably huge clusters of tangled roots. No one carried more than 150 of them at a time. (As soon as one wag saw these monsters he snickered, "Anything smaller than 18-inches is a *cull*.") When we're bagged up, we're ready to plant.

5/27/89

God only knows when this showery, cold, miserable weather will break. I do intend to go on with the lexical letter, but not now.

An interesting thing happened to me today. L turned up on the slope to photograph me as I worked. She took three portrait shots with the block and Gibralter peak in the background, then a photo of me planting. I have no idea how they turned out, but she has promised to send me copies. Ah well, we laborers plug away while the Dow rises and falls. All this fucking education and here I am again. Still, there are long moments when I wouldn't be anywhere else.

5/28/89

When we bag up we're ready to start our run. Shovel in hand, I waddle under my load of trees. The first 100 or so always seem quite slow. Each movement emphasizes the weight I carry, and my rhythms only come on gradually.

photos by Lorraine Gilbert

My shovel nose probes for a *microsite*. When it finds dirt I *screef* a patch clean, pound in a *straight-back hole*, slip the plug in to the *root collar* (*laterals* have to show but the *top of the plug* must be covered), and hammer shut the hole. And as that first plug goes in I often retaste a bit of my breakfast.

The mechanics of planting never change, but each tree goes in the ground a little bit differently, and we get fined for all sorts of things. If the *screef* isn't large enough in grass, we get fined. If the tree is *too deep*, *too shallow*, *L-rooted*, *J-rooted*, leans more than 7° (a *leaner*), and/or the plug is *clipped*, we get fined. We also get fined for *spacing*—that is, putting trees into a given *plot* of ground. Too many and we're fined for *excess*. Too few, we're fined for *missed spots*. We're fined for trees too close together. We're fined if our planted trees are too close to *naturals*.

Sound complicated? And boring? It is. It doesn't take much *screefing* the *duff*, dodging the naturals (which tend to run in packs), and fighting the *fuck brush*, or *slash*, or *schnarb* before planters start thinking about anything but planting trees. And that's when we get fined. I'll go into more of this later, but for now it's just too depressing. And there aren't any *checkers* breathing down my neck right now.

Some of the lazier—or more frustrated—planters find novel ways to take revenge on trees. One fellow I knew insisted that heavy *culling*, throwing away 10-20% of the stock, was a valid practice. Another, a fellow named California Bill, decided that *honking* was the way to go. Old Bill tried stuffing bundles of trees down the gopher holes he found on his blocks. Unfortunately for Bill, the gophers didn't like his plan. They pushed the bundles back out onto his line, and Bill wasn't simply fined: he went *down the road*.

5/30/89

Yesterday I got ill. A cold combined with some brief kind of flu laid my poor old body low. Since this experiment started, three weeks ago, I've lost the eight pounds it took me two years to gain, and I seem older and slower.

The weather has finally broken. The mountains look frigid in their new layers of snow. We're living almost at snowline.

5/31/89

Since the only trees that survived this part of the fire crouch in the little valley where we have camped, I've set up my tent at the edge of the camp closest to the thickets. Tonight the wood thrushes and robins began their summer cho-

rus. As I returned to my green half-dome tent a ruffed grouse swept out of the twilight, passing so close by my head that the air rushed through its feathers like the low roar of wind-fanned fire.

6/02/89

Today we got into a block of *cream*—like cats to a saucer. My planting partner and I put 960 trees into a small piece of great ground very close to the road—and had great fun.

6/07/89

It's been a wild day. Nine of the most experienced planters in camp ran amok, and *creamed off* a whole mountainside. That is to say, they cut enormous chunks of the best ground in our new block for themselves. R had left D in charge, and he went screaming mad. There's nothing but bad ground left for the slower planters, and D swears that as soon as those *highballers* have finished the sections they're planting, they'll be working in shit so deep they'll have to tilt back their heads to breath.

The Varied Thrushes have reached the high country, buzzing that strange song of theirs.

6/11/89

I can hardly belive it. I'm an old *pud*, but I'm still in the money. I'm having fun, too.

New folks have begun arriving, to replace the planters who left. New couples bring some sanity with them. We'll need it, too, because by the day after tomorrow we should be up to 24 planters, from the 8 who struggled on just a few days ago.

6/12/89

The lunacy begins! The highballers are arriving. Most of them are young and wild, all balls and strutting energy. As I looked at one young fellow's glazed eyes this evening, I imagined him thinking about nothing but trees. I could read the numbers on his greedometer.

Now the *green* planters will get some seasoning. If their attitudes are bad they'll try keeping up to the big guns, and when they can't match the numbers they'll get frustrated and doubt themselves.

So far this season I've deliberately held myself in check. But I don't want to return to excessive *pudding*. So the circus draws me in. Right now I'm dreading

photos by Lorraine Gilbert

tomorrow. We're supposed to move to a new block, which may force me to return to that most crippling of all planting tools, the mattock. I know only that we'll face the fiercest screef we've seen all year. I already ache, and heavy screef broke D's back. Later we're supposed to move to another block, which will require a 1-1/2 hour commute, each way. Just the thought of commuting 3 hours a day exhausts me.

I long for rational attitudes, honest claims to ignorance. I wonder about all of us. I've paraphrased a quote that R gave me, to help me tough it out:

> "Across the road from my cabin was a huge clear-cut—hundreds of acres of massive spruce stumps interspersed with tiny Douglas firs—products of what they call 'Reforestation,' which I guess makes the spindly firs en mass a 'Reforest,' which makes an individual spindly fir a 'Refir,' which means you could say that Crestbrook and the B.C. government, has Refir Madness, since they think that sawing down 200-foot-tall spruces and replacing them with puling 2-foot or 6 or 8 inch Refirs is no different from farming beans or corn or alfalfa. They even call the towering spars they wipe from the earth's face forever (to print a single issue of the Sunday New York Times) a 'crop'—as if they'd planted the virgin forest! But I'm just a writer and maybe missing some deeper significance in their strange nomenclature and stranger treatment of primordial trees.*
>
> *adapted from David James Duncan, The River Why.

We're planting a burn, which sounds like a noble enterprise except that it's already restocking itself. The regen on some blocks is so thick that forestry spacing regulations prevent us from planting the seedlings we carry. The companies and forestry know so little about natural mechanisms of reforestation that they're still experimenting. They scarify some ground—turn it into furrows—then demand that we plant in the rock-hard dirt at the furrow bottoms. At this point their survival plots indicate that the trees planted according to their specifications are already dying in the sun. Our Refirs aren't doing well. Too many theories and too much politics. And the government is already selling 25-year leases to transnational conglomerates.

Lately I've been talking to R about his view of the planting situation. We can both clearly recall why we got into this business: we thought it was a way to help reclaim some of the devastation we saw. But he's getting quite cynical about our place in the system:

*

Companies view forests as expendable and short term, in much the same way as they view the rest of our economy. They see trees as dollars, but forest ecosystems that have taken thousands of years to emerge do not take easily to short crop rotations. Taking a huge piece out of the balance tips it. And arguing "fact" with professional foresters often collapses, because "facts" can be manipulated to enhance expedience, and emotionally charged points of view are dismissed as radical. But a dialogue based more on underlying feelings than on "scientific fact" might be a good thing. Perhaps even foresters need to listen more to those voices inside that let them know what is right.

Planting isn't open licence to cut more. We're told now that we plant trees to reforest areas that will not naturally regenerate. Our consumerism fuels the demand for wood-based products, but our social attitudes are slowly changing. Big business is scared. It has assumed its "right to harvest". The public needs to know that transnationals spend millions of dollars on advertising propaganda to cover their abuses. Still, though we blame them and our governments for the greed and excess, we're all entwined in the mis-management of our forest resources. The way our forests are treated by large corporations must change, as must our demands on the resource. Looking to the future, planting should be minimized, in conjunction with reduced cutting and truly sustainable forest management.

For years I've struggled with my conscience so I could work and live in the woods. I've made a living in an industry that I criticize freely. Though I'm watching the destruction of our resource, the "forest managers" expect me to say that what I see out there is good. That we're doing a fine job reforesting the devastation and everything is O.K. That's not how it feels. I've seen too many mountains slide into creeks; too many washed out roads; too many muddy rivers; too many cut blocks that never should have been logged. My views have changed.

Going treeplanting those first years was a "save-the-world" feeling, an alternative lifestyle as exciting as it was important. I still have that passion for life in a planting camp, but no longer feel that we're much more than a cog in an industry wheel. It's hard, because many of us involved in planting share my views, yet we find ourselves working to perpetuate the very system we despise. Perhaps this is why we are such a non-vocal work force: we've come to feel that we're betraying our deepest selves. Planters and contractors have to start speaking out, and not in support of the industry, in support of what's true for them.

photos by Lorraine Gilbert

Discover a wilderness that's a cut above the rest

Super, Natural British Columbia

123

JERRY SCHROEDER

MATRIX MANIFESTO

thebushisstillourstrengthgivingusthemagicalspacetooperateinconjunc
tionwiththevariousenergiesthataretherethisisnotsomethingasobviousa
santhropomorphicentitiesalthoughtheytoodoexisttherebutconfigurati
onsofphenomenalspaceofwhichthismodeofwritingmatrixwritingisanex
pressionthepurposeofthiswritingismultiplexinfiniteperhapsbutitiscana
dianwritingformebecauseitallowsonetohideandyetbemanifestlyobviou
stoanyonewhocomesacrossithologrammaticspacemagicalanarchyyou
aregoingtogetitevenifyoudontbutatthesametimethetextismultidirectio
naltheexampleyouseehereissimplelefttorightthissimplybecausethisisa
moreovertlypoliticalintheexotericsensethatiswhocancensorthemselve
sinordertosensorthisyouhavetosenseyourownunconsciousyourownsu
perconsciousthelanguageofyourguardianangelisalwaysjustaspaceawa
yonanypageofwritingtheeffectofmatrixwritingisastheeffectofourbusha
blurthatisimitatedbytelevisionelectronspraybutthatstuffisonlyaminisc
ulechildbratsimpulsecomparedtotheenergymanifestandpotentialandm
agicalanarchykineticineveryletterofthematrixeveryblinkoftheeyemagic
alanarchyisanewuniversethispieceismorelinearthanmostexamplesofth
iswritingbutevenherethealeatoryenergiesthefoolsrandomnesstheainso
phnothingtheonlymagictrueisanarchynoanarchyismagicatallriskandn
oneananarchycanbeinthiscountrysototalthatnoonewillevenbeabletop
redictwhetherornotthegunswillworkthusdoingawaywiththatshitcomei
nlookinanydirectionmagicalanarchyandyouwillseethewordsandsound
sofimaginationsendlessbushformingthesearesoundsandwordsfromthe
wildernessbackofthemindhowdoyoudividelanguageourgovernmentsal
waystrytothisimplodesandthenexplodeswhatevertheysaymakesthemc
ontinuouswiththeunconsciouswecanwriteinanydirectionandalldirecti
onsmagicalanarchythisformeisthepotentialityofthelanguageofthistruly
infinitespacewhatisthemessagewhatisnotnoonecandecideandsoeveryt
hingismanifestatonceifyoutraceadiagonallinedownthepageandthenan
otheroneonanotherangleathreedimensionalobjectwillcomeoutofthepa
gemagicalanarchysothatlanguageisrestorediconicitybutnotadetermina
teonebutratheranaleatoryonethatisthepulsepulsenow

CAPTAIN PAUL WATSON

IN DEFENSE OF TREE-SPIKING

Tree-spiking is one of the most effective tactics yet developed to protect old-growth forests. It is a controversial tactic, but the most effective tactics are always controversial. Why tree-spiking? As the originator of tree-spiking as an environmental tactic, I feel it is my responsibility to defend its legitimacy.

As a child I witnessed my father break a chain saw on a horseshoe that had been nailed to a tree a century before and became over time an internal armour protecting the heart of the elderly and noble being. I was delighted. In the mid-sixties I spiked some trees to protect them from developers in my neighborhood. It was not successful. The trees were cut down, but with the small satisfaction of two broken chain saws.

Then, in 1982, the Grouse Mountain Ski Resort in North Vancouver, British Columbia announced that they were selling the timber rights to the south slope of Grouse Mountain. The decision meant that loggers would bald face the mountain overlooking the city of Vancouver. The public was outraged. The North Vancouver City Council was unsuccessful in stopping the decision from going ahead. Despite petitions from school-children and appeals from prominent citizens, the trees were doomed. The resort would not relent.

I organized a small cadre of concerned eco-activists and we formed the group called the North Vancouver Garden and Arbor Club. We started out early on a Sunday morning, each armed with a hammer and a backpack filled with metal spikes. The six of us were able to successfully spike some two thousand trees. At the same time we pulled out every survey stake we could find. We posted over three dozen warning signs stating that the entire condemned lot had been randomly spiked. Then we drove into Vancouver and dropped off press releases to the media.

The next day the shit hit the fan. The Vancouver *Sun* and the Vancouver *Province* both ran the story on the front page with banner headlines. We followed up by interviews with television stations—all of us wearing masks and identifying ourselves as spokesperson Wally Cedarleaf.

Within a day, the sawmills stated flatly that they had no intention of buying logs from the spiked lot. The deal was off. The Grouse Mountain Resort people were furious. We were denounced as terrorists and criminals by those we thought were our allies: the North Vancouver City Council, and Greenpeace and assorted other eco-bureaucrats. We didn't give a damn—the fact was that the trees were saved, Grouse Mountain would remain intact. It was a tactic that worked.

The Royal Canadian Mounted Police (RCMP) investigated the case and their sleuthing led them to our doorsteps, where we were questioned but not charged. The logging interests were quick to realize that any publicity over such a simple tactic would do them more harm than any benefit they would derive from prosecuting us. Not only was it a tactic that worked, it was a tactic that we could get away with.

Prior to the spiking I had consulted a good friend who was an arborist. I asked him for pointers on how to spike the tree without causing it any harm. He provided me with the advice that I needed. I then made enquiries of the logging industry while pretending to be an insurance investigator. I asked if there were safety mechanisms on chain saws that would prevent the chain from breaking and striking the operator. I was assured by the industry that such an accident could not happen, for all the chain saws used had chain guards to prevent a broken chain from whipping back into the face of the logger. I was also told that the sawmills required safety shields between mill saws and their operators.

Again posing as an insurance investigator, I asked, "Is it possible for a logger or a sawmill worker to be injured if the mill saw should strike a metallic object embedded in a log?" The answer from three different industry spokespeople was a definite "No." The companies I questioned were McMillan Bloedel, Crown Zellerbach, and Weldwood Lumber.

Therefore, I concluded that tree-spiking was a perfect tactic. It would not hurt the tree. It would not hurt the loggers or sawmill operators. It was simple and easy to do. Materials were easy to obtain. It was not illegal. It could not even be defined as damaging property, since trees—being living sentient beings—are not and never will be human property. Recognition of trees as property is a clear statement of anthropocentric thought.

A few months after the spiking of Grouse Mountain, I ran into Mike Roselle in a Greenpeace hang-out in San Francisco. Another participating member of the Garden Club and I told Mike about the incident and the tactic. He was thrilled with the idea, and because of Mike many others became involved.

Thus it was with both pride and satisfaction that I relished reports of tree-spiking from California, Oregon, Washington, and Alaska. One report came from the Bahamas and another from Sweden of spiking operations that had saved forest land. Native Indians spiked trees on Meares Island in British Columbia. Tree-spiking was becoming epidemic. For the first time, the logging industry found itself on the defensive.

The industry reacted with propaganda about the dangers of tree-spiking to humans, conveniently forgetting that only a few short years earlier they had informed me (in my insurance-investigator guise) that an injury was not possible. Industry money was channelled into lobbying politicians to pass laws making tree-spiking illegal. The industry began to spend large sums on security and investigation. But the forests are vast and detection is difficult, and all the new laws and pumped-in money have not paid off with the conviction of a single tree-spiker.

Tree-spiking is also a tactic that keeps the issues of old growth forests and clear cutting in the news. It is itself a controversial issue, and as such is guaranteed to provide consistency to discussion in the media and among the public. With the tactic of tree-spiking the defenders of the forest have a weapon with which to keep the logging industry and their lackey workers on the defensive.

Tree-spiking has continually stimulated the imaginations of many eco-defenders. The original tactic has benefitted from the addition of ceramic spikes, the use of augers, and the employment of twist nails, and thus the trees have benefitted. When the industry threatened to log spiked trees to spite our efforts, I suggested that ecologists escalate our campaign by spiking cut logs both on the floating booms and in the industry yards. Escalate if you like, you bastards, and we'll go for the heart of your operations—your machinery. Thus we have found that tree-spiking can be both a defensive and an offensive tactic.

In a biocentric context, tree-spiking is simply a form of preventative medicine. It is the inoculation of a tree against the disease of logging. But in the context of our society, money talks, and industry money has successfully swayed anthropocentric opinions against tree-spiking.

Unfortunately, there was a weak link in our movement. The anthropocentric socialist types, whose hearts bleed for the antiquated rights of the workers were won over. Concerned that the logger was a "victim", these so-called defenders of the forests have proceeded to weaken our one totally effective tactic by denouncing it.

I was in attendance at the Environmental Law Conference in Eugene, Oregon in the spring of 1990. Judi Bari and Daryl Cherney said that there was unanimous consensus at the tree-spiking workshop that the tactic should be retired. There was not! Judi Bari even told me at the conference that she considered me to be the enemy, but many Earth Firsters were in opposition. It was a tragedy that Judi and Daryl were hurt when their car was bombed.[1] We will probably never know what really happened, but it will be a greater tragedy if the bombing continues to give martyr status to two people who have seriously compromised the established principles of Earth First!

Redwood Summer was not an Earth First! type of operation. Civil disobedience is costly to its participants, both financially and physically. It is a tactic that springs from the deep Judeo-Christian ethics of self-sacrifice and voluntary self-inflicted persecution. It was not a tactic that was ever practiced by North American native peoples. The establishment loves CD. The authorities are trained to deal with it, there are no surprises.

The Redwood Summer people would have us believe that the loggers are not our enemies. Judi Bari considers them her allies, while at the same time accusing me of being her enemy. The reality of her views is plain. She is acting from an anthropocentric ethical foundation, while I come from a biocentric base.

The hands of the individual who would destroy a tree are the hands of a person prepared to murder a sacred and respected citizen of this planet. Livelihood, material well-being, these are not sufficient justification for this crime against nature. Loggers are just pathetic foot-soldiers for the corporate generals of the logging industry. Certainly they are being exploited by the companies, but they have made the decision to be exploited. The trees have not.

Yes, I realize that humans use wood and believe themselves dependent upon the cutting of trees. I also realize, however, that to a vastly reduced population wood could be made available without killing trees. Dead wood; weather preserved wood; living planks cut from living trees (a practice that provided Northwest coastal Indians with planks without depriving the world of a tree); cotton and papyrus for paper; these sources are all alternatives to the wholesale destruction currently practiced by the logging industry. There are alternatives, the most important being disciplined conservation. Yes, this is extreme, but so is massive clear-cutting to provide cheap logs for Japanese mills and bags of redwood charcoal for California cook-outs. I could occasionally even condone the cutting of a living tree: if it was diseased, and done with the proper respect, and used for a noble purpose. Unfortunately, 99.9% of all trees killed are in good health and are used for ignoble purposes.

A few years ago, a Santa Cruz reporter told me that she did not believe that all the redwoods in California were worth the life of a single human being. What incredible arrogance. This opinion is the extreme view of anthropocentric Judeo-Christian thinking. I am of the extreme opposite view. To me, all of the human beings in California are not worth the extinction of one of the mighty and revered ancient forest dwellers we have chosen to call redwoods.

The debate really comes down to this: Is Earth First! a movement of anthropocentrics, a movement of biocentrics, or is it a little of both? Can the anthropocentric mind-set work harmoniously, or even work at all, with the biocentric mind-set? One thing is certain, that there is a vast chasm between the two modes of thought. Perhaps there is a need for two Earth First! groups, one for anthropocentrics and the other for biocentrics.

As for myself, I do not believe in loggers, I believe in trees. I do not believe in fishermen, I believe in fish. I do not believe in miners, I believe in the rocks beneath my feet. I do not believe in pie-in-the-sky spirituality, I believe in rainbows, rivers, mountains, daffodils, and moss. I do not believe in environmentalists, I believe in the environment. I am a proud traitor to my species, in alliance with my mother the Earth in opposition to those who would destroy her; those who would tear down the sun to make a buck; those insignificant parasites who believe that the Earth is here to serve human interests.

The Earth abides. We overly glorified primate apes will pass, for we are a stupid species, incapable of relating intelligently to nature, with harmony and respect. We have chosen not to consider ourselves to be interdependent, and have bestowed divinity upon ourselves to justify our separateness from the divine beauty of the living Earth. We must either change or pass, and in our passing the rocks will scream joyously at the Earth's liberation, which will be their reward for our disappearance. Or, if we survive, it will be as equal citizens, who have finally realized that the path to bliss lies in surrendering to nature, not dominating her. But to survive we will have to endure the humiliation of voluntarily giving up our anthropocentric throne of domination.

If we are removed from the Earth, the loggers will slowly fade from her consciousness like unpleasant and distant memories. If we survive, the loggers will also fade from the consciousness of humanity, as perverse and embarrassing aspects of our once primitive selves. Either way, the logger is a nothing, an insignificance, a virus, a rot, a disease and an aberration against nature, and I for one will not weep a single tear at his demise.

To sum up, I would like to repeat that tree-spiking is a tactic that works. It does not hurt trees. It does not injure people. It is simple. It is not costly. The logging barons have little defense against it. They moan and they groan and they gnash their teeth, but they can do little—except of course to employ the old tactic of divide and conquer. They can manipulate members of our movement and spread division and hatred among them by exploiting their anthropocentric Judeo-Christian morality. In this way they can spread their rot among us and destroy us.

But whatever political stance that the Earth First! rank-and-file takes—the reality is that tree-spiking will continue. It continues in northern California, even more covertly, because it is now plain that advocates may fall victim to former brothers and sisters. Continue it shall, despite the laws of society, despite the so-called "rights" of the loggers and their ilk. Tree-spiking is an idea, and an idea is impossible to kill. It will continue, and I will continue to advocate it until the day I die. No compromise, not now or ever.

---

1. Jordan, I have no idea who bombed the car. Our group has never been suspect, and we are not concerned if people think we are or not. I do stand by my concern that the bombing gave martyr status to two people who have compromised a very effective tactic.

Joyce Nelson

SPEAKING THE UNSPEAKABLE:
UNDERSTANDING ECOFEMINISM

Whatever is unnamed, undepicted in images, whatever is omitted from Biography, censored in collections of letters, whatever is misnamed as something else, made difficult-to-come-by, whatever is buried in the memory by the collapse of meaning under an inadequate or lying language—this will become, not merely unspoken, but unspeakable.

– Adrienne Rich[1]

Daring to speak the unspeakable is what characterizes every liberation movement, and in our time we are witnessing an extraordinary collective phenomenon of new naming, renaming, unburying, remembering and rethinking in virtually every field of thought and endeavour. This challenge to patriarchy in all its forms is coming from every oppressed people on the planet. As black Nigerian writer Chinua Achele has put it, "The great excluded are starting to make trouble."[2]

Not only are we starting to make trouble, we are making links among ourselves and among previously disparate and isolated disciplines, fields, facts, and phenomena: links which certainly do trouble that privileged point of view from which most thought has been thought (and most words written) over centuries. As previously excluded voices struggle out from under oppression and imposed silence, their contributions change the entire picture.

Consider, for example, Eduardo Galeano's trilogy, *Memory of Fire*—a telling of the past five hundred years from a Latin American point of view.[3]

By filling in what had previously been unnamed, undepicted, omitted, censored, misnamed, buried, and unspoken, Galeano has not only challenged the prevailing historical portrait conveyed by most First World accounts, he has given all of us some missing pieces of that fragmented jigsaw puzzle called patriarchy.

As we put that puzzle together, we are able to see its picture as entirely arbitrary, a world-view that benefits only a tiny few, at the expense of most other beings on this planet and of the planet itself.

Over the past dozen years or so, but especially during the otherwise dismal 1980s, a number of pieces of the puzzle have been added, leading to a critique that goes right to the core of the western patriarchal paradigm. Part of the developing critique has been the rise of "ecofeminism" which, in essence, bridges the gap between ecology and feminism: strands of analysis which have existed side by side over past decades without necessarily intertwining. Thus, there have been any number of environmental analyses and books which illuminate the process of ecological degradation, but which fail to make the connection between planetary exploitation and other forms of social injustice and inequality. Similarly, any number of feminist texts have explored the politics of patriarchal society without broadening and deepening the focus to include the exploited planet. By making explicit the connections between an unjust and misogynist society and a society which has exploited "mother earth" to the point of environmental crises, ecofeminism has helped to highlight the deep splits in the patriarchal world-view.

Patriarchy's Shadow

As women have long recognized, our oppression is primarily based on body difference. Our women's bodies, which bleed, conceive, give birth and lactate, have been perceived under patriarchy as "closer to nature" than the male, closer to the animal realm, and we have thereby been deemed "inferior" to men. The second wave of feminism in this century necessarily rejected this patriarchal projection by asserting that "anatomy is not destiny" and by struggling for equal opportunity in all professions, for control over our own bodies, and for social change in a deeply misogynist world—struggles which obviously continue.

It may be fair to say that ecofeminism has taken the critique deeper to ask: why is it that men feel "superior" to nature, cut off from the natural realm? Why is it that men perceive their own bodies as *not* "close to nature", not even part of nature? By thereby changing the framework of analysis to highlight the mind/body split so central to patriarchy, ecofeminism reveals the basic fault-line in the patriarchal zeitgeist.

That fault-line is hierarchical dualism. Where there is only difference, Western patriarchy perceives not just "opposites" but a hierarchical relationship between opposing terms. Thus, patriarchy's perception of the female as subordinate and inferior to the male is recapitulated in the culture/nature dichotomy wherein non-human species and the Earth itself are perceived as subordinate and inferior to "mankind". Focusing on this prevailing anthropocentric view, Elizabeth Dodson Gray writes in *Green Paradise Lost* :

> Ultimately, the problem of patriarchy is conceptual. The problem which patriarchy poses for the human species is not simply that it oppresses women. Patriarchy has erroneously conceptualized and mythed "Man's place" in the universe and thus—by the illusion of dominion that it legitimates—it endangers the entire planet.[4]

Gray and others have traced the conceptual "error" in the West back to the three thousand year-old creation myth expressed in the first chapters of Genesis: with its command to "subdue the earth" and "have dominion over" all living beings; and its narrative which "explains" male dominance in Chapter 2 through Adam's creation first, his naming of all reality, the birth of Eve from his side, and the Eve-serpent collusion.

As creation myths go, Genesis is a relatively recent one, recorded when patriarchy was still in the process of becoming entrenched. The ancient Hebrews did not invent patriarchy—which was well under way at least a thousand years before Genesis was recorded—but they too were caught up in its zeitgeist.

While there are undoubtedly profound meanings in our Genesis myth, it has traditionally been understood to mean that Eve and the wily serpent were responsible for the "Fall of Man." By yielding to temptation and then tempting Adam to eat the forbidden fruit, Eve is perceived to have caused the wrath of Yahweh, resulting in Paradise Lost. But if we ask what the "Fall of Man" was, we recognize that it was a fall into consciousness—specifically consciousness of the body. Genesis tells us that after eating the fruit, Adam and Eve "knew their nakedness" and hid from Yahweh, who angrily asks: "Who told you that you were naked?"

Thus, at issue in the first three chapters of Genesis is body consciousness—the gaining of carnal knowledge or the knowledge of embodiment, incarnation. As the result of this supposed transgression, the angry Yahweh splits off from his creation: a breach central to that other patriarchal dualism expressed as a spirit/matter opposition. Genesis thus posits a hierarchical "chain of being", with the sky-god Yahweh at the top of the ladder, the angels a bit lower, then Adam, then Eve, then all other species, with nature (and the devil) at the bottom. For our purposes here, the most resonant moment may be Genesis 3:17, in which the angry God curses the very ground because of Adam and Eve's transgression.

A thousand years later, institutionalized Christianity (as of the third century A.D.) amplified that curse into a view of earthly life itself: "corruption" with both body and woman the signs of defilement keeping Man from a most unearthly heaven. Over the centuries, Western patriarchy has given us a series of deep splits or false oppositions that have been pitted against each other in our psyches and in the external world. Those splits are these: an absolutely good God vs. an absolutely evil Devil; light vs. dark; male vs. female; mind vs. body; spirit vs. matter; human vs. animal. But under patriarchy, these so-called "oppositions" have been scripted to mean that one must triumph over the other. The absolutely good God must triumph over the absolutely evil Devil; light must triumph over dark; male is superior to female; mind is triumphant over body; spirit is better than matter; humans are superior to all other species.

But perhaps the most subtle, yet most damaging, split is the spirit/matter duality, reinforced by Yahweh's curse of the very ground. Even three thousand years after Genesis was first recorded, that curse still reverberates through Western patriarchy. As Jamake Highwater, author of *The Primal Mind*, has noted:

> For most primal peoples the earth is so marvellous that their connotation of it requires it to be spelled with a capital 'E'. How perplexing it is to discover two English synonyms for Earth—'soil' and 'dirt'—used to describe uncleanliness, soiled and dirty. And how upsetting it is to discover that the word 'dirty' in English is also used to depict obscenities.[5]

Writing from a cultural perspective that considers the ground itself as sacred, Highwater reveals the extent to which even our dominant language reflects patriarchy's profound dis-ease, unease, about both embodiment and being grounded in the natural realm.

In Jungian terms, body and nature have been patriarchy's "shadow": rejected, feared and despised as the inferior and loathsome "evil" side of the human condition. As a result, whatever patriarchy has perceived as "closer to nature" has also been perceived as "further from God"—an obvious prescription for exploitation. Not surprisingly, the patriarchal shadow has been projected onto women, people of colour, "primitive" societies, peasant peoples, nonhuman species, and the planet itself. Since, in terms of hierarchical dualism, "further from God" means "closer to the Devil", exploitation has over the centuries rarely troubled the patriarchal conscience.

Thus, it is no accident that the so-called Age of Enlightenment, which began in the 16th century, coincided with the onset of the slave trade, the plundering and decimation of indigenous peoples of the New World, and the centuries of witch-burnings. A zeitgeist which posits light-male-mind-spirit on the side of God, and dark-female-body-matter on the side of the Devil, can easily perceive the "other" as not human, "mere animal" or "devil".

These historical phenomena were an intrinsic part of a Scientific Revolution which would take the Western patriarchal paradigm to its logical conclusion: the triumph of Mechanism over Vitalism in the Cartesian world-view.

The Death of Nature

Before the Age of Enlightenment, nature was perceived of as "inferior", and "feminine", but nevertheless alive. Under Descartes, Locke, and others involved in the Scientific Revolution, the entire cosmos would henceforth be perceived as a mechanistic "clockworks" set in motion by an aloof, transcendent, and finally absent deity. All animal species were perceived as unfeeling "machines", and matter itself became mere "dead matter" to be manipulated by the superior white male mind. This denial of life itself to the natural realm (including the body) was patriarchal split-consciousness taken to its ultimate, but it coincided with other (unspoken) losses, including the loss of meaning and feeling, and certainly the wilful loss of millions of people perceived of as less than human.

As Carolyn Merchant has written in her extraordinary book, *The Death of Nature*:

> *The removal of animistic, organic assumptions about the cosmos constituted the death of nature—the most far-reaching effect of the Scientific Revolution. Because nature was now viewed as a system of dead, inert particles moved by external, rather than inherent forces, the mechanical framework itself could legitimate the manipulation of nature. Moreover, as a conceptual framework, the mechanical order had associated with it a framework of values based on power, fully compatible with the directions taken by commercial capitalism.*[6]

The triumph of Mechanism over Vitalism, finally achieved by the end of the 19th century, found its ultimate expression in a 20th century which has moved relentlessly toward planetary annihilation. It is as though patriarchy itself in all its forms, so long estranged from body and nature, is soaring off to that unearthly perfection of mind and spirit called "heaven". In the process, it is killing off 150,000 species per year in its continuing rape of the Earth, waging wars of oppression across the planet to feed its power-drive, spending $2 million every minute on military weaponry, and eliminating diversity itself under the aegis of that modern monotheism called Technocracy. Whatever else it may be, ecofeminism is nothing less than the transformed return to Vitalism (but devoid of patriarchal projections) as a conscious political and spiritual challenge to the prevailing Mechanical zeitgeist. In its reweaving of the ripped web of life, ecofeminism asks us to rethink all hierarchical dualisms and thereby change everything. It may be fair to say that neither feminism nor environmentalism has, by itself, gone so deep.

Such a critique helps us to understand the phenomenal blossoming throughout the 1980s of Earth-centered spirituality in a wide diversity of forms and practices. But common to each are three core concepts: (1) immanence—the concept that sacredness is inherent in all Creation; (2) interconnection—that all parts of the living cosmos are linked; and (3) compassion—the ability to see ourselves as answerable and accountable to those who are different from us, to value all other lives as we value our own.

But ultimately, ecofeminism challenges the very basis upon which all current economic systems have been built: the belief that sees "the other" as a resource to be exploited for profit. Whether that other is an oppressed class, race, sex, or the planet itself, all are linked by our shared oppression in a system that must rank Being itself for the gain of the few. As Judith Plant, editor of *Healing the Wounds*, writes in her introduction:

> ... there is no respect for the "other" in patriarchal society. The other, the object of patriarchal rationality, is considered only insofar as it can benefit the subject. So self-centered is this view that it is blind to the fact that its own life depends on the integrity and well-being of the whole.[7]

An alternative paradigm based on immanence, interconnection, and compassion thereby challenges every patriarchal institution on the planet. Such concepts provide an imperative toward action in the world: an activism that links the political and the spiritual. As Starhawk writes, "instead of replacing political action, earth-based spirituality provides a repository of energy that can resurge in new cycles of political momentum."[8] Ecofeminism is the inheritor of feminist spirituality rooted in Earth-centered traditions.

The richness of ecofeminism is in the extent to which it makes explicit the interconnection of human systems of oppression and posits a vital alternative to the patriarchal paradigm based on hierarchy and dominance. Into the 1990s, ecofeminism will continue to speak the unspeakable in a society which wants us to remain ignorant of interrelationships, isolated from one another, and fragmented in our efforts toward social change.

---

1. Adrienne Rich, On Lies, Secrets, and Silence (New York: W.W. Norton and Company, 1979), p. 199.
2. Chinua Achebe, remark at the 54th International PEN World Congress, September 1989, Toronto, Canada.
3. Eduardo Galeano, Memory of Fire. Three volumes (New York: Pantheon Books, 1982, 1984, 1988).
4. Elizabeth Dodson Gray, Green Paradise Lost (Wellesley, Mass.: Roundtable Press, 1979), p. ix.
5. Jamake Highwater, The Primal Mind : Vision and Reality in Indian America (New York: Meridian, 1982), p. 5.
6. Carolyn Merchant, The Death of Nature : Women, Ecology and the Scientific Revolution (New York: Harper & Row, 1980), p. 193.
7. Judith Plant, "Toward A New World: An Introduction," in Judith Plant, ed. Healing the Wounds: The Promise of Ecofeminism (Toronto: Between the Lines, 1989), p. 2.
8. Starhawk, ibid. "Feminist, Earth-based Spirituality and Ecofeminism," p. 177.

Marc Drouin

HYDRO-QUÉBEC: POWER POLITICS OR BUST

Until now, development has been part of a mentality and the interests of minority groups who have enriched themselves upon our territories.

— Rigoberta Menchu, *Stolen Continents*, 1992.

The conflicts which are part of this resistance have been, and continue to be, more than a simplistic war between races of people; the Lakota realized this by recognizing the economic propensities, not the race or culture, of those they called Wasi'chu.

— B. Johansen and R. Maestas,
Wasi'chu: The Continuing Indian Wars.

Introduction

Since the New Year, a number of events have taken place in Québec with regards to Hydro-Québec and the Québec government's efforts to maintain their hold on the "terms of reference" which guide the debate on energy policies in this country. What follows is a brief look at some of these events and their recent history. While overtly repressive in their intent, some of these events have fuelled a growing solidarity between Native and non-Native people, a solidarity which needs to develop while deepening its roots in common understanding and experience.

Resistance to the continued destruction of the Land is bringing people together while questioning the illegitimate right of a small elite in Québec to impose with impunity its policies of environmental destruction and social impoverishment. Behind these individuals lie the courts, the police forces, the public image makers, and an army of consenting technocrats whose actions and policies only serve to rationalize and pursue five centuries of arrogant conquest and blatant contempt for First Nations, their history, and their aspirations for the future.

The Coalition for Nitassinan and the Law

The Coalition for Nitassinan was founded in January 1992 by members of the Innu Nation who live in *Mani-Utenam*, one of twelve Innu settlements located in what we refer to today as Québec and Labrador (Newfoundland), in north eastern North America. The Coalition is a grassroots, community-based organization and is continuing the Innu Nation's struggle for sovereignty and the recognition of its historical rights as a First Nation which has never, in the colonial history of this country, ceded its land or the resources it contains.

On February 2nd, in Sept-Iles, located on the North shore of the St-Lawrence river, Québec superior court judge Ross Goodwin sentenced four members of the Coalition for Nitassinan to jail and fines. The "guilty" had defied a Band Council[1] injunction launched against members of the Coalition, outlawing any forms of public protest. They peacefully erected a road block near their settlement on December 12th, 1992, in protest of a 3 billion dollar hydro-electric project slated for the Saint Marguerite river which runs on Innu land.

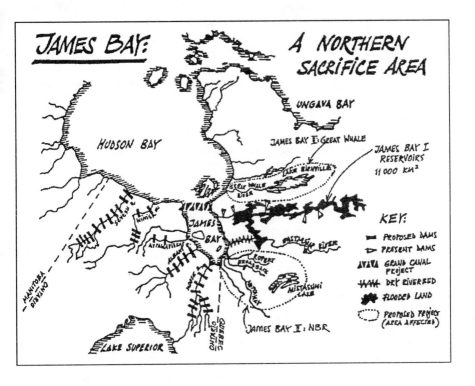

The Band Council came out in favour of the project, known as SM-3, despite public hearings and polls organized in *Mani-Utenam* which indicate that 80% of the local population reject the project. SM-3 is Hydro-Québec's fourteenth project on land that the Innu Nation has occupied for over 9000 years. The Band Council injunction was used in order to lay some 70 criminal charges against men and women who wish to organize, walk, sing, demonstrate, and ask too many questions...

The Superior Court judge decided to sentence the four members of the Coalition on the opening day of government sponsored environmental hearings looking into the SM-3 project. For the duration of the hearings in Sept-Iles, from February 2nd to the 12th, Gilbert Pilot, one of the project's most vocal opponents from *Mani-Utenam* sat in a Baie Comeau jail, fasting in protest.

For forty years, the Innu Nation has watched corporate and government interests sink mines, dam rivers, and turn their hunting grounds into bombing ranges. Today, the British, Dutch, and German Air Forces practice low-level flying with their 30-ton war planes, 100 feet above the ground at speeds of 600km an hour. Canada has reaped billions in revenues from Innu land and multinationals have grown fat from the "earth's bounty," while the Innu way of life has been criminalized. Courts and wildlife authorities incessantly harass the Innu who hunt and fish on their land to feed their families, and who cut wood to heat their homes without the proper State "permits" and licenses.

While the Canadian, Newfoundland, and Québec governments continue their illegal occupation of Nitassinan, pillaging and "developing" all the way to the bank, the media in February briefly cast its attention on the Innu community of *Utshimasit*, located on the coast of Labrador, where at least six children had collectively attempted to commit suicide by inhaling gasoline in an abandoned shack and then freezing to death in their unconscious state. The media conveniently overlooked the link between the destruction of the Land and the resulting annihilation of a Nation and its social fabric. As Utshimasit was portrayed as an isolated incident, this continent's history of genocide slowly crept along its way...

Hydro-Québec and the Law

In December 1992, Hydro-Québec created its own police force called Sureté d'Hydro-Québec, to be administered by a retired Sureté du Québec (SQ)[2] bureaucrat. This new security force can count on 200 trained officers and an initial budget of 26 million dollars (CND), as well as the legal right to arrest, raid, and investigate whom it chooses while being able to call upon the "expertise" of other police forces and intelligence agencies located elsewhere in North America.

According to one of the first news reports on this new repressive entity, aired by CBC-TV on February 7th, the Sureté d'Hydro-Québec will be focusing its attention on Native "radicals" and environmental "extremists" in Québec and abroad. Of course, the main threat posed by these Native and non-Native groups and individuals is not "terrorism" but their unequivocal No! to hydroelectric mega-development—a response which goes well beyond the acceptable bounds which govern the debate on energy policies in Québec.

Hydro-Québec and Ecologists Inc.

From the stick-to-more-acceptable methods to be directed toward average energy consumers, who have had to face hydro bill increases totalling 24.84% in twelve months from 1990 to 1991, and a further possible increase of 2.3% asked for by Hydro-Québec for 1993, an environmental think-tank in Québec known as GRAME (Groupe de recherche applique en macroecologie) offers a report published in February, entitled "Rehabilitating hydro-electric power and denouncing lies."

GRAME was founded in 1989 by Luc Gagnon who has been working for the last year for Hydro-Québec's environmental services. GRAME has also managed to squeeze 20,000 dollars from Hydro-Québec in order to "improve its analytic and comparative models which make hydro-electric power the champion among methods of sustainable development" (*Le Devoir*, 15 March 1993).

GRAME presented its 67-page report to a parliamentary commission on energy on March 16th in Québec City. It served as an introduction to the "new Union for Sustainable Development" composed of "sincere, experienced and informed" environmentalists including Francis Cabot, an American business-man. Cabot spoke before the commission of the "environmental fascism" of opponents to the infamous Great Whale hydro-electric complex, borrowing from the libelous if not insane remarks of Richard Le Hir, vice-president and director general of the Québec Association of Manufacturers and principal instigator of a pro-Great-Whale coalition, who labelled, in 1992, all opposition to mega-progress as "eco-fascism".

Following their presentation to the commission on March 16th, the mem-bers of this Union for Sustainable Development asked the Québec government to dig further into the public purse in order to finance their "scientific" and "ratio-nal" work. Against the onslaught of lies and demagoguery emanating, according to them, from English Canada and the United States and directed toward hydro-electric power and Hydro-Québec, these well paid "experts" wish to put the debate rising around mega-development back on the right track.

GRAME's report states: "we cannot let organizations which use lies in lieu of arguments to establish the terms of reference for such important matters." Gen-erous subsidies from the government—in these times of drastic cuts in social spending—would allow these experts to "defend our interests" anywhere abroad where Hydro-Québec and its projects are being criticized. In its campaign against lies and demagoguery, however, GRAME seems to have overlooked an embar-rassing news item published on February 15th by *Le Devoir*, a Montréal news-paper. It appears that a Hydro-Québec engineering subcontractor, SNC-Shawinigan, falsified a study a year ago and inflated by 40% the production costs of a wind-generated electrical project on the Lower North shore of the St. Lawrence river. Because of the study, Hydro-Québec abandoned the project and opted for yet another hydro dam on Innu land...

Public Relations and Crisis Control

On the international level, Hydro-Québec is also trying to remake its public image, tarnished by more than twenty years of major flooding, an astronomical debt burden of 33 billion dollars (which is expected to reach 38 billion dollars by 1995), miscalculations such as methyl-mercury and cadmium poisoning, and methane and carbon monoxide leaks into the atmosphere from flooded marshes and woodlands[4]. According to the Montréal chapter of Greenpeace, Hydro-Québec is working with the American public relations firm, Burson-Marsteller, the largest in the world, whose clients have included Nicolae Ceausescu's regime, the 1976 military junta in Argentina, the owners of the Exxon Valdez, and Union Carbide following that company's criminal negligence in Bhopal, India.

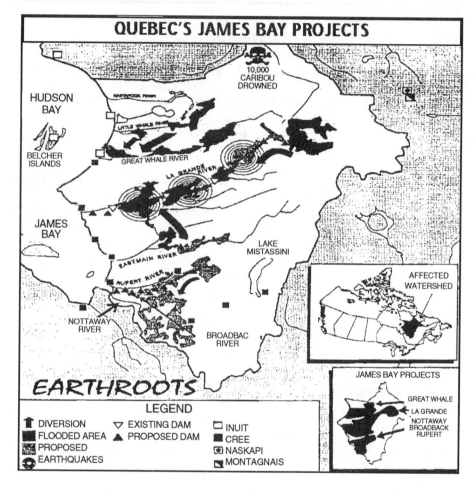

Also working for "our" State-owned monopoly are US advisors brought together by Québec premier Robert Bourassa. Each member of this select committee is paid 2,500 dollars annually and 1,500 dollars for each day they work on Hydro-Québec's behalf. The utility won't provide a full list of the committee's members, but has confirmed that members include James Schlesinger, CIA director under Richard Nixon, Defence Secretary under Gerald Ford, and Energy Secretary under Jimmy Carter. He is also a senior economic advisor to the Wall Street brokerage firm Lehman Brothers, which underwrites Hydro-Québec's foreign debt. He was appointed by Bourassa in 1986, and is now chairman of the advisory committee (Montréal *Mirror*; March 25 - April 1, 1993).

Also on the committee: John Dyson, former chair of the New York Power Authority, forced to resign because of conflict of interest charges; Guy Nichols, former chair of the New England Electric System; Edmund Muskie, former Maine Senator; and William Simon, the former US Treasury Secretary and consultant to Bechtel. He sat on the committee until 1988.

In the late 1960s, the San Francisco-based engineering conglomerate Bechtel built the Churchill Falls hydro complex, then the largest in the world. The project flooded 6,700 km² of Innu Land in Labrador including ancestral burial grounds. Through a secret deal with Hydro-Québec made public in November 1972, Bechtel was awarded the management contract for the La Grande complex and James Bay I. Bechtel is expected to bid for further Hydro-Québec contracts in the future.

Hydro-Québec and Secret Contracts

During the darkest years of Maurice Duplessis's rule in Québec, iron-ore was sold to American multinationals at 1 cent a ton. Today Hydro-Québec sells some of its electricity at 1.2 to 1.5 cents per kilowatt-hour (kwh), well below the cost of production estimated at least 3 cents per kwh. Over the years, the Bourassa government in Québec and Hydro-Québec have signed 13 secret contracts known as shared-risk agreements. In the Spring of 1991, the contract signed with the Norwegian transnational Norsk-Hydro revealed that from 1988 to 1990 the magnesium plant was buying electricity at 30% the going rate paid by average energy consumers in Québec.[5]

While Norsk-Hydro benefits from preferential rates which also fluctuate according to the price of magnesium on the world market, average consumers must deal with continually increasing rates, now priced at 4.8 cents per kwh. Over the last ten years, as corporations were getting their electrical power for next to nothing, the rest of us watched rates increase faster than the rate of inflation (*Le Devoir*; 19 March 1993).

According to its contract with Hydro-Québec, by 1993 Norsk-Hydro was to pay 75% of the going industrial rate. At the end of March this year, however, a report from Hydro-Québec was made public, revealing that its series of secret contracts would cost 2.9 billion dollars in lost hydro revenues between now and the year 2010 (*La Presse*; 31 March 1993). Such a loss for the State-owned utility means more financial costs for Québeckers.

Hydro-Québec and Big Business

Hydro-Québec sells electricity to some 13,000 companies; of these, 175 of the largest corporations consume 85% of the electricity allotted to industry in Québec. As their consumption increases, the price they pay for electricity decreases. In 1990, one quarter of all of the electricity produced by Hydro-

Québec was exported or used in the production of aluminum. If James Bay II is ever built, 60% of the power will go to aluminum smelters, 20% to exports and only 5% to 10% to Québecker's needs—if demand even increases that much in real terms.

Energy consumption in Québec is at the same level it was in 1973, having decreased by 1.7% from 1989 to 1990. There are 485 hydro dams in Québec and with a third the population of New York State Québec is one of the leading per capita consumers of electricity in the world. But who is consuming this energy? Who is paying for it? And who is making profits while demanding more and more dams? These are important questions and they need to be answered.

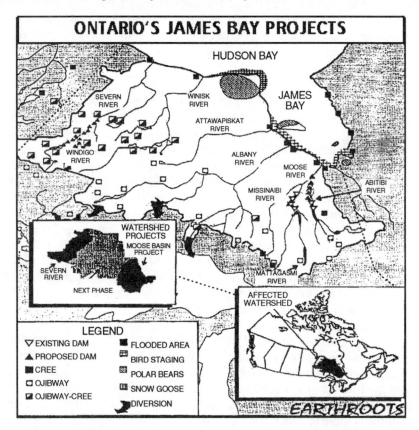

The 13.1 billion dollar Great Whale mega-project announced by premier Bourassa in 1988, and expected to produce 3,168 megawatts of power, was conceived in order to meet the needs of four aluminum smelters—two American, one French, and one German. There are ten aluminum smelters in Québec, each annually consuming as much power as an average-size city during the same time period. While recycling allows for the production of goods using far less energy,

aluminum can be recycled using 90% less energy than required to produce it from scratch. So why do we need more smelters?

On the supply side of the Hydro-industrial complex in Québec are construction and engineering firms, like the SNC group whose president and CEO, Guy St. Pierre, is a good friend of Robert Bourassa and an ex-Liberal Party minister. Undergoing restructuring but still breathing and closely associated to SNC is Lavalin, an engineering firm which saw the light of day thanks to James Bay I, and which managed to survive thanks to environmental impact studies on Cree and Innu land paid for by Hydro-Québec, the federal Department of National Defence, etc. Also in the fray is the Simard-Beaudry company which also worked on James Bay I, building three dams, and which completed a contract at the La Grande 3 dam a few months ago. That company is partly owned by the family of Andre Simard, Robert Bourassa's wife. All of these companies and many more live or die according to Hydro-Québec or mega-development schemes.

The White-Male-Builder-Establishment

On the morning of November 23, 1991, the headline on one of Montréal's leading newspapers, *La Presse,* read: "Great-Whale: forge ahead despite the Indians. Québec decision makers massively support the hydro project." According to the article which followed, 205 individuals had been surveyed over a two week period and all were chosen because of the positions of command they hold within their respective spheres of business activities. Two-thirds of them wished to impose the Great Whale hydro complex on the Cree people of the Hudson's Bay region if the provincial government failed to reach an agreement with them.

According to the article, 93% of respondents to the survey were men, 78% were 43 years of age or older and 63% of them earned 100,000 dollars a year or more. No less than 84% of these decision makers were in favour of mega-development and the Great Whale project. Once again, predominantly white men who have managed to scale the upper echelons of Québec's corporate hierarchy are speaking in the name of six million people. What they say counts, and the majority of us have never been consulted on the matter of energy policies let alone seen their long term plans. These men are paid phenomenal salaries to conceive, develop, and promote projects which in their costs and magnitude have entirely eclipsed Québec's industrial and economic development, now and for the future. For this Hydro empire, an 11,000 dollar debt hangs over the head of each man, woman, child and elder in Québec.

Our participation in any kind of decision making process with regards to energy policies is irrelevant. They expect the population to stand around as what is left of our social infrastructures disintegrate, and to nod approvingly as they demand we tighten our belts and pay higher bills. In real terms, this generation will be asked to bear the economic costs, but the next will also have to deal with the environmental destruction and its consequences. For all we know, these decision makers have mortgaged our future well into the next century.

Conclusion

The Great Whale project is only one in a series of dams and projects that make up Hydro-Québec's development plan known as James Bay II, a 62 (plus) billion dollar extravaganza to be built over the next ten years—if demand for electricity can be inflated, and if the proper financing can be arranged in these

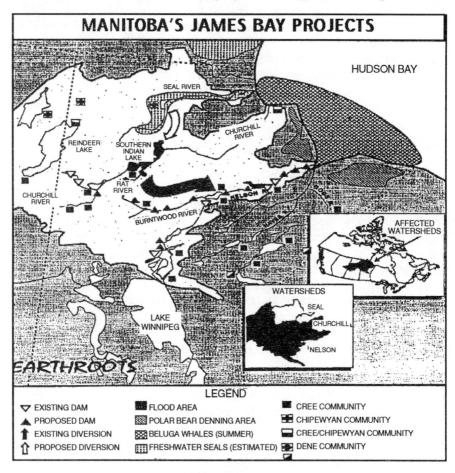

MANITOBA'S JAMES BAY PROJECTS

HUDSON BAY

SEAL RIVER

CHURCHILL RIVER

REINDEER LAKE

SOUTHERN INDIAN LAKE

RAT RIVER

CHURCHILL RIVER

BURNTWOOD RIVER

NELSON RIVER

AFFECTED WATERSHEDS

WATERSHEDS

LAKE WINNIPEG

SEAL

CHURCHILL

NELSON

EARTHROOTS

LEGEND

▽ EXISTING DAM	▨ FLOOD AREA	◼ CREE COMMUNITY
▲ PROPOSED DAM	▧ POLAR BEAR DENNING AREA	▦ CHIPEWYAN COMMUNITY
⬆ EXISTING DIVERSION	▩ BELUGA WHALES (SUMMER)	◻ CREE/CHIPEWYAN COMMUNITY
⇧ PROPOSED DIVERSION	▦ FRESHWATER SEALS (ESTIMATED)	▨ DENE COMMUNITY

hard economic times. And if Hydro-Québec and the decision makers don't get all the money they need to build a few big dams in Cree territory near James Bay, then they'll build a series of "smaller" dams like SM-3, Lac Robertson, *Ashuapmushuan* in Nitassinan. The important thing is to keep the economic machine chugging along in Québec and the inlaws happy, including Uncle Sam. Meanwhile, helping fuel the economic machine are recent government cuts in unemployment insurance, welfare, health care, education, social housing, and day-care. And the list goes on.

Short term profits are what the decision makers are after, and in Québec the best way to get them is by turning the earth into a commodity and that commodity into capital. The environmental or human side-effects of such a process are secondary, if considered at all, because the system we live in is economic, not social.

So raging Northern rivers are dried up or turned into toxic reservoirs, Cree elders and children can't eat the fish, and the Innu are being jailed for trying to defend what's left of their homeland. Down south, in urban civilization, the shores of the St. Lawrence river are littered with 70 major industrial plants which discharge toxic effluents at a daily rate that defies the human imagination.

Profit is the bottom line and the idea behind the *Wasi'chu* principle is to take more than you put in. What was called "conquest" five centuries ago is what, to some extent, we now call a "wise economic investment" or "economic growth." The decision makers then were just as blind and criminally negligent as those we have today. The consequences of their actions must either bring us together to live and organize differently, or we'll die off like rats in our own waste before the end of the next century. Progress must be redefined and many of us refuse to just wait things out and see what will happen. The time to act is now, to build links of solidarity and put an end to this five century old war that the *Wasi'chu* today continue to wage against the Earth and the First Nations of this continent.

---

1. The Band Council is the Indian Act form of government imposed on Native Nations in Canada. In the years following World War II the Indian Act, still in effect today, influenced the creation of the racist Bantustan reserve system in South Africa. The Band Council is still the only form of political organization for Native "communities" deemed "legitimate" by the federal government.
2. The SQ was responsible for the July 11th, 1990, armed assault against the *Kanienkaha:ka* (Mohawk) community of *Kanehsatake* and to this day continues its harassment of that Nation.
3. Peru's "global" debt burden in 1993 is 22 billion dollars; *Le Monde* Diplomatique; April 1993.
4. An estimated 184 million tons of "green house gases" have leaked into the atmosphere following the flooding of Northern lands and the decomposition of organic matter. *The Amicus Journal*;"James Bay II"; Andre Picard; Fall 1990; pp. 10-16.
5. Option Paix; vol. 9, no. 2; Summer 1991.

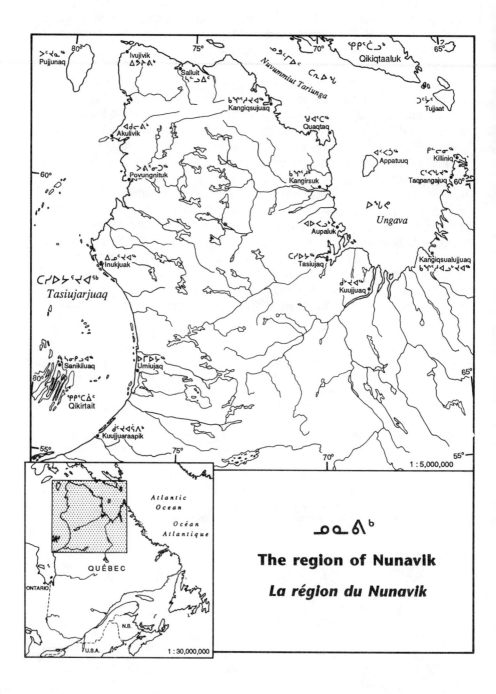

The region of Nunavik

La région du Nunavik

146

ᓄᓇ ᐃᓪᓗ ᐊᑎᖁᑎᓪᓗ
ᓄᓇ ᐊᖕᒥ
PLACES AND NAMES IN NUNAVIK
LIEUX ET NOMS AU NUNAVIK

ᐊᓪᓚᑎᒐ ᑲᑎᒪᔪᓕᕆᓂᐅᔪᒃ ᔪᓕᐅᑕᒃ
Editor/*Éditeur* : Ludger Müller-Wille
ᓄᓇ ᐃᔾᑦᑕᕐᓂᐅᔾᑯᑦ: ᓂᒃᒃ ᓴᔪ
Cartography/*Cartographie*: Richard Bachand

ᓄᓇ ᐃᓪ ᐊᑎᖁᑎᒃ ᖃᕐᒋᐹᕋᕐᓗ ᑲᖓᕐᓱᔪᐊᕐᓗ	Place Names in the Environs of Kangirsujuaq	Noms de lieux dans les environs de Kangirsujuaq

ᓄᐃᑕᒃᑕ 25, 1980-ᐅᓐᓗ ᑲᖓᕐᔪᕐᑕᒃ ᓄᓇᓕᒃ ᑲᑎᒪᔨᖏᓐᓄᑦ, ᓄᓇᓕᒃ ᖃᐃᒃ ᕚᒃᑕᒻ ᐊᒃᑲᓐᓕᐳᓐᒥ ᑦᐹᑕᓐᖑᔪᑦ, ᔪᐳᑦᐱᓐᒥ ᐊᓪᓚᑕᖓᕐᑦ "ᓇᓕᐹᑦᑎᐳᓂᕐᓂᒃ ᓄᓇ ᐃᔾᑦᓗᒃ ᐊᖕᑦ ᑲᐳᓐ ᑦ ᑕᐳᓐᓂᒃ ᑕᓚᒃ ᑲᖓᕐᔪᕐᑕᒃ ᐊᑦᐹᓴᒃᑐᒃ ᐊᓪᓚᓗᒋ ᐊᖃᑦᒋ ᑕᐹᓚᓐᓴᐳᒃᑕᓐᒃ." ᑦᐳᕐ ᖁᐹᕐᐱᕐ.

On November 25, 1980 the Inuit Community Council of Wakeham Bay, as Kangirsujuaq was then still named officially, wrote in a resolution, "The project of the maps being named here in Kangirsujuaq is approved and to be put into effect by Avataq." This sentence endorsed the work Zebedee

Le 25 novembre 1980, le Conseil municipal inuit de Wakeham Bay, ainsi que s'appelait encore officiellement Kangirsujuaq, rédigea une résolution : «Le projet de cartes géographiques portant des noms d'ici, à Kangirsujuaq, est approuvé et sera mis en oeuvre par Avataq.» Cette phrase sanctionnait le

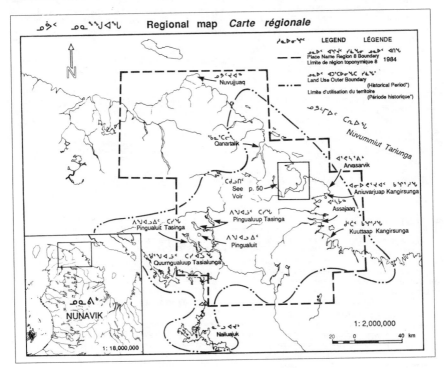

ᓄᕐ ᓄᓇᕐᔪᐊᑦ Regional map *Carte régionale*

LEGEND   LÉGENDE
ᓄᓇᑦ ᐊᑎᖁᑦ ᕐᐃᖕᓗ ᓄᐹᑦ ᐊᑎᖕᓗ
Place Name Region 8 Boundary   1984
Limite de région toponymique 8

ᓄᓇᑦ ᐊᑦᑦᑕᕐᓂᖕᑦ ᕐᐃᖕᓗ
Land Use Outer Boundary
(Historical Period")
Limite d'utilisation du territoire
(Période historique")

ᓄᕕᔾᔪᐊᖅ
Nuvujjuaq

Nuvummiut Tariunga

ᕐᐹᑦᑕᖕ
Qanartalik

ᐊᕐᕙᓴᕐᕕᒃ
Arvasarvik

ᑕᐳᓐᒃ
See p. 50
Voir

ᐊᓗᐳ ᐁᕐᕿᔾᕐ ᐸᔪ ᕐᐃᖕᑦ
Aniuvarjuap Kangirsunga

Assajaaq

ᐊᔾᕐᐳᔾᕐ ᓯᕐᕿ
Pingualuup Tasinga

ᒃᑯᑦᑕᐳ ᐸᔪᕐᕕᖕ
Kuuttaap Kangirsunga

ᐱᖕᐳᓗᐃᑦ ᑕᓯᖓ
Pingualuit Tasinga

ᐊᔾᕐᐳ ᐁᕐᕿ
Pingualuit

ᖂᕐᖕᐳᐊᓗᐳ ᑕᓯᐊᓗᖓ
Quurngualuup Tasialunga

ᓄᓇᕕᒃ
NUNAVIK

1 : 18,000,000

ᓇᓕᐳᐊᔪᒃ
Naliuajuk

1 : 2,000,000

20   0   40 km

ᓇᓄᓇᐃᕐᓯᓯᒪᔪᖅ ᐱᓇᓱᑦᑕᕕᓂᖏᓐᓂᒃ ᔭᐃᐱᑎ ᓄᖕᖓᐅᑉ ᐱᓇᓱᖃᑎᖃᕐᓱᓂ ᒫᑎᐅᓯ ᓂᖏᐅᕈᕕᒻᒥᒃ, ᓈᓚ ᓇᑉᐹᓗᒃ ᐊᒻᒪᓗ ᒫᑎᐅᓯ ᓴᑭᐊᒑᕐᒥᒃ, ᑲᑎᑎᕆᑦᓱᑎᒃ ᐃᓄᐃᑦ ᓄᓇᖓᑕ ᐊᑎᖏᓐᓂᒃ ᑲᖏᕐᓱᔪᐊᒥ ᓴᓂᐊᓂᓗ. ᑕᐃᒪᐃᑦᑐᓴᐃᓐᓇᑲᓵᖅ ᓄᓇᓂ ᐊᑎᖏᓐᓂᒃ ᐱᓇᓱᓐᓂᖅ ᐱᓇᓱᑦᑕᕕᓂᐅᒻᒥᔪᖅ ᑲᒪᒋᔭᐅᑦᓱᓂ Bernard Saladin d'Anglure-ᒧᑦᓗ Louis-Jacques Dorais-ᒧᑦᓗ ᓴᓂᐊᓂᑦᓴᐃᓇᖅ ᔫᓚᐃ 1968-ᒍᑎᓪᓗᒍ. ᐃᓄᓐᓂᒃ ᐱᓇᓱᖃᑎᓕᕕᓃᒃ ᐊᓪᓚᓯᒪᔪᕐᓂ ᐊᑎᖃᕐᑎᑕᐅᔪᓂᒃ ᒪᓯᐅ, ᒫᑯᓯ, ᒫᑎᐅᓯ ᐊᒻᒪᓗ ᐱᑕ. ᕖᕗᐊᕆ 1984-ᒥ, ᑲᒪᔨᐅᑎᓗᖓ, ᔮᓂ ᐹᓚᓴᓗ ᕿᐊᓚᓐ ᐅᐃᑖᓗᑦᑐᓗ ᐊᐱᕐ-ᓱᑐᕕᓃᒃ ᓈᓚ ᓇᑉᐹᓗᒻᒥᒃ ᔫᒋᓂ ᐃᕐᓂᒥᓪᓗ. ᖃᐅᔨᒪᒐᑦᓴᓕᒫᑦ ᐃᓚᓯᒪᑦᓱᑎᒃ ᐊᑎᕐᓂᒃ ᐱᔭᐅᔪᕕᓃᑦ ᒪᑭᕖᒃᑯᑦ "ᐃᓄᐃᑦ ᐆᒪᔪᓂᓗ ᐱᕈᕐᑐᓂᓗ ᖃᐅᔨᒪᓂᖓ ᓄᓇᐅᑉ ᐊᑐᕐᑕᐅᓂᖓ ᓄᓇᙳᐊᓕᐅᕐᓂᖅ" (1983) ᑲᑎᕐᓱᑕᕕᓃᑦ ᐊᒻᒪᓗ ᐊᑕᐅᓯᙳᑎᑕᐅᑦᓱᑎᒃ ᐊᑐᐊᒐᕐᒧᑦ <u>ᐃᓄᑦᑎᑐᑦ ᓄᓇᐃᑦ ᐊᑎᖏᑦᑕ ᑲᑎᕐᓱᑕᐅᓂᖏᑦ ᓄᓇᕕᒻᒥ</u> (1987). ᑖᓐᓇ ᓄᓇᙳᐊᖅ ᓯᑕᒪᓃᑦᑐᖅ ᐃᓗᓐᓇᖏᓐᓃᔭᒐᓂ ᓄᓇᙳᐊᓕᕆᔪᓯᒥᒃ ᓄᓇᙳᐊᓂ ᓯᑯᑦᓴᔭᓂ ᐅᑯᓂᖓ (25E-12 & -13; 35 H-9 & -16); ᑭᑎᑦᔪᑎᓕᐅᕐᑕᐅᓂᖏᑦ ᐱᔭᐅᓯᒪᔪᐃᑦ ᐃᓕᒃᑯᑦ ᓄᓇᙳᐊᓂᑦ ᓯᑯᑦᓴᔭᓂᑦ ᐊᑎᖏᑦᑕ ᑲᑎᕐᓱᑕᐅᓂᖏᓐᓃᑐᓂᑦ.

ᐊᑏᑦ ᐊᑐᐊᕐᑕᐅᕆᐊᓪᓚᕋᑦᑕᓯᒪᔪᐃᑦ ᐃᑉᐱᕆᔭᐅᑦᓯᐊᕿᓱ-ᐊᒻᒪᓇᑦᓱᑎᒃ, ᑭᓯᐊᓂ ᑖᑦᑯᐊ ᐊᑏᑦ ᓄᐊᑕᐅᓯᒪᒪᑕ ᐊᒥᓱᓂᒃ ᐊᐱᕐᓱᓯᒪᒪᑕ ᐊᑦᔨᒌᑦᔭᖏᑦᑐᓂᒃ ᐊᐱᕐᓱᑎᖃᕐᓱᑎᒃ 20 ᐊᕐᕿᒍᐃᑦ ᐅᖓᑖᓄᑦ ᓈᓯᒪᓕᕐᑎᓗᒋᑦ, ᐃᓚᖏᑦ ᐊᑦᔨᒌᓗᑐᙱᑐᐃᓐᓇᓇᐊᓖᑦ, ᓄᐃᑕᖕᖏᑐᓂᓗ ᐊᓪᓚᓗ ᐊᑦᔨᒌᙱᑐᑦᑕᖃᑐᐃᓐᓇᓇᐊᓕᒃ ᑕᕐᑕᕐ ᐊᑐᕐᑕᐅᔪᓂᒃ ᓄᓇᐃᑦ ᐊᑎᖏᓐᓂᒃ ᑲᖏᕐᓱᔪᐊᒥ. ᓄᓇᐃᑦ ᐊᑎᖏᑦ ᐱᓪᓚᓐᑦ ᐊᓪᓚᓗ ᓱᖏᐅᑎᔭᐅᔫᑦᓱᑎᒃ ᐅᓪᓗᑕᒫᕐᓯᐅᑎᓂ ᐊᑐᕐᑕᐅᓱᑎᒃ ᓄᓇᓕᓐᓂᒥᐅᓄᑦ. ᖃᖓᒍᓗᑐᐃᓐᓇᖅ ᑕᒪᓯ-ᒪᔭᐃᓪᓘᓃᑦ ᐃᓚᔭᐅᕆᐊᓖᓪᓘᓃᑦ ᐋᕿᑕᐅᑐᐃᓐᓇᓇᐊᓖᑦ. ᐃᓘᓐᓇᑲᓵᖏᑦ ᐊᑏᑦ ᓄᐊᑕᕕᓃᑦ ᖃᒻᒥᖅ ᖃᐅᔨᓯᐊᕐ-ᑕᐅᒪᑦ,ᑕᐃᒪᐃᓐᓂᖃᕐᑎᓗᒋᑦ ᐊᖏᓪᓚᓇᑦᑕᐅᓯᒪᔪᐃᑦ ᑯᐯᒃᑯᑦ ᑲᕙᒪᒃᑯᖏᓐᓄᑦ ᐅᑯᐊ ᐅᑦᑑᑎᕆᓗᒋᑦ ᑲᖏᕐᓱᔪᐊᖅ (1980) ᐊᒻᒪᓗ ᖄᕐᓂᐊᖅ, ᓴᕐᕙᓕᐊᖅ, ᐊᕕᒍᑎ (1990) ᐊᓯᖏᑦ ᓄᐃᑖᓕᕐᑐᐃᑦ ᓄᑖᓂ ᓄᓇᙳᐊᓂ. ᑕᐃᒪᐃᒐᓗᐊᕐᑎᓗᒍ ᑕᒪᓐᓇ ᐱᓇᓱᐊᕐᑕᐅᓂᖓ ᓱᒃᑲᐃᙲᖏᓐᓈᑐᖅ. ᐃᓄᑦᑎᑐᑦ ᓄᓇᐃᑦ ᐊᑎᖏᑦᑕ ᑲᑎᕐᓱᑕᐅᓂᖏᓐᓂ ᓄᓇᕕᒻᒥ, ᐱᑕᖃᓕᕐᒥᔪᖅ ᓄᓇᙳᐊᓂᒃ ᐃᓄᑦᔪᐊᑉ ᓴᓂᐊᓂ ᐃᓄᑦᑎᑑᑐᐃᓐᓇᑐᓂᒃ, ᑕᒪᓐᓇ ᐱᑕᖃᕐᑎᓯᒐᓱᐊᕐᑐᖅ ᐃᓄᓐᓂᒃ ᐊᓯᖏᓐᓂ ᓄᓇᓕᓐᓂᒃ ᓄᓇᕕᒻᒥ ᖃᐅᔨᒪᔭᐅᕆᐊᓕᓐᓂᒃ ᖃᐅᔨᒪᑎᓯᓗᒋᑦ ᓯᓚᕿᒐᓱᐊᕐᓱᓂ ᐃᓄᐃᑦ ᓄᓇᒥᓂᒃ ᖃᐅᔨᒪᓂᖏᓐᓂᒃ.

Nungak had carried out with Mathew Ningiuruvik, Naala Nappaluk and Matiusie Sakiagiak on recording the Inuit place names in the environs of Kangirsujuaq. Similar place name work had been done in the area under the direction of Bernard Saladin d'Anglure and Louis-Jacques Dorais in July 1968. They worked with Inuit whose names were given in the report as Masiu, Markusi, Matiusi and Pita. In February 1984, under my direction, Johnny Palliser and Helen Oweetaluktuk interviewed Naala Nappaluk and Jugini Irniq. All this information, with additional names obtained from Makivik's "Land Use and Ecology Cartography Project" (1983) was compiled and integrated into the <u>Gazetteer of Inuit Place Names in Nunavik</u> (1987). The place names shown by numbers on the regional map and included in the list are taken from the Gazetteer. This map straddles the area of four adjacent topographical sheets (25E-12 & -13; 35 H-9 & -16); the numbering is thus maintained per map sheet as in the Gazetteer.

The list of names has been checked with particular care, but since these names have been collected from many individuals by different people over almost 20 years, some variations, gaps and differences might exist with the current usage of names in Kangirsujuaq. Place names are dynamic and are often adapted to the current needs of the local population. Corrections and additions can always be made. Most of the names collected in previous surveys have been officially accepted by the government of Québec; some examples are Kangirsujuaq (1980) and Qaarniaq, Sarvaliaq, Aviguti (1990) and others which will now appear on newly printed topographical maps. But it is a slow process. The Inuit Place Name Map Series of Nunavik, which now includes maps of the region around Inukjuak solely in Inuktitut, is a way of providing the Inuit of other regions in Nunavik with an essential resource to maintain their geographical knowledge.

Ref: ᐃᓄᑦᑎᑐᑦ ᓄᓇᐃᑦ ᐊᑎᖏᑦᑕ ᑲᑎᕐᓱᑕᐅᓂᖏᑦ ᓄᓇᕕᒻᒥ (ᑯᐯᒻᒥ ᑲᓇᑕᒥ) - Müller-Wille, Ludger. Gazetteer of Inuit PLace Names in Nunavik (Quebec, Canada). Répertoire toponymique inuit du Nunavik (Québec, Canada) Avataq Cultural Institute, 1987.

travail accompli Zebedee Nungak avec l'aide de Mathew Ningiuruvik, Nala Nappaluk et Matiusie Sakiagiak pour retrouver les noms de lieux inuit des environs de Kangirsujuaq. Une recherche semblable de toponymes avait été conduite dans la région en 1968 sous la direction de Bernard Saladin d'Anglure et de Louis-Jacques Dorais. Ces anthropologues avaient travaillé avec des Inuit dont les noms figurent dans leur rapport comme étant Masiu, Markusi, Matiusi et Pita. En février 1984, sous ma direction, Johnny Palliser et Helen Oweetaltuk ont interviewé Nala Nappaluk et Jugini Imiq. Toute cette information, ainsi que d'autres noms tirés du Projet de cartographie de l'utilisation du territoire et des connaissances écologiques (1983), de la Société Makivik, a été compilée et intégrée au Répertoire toponymique inuit du Nunavik, paru en 1987. Les noms de lieux présentés par numéros sur la carte régionale et dressés en une liste sont tirés du répertoire. Cette carte régionale recouvre quatre secteurs adjacents (cartes topographiques 25E-12 et 13; 35H-9 et 16); les numéros apparaissant sur les cartes topographiques sont donc les mêmes que dans le répertoire.

La liste des noms de lieux a été vérifiée très soigneusement, mais comme ces noms ont été recueillis chez un grand nombre d'individus, par différentes personnes, au cours d'une période de presque vingt ans, il est possible qu'il existe quelques variantes, des vides et certaines différences dans l'usage courant des noms de la région de Kangirsujuaq. Les noms de lieux possèdent leur dynamique propre et résultent souvent d'une adaptation aux besoins d'une population à une époque donnée. Des corrections et des additions peuvent toujours être faites. La plupart des noms recueillis lors des relevés précédents ont reçu l'approbation officielle du gouvernement du Québec, tels que Kangirsujuaq, en 1980, et Qaarniaq, Sarvaliaq et Aviguti, en 1990, ainsi que d'autres qui apparaîtront désormais sur les nouvelles cartes topographiques qui seront imprimées. Toutefois, le processus est lent. La Série de cartes toponymiques du Nunavik, qui comprend maintenant des cartes de la région des environs d'Inukjuak avec des noms en inuktitut seulement, offre aux Inuit des autres régions du Nunavik un outil essentiel pour les aider à préserver leurs connaissances géographiques.

ᑲᖕᐯᔾᒃᒃ ᓴᓂ ᐋᓯᓂ ᓄᐄ ᐄᑦ ᐊᑎ ᖕᑦ
Place names in the environs of Kangirsujuaq
Les noms de lieux aux abords de Kangirsujuaq

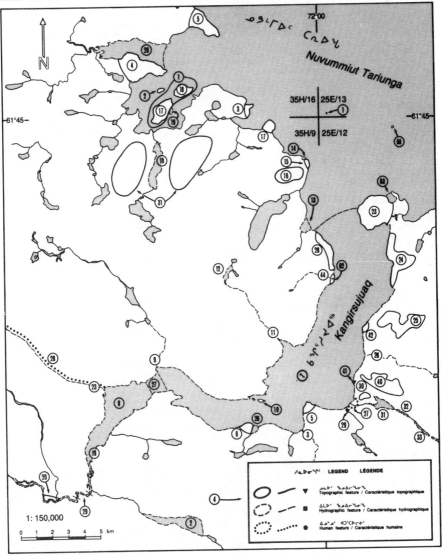

ᓄᓇ ᐃᑦ   ᐊᑎᖕᒋᑦ   ᑲᖏᕐᓱᔪᐊᖅ   ᓴᓄᐊᓂ   ᓄᓇᖕᖑᐊᑦ   ᑭᑎᕐᑎᖕᑎᒍᔾᑐᑦ

List of Place Names Around Kangirsujuaq by Map number

Liste des toponymes des environs de Kangirsujuaq par numéro de carte

Topographical Map 25E-12

23	ᓂ ᐊᖁᖕᖑ ᑦ	Niaqunnguut	cape/*cap*	it looks like heads/*ressemble à des têtes*
24	ᐃᑦᑐᐃᑦ	Ittuit	cliff/*falaise*	old men/*vieillards*
25	ᖃᕐᓂ ᐊᖅ	Qaarniaq	mountain/*mont*	white surf/*vagues écumantes*
26	ᐊᕕᒍᑎ	Aviguti	creek/*ruisseau*	place to separate/*lieu de séparation*
27	ᑲᖏᕐᓱᔪᐊᖅ	Kangirsujuaq	settlement/*village*	huge bay/*baie immense*
28	ᓯᑐᓂᖅ	Situniq	cliff/*falaise*	slide/*glissement de terrain*
29	ᖁᑎᐊᓗᒃ	Qutialuk	site/*site*	big foothill/*grand contrefort*
30	ᐅᒥᐊᖕᖑᐊᖅ	Umiannguaq	hill/*colline*	it looks like a boat/*ressemble à un bateau*
31	ᑕᓯᐊᓗᒃ	Tasialuk	lake/*lac*	big lake/*grand lac*
32	ᑕᓯᑯᑕᐊᒍᓗᒃ	Tasikutaaguluk	lake/*lac*	small, long lake/*petit lac long*
33	ᑕᓯᑯᑕᐊᖅ	Tasikutaaq	lake /*lac*	long lake/*lac long*
34	ᑭᕕᓂᓕᒃ	Kivinilik	lake /*lac*	water on ice/*eau sur la glace*
40	ᖃᕐᖃᐊᓗᒃ	Qarqaaluk	mountain/*mont*	big mountain/*grosse montagne*
41	ᓄᕗᑲᓛᒃ	Nuvukallak	point/*pointe*	small point/*petite pointe*
42	ᖃᕐᓂ ᐊᖅ ᓄᕗᐊ	Qaarniaq Nuvua	point/*pointe*	Qaarniaq's point/*pointe de Qaarniaq*
44	ᓴᕐᕓᓕ ᐊᖅ	Sarvaliaq	river/*rivière*	leading to the rapids/*mène aux rapides*
62	ᓴᕐᕓᓕ ᐊᑉ ᓄᕗᐊ	Sarvaliap Nuvua	point/*pointe*	Sarvaliaq's point/ *pointe de Sarvaliaq*
63	ᓂ ᐊᖁᖕᖑᑦ ᑲᖏᕐᓱᖕᒐ	Niaqunnguut Kangirsunga	cove/*anse*	Niaqunnguut's bay/*baie de Niaqunnguut*
65	ᑲᐅᑦᑐᐊᐱᒃ	Kauttuapik	island/*île*	small place of hammering/*petit lieu de martelage*

Topograhical Map 25E-13

1	ᖃᐃᕐᑐᐃᓈᖅ	Qairtuinnaq	island/*île*	all but solid rock/*seulement du roc solide*

Topographical Map 35H-9

2	ᑕᓯᐊᓗᒃ	Tasialuk	lake /*lac*	big lake/*grand lac*
3	ᐊᓛᖅᐱᐊᑉ ᑰᖕᒐ	Allaaqiap Kuunga	river/*rivière*	Allaaqiaq's river/*rivière d'Allaaqiaq*
4	ᐊᓛᖅᐱᐊᖅ	Allaaqiaq	lake/*lac*	shining/*qui brille*
5	ᖃᕐᒪᐃᑦ	Qarmait	point/*pointe*	(old) sod houses/*(vieilles) maisons de tourbe*
6	ᐊᕐᐱᐊᕋᐃᑦ	Arpiarait	point/*pointe*	many small cloudberries*/*nombreuses petites mûres**
7	ᑲᖏᕐᓱᔪᐊᖅ	Kangirsujuaq	bay/*baie*	huge bay/*baie immense*
8	ᑕᓯᐅᔭᖅ	Tasiujaq	bay/*baie*	it looks like a lake/*ressemble à un lac*
9	ᐃᒥᕐᑕᕕᐊᓗᒃ	Imirtavialuk	creek/*ruisseau*	big water-fetching place/*lieu où on puise de l'eau*
10	ᖅᐱᕐᑖᔪᒃ	Qikirtaajuuk	islands/*îles* (2)	the two small islands/*deux petites îles*
11	ᐸᐅᓯᐊᖅ	Paussiaq	river/*rivière*	it looks like soot/*ressemble à de la suie*
12	ᐸᐅᓯᐊᑉ ᑕᓯᖕᒐ	Paussiap Tasinga	lake/*lac*	(person's name) lake/*lac à (nom de personne)*
13	ᖃᒡᒋᐊᓗᒃ	Qaggialuk	bay/*baie*	big gathering place (snowhouse)/*grand iglou de rassemblement*
14	ᐃᕿ(ᒃ)	Iqi(k)	cove/*anse*	corner of the mouth/*coin de la bouche*
15	ᐃᕿᐅᑉ ᓄᕗᐊ	Iqiup Nuvua	point/*pointe*	Iqi(k)'s point/*pointe d'Iqi(k)*
17	ᐅᖃᒻᒪᖅ	Uqammaq	cape/*cap*	it looks like a tongue/*ressemble à une langue*
18	ᑭᓱᐅᔭᖅ	Kissuujaq	lake/*lac*	stew pot/*pot-au-feu*
19	ᐃᖃᓪᓕᕕᐅᑉ ᑰᖕᒐ	Iqalliviup Kuunga	river/*rivière*	river of the fishing place/*rivière de l'endroit pour pêcher*
20	ᐃᓪᓗᐊᕐᔪᐃᑦ	Illuluarjuit	shore/*rivage*	poor houses/*maisons en mauvais état*
23	ᑰᒃ	Kuuk	river/*rivière*	the river/*la rivière*
26	ᐊᕐᐱᐊᕋᐃᑦ ᑲᖏᕐᓱᖕᒐ	Arpiarait Kangirsunga	cove/*anse*	Arpiarait's bay/*baie d'Arpiarait*
27	ᖁᐅᕐᖑᖅ	Quurnguq	narrow/*goulet*	the narrows/*le goulet*
28	ᐊᒡᒍᓕᐊᕆᐊᖅ	Agguliariaq	route/*route*	facing the wind/*vent devant*
29	ᕿᓚᓇᐅᑦ (ᕿᓚᓇᐃᑦ)	Qilanaut (Qilanait)	channel/*chenal*	the (water) rising/*la crue*
31	ᑭᓱᐅᔭᓘᒃ	Kissuujaaluuk	mountains/*monts* (2)	the two big stew pots/ *deux gros pot-au-feu*

Topographical Map 35H-16

1	ᕿᕐᑕᑲᓛᒃ	Qikirtakallaak	islands/*îles* (2)	the two small islands/*les deux petites îles*
2	ᐱᓯᐅᓛᕐᓯᑎᒃ	Pissiulaarsitik	island/*île*	Arctic tern** colony/*colonie de sternes arctiques**
3	ᐃᕿᒃ	Iqik	point/*pointe*	corner of the mouth/*coin de la bouche*
4	ᐊᑯᓕᕕᒃ	Akulivik	point/*pointe*	in between/*entre-deux*
5	ᐃᖕᒋᐅᓕᑦᑑᖅ	Ingiulittuuq	cape/*cap*	continuous big surf/*grosses vagues continuelles*
17	ᕿᕐᑖᓗᒃ	Qikirtaaluk	island/*île*	big island/*grande île*
18	ᕿᕐᑕᑲᓛᒃ	Qikirtakallak	island/*île*	small island/*petite île*
19	ᑭᓴᕐᕕᒃ	Kisarvik	anchorage/*mouil.*	place to anchor/*mouillage*
20	ᑕᓯᐅᔭᖅ	Tasiujaq	bay/*baie*	it looks like a lake/*qui ressemble à un lac*

* Arpik - Rubus chamaemorus
**Pissiulaaq - Sterna paradisaea

150

MILTON BORN WITH A TOOTH
MESSENGER OF THE RIVER

Milton Born With A Tooth laughs when asked if he's a militant. It's as if he's asking, "How can you be militant when you are doing what would be perfectly natural for you or your ancestors to do?" And so he laughs. In fact, he laughs often and easily, contradicting the image one gets from the media of the Leader of the Peigan Lonefighters' Society. The word that is used to describe Born With A Tooth most often in the press is "Militant". But to meet and talk with Milton Born With A Tooth is to understand that he is very much a man of peace. And a man at peace with himself and the decisions he has made.

I spoke to him at the home of an upper middle class family on the outskirts of London, Ontario. They were the epitome of the yuppie family as presented on the television program "Thirty-something," Canadians who had success within the mainstream structure, but are well aware that things are not quite what they seem, and not everyone is living the Canadian Dream. Born With A Tooth spoke that evening at a conference on Natives and the Justice System organized by the London Chapter of CASNP (Canadians in Association with Native People). The majority of the audience was non-Native, and many openly wept. Other people who have seen Born With A Tooth speak on a number of occasions say that it's a common response.

Milton Born With A Tooth speaks from the heart with the voice of the river.

Miles Morrisseau: Who are the Lonefighters and where did they come from?

Milton Born With A Tooth: It's always been there. In the early 1900s, when they outlawed religion and doing rituals and things like that, everything ceased. And after the 1940s, after what Hitler did to the Jews, the United Nations passed the Genocide Act. After that the Canadian government realized they had to change their policies. That's when they said, "You could do your rituals again." "But certain parts," they said, "you can not do." They called them too "Barbaric", such as the Sundance ceremonies. The (Lonefighter) Society itself is one that never bothered to come back into the open. In a way, my father was part of that. And where I come from, and the group of us that started it, we are direct descendents from those people who ceased to take part in the process.

In doing what we did on August 3 [1990] and before that, we more or less wanted to show that what we were doing was all connected to preserving our true identity. This (Lonefighters') Society is one that never went through that assimilation process and so it's not tainted by interference. Like some of the ceremonies today are interfered with, and some of them watered down. So by using the Society, it was a Society that was very strong in our culture, and part of what we know of the medicines that it had, it had medicine that was very strong and very rarely used. What made them strong back then was how closely they were connected to the rituals and the medicines. They have never lost a battle since the beginning of time. Their ultimate goal and only goal is "to Protect" the boundaries.

So that's how we were able to do what we did last year. We used something that had always been there but had kind of been forgotten. See, the anthropologists and the Christian people never got hold of this Society, so they never had documented it. All we know is from being hereditary people to this Society. So most of the knowledge, people cannot relate to, which is good. Because it gave us an advantage last year, no one could pick it apart and have advance knowledge of what we would do. So, whatever we brought out with it, that's what they had to understand it to be.

We did the things that were meant and we had to go about doing. We chose "the pipe carrier" and all the necessary personal things for this to continue. And as we went about doing these things we got stronger in our understanding of what we had to do to protect the river.

It didn't start August 3, it started months before that in the winter time. All the individuals who started, I had to go talk to them one by one. A lot of people on our reserve were very surprised by who was there, because these were very individualistic-minded people. Like you, on your reserve, probably know people who no matter what you tell them they'll never do anything. They're the kind of people you can't tell anything. But it was those kind of people who joined the camp, who started things off. And these were people who could survive on their own, they didn't need anybody, and when it came down to it they'll use these too (Milton holds up his fists). Some people referred to them as the "badass people", but yet they were the people who did not need to rely on other people. They had their own way of thinking and their own answers. And yet, we were very committed to the culture in one aspect or another. We were the ones who would make time to go see the elders. We would be the ones who would do the little things, when we did get too much we would share. And it's not like we did it purposely, it's just something we did because we knew what hard times were. We knew what it was like to be in the cities. We knew what it was like to be in jail, what it was like to be homeless, to get beaten up, we knew all these things.

In getting to August 3rd, and following through the process of this ritual...that's what came out: "The trueness of everything... of every little bitty thing." And while we were doing it that's how we really were able to come together to what our ultimate goal was. The separation between "do we let this happen, or do we not?" And if we do let it happen then we let it, and if we don't we don't, we go out and we stop it.

M: How did the group come to find that through the Lonefighters' Society there was an avenue to try to stop the construction of the Dam?

BWAT: It's where we go. You know, we're too used to this non-Native White Man world, however we chose to call the outside world. Kind of like when the government came to talk to us in the camp. They wanted to know where we got the plan. And so we told them. Because we didn't get it from them, they did not know the procedures, and that's where we had an advantage. And if Native people are ever going to do something in this country, we have to go back to what makes us who we are. People might think it's funny that the tree has something to offer, but it does. I mean that's really serious, what was said back in earlier times can still be said today, we still can make that connection to our way of life. And our way of life is the environment. Now we have a word that makes sense, eh! Before we used to talk about the water spirits, the tree spirits, the beaver spirits, and all these other spirits and people were kind of...(shrugs his shoulders), but now we have a word that says "environment", and now it clicks in. So that has made it a little easier for the skeptics, and even for our own people, who have kind of shunned away from that saying, "Leave that beads and moccasin way of life." They say it's dead and gone. That's why nothing worked right for Indian people, because we refused what made us who we are. The A, B, Cs and the 1, 2, 3s and Einstein, Julius Caesar, and Jesus Christ, those are not what makes us strong. What makes us strong, in my way of thinking, is "Sitting-on-the-Eagle-Tail, Brings-Down-The-Sun, Iron Shield." We'd say all these other people, and we would look at the berries, the roots, the herbs and all the animals in our domain, those are the things that made us strong. That's what we went back to.

I tell a lot of people now, what we did last year was not human. Part of what we were involved in, that we didn't know but we felt was very strong. And as we were doing every inch, of every second, of every detail it became more apparent that there was something else there. Not only did we know that "The Oldman River Dam" project, and its real reason for building it, we knew that there was something else there, and we knew there was something else there for us, as to who we were and how we can best protect ourselves— because there is just a little bit left. When you get desperate, when you get right to that last line, to what I did... When you get to end, that's where you find what is really sacred, and what's missing and what's not missing.

Even though not long time, you get rid of all the things that don't really matter, that are just distracting, and you go to the core of things, and that's what we were able to see. So that's what came out of it, when we say it was not human. Because some of our elders came to us, some of our old people— I hate to call them elders, it's the wrong word for them because no one was special in our way of life. Each one we respected, it wasn't we respected the human being, we respected this human being because it respected a certain ritual, a certain medicine it had. And because it respected that, it respected its ability that it had to be shared. Now we have some of these so-called elders that want to maintain and say, "Me powerful. You got listen to me or I will tell you no secrets." Because of boarding school, white man thoughts have made him think like a business man. You know: "Get Gain and Gold."

That's why we have a fight amongst us. So us, we just say, "Bullshit!" We want the truth, we want to share, and we want to exist, and most of all we want to protect, because we see what's important.

And so some of these old people, the knowledge carriers, said, "Do you know what you guys are doing?" And we said, what is it? They said what we were doing was a prophecy that came a long time ago. It talks of two dams, the first dam was built in 1922, the second one they're building now. They say the second is going to break. They didn't say how it was going to break, but it's going to be culture that will break it. See, prophecy was never direct as to how we would see it, so it was a matter of it all fitting into place. And then we all came at ease, because we were so intense, we knew there was something there and the more we knew the stronger we got, and the more we wanted to protect.

Some of the things we did during the time we were finding out these things, like we got our bulldozer stuck, a D-9. Can you imagine the size of a D-9? And we got it stuck in the swamp, and everybody we called said forget about it, you'll have to get another D-9 or a D-10, a bigger one with a winch to pull it out. And that evening we got it stuck everybody just kind of,...it was the third day we were into it and it kind of broke our spirits. We were kind of down. We thought, "Jeeze. We need the bulldozer, because it's doing our thing." So the next morning we had a sweat, and during that sweat we almost forgot about the bulldozer being stuck. We come out and we were joking. We started talking about winter time, and we started talking about our vehicles. When we get stuck on the reservation we never have enough money to call the tow truck. And how we got out, we talked about it. And then it dawned on us. Bulldozer no different than car, only bigger, but we can do the same thing. We had two shovels. It took us four and a half hours to dig it out, the mud was seven and a half feet deep. That's how low the thing had sunk. But we never stopped to see that. Now I stop, and it kind of scares me a little, because that's the kind of strength we had. We got it out in no time.

At the same time, the media was making reports and laughing, saying, "Those stupid Indians got their bulldozer stuck." But they couldn't see what made it go beyond, and made it a thing that was extraordinary.

M: How important was what was happening out in Oka to what happened with the Lonefighters in Alberta?

BWAT: See, kind of in a way the judge talked about that, everybody talked about that, and while we were going through it everybody kept telling us that we were using the Mohawks to get away with it. And here our plans started way before. And they were saying that Elijah Harper was partly responsible for inciting us. But when they found out that this thing came way before Elijah and way before the Mohawks. And what we have to say is what happened with the Mohawks started a long time ago as well, and what Elijah did started a long time ago as well. It's just that we were living in those times. It's not like we timed it. Elijah go first, and then the Mohawks second, and then Lonefighters. No. It was, we followed this certain way that was not human, and that's what gave us the strength.

So what happened in Oka, we didn't think nothing about, though we felt what they felt. We listened to the radio and we watched the news. And when we were asked, "What are you going to do for Oka?" we would say, "We can't do nothing except pray, and we can understand and in our own way keep up the struggle." But we knew that if we maintained our direction, the way it came out is now we have something to offer.

See before our issue really broke out, on September 7 and 8, on August 31 I came down to Montréal. I came down to Kanehsatake, and nobody knew. I snuck across the border because the cops were already looking for me. I took off to Boston, some people came and got me and took me to Vermont, we waited for a little while and then some people came and got me and took me to Montréal. I went to Dorval, where they were having their negotiations. That's where Joe Norton, Mike Myers and all those people were surprised. They said, "Hey. What you doing here? We just been seeing bits and pieces about you guys on the news." I said, "I come to ask you. We understand you. We really feel for you, but the attention is on you guys. There's other problems across this country." I knew the RCMP was going to invade us so I told them, "I just want you to be aware that something is going to happen out here." That's when I first met Elijah, because he was out there at the same time. So I stayed out there for a day and a half, and Joe Norton was kind enough to let me speak to the people they were speaking with, because a lot of people were there offering their support. They wrote me out a support letter. I was the only one who left there with a support letter. Everyone was there to offer support; me, I was only there asking for support. (Laughs)

So I went back. It was all I needed. I went back September 5, and on the night of September 6 and the early hours of the morning of September 7, that was when it happened.

M: Warning shots were fired. How did that come about? What happened that morning?

BWAT: It was very simple. Already the government had told the Chief and Council if they were going to move into the area they were going to tell the Chief and the Council first. The Chief and Council and me had a good relationship up to that point. That's another thing that's been misconstrued, that I never listened to the Chief and Council. Well we started with them and their knowledge. For that day, they had told the Chief and Council that they would come in. The morning of the seventh, they moved in that morning, no warning, we were still in camp. There wasn't very many of us there, because it was a Friday. We were on the reservation and people had gone back to their homes to get a few things. Because it was on our own territory.

It just so happened that they passed by this one house and the people seen this long line of RCMP cops and these semis with bulldozers and front-end loaders go driving by. They jumped in their car to come and warn us. We were still sleeping, it was seven o'clock in the morning.

So, it was kind of like, that's where the real thing was as to one part of what had to be dealt with. We had dealt with everything real seriously and there wasn't a decision left. We had already made a decision way ahead of time between us. We had said that there was going to be a sacrifice, I was to be the sacrifice. That's why I am the leader of the Lonefighters' Society. The thing is, I am not a leader of the people, I am a leader of the Society. I have to maintain its credibility. So therefore if anything was going to happen to our whole action, I was the first. So that was understood.

When it came down to it and when they moved in that morning, it was my decision and the rest knew what my decision was. The thing was that these people gave us no respect. For thirty-four days we were there with an open door policy that we were willing to sit down and deal with the issue, but they never chose to come through it. So when they came marching down like they did...and they chose all the RCMP...like maybe on your reserve you have certain cops that you just hate, and they hate you and mess with you all the time. While they chose all those cops to be on the front line and they had a real shitty attitude like, "Watch what we're going to do now." They marched in like that. And see, people don't know that. And the government officials who came were really happy to follow these guys because they knew that.

And we asked them to get off the land, they were trespassing. They didn't listen, so I did what was done. I fired two shots to warn them. And it worked, the warning worked. And now one of my charges, they have me assaulting ninety police officers. But the thing was they knew, and when we went through trial this came out, they knew we only had one gun. We used it for hunting, we were living there at the time. So they knew we knew we only had one gun because they had infiltrated our camp weeks ahead of time. We knew they were out there. We had nothing to hide.

They knew that ahead of time...so why did they have to bring such an awesome force? While at the same time, in a town called Provost, Alberta there was a gathering of the Aryan Nation and Ku Klux Klan. They were doing a cross-burning ceremony. They had punched out a few reporters and they had harassed some of the local people there. Some of the local people called the RCMP to send some people out there to stop it. And at that time they said they couldn't deploy any RCMP because they were all down south. They had AK-47s and they were shooting up in the air and threatening. But the thing about it was that the word came from Ottawa why the RCMP had to be down at the reserve. It was all planned, just like in *Kanehsatake* the word came from Ottawa.

The funny thing about it too is that one of these Aryan Nation guys killed an old Indian man three months ago. He went to trial a month ago and he got four years. And they wanted to give me fifty-seven years for firing two warning shots.

M: What was the experience in court like? I understand they chose the jury from a community of irrigation farmers, it was like the mice trying the cat...(Milton begins to laugh). I did laugh the first time I heard it too, it just seemed so strange.

BWAT: I laughed all the way through because I got to see these people and I knew what they were all about. The judge told the jury, "We have to find out which charges he's guilty of. It shouldn't take very long." And the jury felt the same way. So it was a joke. But the thing was, I was able to get observers from across the country to see that. Very rarely does the outside world get to see how we're treated. And my case is not that unique. There are a lot of our people in jail because of that, because there is nobody there to watch it, and it's no different. It's just that I had an opportunity to acquire that kind of observation, and they got to see what we really go through when we go into court. The judicial system...you know where they got the woman with the two scales, we're not even on there, on either scale. It's just them. There has to be a third scale, that's all there is to it.

M: But that system has control over your life. It will decide whether or not you're a free man.

BWAT: The thing is, when we started out we chose a sacrifice. I am that sacrifice. I ain't in it to win or lose. I'm just in it to make my enemy's life as miserable as he makes mine. And while I'm doing that I'm exposing the system for the rest to see. The rest depends on how much people are willing to say, "Here is something that we can measure as to what's wrong." And if they choose to do something about it that's up to them. But next time something comes up again, these people will know that we will never win in the courts. Never. There isn't one court that is going to deal with us fairly.

M: You started a process when you went to Oka, with the connections you made there towards making a National Alliance. Can you tell me where that's at?

BWAT: Already been doing that. And in a way, it was already done with what we did, because now we are finding a lot of connections to the real issue. Like I said before, "There was something far greater than them building the dam strictly for farmers." Now we are finding out what some people refer to as "the Grand Canal Scheme." The Northwestern Alliance of Power Association deal that was made in the late 50s and early 60s. What they want to do is build a series of dams with connecting dikes and canals, to where they'll be able to connect it all together from the area where I come from in the North, to northern Saskatchewan and then into Manitoba, Ontario, and James Bay. See the real issue behind James Bay is not just power, it's the selling of water. The United States is at a point where its water crisis is becoming far greater than any other situation they are facing. We have uncovered what I've been referring to as "the Real Watergate." When meeting with Joe David in *Kanehsa-*

take, he produced a map that shows some of the things that will be coming out of James Bay II. And one of the main transmission line happens to run through *Kanehsatake*. So, I mean, it's connected.

I've just been visiting the people out in Saskatchewan for the past six days before I came out here. And the question that we came out with is: "Why is the Rafferty Alameda Project sitting in the middle of nowhere, built with no water around it?" It's like it's waiting for something.

This scheme plans to flood all of northern B.C., Alberta, Saskatchewan, Manitoba, Ontario, and, we know, Québec. So we are talking about a massive amount of land being destroyed. And the only way they can get away with that deal; again, we are in the way of progress. Why did they send an army into Oka? To us it didn't make any sense. It couldn't be just over a golf course, it had to be something far greater. Now we are starting to piece it together. For us it's the same thing. Why are they building a dam without a license? Why are they willing to break their own justice system so blatantly?

Look at the people in this house. We are talking about upper middle class people who are willing to invite someone who everyone is saying is a violent man into their home. Why? Because they see their system being abused to a point where they are starting to ask if there is something far greater. That's kind of where this alliance is coming in. But this alliance has always been there, we are just following the old ways of connecting, and that's because we care about our territory, we care what happens to it.

M: You've travelled across the country, spoken to a variety of groups of people. Do you get a sense that people are ready and willing to make things change?

BWAT: Yes. I think once they see the real facts, they will feel the same things we feel, they will see the same things we see. Then we will be able to measure that with, "Now we know what Indian people are all about, now we can really tell." Because they've been listening to our sell-out Chiefs. And me and you can agree what sell-out Chiefs are all about. I mean, we have too many of them. They are the ones that are making it real hard for the non-Native world to accept us. Because here is us living this life, and there's our chiefs saying a whole other thing. Now the province is telling us, "Well, we can't deal with you because your chiefs did this." And what we were telling them back home is, "Yes, the chiefs sold out. But we didn't." The chiefs ain't sole power within our own domain. When the governments made an agreement with the people, there was no chief and council. The Indian Act wasn't in place. What was there? What was signed? Who did they sign agreements with? Who did they recognize? They recognized the people. That's who was there. So what we've done is follow that original agreement. What everybody calls a treaty.

And the people at that time were still people who were rightly connected. To be able to speak in our own terms, to explain it in our own terms. Now when we try to explain it, when we get into the courtroom or whatever, we have to explain things in what they call layman's terms. And that's how come we confuse the issue, because when you explain it that way it's like a watered down, not really sincere feeling or approach. And whoever we're talking to can't get it, but when we use our own way and we explain it with, that they got no choice but to feel it. And that's the point we got to last year, where we said we're going to die, and everybody said, "Oh, you just want to get into war." But that's not it, because when you find that you really want to preserve the culture, and when you understand how sacred it is and how special it is, then the ultimate decision is that it's worth dying for. It's that simple. And when you get that far and accept it, then solutions come and you can explain things a hell of a lot better. Because you don't use their way, and you don't fear their way. Then armies, governments, and policies don't bother you any more. That doesn't phase you.

The real issue is that our lifestyle is still here. The trees are still here, the water is still here, the roots and herbs are still here. But that's where we get down to it:...is knows how to connect with them? That's where the extinction lies. That's where the seriousness of where we are is at. We don't have that many people left that can be truly considered fluent. Very rare. And every nation is like that, and mine is the same.

M: The media always refers to you as "the Militant" Lonefighters' Society. What does that mean to you? Militancy? Is that part of the stand that the Lonefighters are willing to take?

BWAT: You have to be a bit cheeky about it, and take the word and look it up in the dictionary. Militant means "Passive. One who will protect." So to me it's alright to call me that. You can look at it the other way; all they did was spell my name wrong. My name is Milton; not Militant. That's how I look at it, both ways. I don't mess with that word, because proof is enough about what we want to do.

M: But surely there is a sense in many communities of frustration and anger. And you must be getting that feeling as well, that...you can speak to the government; you can get the Canadian people on your side; you can get the whole country on your side, for that matter; but what does it take to get the government, what does it take to get the justice system or the politicians to change their direction? Can that be accomplished through peaceful means, or do you have to put a gun to their head before they will say, "O.K., O.K., we'll think about it"?

BWAT: You're going to have to get to the seriousness of it. The thing is, if they cannot change, if they cannot stop trying to prove to people something that does not exist—the Assimilation Process. I'm one who has proven that the assimilation process does not exist, that it's a farce. And all this billion dollar spending on it did not work. That's what's going to break them down. It's not going to be this one day, all of a sudden they're going to say, "Whoops!" Nah. It's not going to be like that. It's going to be a long drawn-out and painful process, because the people who continue that process are our taxpaying people, are the ones that vote, are the ones that keep this machinery going. Because they do not know the truth. And we have a lot of false people right now who are explaining the truth. We've got people like George Erasmu;, and we have people like my own chief, we've got chiefs across the country. We have all these false people out there explaining. But they're (the Canadian Public) going to have to hear it from us. And the way it's going to be changing is when we come to that point.

Do we really want to protect and preserve our way of life? Or at what cost are we willing to sell out? The test is going to be there. I've gone this far, years and money, and all that they put before me has not phased me. I'm still only the same thing.

That's what's going to change. Is that if we really become serious. Do we really want to become who we are? Or do we want that image? How best we can camouflage it with lies, with makeup, with whatever. The thing is, that's what it will take.

We say we do things for the future generations. But we're not doing it no more. We're doing it just for the Me Time. That's what we want to do. We want to live good. For our time. The thing is, we forget that we cannot do it in one lifetime.

Joe David

HOW TO BECOME AN ACTIVIST IN ONE EASY LESSON

October 4, 1991

The voice on the other end of the telephone said, "Congratulations." For what? I wondered. "It's been a year since you were released from jail last fall." The fact that someone else was marking the calendar, when I wasn't, surprised me. Until then, I hadn't even thought about it. Since that phone call, I've hardly thought of anything else.

Sometimes, it even seems as if people would like to forget the whole thing. When they invite me to speak at churches, universities, or meeting halls, it seems as if they consider me entertainment. It's as if they're watching me spill my guts in front of them. They seem detached, untouchable, like they're watching something on TV.

I get tired of it, because I want them to take responsibility, individually and collectively. They seem to want me to do something for them; to keep fighting the battles and never give up. To ease their guilt. They can't understand that I don't have the answers and I can't fight for them. They can't see that I need help.

One professor drew me aside one evening. He told me how guilty he felt about the way his country treats aboriginal people. I understood how he felt. But I also got pissed off at him because I couldn't fathom his not doing anything or not knowing what to do. After all, he was the educated man in an influential position and he had the power to influence others. Instead, he chose to do nothing.

I'm tired of the lip service. I'm the one who comes from a powerless group of people. Yet I'm always asked to suggest what to do, that they write letters, that they lobby, that they demonstrate, somehow. The constant refrain of, "I'm only one person" or "I feel so powerless" is a cop out. Because I know it always starts with just one person.

One year ago today, I was just being released from army custody. I have been wrestling with so many strong emotions since last year that I feel I'm only now beginning to regain my balance.

I've watched the media come and go in this story. I've watched as politicians and native leaders postured and discussed "Oka," the dry analysis rarely helping my community or the people most hurt in the "crisis". I've become disheartened by the empty rhetoric, the almost assured and predictable end to this tale.

On February 5, 1991, I began acting as a coordinator for the legal defense— my own defense and the defence of the Mohawks from my community who were charged. It was on this day that we showed up in court and our lawyers announced they were withdrawing from our files, citing lack of funds. They weren't being paid, they said.

Confusion. It caught most of us by surprise. Until then, we assumed we were being taken care of. I remember pandemonium in the courtroom, panic and maybe a little fear. I remember thinking it's a much less honorable place to fight for our rights than in the pines, and that we weren't prepared for this kind of battle. I think we all thought that the amount of support would have translated into enough donations to pay for the lawyers. Or, at the very least, some lawyer or lawyers would surely volunteer their services. I suppose it was naive to think that, having just come out of a showdown with the Canadian army, we were going to be allowed to rest. Naive also to think that at some point I would get my life back; this land dispute has already eaten up almost two years of my life.

In February 1991, some of us with charges got together. Not having any lawyers and not feeling confident in the people who had, until then, been acting as a coordination team, I felt that if anyone should be giving direction to the lawyers, it should be someone from *Kanehsatake* able to bring up issues in court specific to that community and speak of what happened at Oka with authority; and people with charges representative of the three communities most directly involved. I teamed up with Joe Deom from *Kahnawake* and Lorne Oakes for *Akwesasne*. Since that time I feel I've been on a treadmill, being whipped and urged on by the possibility of jail. When we brought in our latest lawyer, he went to St. Jérôme and tried to get a sense of how things were going in court. He said the Crown prosecutors were walking on air, they felt they had the whole case in the bag. It's an infuriating position to be in, with almost no money to pay these lawyers and not a lot of help on the scale we need. In the face of the massive propaganda campaign against the Warrior Society, sowing doubt and confusion, chipping away at our support, it's imperative to point out that not everyone charged is a member of the Warrior Society. In fact, it's not only Mohawks, but also five other nations from British Columbia, Saskatchewan, Ontario, Nova Scotia, and one French Canadian who have been charged; and that the issue had nothing to do with contraband cigarettes or gambling, it was purely a land-claim issue.

My life has always been fairly quiet and uncomplicated in *Kanehsatake*. I kept a low profile, concerned myself with my art and my friends. I watched the ongoing political problems of my community from the outside, rarely getting involved.

I grew up with a rich family history that few Canadians can identify with. The Mohawks have occupied this territory from time immemorial, thousands of years. My parents often talked about my grandmother Lena, and how in 1950 she tried to stop a sawmill in the same pine forest that I was arrested in. She was beaten up by one of the men working for the company that claimed to own the pines, charged with assault, and hauled off to jail in St. Jérôme, the same town, where forty years later over sixty Mohawks are being criminalized for the "Oka crisis," myself included.

Nothing's changed. History just keeps repeating itself.

Dating from the first days of the Christian intrusion into our lands there has been a steady stream of petitions demanding to have the various levels of the colonists' governments recognize our legitimate claim to our territory. In 1781, 1788, 1794, 1802, 1818, 1828, 1839, 1848, 1869—all the way to 1990.

Throughout our history my people have been oppressed to the point of slavery, forbidden to cut wood even on our own lands. "The Indians would cut wood for making lacrosses or snowshoes or baskets for sale," wrote Amand Parent, the Methodist missionary who arrived in Oka in 1871. "They would be arrested, and dragged twenty miles for trial. There they would be bailed out. Some months after, they would be heard before the court. The juries would disagree, or acquit them. They would hardly arrive home again before another arrest, and the round would be followed once again."

We, at least my generation, have grown up being taught some of the things my parents knew and we're learning more all the time. That the goal of the government is total domination over native people, and if that can't be achieved in such ways as assimilation, then it will be done by annihilation.

I'm thirty-four years old, and the intensity of my life these days is hard to cope with. I'm really amazed at how pervasive and deeply rooted racism is in this country. I've tried to cope with racism all my life because, from learning about my history, my culture, I learn about the Indian nations wiped out by guns, starvation, and smallpox-infected blankets.

I've become a racist. My people are becoming racist.

I don't want to be. And I don't want them to be.

Today we know so much more about our history. It makes us both proud and angry. It's a deep anger, one of betrayal. My people have tried so hard to accommodate, but when you corner or attack any animal or person, their instinct is to fight. We are backed against the wall. We have almost no land left, and the government has successfully stalled our land issue long enough for the Canadian public to think it's all taken care of. Long enough for people to forget.

I really believe a similar confrontation will come to pass, that history is going to repeat itself. Because the paternalistic attitude will be maintained, if only for economic reasons.

July 11, 1990 was not the first time there's been an armed confrontation. In 1909, Joseph Kanawatiron Gabriel, my great-grandfather rallied forty men to try to stop a Canadian Northern Railway track that would have crossed two hundred and fifty meters of what we considered our traditional land. The Sulpician priests had been selling land, in violation of the land grant of 1717, and they also gave permission to the Canadian Northern to pass through the territory.

INDIANS THREATEN WAR AGAINST RAILROAD MEN, the headlines read. CANADIAN NORTHERN CONSTRUCTION GANG AT OKA STOPPED BY FORTY ARMED WITH REVOLVERS, SHOTGUNS, AND BLUDGEONS. CHIEF KENNATOSSE GABRIEL THEIR LEADER THREATENS SERIOUS TROUBLE IF THEIR LAND IS CROSSED.

They were successful, but Joseph Kanawatiron Gabriel was forced to go on the run for years. Thousands of dollars were spent in the hunt to have him arrested. Eventually the charges were dropped.

I'm told the "Oka crisis" cost upwards of two hundred and fifty million dollars. Apparently, the bills are still coming in. It would have been much cheaper to have dealt honorably with us for once. Maybe corporal Marcel Lemay would still be alive, too.

Why does it take so much? Especially in a country that would like to see itself as a leader in the field of human rights. "Might is Right" is still the doctrine practiced. Manifest Destiny is alive and well in Canada, and as long as nobody says anything against the policies except the Indians, it will stay just as it is.

I've gotten so cynical over the past year, but then, my entire community has been the victim of a massive assault: government, police, army, media, the curious and the wannabees have all been such a drain on my energies.

I don't believe I'll see justice. There's no such thing as justice for native people. The court system is just another big stick to intimidate my people. Tie us up. Make us toe the line. Meanwhile, international law and human rights are being violated. I'm caught up in the genocide machine and, if anything, I'm getting more militant, more angry, becoming more of a nationalist Mohawk. I've been radicalized, and all I wanted was a peaceful, quiet family life.

I remember being in the treatment centre last year, thinking I was never going to leave that place alive. My memories of that time are very hard to deal with. The psychological warfare used to wear us down and demoralize us has, for the most part, worked. Very high level propaganda and psychological experts were brought in to use against us, but when I tell white people that, they can't believe their governments would do such a thing.

I opposed the weapons throughout the spring of 1990, and I was called "Gandhi" because of it. Yet I'm one of the few from *Kanehsatake* charged with possession of a weapon. But both personally and for my community I don't believe there was ever any choice. The "crisis" happened as much because of the governments' attitude as because of our resolve to finally have our title to our land recognized.

My role in the "Oka crisis" was inevitable because of my great-grandfather and my grandmother, my parents and the history of my community, but also because of the two governments' intentional disregard of natives' legitimate protests and demands. There are more people just like me, and more on the way. In James Bay, in British Columbia, all over this country, the frustration is reaching explosive proportions. The Lubicon people wouldn't cooperate with the governments' demands. The governments' response was to create another band, enticing the more malleable people with money, creating a band that would sell out.

The new constitutional proposal being pushed by the Mulroney government speaks of the fundamental "duality" of Canada. This is a slap in the face of aboriginal people. Almost as bitter a joke as Québec's assertion that it is a "distinct society".

photo by Linda Dawn Hammond

Arthur Kroker

THE MOHAWK REFUSAL

It is appropriate to reflect on Virilio's *Pure War* in Montréal, a city which in the early 1990s was the scene of the violent application of the Canadian war machine against its original aboriginal population, the Mohawks. A city, that is, which in the summer of 1990 experienced as part of its cultural politics the invasion of the aboriginal lands of the Mohawks surrounding Montréal by all the policing strategies of the state: 6000 soldiers of the Canadian army, complete with tanks, armoured personal carriers, and even TOW missiles, the greater part of the Québec provincial police, and the RCMP. And all of this array of the power of the state against, in the end, less than 50 Mohawks who only wished to prevent the destruction of a sacred pine grove of their ancestors by developers intent on extending a golf course to eighteen holes. (In a perfect Virilian gesture the Mohawks not only reclaimed the sacred pine groves at Oka, but also took physical control of the Mercier bridge—one of the main traffic arteries between the south shore suburbs and the island of Montréal.) If in cultural politics we should be able to read the universal in the particular, to decipher a larger war logic in local applications, then Oka is Pure War in Virilio's sense.

First, it is about an urban space, not as a site of commerce, but as defined in relation to war. That's Montréal, which has always been a site of war first, and of commerce second. A city of two founding exterminisms: the original genocide of aboriginals by French colonizers who, speaking the language of Christian salvation, imposed the spatial logic of "enlightenment" on the northern tier of North America; and then the attempted exterminism of the local French population by English colonizers, for whom the "conquest of Québec" was most of all about suppression of a Catholic French America by a Protestant mercantilist logic. Montréal, then, as a Virilian space: an intensely urban zone as a spatial vector for the war machine: a site of maneouvre, negotiation, and conquest—a violent scene of sacrificial power.

photo by Linda Dawn Hammond

Second, Oka is a matter of tactics, strategy, and, most of all, logistics. Just as Virilio has theorized in *Pure War*, it is about an indefinite preparation for war, involving the colonization ("endocolonization") of local populations. Thus, for example, the Canadian military stated that this "conflict" could be over in two or three minutes, but the real war was a "media war" to win over the consciousness of the civilian population. Here, logistics could be an endless preparation for war: control of food, communications, space. And all of this accompanied by constant armed helicopter flights over Montréal in the summer of 1990, as if to demonstrate symbolically the state's control of the local population. Is this not what Virilio has described as "state terrorism"—the act of war without a declaration of war, so that there is no formal protection of civil rights, and no political rights for international agencies to intervene on behalf of the Mohawks. And is the indefinite occupation of Oka and the ceaseless police raids into other aboriginal territories not an indefinite preparation for war in another way: not really about the Mohawks at all, but a violent warning to all the First Nation peoples, most of all to the Cree in Northern Québec, not to intervene physically (by blocking roads) or legally (by court actions) in the future construction of James Bay II, the Great Whale project (the state-driven plan for a vast extension of hydro-electrical development on aboriginal lands in Northern Québec)? Oka, then, is a pure technological war between the energy requirements of the high-intensity market society and the irrepressible demands of aboriginal peoples for control of their territory. A technological war, that is, where the war machine has come inside of us and taken possession of our identity. Virilio is correct: "All of us are already civilian soldiers. We don't recognize the militarized part of (our) iden-

photo by Linda Dawn Hammond

tity, of (our) consciousness. And anyway, what is so dangerous about the Mohawks, about the sovereignty claims of the First Nations?" Virilio states that the war machine is the crystallization of science as the language of power, of the depletion of the energies of society, and their draining away into the war machine. Maybe that is what is so threatening about the struggles of the First Nations. It violates and refuses the genetic logic of the technological dynamo.

Consequently, a politics of remembrance of twenty-five thousand years of aboriginal history versus what Virilio describes as the extermination of time (in favor of a purely spatialized power) in technological societies. Here, real tribal consciousness and real grounded sovereignty—duration and a vital sense of sedentariness—militate against the pure mobility of the war machine. And not just memory, but the cultivation of a dynamic ecological relationship among land, economy, and culture on the part of the Mohawks now stands opposed to the disappearance of territory into abstract vectors of speed in consumer culture. This is perfectly captured by the bitter political struggle between the peoples of the First Nations of Labrador and NATO over low-level training flights by fighter jets. In Virilio's war machine, it is always land without history, people without remembrance, space without a sense of duration–the abstract control of territory against the loss of history of territory.

Finally, what makes the Mohawks really dangerous for the Canadian state is their creation of a model of democratic politics based on matriarchal principles of rule. Here, the traditional form of the Longhouse society militates against rule by the technocratic specialists of the war machine. Virilio says that in the war machine, there are no longer any priests who could mediate death. Now, the leaders of the war machine can speak triumphantly of mega-deaths, because death is also total release from the earthly constraints of gravitation. In this sense, the Mohawks are like gravity, a fall into real time, whose very communal existence militates against the pure speed, the will to endless circulation of the war machine. If the peoples of the First Nations can be so oppressed, not only in Montréal but also in all of the Americas from the United States to South America, maybe that is because they are the bad conscience of what we have become in the society of speed and war: perfect sacrificial scapegoats for feelings of anxiety and doubt about that which has been lost in the coming to be of the technological dynamo.

R.M. Vaughan

LOBSTER IS KING: INFANTILIZING MARITIME CULTURE

"The Maritimes and the US South share one thing—they're both lands of defeat."

– David Adams Richards

Atlantic Canadians are surrounded by decline. All of our symbols and systems of self-reference point us to a pre-Confederation era, to a time in our history we are told we have escaped from and yet by which we are still defined. This double bind is archetypally colonial—a paralyzing system of reference that disallows forward movement. We are effectively severed from the strengths of our past at just the same moment as we are asked to celebrate our heritage. Like many occupied peoples, we are no longer able to judge what is a true representation of ourselves.

(1) To understand regional differences in Canada it is essential to understand that Canada is a failed experiment—a "last days" excess of two colonial powers gone to seed.

Canada attempts to unite a continent's worth of diverse people under a flawed (and half-hearted) liberal agenda of false pluralism and deceptive commonality. British Columbia is not Ontario, Québec is not Newfoundland, and none of the south will ever be part of the north. Nevertheless, the illusionary politics of "from sea to shining sea" (from the national anthem) is not only indulged, but is often enforced to the detriment of the "regions" that do not comply with centralized policy.

Thus, to grow up in Atlantic Canada is to grow up in opposition to the federalist agenda. The very presence of the Atlantic provinces speaks the lie of federalism. A thousand miles and a linguistic bloc away from the capital and its old dreams, the Maritimes further exaggerate the impossibility of uniting a diverse continent.

The Atlantic provinces are a geographical hyperbole in the national text, and the people who live here have provided the centre with a key mythology in the narrative of nation building—the mystery of the folk, the feudal drama of an early "homeland" people who mark the beginning of the time line of progress.

In the Canadian federalist myth system, Atlantic Canadians are the equivalent of the Japanese rice paddy workers who always seem to be photographed stooped beneath futuristic monorail systems, or the peasants bringing up the rear in Soviet constructivist panoramas. We are a national image bank for an insecure country trying to sell itself on the global market. The stereotype of the lumpen "Maritimer" reaffirms the schema and morality of centralist "world class" progress.

169

Throughout my life in New Brunswick, I have been inundated with centrally-generated images of my provincial self that have never accurately spoken of or for me. I was told by a centralized media that I was part of a community of people who were primarily supported by primitive resource industries and who abided by simpler (and slower) philosophies of life—philosophies that stemmed from a magical past long since discarded by the newly urban and aspiringly urbane of the nation's centre. To grow up in Atlantic Canada is to grow up the poor cousin of arriviste relations.

(2) Four symbols dominate popular representations of Atlantic culture: the aging, gnarled seaman, or "Salty Dog"; the common gray seagull; the lobster; and the wooden lighthouse. These figures are constants in the barrage of mass media images of Maritime life, and are used as marketing reference points in all federal economic and political strategies. They are the visual canon of a systemic prejudice that reads Atlantic Canadian life and people as parochial, technologically outmoded, and, ultimately, powerless.

Upon closer inspection, the seemingly harmless, if not whimsical "trademarks" of Maritime culture are actually indexes of the attrition of the very culture they ostensibly herald.

Although my background is typically middle class and suburban, I cannot remember a time when I, as a "Maritimer," was not represented in the national media as a caricatured fisherman—preferably old, preferably toothless. This "Salty Dog" character appears in almost every representation of the Maritime population and is mass produced as a tourist curio throughout the area.

Dressed in a yellow slicker, stoop shouldered and narrow-eyed, the "Salty Dog" projects an image of wily (but uneducated) harmlessness and whimsical (but uninformed) folk wisdom. He is the Canadian equivalent of Aunt Jemima or the locals from *Deliverance*, and he is used to sell everything from fish sticks to Maritime vacations.

Very few Atlantic Canadians work exclusively in the harvesting of natural resources. However, we are frequently described as having a "resource dependent" economy by the national media. The subtexts of "resource-based" are "antiquated" and "outmoded" (and thus burdensome).

I've never met an actual fisherman, let alone a toothless one. I've never been on a trawler. I don't particularly like lobster. Yet, this character represents me and is inscribed in my psyche. Psychologically colonized, I find the "Salty Dog" as difficult to give up as it is to accept, largely because the alternative is assimilation into the global facelessness cultivated by the centre.

Other images work similar tricks. In any proper folk mythos there are accompanying animals that act as symbolic complements to, if not extensions of, the falsified character of the people.

The seagull, although found in equal numbers throughout Canada, is never far from sight in mass media depictions of the Maritimes. A scavenger bird living off carrion and garbage, the seagull is without majesty (and thus ideologically impotent) or particular interest as a bird. They are as common as mice, and a convenient, subconscious reminder of the national perception of Atlantic Canadians as the bottom feeders in the economic food chain. The bird makes an annoying squawk, typical of the griping poor. The seagull is a beggar.

Equally prevalent is the image of the lobster: a hapless, prehistoric creature that willingly wanders into the most obvious of traps in order to later be boiled alive. It is said to let out a pitiful whine as its exoskeleton contracts in the scalding water.

Gerry Gilbert

Outside of the context of Maritime life, the lobster is a food signifying wealth and middle class achievement. It is a luxury, or "gourmet" dish. However, depictions of lobster in images of the east coast refer exclusively, and deceptively, to the mode of harvesting—the antiquated wooden traps.

Atlantic Canadians are not often imagined eating the expensive seafood they catch. Instead, the lobster signifies our supposed economic dependence on dwindling natural resources, and reinforces the folk stereotype of a semi-magical (and primitive) "connectedness" to the ecology of the sea. It would be disruptive to depict Atlantic Canadians partaking of a commodity the rest of the country considers glamorous.

Finally, the lighthouse is possibly the strongest and most frequently invoked symbol of the declining fortunes of the east coast. All but useless since the arrival of sonar technology, and no longer operated by hand, lighthouses continue to be maintained both as navigational beacons and, more prominently, as graphic icons that foster an orchestrated nostalgia for the "golden era" of Atlantic Canada's now moribund seaport economy.

Replicas of clapboard lighthouses are erected in land locked communities to attract tourists. Thousands of businesses adopt the symbol as an "inside" reference to Maritime ownership. Even the federal government's Atlantic Canada Opportunities Agency (ACOA) uses a lighthouse image in its official letterhead: a surprising choice considering ACOS's mandate—to revitalize Maritime industries by providing aid for technological upgrading. Ironically, the lighthouse logo is more potent as yet another sign of the fatalism with which the central government approaches Atlantic Canada.

(3) The stereotypes used to market "life in the Maritimes" constitute an act of cultural impeachment; a replacing of the diversity of the east coast with a culturally resonant, supposedly benign, one-note ideal.

In order to build a strong economic engine, a new nation needs a labour class. By presenting Atlantic Canadians as uneducated, fearful, and empowered only within a very specific set of working and lifestyle conditions, the centre of Canada has discovered a semiotic basis for the creation of an abundant source of cheap, moveable labour.

If Atlantic Canadians are read as a population in need, the federal government can subsequently exploit east coast people without guilt or hesitancy— the dominant stereotypes are read as actual, and the slow erosion of Maritime culture via a population exodus becomes not only excusable, but is considered a generous response. Canada's own little Third World.

It is not coincidental that Canada's foreign policy and "developing world" aid strategies (moving capital from North to South) parallel the welfare state "transfer payment" model of domestic economic aid (moving capital from West to East).

The end result of Canada's regionalistic stereotypes is the infantilization of the Maritime people. Conversely, decades worth of federal paternalism have generated a predictable resentment among central Canadians towards their supposedly ever-needy and plodding east coast neighbours. The final irony of years of systematic misrepresentation of Atlantic Canada is that it may ultimately hasten the collapse of the federal agenda.

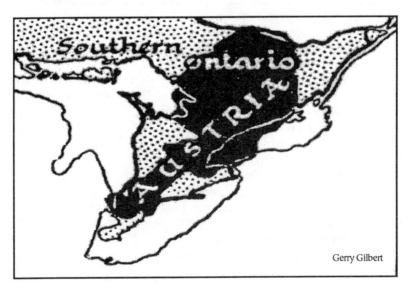

Gerry Gilbert

DAVID L. BENSON

A NEWFOUNDLAND PERSPECTIVE
ON CANADA'S 125th BIRTHDAY

Transfer payments
mean that we can buy
the things our resources make
with our electricity,
somewhere else.
Occasional chastisements
from State Controlled Radio
mean we even feel grateful
for the opportunity.
All of this means, of course,
that explosives
can be diverted
to make fireworks
to celebrate imperialism.
Fireworks are pretty
and encourage us to look up...
So we won't see
the red maple leaves
falling from the trees.

BHARATI MUKHERJEE
MOSAIC? WHY NOT FUSION?

Bill Moyers: Have you experienced any racism here (in the US)?

Bharati Mukherjee: Not in the United States, not personally, no.

Moyers: Where have you experienced it?

Mukherjee: In Canada. And I think that...

Moyers: You moved to Canada after you came here in '61, didn't you? You stayed [here] a few years and then went to Canada?

Mukherjee: My husband and I, when we were—when Clark and I were looking for our first jobs after our degrees from the University of Iowa, we looked only in Montréal, and went there in 1966; and in the beginning, Montréal was a perfect city for a biracial, bicultural, multilingual couple like us. And then, by the early 70s, 73 especially, I'm afraid racism reared its ferocious head, and by 1980 I felt that not only was racism institutional there, but had gotten, by 77, 78, particularly physically virulent.

Moyers: Did you experience it physically?

Mukherjee: Yes. Absolutely.

Moyers: Was there violence?

Mukherjee: I mean, I don't want to go through a litany of harassments, but being spat on or being thrown to the back of the bus, or being ejected from the lobby of a fancy hotel, being called a whore, these are not just my personal experiences, but they were every south Asian-Canadian's experiences during the 70s. And I blame some of that on the mosaic theory of absorbing immigrants.

Moyers: That culture is a variety of pieces that are put—placed together side by side: they don't blend or fuse into each other?

Mukherjee: A mosaic. Exactly. Where the government and the national mythology encourages the newcomer to hang on to Old World cultures, Old World psyches. And I know that the intention is good, or was good, but the consequences on the non-Anglo immigrants is to marginalize them.

SWITCHES

Michael William

璽顓
沙地士
山呀士下巴
沙面李巴
山汝治
所路市丙令埃崙
審市嘩利
四埃崙
士墨架文
所市滑
澀譬粦
昔儉麼士
雪汝埃崙
市卷拿
市結地桀
士弩數隙
心文弩士
市卑路尾申
市卑森
市片士卑唎治
市疋砧
市丹利
市地廠
嫣利尾善
市鑫汝隙
市胆瀝
所嫣
沙利仙呀
夭寅米
云巧巴（即咸水埠）
云永路
溫晏呀
云宵

JIM CAMPBELL

THE LITTON BOMBING: 10 YEARS LATER

On October 14th, 1982, a powerful truck bomb exploded outside a Litton Systems plant in the north end of Toronto, injuring seven people and doing five million dollars worth of damage. A few days later a communique was released from a group called Direct Action claiming responsibility. The communique apologized for the injuries, but expressed no regrets for the attack. It was an attempt to bring attention to Litton's role in building the guidance system for the Cruise Missile, a first-strike weapon which threatened the precarious balance of terror that existed between the US and the USSR.

A few months earlier, another Direct Action bombing completely destroyed a nearly completed B.C. Hydro substation which was part of an electrical grid that was to connect the British Columbia mainland with Vancouver Island, a project opposed by local residents as being the beginning of devastating industrial development in this wilderness area. A month later, three outlets of Red Hot Video were firebombed by a group calling itself The Wimmin's Fire Brigade. This rapidly expanding chain specialized in violent porn videos, including the "snuff" type. Local women had begun to organize opposition to this exploitation, but the chain had continued to grow and prosper. The firebombings, while igniting a huge debate about exploitation, violence against women, and censorship, were broadly supported by the Vancouver women's community.

In January of 1983, Ann Hansen, Brent Taylor, Doug Stewart, Julie Belmas, and Gerry Hannah were arrested in British Columbia and charged with these actions as well as conspiracy to rob a Brinks truck, weapons offenses, and other relatively minor criminal charges. In Toronto, the offices of a peace group that was organizing against Litton were searched by the local police, along with the homes of some of its leading members. In Vancouver, shortly after the arrests, four houses of people doing support work for the Vancouver Five, as they came to be called, were searched.

The Trial

In June of 1983, Bulldozer (the collective) was also raided. Virtually everything associated with *Bulldozer* (the magazine) was confiscated, including an issue in production. We were threatened with a charge of seditious libel, which apparently meant that we were calling for the armed overthrow of the state. Though nothing ever came of that, Colleen Crosbie, a midwife living with us, was charged with procuring an abortion. Information to lay the charge had come to the attention of the police from wire taps and room bugs to which we were subjected. Crosbie was offered a deal, where the charge would not be pressed if she told all that she knew about Bulldozer's connection to the bombing. Her refusal to cooperate took us into a legal fight costing thousands of dollars. Eventually, all the charges Crosbie faced were dropped.

In June of 1984, the first of four scheduled trials was coming to a close. The defence had lost a bid to throw out hundreds of hours of tape recordings made by room bugs, and all five defendants copped pleas. They received what were considered by many to be unduly harsh sentences. Hansen got life, Taylor was given 22 years, Belmas, only 20 when the bombings occurred, received a 20-year sentence. Hannah got ten years and Stewart six, the sentences of the latter two reflecting the fact that neither of them was linked to the Litton action. (Julie Belmas eventually broke rank. She testified against Taylor and Hansen at her appeal, sabotaging their appeals, in exchange for a 5-year reduction in her sentence. All contact was broken off with her by the other four and their supporters.)

All five have now been released from prison, with Hansen and Taylor having served about 7 years, including pre-trial detention, before receiving day parole. We honour the Five for their courage and feel that they made an invaluable contribution to the struggle in Canada, even if proof of such a contribution must remain subjective. This chapter in the history of Canadian anarchism has come to a close. But the personal sacrifices made by these comrades surely demand that we re-examine these events in order to learn from that experience. Though we will draw out some of the mistakes we feel were made by Direct Action and their supporters, our intention is not to trash anyone.

Direct Action was technically competent, as the two five million dollar bombings would suggest. And politically they were very developed. The communique, an essay really, released after the Litton action is as relevant today as when it was written. The issues that the Five addressed in their armed actions and in their broader politics—the Native struggle, violence against women, destruction of the earth from unchecked industrialism, prisons, imperialism, nuclear and non-nuclear war—are more critical today than ever before. The actions and trial in Vancouver did provide an opportunity to discuss these issues in other political circles.

The injuries of seven people in the Litton bombing, the majority of whom were plant workers, gave a negative cast to the bombing. Direct Action apologized for the injuries and explained their error as believing in the image of cops and security guards as super heroes. They had placed themselves at risk of arrest to ensure that the workers be given sufficient warning. But three security guards at the main gate failed to notice the van being driven and parked 100 yards from their glass-encased booth. Security also failed to understand the warning called in at that time. They called the cops but did not begin to evacuate the factory. It took the police ten minutes to arrive on the scene, and the bomb exploded twelve minutes early, probably due to police radios, just as people were leaving the endangered areas. The interference of police radios with the remote detonator could probably have been foreseen and prevented.

The size of the bomb itself was questioned by Doug Stewart, writing in *Open Road* after their conviction. He suggested that medium-level attacks such as arson and mechanical sabotage are easier to do than bombings. And large-scale actions virtually demand that the guerillas go underground. Direct Action understood that they had to break off contact with other political people; that to do actions in one city, they should live in another. But this demands enormous emotional and personal sacrifices. Indeed it was the failure to completely cut off ties with friends and lovers that left a trail for the local police. Smaller actions are technically simpler and allow, as Stewart says, "a group to come together easily around a particular issue." Medium-level activity also "has a much less intense impact on one's personal life. If you are not underground you are less emotionally isolated, and the overall stress level is very much lower. Capture for a medium-level action would be much less devastating in every way. A two- or three-year sentence is no joke, but it is substantially easier to deal with than a ten- or twenty-year one."

There was also a romanticization of guerrilla politics shared by both Direct Action and their supporters that undercut our ability to respond to the arrests. Direct Action never planned on what would happen if they got arrested. Nor had the milieu out of which they had arisen seriously thought through how we would handle a political trial, even though we covered armed resistance in the US and Europe in our newspapers, and at least talked of the possibility of it happening in Canada. "Romantic" is used in the sense that it is one thing to imagine going down in a hail of police bullets. It is something else to sit in some detention centre, facing many years in prison, trying to figure out a trial strategy. Similarly, for those of us on the outside, it is straightforward to reprint communiques from underground comrades. But it is much more difficult to handle raids and lawyers, harassing arrests, and to watch other friends and comrades distance themselves just when their support and work is needed the most. One must be able to handle high-stress politics for what could be a period of years, while advancing politics that may not even be supported by one's own friends and political associates, let alone by the wider society.

In the initial confusion, the right to a fair trial became the main demand. Since it did seem possible that the room bugs which provided the main body of evidence might be thrown out, this strictly legal course was hard to resist without prior political clarity as to how trials should be conducted. The right to a fair trial must not be ignored, if the battle is going to be fought on the legal terrain at all. But it is the state's battleground, and their first weapon is criminalization. The Crown (prosecution) split the indictments into four trials, the first of which was on the least overtly political charges: weapons offenses and conspiracy to rob a Brinks truck. While it may be obvious to those who have a certain political understanding why guerrillas need weapons and money, television pictures of a desktop full of weapons and reports of meticulous planning for a raid on a Brinks truck were calculated to defuse claims that the Five were principled political activists. The fight for a fair trial did draw support from activists, progressive journalists and lawyers, and people concerned with human rights. But it does create real problems if the trial is made to appear "legally" fair. Or when, as happened, the Five eventually pled guilty. Some people who did support work felt manipulated into supporting "guilty" people, even though we tried to make it clear that there is a difference between pleading not guilty and being "innocent".

The situation was not entirely grim, however. The members of Direct Action were all respected activists known for their militancy. Though this meant that the political police (and a lot of other people) had a good idea as to who the bombers were right from the beginning, it also meant that the efforts to portray them as terrorists did not entirely succeed. In spite of protests from the lawyers, the Five gave interviews and statements that defended the politics behind the actions. While one of the support groups in Vancouver did push the "right for a fair trial" strategy exclusively, the Free the Five Group built support on the basis of resistance to the corporate state and their way of doing things. There was a show of support in the courtroom and outside the courthouse.

Community Support

Direct Action had developed out of specific political communities, and these communities stuck with them. A number of newspapers directly associated with these anarchist-resistance politics, and information on the case put out by the support committees in various cities did reach beyond our own circles. Other alternative papers offered sympathetic coverage, though some anarchist papers were hostile at first. (The "socialist" left ignored the whole affair.) The women's community in Vancouver was particularly supportive. The circles immediately around the Five were primarily women, with a number of them later moving to Toronto where they have been one of the cores of a large anti-authoritarian women/lesbian community.

In Toronto, support for the Five came from some of the pacifists who had been campaigning against Litton, though most tried to distance themselves as much as possible. After the raid on Bulldozer, our support came from our native comrades, in particular the Leonard Peltier Defence Committee, and lesbians who could relate to the social and psychological marginalization that is one of the main goals of such raids. The midwives and pro-choice movement were also supportive, even though both were engaged in their own struggles for political legitimacy.

Generally, the response in Toronto was contradictory. While there was little overt support for armed resistance, there was political sympathy and personal support. Whether more political support could have been mobilized is an open question. Many political people upon first hearing of the bombing had a very positive response—they identified emotionally with this blow against the Empire. But then this supportive gut reaction was replaced by an intellectual distancing from the implications of such a response. A campaign to build support for resistance politics among the activist communities would have had to counter the critiques of armed actions, while at the same time building on the initial response.

Isolation

There was a choice as to whether there would be a trial in Toronto for the Litton bombing. But the small anarchist community, of which Bulldozer was a part, was new to Toronto. In our relative isolation, it was difficult to imagine taking on what would have had to be a major effort to present the politics behind the bombing to a hostile mass media. Yet not doing so meant that there was never a longer-term focus nor sense of direction for those who might have been willing to come forward with more active support.

Overt political actions such as these bombings—propaganda by deed, as they are known—are not understood in a non-political society. Major bombings are simply one more spectacular act in a world considered to be increasingly mad. Even though few people will understand the motivations behind the attack, the positive side is that there won't necessarily be a major reaction against it either. Indeed, it is an error to think that something like the Litton bombing will act as a "wake-up" call for the people to do something about a critical situation facing them. But, properly explained, it can make a difference to those people who are already concerned about the situation, and who have become frustrated with other methods of dealing with the issue.

Guerrilla actions are not ends in themselves; that is, a single act, or even a coordinated series of actions, has little likelihood of achieving more than some immediate goal. Such actions are problematic if it is assumed that they can be substituted for more above-ground work. But if they can be situated within a broader politics, as one tactic among many, then they can give the above-ground movements more room to maneuver, making them both more visible and more credible. At the same time, activists are given a psychological lift, a sense of victory, regardless of how fleeting, so that they can go about their own political work with a renewed enthusiasm.

There are different ways to determine whether Direct Action's armed resistance has had an impact on the politics of the country. The first, of course, would be whether or not militant tactics have continued to be used. In Ontario, the answer is no, although the Animal Liberation Front did do some actions in the mid-eighties. In British Columbia, however, over the last two years there has been a great deal of ecotage (ecological sabotage) against the logging of some of the last wilderness areas. Though these tactics were initially developed in the US, Direct Action was one of the sources of inspiration.

The second criterion is whether or not the politics expressed by the guerillas have been perpetuated. A relatively small but very active milieu of young activists adopted many of the politics around Direct Action, and developed them through such projects as Reality Now, the Anarchist Black Cross, and Ecomedia. They were also instrumental in working in the peace, punk, and Native support movements, helping to ensure that such politics did not end when the Five went to prison. Repression is most effective when it is able to keep the radical ideas from being transmitted to a new generation of activists. If the ideas can be passed on, then the next wave of activists develop their politics from the base that has already been created. Nor does the inter-generational politics just flow one way. Bulldozer itself owes its continued existence to the energy and enthusiasm of these younger anarchists. We were brought out of a period of burnout, despair, and inactivity after the trials by those who passionately raged at injustice, who could still feel that through our activity we can make a difference. We re-learned much that we had forgotten.

For most North American activists, armed struggle is reduced to a moral question: "Should we or should we not use violent means to advance the struggle?" Though this is relevant on a personal level, it only confused what is really a political question. Most radicals, at this point in time anyway, are not going to become directly involved in armed attacks. But as resistance movements develop in North America—and they had better or we are all lost—it is inevitable that armed actions will be undertaken by some. The question remains whether these armed actions will be accepted as part of the spectrum of necessary activity. Much will depend on whether people suffer harm or injuries. Far from being "terroristic", the history of armed struggle in North America shows that the guerillas have been quite careful in selecting their targets. There is a major difference between bombing military or corporate targets, or even assassinating police in response to their use of violence, and setting off bombs on crowded city streets. The left in North America has never used random acts of terror against the general population. To denounce any who would choose to act outside of the narrowly defined limits of "peaceful protest" in order to appear morally superior, or to supposedly avoid alienating people, is to give the state the right to determine what the allowable limits of protest are.

The Litton bombing was by no means politically definitive either at the time it took place, or now. But it is not entirely coincidental that ten years after the Litton bombing the radical political communities and movements in Toronto are much larger than they were then. The ideas that were being advanced by the Five and their supporters are now shared by a much wider element of the independent and anti-authoritarian left. It is not that we "won" people over to our political line. But we have contributed to a critique of North American society that others have found useful. In turn, we have learned from many other movements, perspectives, and peoples.

Canada is a much more profoundly politicized society now than it was ten years ago. There are many different reasons for this political development. In particular, the armed self-defence of Mohawk land in 1990 and the massacre of fourteen women by a man "hunting" feminists in Montréal in 1989 resulted in an understanding that social conflict cannot be contained within the limits of parliamentary politics. The iron fist of reaction has been exposed, even as the necessity for radical change becomes ever more apparent. Our voice has been one among the many that have aided in the development of this more radical understanding of Canadian society. The bombings ten years ago were a challenge to radicals and activists to get down and bring about the changes we know must take place in Canada. Since that time the global situation has only become more critical. Even if we choose not to use the same tactics as Direct Action, their courage in acting surely demands that we refuse to compromise our efforts.

JIM CAMPBELL

RIOT ROCKS TORONTO

On May 4/92 the biggest "riot" in recent history struck downtown Toronto. Influenced by events in Los Angeles, but fueled by the reality of police racism and violence in Toronto, angry demonstrators smashed store windows, threw rocks and bottles at the police, and did a bit of looting. A rally had been called by the Black Action Defence Committee (BADC) in solidarity with the protests in the US after the Rodney King verdict, as well as to protest the recent acquittal of two Peel Regional Cops for the killing of a local Black teenager in 1989. The fatal shooting of Raymond Lawrence, a young Black man, by a member of the Metropolitan Toronto police on May 1/92 added to the grief, frustration, and rage felt by those attending the demonstration. The media's repeated cries about the "unfortunate" timing of Lawrence's murder—as though there might be times when the killing of an African is "fortunate"—added to the fury. In the past four years, four Blacks have been killed, with another four wounded, by police in the Toronto area. In spite of protests, liberal articles in the media, and government reports, the police still regard it as their right to shoot and kill as they so desire.

The demonstration heated up quickly as four members of the fascist Heritage Front were chased when they showed up to counter-protest. After marching up Yonge Street, a thousand people sat down at a major downtown intersection. After an hour the march continued. Windows were broken at a downtown courthouse as a group of forty youths rushed the building. Continuing on to City Hall, bottles and rocks were thrown at mounted policemen who were blocking the entrance. No city official could be bothered to speak to the rally even though council was in session, so the crowd headed back to Yonge Street (Yonge Street is Toronto's commercial heart. Filled with fast food places, cheap electronics stores, small businesses, and flanked by major shopping malls, it has long been a hang-out spot that is usually crowded with an amazing mix of people.) For several hours the cops held off as a core of people continued to do the riot thing. Hundreds of people, though not participating in the rock throwing or looting, stayed with the window-smashers, providing them with needed cover and support. As streets were taken over, passers-by joined in and others came downtown as radio and TV spread the news about what was happening. Away from the intensity of the window-smashing, the streets, suddenly freed of vehicle traffic, took on a festive air as people debated and watched what was going on. In the end, thirty people were arrested, with all but seven being released by the next morning.

The media, politicians, and police went predictably crazy. It shocked all the little burghers to think that Toronto, "the city that works," could seem, well, so *American*. Compared to the television image of the menacing underclass of the big American cities, those marginalized by Canadian society always seemed relatively harmless. The media went on and on about the "violence" of that evening, of which it had a distorted sense, since the majority of threatening incidents were directed at journalists and their ever-present cameras. For the demonstrators there was a sudden sense of power and possibilities, however awkward it felt. The streets were ours for a brief moment. Curiosity rather than fear seemed to be the shared emotion for those who, as spectators, also thronged the streets and sidewalks.

Whereas it was generally easy for Canadians to accept that deep-rooted racism in the US provoked the uprising in Los Angeles, the riot here was regarded by many as a copy-cat affair and not due to systemic racism in Canadian society. The participation of white people in the street action was seen as evidence that looting was the motivating factor that evening—as though opportunism was the only basis on which Whites would participate in an anti-racist event. But the rally and later events were among the most racially mixed demonstrations to be held in this city—Natives, Latinos/as, and Asians, as well as Blacks and Whites came together in a shared anger at the unapologetic racism of the police and the inadequacies and/or refusal of the justice and political systems to stand against them.

Black Activists Attacked

Though relations between the police and black community have been severely strained, rather than trying to resolve these tensions the police department has been consciously attacking Black activists. It spent at least $500,000 to entrap Dudley Laws, a prominent Black civil rights activist and a leading member of BADC. Laws, charged with conspiracy to smuggle illegal aliens into the US, was subjected to wiretaps and heavy surveillance as twelve cops worked full-time on his case, even as they whined that they needed more money to save Toronto from crime and indecency. The Toronto cops actively participated in the case even though immigration is normally the work of the Mounties. Other Black activists have been directly attacked. A local artist and activist had her arm broken when she was physically assaulted as she was singled out for arrest after an earlier demo. And in a case going back to 1990, when eleven people were arrested after police attacked a demonstration protesting a racist exhibit at the Royal Ontario Museum, Oji Adisa was given ninety days in jail for assault. The judge made it clear that the sentence was related to his role as a leader of the protests.

Some liberal commentators used the fact that more non-Blacks have been shot and/or killed by the police in the last four years to obscure the fact that Blacks, who are only about 10% of the local population, are disproportionately subjected to police violence. All this shows, though, is that along with their racist attitudes there is a major problem with police use of violence, both lethal and non-lethal. Nor is Toronto alone in this problem. Racism and frequent brutality have been documented in the actions of the police in Vancouver, Halifax, and Montréal. Across the country the police beat and oppress Natives, Asians, Blacks, Latinos/as, and poor and working class Whites—a multicultural society offering them plenty of targets for their abuse and ignorance.

The problem goes beyond the prejudices of the police (though they are ignorant fuckers). Multiculturalism has been the official ideology of the Canadian state since the early seventies. The official lie has been that Canada is not a melting pot, but a mosaic where people can come from around the world and maintain their own communities with their own values. But reactionary and conservative elements have never accepted this vision of Canada where immigrants and refugees from the Caribbean, Africa, Asia, and Latin America could become fully functioning members of Canadian society on their own terms. The police, reflecting their historical roots in the British colonial police, see themselves as being the last line of defence in protecting "White" Toronto from these changes. The best way to do this is to marginalize and criminalize anyone who does not fit in. As the children of immigrants discover, skin colour alone can determine whether or not one is considered acceptable.

Social Explosion

All the elements for a social explosion were here: police violence, racism, poverty, corporate greed, conspicuous consumption, political indifference, unfulfilled promises, homelessness, unskilled youth, and racial polarization. But what happened that Monday evening was not just an outpouring of rage and despair in response to deteriorating social and economic conditions. The events took place within a context of increasing political awareness. Although the media, police, and politicians tried to label it as the work of hooligans and thugs, it was clear that their real concern was that it had a conscious element to it that threatened them in a way that other riots that occur with some regularity on Yonge Street, for any number of reasons, do not.

Though police shootings of Blacks has been a primary political focus for the Black community, racism has become a key issue in the schools and universities, among writers and artists, in the women's community, and in the work place. The struggle against racism by people of colour in a country of immigrants, as Canada is, takes a different form than that of the US, where the black and white communities face each other over what seems at times to be an unbridgeable gulf rooted in the centuries of slavery. Immigrants, almost by definition, are optimists. Though there has been a radical leadership, particularly from the Caribbean (and the historic black communities in Ontario and Nova Scotia) that exposes racism in Toronto, the majority of immigrants don't make waves. But it is their children, raised with higher expectations, who run into the institutionalized racism in the schools, the lack of equal access to jobs, and police harassment on the streets. As happened in England in the 1970s, it is these young people who radicalize the fight against racists and racism. Aiding this process is the awareness of and often connection to the struggles of African people in the US, the Caribbean, England, and Africa itself.

It is not just those of African heritage who are resisting racism in Canada. Many other immigrants—South Asians (from Sri Lanka, India, and Pakistan), South East Asians (from Vietnam, Hong Kong, China), Latin Americans, and those from the Middle East—are all discovering the racist reality in Canada. Nor is racism a new phenomenon here. The indigenous people in Toronto have also been struggling for their rights as urban natives, and against the prejudice and racism they face in the city, as part of their historic struggle for self-determination and survival. The African community in Canada, which goes back to the very beginning of non-Native settlement, began in the chains of slavery. There is pride that Canada was a haven for escaped slaves from the US before the American civil war. Little mention is made of the fact that most of these former American slaves chose to return to the US after emancipation, since their conditions here were no better than what they experienced on the other side of the border.

Anger at racism and police violence, and the failure of any level of government to take these issues seriously, motivated many Whites that night along with those people who are directly experiencing that racism. But there were other reasons for the anger as well. Gays and lesbians, who were well represented, were incensed because two days earlier the police had raided a local gay bookstore, seized a lesbian magazine, and laid a charge of obscenity. Women of all races, who also participated in large numbers, have seen ever-increasing levels of violence directed against them, even as a backlash is regularly mounted in the press against the gains that a small number of women have made. Rising levels of poverty and homelessness, along with the loss of tens of thousands of jobs in the recession, have made a mockery of claims that Canada has a "kinder, gentler" form of capitalism. The "business as usual" attitude of the social democratic provincial government in Ontario, elected less than two years ago with hopes that social issues would have political priority, has forced many activists and radicals to reconsider the role of parliamentary politics and the ways in which change will come about.

Over the past several years, a non-parliamentary opposition has strengthened in Canada. In spite of the clever and elaborate schemes of the state to buy people off and incorporate popular struggles, the women's movement, the unions, the gay and lesbian movement, immigrant communities, people of colour, and particularly the native people have gained in momentum and clarity. Much is owed to the courageous armed self-defence of the Mohawk people in 1990 against the army and police threats against their land, for they showed that there were many ways to struggle in honour and principle. In spite of all the difficulties—the struggles against racism, chauvinism, sexism, class distinctions, and homophobia within these movements—there has been a gradual coming together of forces. Issues are no longer considered in isolation from each other. People have been in a process of learning how to give support to each other. It has not been easy, and there is a long way to go, but an emerging culture of resistance offers some possibility of practical unity against the oppressor—a unity which begins as we come to understand that we need not feel threatened by the gains of others.

New Level of Resistance

The mini-uprising that evening offered evidence of a new level of resistance in Toronto. By itself, it momentarily brought about an increase in the attention paid to the issue of racism directed against the Black community. But

photo by Carole Beaulieu

it also showed a new willingness to go outside of the confines of acceptable protest. The militant action had a sense of inevitability, shared by both activists and many ordinary people, given the unresponsiveness of the system to racism and police violence combined with hard economic times. Three days after the riot, twenty-five hundred people attended a rally previously scheduled by the Black Action Defence Committee. The politicians, media, and police had all called for BADC to cancel the event. This show of support, in spite of dire warnings of violence that kept some away, confirmed that the attempts by the authorities to isolate the political elements of the Black community would not work.

As opposition is slowly transforming itself into resistance, the forces of reaction are growing. The racism of the general population is increasing and becoming more open. Skinheads are organizing themselves and are working with the fascist Heritage Front. For a week after the riot, the Police Public Order unit—a riot squad, by another name but with specialized training—patrolled Yonge Street and forced confrontations with young people, arresting several. The campaign against the leaders of BADC continues without let up, blaming them for stirring up trouble even though the official report of the riot confirmed the extent of the racism in Ontario, particularly against Blacks. The media has recently carried scare stories about "Black Muslims" being a threat, with pictures of pigs with machine guns providing "protection" for a trial for people charged with conspiracy to bomb a Sikh temple. Though the connection has never been made clear, the propaganda impact is readily apparent: that Black radicals are inherently dangerous. But, as always, it is those who seek to maintain the status quo at all costs who are endangering social peace. By refusing to address the serious social issues with which we are being confronted, they will only add fuel to the fires to come.

PRISON: The Ultimate commodity

In a world where everything is bought and sold—including, and especially, our lives—that even prisons have become a kind of ultimate commodity is no surprise. Only by abolishing money and killing the law of value can we start to abolish the nightmare, and empty the prisons once and for all.

art by Peter Sandmark

ROY GLAREMIN

WORD FROM THE PRISONS, 1992

At first I thought it would be easy to describe the current state of programs and resources for prisoners in Canadian federal prisons. Having started to do that two weeks ago, and still being somewhat unsure of how best to proceed, I have changed my mind. The difficulty I am having lies with the fact that the Correctional Service of Canada (CSC) is moving forward and backward at the same time. The result is that conditions in federal prisons are in a state of flux.

I started my sentence in 1977, the same year the government appointed a parliamentary sub-committee to investigate the then seriously troubled prison system. For six years, beginning with the infamous Kingston Riot in 1971, Canadian prisons had been upset by work strikes, full-scale smash-ups, and hostage-taking incidents. Goon squads were running amok, beating and gassing prisoners routinely, without justification. The government's intervention marked the beginning of reform within the prison system, reform that continues today, fifteen years later.

Past practices and their consequences proved to be considerable obstacles to that reform, especially in the beginning. Past hiring practices, for example, had allowed relatively uneducated and ill-adjusted people into the CSC. The worst of these ill-adjusted CSC employees made all attempts at reform difficult. The idea that prisoners have rights was not only objectionable to many frontline uniformed staff, but also to some of their supervisors and to some managers higher up in the chain of command. This was apparent during the years of open hostility, between 1971 and 1977. Though confrontational thinking had become entrenched throughout the system, reforms began to take place nonetheless.

One of the first reforms concerned the use of excessive force. Prison wardens became accountable for every cannister of tear gas in prison armories. This produced an immediate and welcome change for prisoners, especially for those in maximum and super-maximum security facilities, where most of the incidents involving the excessive use of gas had taken place. The change was so sudden that many men who started their sentences only a year or two before me have, over the years, been surprised to find out that I have never been gassed, even though I spent my first three and a half years in one seg (segregation) unit or another. This reminds me that the CSC's use of long-term segregation to control "rebels" was likewise criticized and curtailed, though that curtailment was much slower in coming than that which restricted the use of gas.

Along with long-term segregation, the CSC routinely used involuntary transfers ("kidnappings") to control prison populations. Rebellious behaviour (which in 1977 would have included, among more serious acts of rebellion, arguing with staff, complaining, and attempting to contact Members of Parliament or the media) was often dealt with by simply kidnapping the "rebellious" prisoners and shipping them off to other parts of the country. The relatively new *Canadian Charter of Rights and Freedoms*, which came into effect in 1982, "helped" the CSC reform its policy governing involuntary transfers.

Several years ago the Federal Court began to order the CSC to reverse involuntary transfers where they were considered punitive, in that prisoners were separated from their families and/or other community contacts, or placed in higher security, and where the CSC could not show sufficient cause for the use of that punitive measure. As a result, the CSC is now quite careful in executing involuntary transfers.

In the seventies and eighties, the CSC operated under relatively loose financial constraints, which made reform easier. In 1980, the Private Family Visiting Program was introduced. It gave federal prisoners seventy-two hours alone with their families in special housing units within each prison every six to sixteen weeks, depending on facilities and the demands placed on them. Last year the criteria used t0 screen visitors were changed to allow partners of prisoners access to the program, even if the partnership is not recognized in law. University programs were also introduced in 1980. These programs see professors teaching classes inside.

Prisoners now have free and direct access to the media, something few people would have thought possible in 1977. "Warden's Courts" are now run by "Independent Chairpersons", who are admittedly paid by the CSC but who are able and increasingly willing to act in a truly independent fashion. Prisoners now have the right to legal representation on all internal disciplinary charges except those stated as "minor". Telephones specifically for the use of prisoners are now located in every cell block. Prisoners are now asked to evaluate recommendations for changes in CSC policies. Again, even if the opinions of prisoners in this regard carry only minimum weight, it would have been considered lunacy even to ask prisoners for their opinions on such matters fifteen years ago.

The reform the CSC has been undergoing is genuine, its effects are significant and far-reaching, and it would, in my opinion, not be overstating the case to say that the CSC has striven to become professional and publicly accountable; which makes recent changes that much more regrettable.

The current tough economic times are having strongly adverse effects on the CSC. Prison populations have already increased far beyond what were supposed to be their maximum sizes, and they are continuing to increase. Staff and post cuts within prisons have left fewer staff to manage these growing populations, and resources for prisoners are shrinking. More prisoners are double-bunked than have ever been before. The fact that this double-bunking has been accompanied by a *decrease* in facilities and resources means that the negative effects of overcrowding (increased rates for deaths, suicides, illness complaints, disciplinary offences and psychiatric commitments, among others) will soon be, or are already being experienced.

The crowding problem will get worse as the current trend toward making prisoners serve more of their sentences before being released becomes further entrenched. Legislation and policies directed at that goal have recently been either tabled, as in the case of the government's Bill C-36, or effected, as has been the National Parole Board (NPB) policy of "tightening up" on conditional release programs. Even among optimists, there is little hope that things will get better in the foreseeable future.

What is the current state of programs and resources for Canada's federal prisoners? It had been very good, but it is deteriorating quickly. In Collins Bay Institution, a medium security prison in Ontario where I am, approximately 40% of the prisoners are double-bunked. Eight years ago no one was double-bunked here. The university program is in danger of being scrapped completely. For almost two years the prison's gym and yard have not been open simultaneously, a result of staff and post cuts. There are no longer enough seats in the dining hall, forcing many prisoners to perch on seats to eat, while keeping one eye on the door, ready to switch seats when those whose seats they are in show up to eat. Disputes over seats are becoming more frequent and have already led to several fights. When the new seg unit opens this year, the range now being used for seg will become part of the population, increasing the population by a further 10% in the process.

More prisoners are now unemployed than have ever been before. Coupled with huge increases in the tax prisoners now pay on tobacco products (a carton of cigarettes has increased in price from $4.50 to $35.00 in the past ten years as a direct result of taxation, while prisoners' pay has increased $.25 per day during the same period), the increased unemployment has caused an increase in incidents of theft from cells and in "muscling". In short, an increasing number of prisoners are competing for decreasing resources, which is causing problems throughout the prison.

The overcrowding problem is clearly undermining the reforms of the past fifteen years. If the mechanisms governing the release of prisoners approaching the end of their sentences are not adjusted to allow those prisoners to be released sooner to make room for prisoners beginning their sentences, which appears unlikely in today's political climate, then Canada's federal prisons will soon experience a different kind of trouble than that of the seventies, though the effects may be similar. Prisons in many US states and in England have given us previews of what to expect.

Unfortunately, my perception is not distorted, which is my way of saying that the Solicitor General of Canada along with the Justice Minister and CSC's managers and the Union of Solicitor General's Employees and all informed outside observers know where the road the CSC is on leads to. From where I am at the moment, things do not look good.

FRANÇOIS PÉRALDI
PSYCHIATRY OR PSYCHOANALYSIS?

One of the more galling charges addressed to psychoanalysis—as much by certain leftist intellectuals, whom we don't confuse with leftist militants so great is the distance separating them (in spite of it not being very fashionable today to call oneself a leftist), as by professionals of the new pan-psychiatry (psychologists, social workers, psychiatric nurses, therapists of all kinds; even a fair number of psychoanalysts, especially in the English Section of the Canadian Society of Psychoanalysis, all of them under the thumb of psychiatry and its administration of mental health)—is that psychoanalysis is only interested in the individual, and by this fact alone can not be thought of as a science. Those making this accusation continue to believe blindly that there is no science except that of the general. Meanwhile, today more urgently than ever, the question of a science of particularity is being posed. Especially, for example, in language studies: the possibility of a science of the word, linguistics being the science of language. For some with bourgeois ideology, in the Marxist sense of ideology (for us the dismantling of the socialist republics does not invalidate the pertinence of the Marxist critique of capitalist societies, quite the contrary), and, according to others with practices too specific to be either economically viable or sufficiently effective, this "outrageous" individualism would situate psychoanalysis in the subjection of people to the Norm required for their maximal exploitation by our capitalist system. A Norm that, not without a profound hypocrisy, the psychiatrists and even certain psychoanalysts unhesitatingly call "normal personality structure", and which they then consider the goal of any possible cure, whether psychiatric, psychological, or even so-called psychoanalytical. These therapists are manifesting a naïveté, whether from cynicism or imbecility. But, surely this attitude and these ideas also demonstrate, on the part of those who profess them, a total absence of political reflection about their own practice—as if politics were a domain totally foreign to therapy, whatever the latter's aims and means.

This reproach of individualism very rarely assumes the status of a full-fledged, formal critique. It is based either on a confusion, or on an ideological phenomenon in expansion in advanced capitalist societies that I would like to call "social alexia".

Most of those who condemn "psychoanalysis" confuse the use to which it is put, here in Québec for example, with the theoretical practice legitimately associated with the name. If it appears that psychoanalytical practice is, by the admission of psychoanalysts themselves, elitist (through its cost, and its ideological and cultural valorization—media-created image rather than actual fact, in any case), normative (that is to say psychologizing and aiming at a complete adaptation to bourgeois norms), and more or less reduced to being only a variation of psychiatric therapies, then this is something to be upset about—but upset with the psychiatrists themselves, and the associations and institutions they have generated.

"Do you still believe in psychoanalysis?", a pundit of the Canadian Society of Psychoanalysis once asked me, half-joking, half-serious. "Myself, I only use it for listening to the free-associations of patients after an insulin coma or electroshock therapy session." Against the express wishes of Freud himself, these psychiatric-psychoanalysts have just about succeeded in reducing practical-theoretical psychoanalysis to a completely degenerate form, a vulgar practical ideology[1], which would be very aptly named *psychoanalysm*. Although there still remain a few cores of resistance to this degradation[2], it would be enough to read the chapter, happily a short one, that Ellenberger devotes to the history of psychiatry in a relatively recent work, *Précis of Psychiatric Practice* (1981), to get an idea of what is meant in the milieu of Canadian psychiatry today by the sacrosanct term of "scientific method" in the context of the history of science. Ellenberger restricts himself to an account of the continuous and linear development of history, of "facts" which establish a so-called "progress" of psychiatry from its origins in Ancient Greece through the inevitable "medieval obscurantism" to the return to the authorities of antiquity before the coming of Reason, which in its turn was a prelude to the positivist technism of the 19th century that finally culminates in the monstrous expansion of supposedly multi-disciplinary pan-psychiatry—a currently fashionable term that is meant to suggest a "bio-psycho-social" approach to man. Unfortunately for this pretty historical fresco of psychiatry, no one today, (at least) since the scientific revolution of the early 20th century, Hegel's studies of history, and, more recently those of Alexandre Koyré (1962, 1968) and Gaston Bachelard (1973) on the history of science, could advocate this view without assuming at the same time a reactionary position—opting for a "continuist" vision of history which would really offer only "the permanent spectacle, without discontinuity, of the human mind working with science." Quite the contrary. Since the efforts of Marx (after Hegel) on historical determinism, and those of Koyré, Bachelard (already mentioned), Canguilhem (1966, 1968), and even of Thomas Kuhn (1962), history, and in particular the history of human knowledge, seems much more today like a series of areas and periods separated from each other by deep "schisms" or "revolutions", which traverse not only the field of economics and relations of force between social classes, but also scientific territories, radically pitting them against each other as well as against the ideologies and philosophies that surround them. On either side of these divisions, one does not think better or worse, but differently, at the same time as ancient, deeply rooted conceptions, no matter how obsolete, endure and are resistant to change.

By applying this discontinuous conception of history, we can denounce the various forms of "recuperation" and reductionism that ceaselessly work against the "Freudian Revolution" (in this *Précis* of Ellenberger's), especially whenever he presents psychoanalysis as a branch of psychiatry, in the name of the continuity of the history of science, culture, and "progress". We may judge by the following:

> *It was also at the beginning of the century that Sigmund Freud elaborated his system of 'dynamic psychiatry'[sic], psychoanalysis.... Let's say only that it was at the starting point of a vast expansion of dynamic psychiatry as much through itself as through its dissidents, Alfred Adler and Carl Gustav Jung, who developed, each on his own, a dynamic original system that differed radically from psychoanalysis. These two systems as well as psychoanalysis far surpass the traditional limits of psychiatry, so that here we find manifesting itself a new tendency that we may call 'psychiatric explosion'.*

Reading the correspondence of Freud and Jung, we can't miss being struck by the insistence with which Jung justifies himself for watering down and reducing to vague notions the key concepts elaborated by Freud, through establishing compromises with the psychiatric establishment, or because of a desire for respectability, or even for more obscure ideological motives that were to make Jung more or less favorable to the great fascist movements of his time. Reading these letters it seems understandable that friendship and collaboration between these two would not continue, given the rigor of Freud's thought. Neither does it make any sense to think of Adler's and Jung's work, for example, or that of Janov, Rogers, Hartman, even Brenner or Arlow, in terms of original discoveries or of progress. These are all, rather, various forms of deviationism and reductionism that attached themselves to the Freudian insights, trying, more or less openly, to bring them into line with pre-psychoanalytic conceptions. Ellenberger ignores or pretends to ignore that the Freudian discovery required certain radical demarcations and breaks with the discourses that preceded it—breaks that many are not capable of effecting or maintaining, either through intellectual weakness or through considerations of respectability in the medical community, one of the most conservative in existence.

It would be the purest of illusions to think that what Ellenberger calls the psychiatric explosion could have anything in common with the socialist revolution in the 19th and 20th centuries. What he calls revolution is rather the rise of psychiatric imperialism in cultural areas (biology, sociology, psychoanalysis), whose epistemological, logical, and political bases are never analyzed, questioned, or even compared.

Speaking of "dynamic psychiatry" in reference to Freud is simply falsehood. An allegation of this sort is of the same kind as that announcing the death of Jacques Lacan in *Le Devoir* as "a great loss for French psychiatry!" This is not only false, but also dishonest, since it appears that anyone saying such things did not even take the trouble to read Freud. Or Lacan either, since the latter, at all events, is reputed to be unreadable. We can quote Freud against Ellenberger and his colleagues in defence of Theodor Reik against North American psychiatrists, the same who today control the International Psychoanalytic Association and its offshoots.

"What ill wind drove you to America? You should have realized how kindly non-medical analysts would be welcomed by our colleagues for whom psycho-analysis is merely the servant of psychiatry. Couldn't you have stayed in Holland any longer? Naturally I would be happy to write any certificate that would be useful for you. But I doubt really that it would be of much help to you. Where over there is there an institution interested in supporting the continuation of our research?"

The letter I've just quoted from is dated July 3, 1938. And so, when he asks "what institution is interested in pursuing" the work of psychoanalysis in North America, clearly hinting that there is none, this question is all the more cruel since the New York Psychoanalytic Society, as well as the American Psychoan-alytic Association, had been founded 26 years before, in 1911. Freud's very sus-picious attitude about the "extraordinary diffusion of psychoanalysis" in North America, and in particular in the psychiatry that it has effectively "exploded", is founded precisely on the notion that what is disseminated by psychiatrists under the name of "Freud's dynamic psychiatry" has really nothing to do with psycho-analytic research as its inventor, near death, was still able to discern. Freud's disillusion with and his rejection of America were greatly justified when, after his passing, the American Psychoanalytic Association wound up investing and controlling the organism that Freud had created to avert for psychoanalysis in North America the fate of the International Psychoanalytic Association. This is why I can't read without amusement the claim by Dufresene and Saucier (1981) that the only psychoanalysts are those accredited by a Society belonging to the International Association. The latter is no more than a puppet in the hands of the American Psychoanalytic Association, disavowed by Freud!

When you've spent some time in the world of psychiatric institutions, the realization is inescapable that if psychoanalysis is moribund—supposing it's not already dead—this responsibility belongs to those whose job it was to keep it alive; to maintain the subversive virulence it owes to its very special status in the scientific field (in the same way as Marxism) of being a theoretical practice rather than a "science", in the obsolete meaning that psychiatrists and psychol-ogists still assign to this term.

We must admit, alas, that the linguistic, anthropological, social-economic, even mythological and literary formation that Freud demanded for all analysts (never recommending medical training, whose only purpose, as he reiterates at the beginning of his professional life, was to make a living), is totally missing in most. And this real cultural vacuum is, as it must be, inevitably filled up, taken over by the enormous mass of ideological and class prejudice. In Québec, just like everywhere else, most psychoanalysts belong to the bourgeois and petit-bourgeois classes, which becomes very obvious when, as happens, they take positions on issues. (I can't help thinking here of the only scientific meeting ever to fill the auditorium of the Psychoanalytic Society of Montréal, which occurred a few years ago—the subject under debate was recourses to law when patients fail to pay!)

So let's out with it: there's nothing to expect from psychoanalytic institutions but the death of psychoanalysis, sooner or later. The symptoms of its agony can be detected in peripheral ways:

> 1) *The issue of dissemination and, in Europe at least, the State's control over its training institutions;*
> 2) *The medical and psychological reductiveness of its discourse;*
> 3) *Its metamorphosis into a toy of the media;*
> 4) *The growing disaffection of young intellectuals toward its training institutes (especially in the United States);*
> 5) *The muting of all creativity in its institutes and associations, as well as in its official publications overall;*
> 6) *This muting of creativity is nothing else than the result of the adulteration, if not pure mutilation of Freud's text, which constitutes the basis of psychoanalysis, by the "didacts" who have assumed charge of it.*

The social alexia I spoke of consists simply in the fact that, in the words of Stéphane Mallarmé answering to the charge of obscurity made by contemporary literary critics in their assault on poetry, "our contemporaries don't know how to read." Most of the opinions, positions, controversies, petitions, and platforms having to do with Freud's texts could be suitably answered in the same fashion.

For example, those who say that psychoanalysis only concerns individuals are saying nothing sensible about theoretical psychoanalytical practice, but show merely that they haven't even read their Freud. By "reading Freud" we mean: isolating from the very complex play of metaphors (physical, neurological, biological, literary, mythological, etc.) paradoxes, contradictions, discursive discontinuities, signs proper to the subject of the enunciation; lines of force structuring this kind of thought around certain key terms—intangible kernels that, more than concepts, are real "fundamental statements" (*Grundworte*)[3], supporting pillars for a new way of thinking about man. Not only concepts, but ones that uncover unexplored territories of the Real, concepts that bring out new facts, or facts already known under another light, concepts which announce the non-thought.

This is the work that Jean Imbeault has been pursuing for years, which led him to publish *The Event and the Unconscious* (1990). It's true also that the scientific revolution of the beginning of the century had forced a reversal of positivistic and objectifying positions, the kind which inclined Claude Bernard to say that before the truth of facts, theory must come second—which one of the psychiatrists mentioned in the *Précis* didn't miss quoting. But they're wrong, both of them, Bernard and the fact-celebrating psychiatrist. With Freud, as in contemporary physics, as in François Jacob's biology as it is introduced so remarkably in the context of changes in his epistemological positions in *The Game of Possibles* (and not that of biologizing psychiatrists, even of Le Vay with his sexual nodule), as with Marx, theory allows us to separate ourselves from the paralyzing terrorism of facts, it allows for their displacement. With theory the new scientific spirit flies highest when the scientist is able to realize, against the tormenting empiricism of common sense, that before being a fact the physical phenomenon is an equation. Psychoanalysis is born not from psychopathology, but from studies on psychopathology, sudden theoretical insights that Freud prudently called "speculations", and within which he created the structure of the unconscious subject. A structure that is *only* theoretical, and which is present as early as 1895 in the letters to Fliess, as well as in the *Draft for a Scientific Psychology*. A purely theoretical structure, without which neither *The Interpretation of Dreams* nor *The Psychopathology of Everyday Life* would ever have seen the day, nor the structure itself of psychoanalytic theory. We can never repeat it often enough: the unconscious is a concept.

There is nothing like this structure anywhere in the varied concepts which—since Plato, if one goes back to the Greeks; since Descartes, if one wants to be more rigorous—the human sciences have created about the subject. This is a structure which appeared, curiously, almost simultaneously (therefore at a very special moment in history, that of the 19th century revolutions) in Marx, Nietzsche, and Freud. This new way of thinking about man, this "new scientific spirit", as Bachelard called it, is totally foreign to the positivist, empiricist rationalism which reigns supreme in psychiatry and psychology today, and which, after having been essential at a certain moment of scientific development in the Age of Enlightenment, has now outlived its usefulness and is, in fact, one of the most serious obstacles to the formation of the new scientific spirit, therefore of psychoanalysis.

This social alexia that we've been concerned with is demonstrable along two axes:

1) the reduction of fundamental statements to simple medical or psychological notions, or even to common sense;

2) the suppression, the erasure pure and simple, of a certain number of these fundamental statements (which are meaningful only in the sense that they are themselves part of a system which works in such a way that they can only act together in the system), which are very resistant to reduction.

Here I am thinking in particular of the death drives (*Todes Triebe*) that Jean Laplanche, surely a better wine grower than a theorist of psychoanalysis, can just sweep away with a brush of the hand, declaring flatly in the early chapters of his course on *Anguish in Freudian Theory* (1980), that unlike Freud he thought that the drives can be none other than sexual. While Freud, evidently for theoretical reasons more fundamental than those of Laplanche, maintained these death drives at the heart of his theoretical elaboration, against all obstacles from their introduction in 1923 in *The Ego and the Id* until his death. (I suppose Laplanche severs in this way the Gordian knot they constitute in the theory, but by simplifying things in this manner he participates very cheerfully in the murder of analysis and in the attempts that others shared in their time [1963-64], of destroying the teaching of Jacques Lacan, whom they not only wanted to exclude from the French Psychoanalytical Society but also to reduce to silence.)

Lacan showed us, in so many ways in teaching us how to read Freud, that psychoanalysis is not a theory of the individual, whether healthy or not, but the science of man as subject, that is as a speaking being; and from this comes his relationship with the world, with others, and with himself unlike that of any other [being] and irreducible to his animality or even his organicity. All through the course of the development of his thinking Freud orients himself ever more closely toward a social and collective conception of the subject. And if it is never fully developed in his works, it is nevertheless present from the time of *Totem and Taboo*, through *Group Psychology and the Analysis of the Ego*, *The Future of an Illusion*, to *The Discontents of Civilization*, from 1913 to 1929, where certain references can be found, along with allusions and incidental remarks that bring psychoanalysis close to that other great theoretical practice, Marxism.

Louis Althusser, great reader of Marx, showed very clearly that there is no incompatibility between Marxist and psychoanalytical theoretical practices. Psychoanalysis and Marxism unfold in the same epistemological area, whose limits they have helped to set, and whose space they have enlarged. We cannot with impunity condemn these two great theoretical practices of our time under the pretext that certain psychoanalysts, even certain Marxists, through their involvement with institutions that are more or less connected with the state (hospitals, universities, etc.), have shown themselves incapable of carrying through all ideological and epistemological breaks that psychoanalysis and Marxism respectively require from the disciplines and the practical ideologies and the philosophies that accompany them like ambiguous fairies from their very beginnings. From having failed to make these breaks, they've made themselves into agents of the recuperation and reduction of psychoanalysis and Marxism in and by the ruling ideology and its practical forms. Such as, for example, psychology and psychiatry, even a bio-psychosocial psychiatry.

When certain psychologists define psychology by its methodology, that is to say by the entire arsenal of sample groups, the control of falsifications, specimens, etc., and when they make this methodology the criterion of all science, they are manifesting a very limited and dated understanding of science. We could counter them with the example of physics, which one cannot deny is a science and yet which does not at all define itself in terms of its method, but by its object and its ways of theorizing this object. When they cook up their little schemes, psychologists are only applying the verification modes of a presupposed body of knowledge. In other words they invent nothing except what they know already to be there. Not because it is really there, but because it is supposed to be. This "supposed to be" is not an ethical thing but belongs instead to a normative and "Norm-enforcing" vision of the world.

The psychoanalytic cure in this *Précis,* which we're using as an example, is presented to us totally as a passage from one state of being to another. Just as if the authors felt that they had to reassure their psychiatric colleagues on the good moral standing, whatever its "scientific" failings, of this slightly daffy cousin. For instance, they describe a man who is suffering from all kinds of symptoms that are described in the good old traditional psychiatric way. A very different kind of relation, however, is established in analysis than with the traditional psychiatrist or psychologist, since the basis of the relation to the analyst is the transference, an activation of the unconscious but one which seems to be reduced here to the reactivation of ancient ways of relating to papa and mama. What seems very strange indeed in the story of this sample cure is that it would have been enough for this man to have rediscovered, thanks to his memories as well as to judicious interpretations and in the transference, these forgotten but repressed relational modes—which obliged him to an exhausting repetition of erratic behaviour in order for his self, which is very close to the bourgeois norm, to control the incorrigible and wild child he was in reality or in fantasy, with the result that he be able to lead a life suitable for the bourgeois world. Conditioning wasn't really the effective factor, but something much more pernicious which the authors gave us a glimpse of at the conclusion of the cure: an identification with the strong self of the analyst whom the analyzand leaves with a kind of ambivalent gratitude, certainly, but the way one leaves a "spiritual father" [*sic*]. I regret it, but I must confess that I know no analyst, and God knows I know a few, that I would consider as a "spiritual father", Lacan least of all. And if the "identification with the self of the analyst" must end the cure, I see no difference between this end of analysis and behavioural therapy of the lowest sort: the alienation of the self of the subject by way of a behavioural norm, in the most abysmal ignorance of what it means for him to be a subject.

The grounding statement of transference must be understood, for example, along with the entirely new problematic of the subject (that is to say, as we've been explaining, man in his rapport with language, the use he puts it to and which structures him in return), through the elaboration of a system of concept-questions:

> *Concept-questions that in psychoanalysis we should never take for concept-responses: to say, and so to allow us to refer by means of a simple indication to this paradigm: that the dream has a meaning, or it fulfils an unconscious, sexual, infantile desire to open research rather than close a question; research that should become more specific in terms of each case as a function of all cases, rather than a temporarily posed question whose resolution would apply to some a certain number of these cases (Schotte, 1964).*

Unlike psychology and psychiatry (even the "psychoanalytical" sort), psychoanalysis does not produce through its methods and its techniques the passage from a state #1 (for example: neurotic or sick) to a state #2 (normal or cured). It opens up for the subject who engages in the analytical experience, and becomes by this fact an analyst, an unlimited future space. It reopens a space of questions, of desires effectively inscribed in the history of the subject, and more exactly, in his childhood narrative. Where he was denied, repressed, even foreclosed, this reopened space restores to him a status of subject-in-process, plural subject, infinitely malleable and not *only* suited to the bourgeois order— provided he hasn't been closed off by a "normalizing" response and interpretation, a "you must", which would subject him again (if only by way of identification) to a factitious unity: a state whose blind stability facilitates the exploitation he is both victim and agent of in our capitalist system.

Transference is what allows the reopening of what had been repressed, closed or foreclosed, and had forced the subject into repetition. Rather than a space of questions and desires which would always lead to the notion of a radical lack [in the subject], we would say that transference in psychoanalysis is more on the order of recognition. Instead of the questions, "But what's wrong with me, Doctor? What am I?" that a specialist would always readily answer: "a neurosis", or an "incurable schizophrenic", there should be substituted a "Who am I?"—which means "What mélange of drives determines my status, my movement as subject, and my inscription in a process that transcends me (and not an order which subjugates me)?"

In other words, transference, so essential to revealing the structure of the subject, is not the simple displacement onto the analyst of feeling lived by the subject in his early infancy regarding his parents, feelings repressed then reactivated in the patient-therapist relationship (which would constitute rather a psychologizing definition). Transference is rather the "activation of the unconscious"[4], insofar as this activation constitutes, properly speaking, the psychoanalytic relation. Because there is a transference to be recognized, psychoanalysis is possible. Because transference is recognized as activation, unmasking of an unconscious which exists only by reason of its having been repressed, there can be analysis. That this discovery is effected in the form of a metaphorical recognition of affective situations previously lived through in the oedipal space of the family matters little. As long as these familial metaphors are taken to be veritable dramatic productions, theatrical and theatre-creating representations of a subject swept by a determinism of drives that are not reducible to trivial family drives. Cute little sexual emotions, to which Laplanche would reduce the drives, are actually concealers of them, and in fact represent, "something serious and formidable that we should approach with circumspection." (Freud)

Through his silence, his sustained attention equal to the use that the analyzand is making of language, the analyst favors the slow emergence of a word at once plural and questioning. A full, true word of the subject, a "Who am I?" modulated in a thousand possible ways to which—contrary to the psychologist, to the normalizing psychologist, doctor or specialist who already knows the answer—he will only respond with a "*che vuoi?*" "What do you want?", also modulated in a thousand ways; from an inarticulate grumble to the most over-refined language in which he finds himself trapped in spite of himself, but that he will only utter in order to sustain the tension of the questioning. Through the forcing of the analyzand's discourse outside the area of an immediate under-standing, of a capture by meaning, so that the subject's self (the images that he has fashioned of himself through the play of successive specular identifications that have, one after another, roused his loves and hates) crumbles before the continually changing yet immutable mirror which never reflects the same image of himself. Finally, the subject of the unconscious emerges, reversing and oppos-ing all defence mechanisms of the self.

We term transference the very possibility of this emergence, of this coming of an unconscious subject "which doesn't appear," as Serge Leclaire and Jean Laplanche (in 1963, when he knew better) wrote, "in the first or third person but in person." This could be manifested by the patient's making an ugly sound like a "Wutze" [pig], lacerating suddenly the polite and well organized talk of his analyst. An insult that conveys all the contained, repressed violence, which by this fact constitutes him as subject of the unconscious now announcing through its incongruity his non-affiliation with the enunciations that surrounded the apparition. Transference is constructed from the very irrepressibility of these signifiers which, in spite of the colossal force of the repressive mechanisms, have produced psychoanalysis in the same way as they have created the human subject in process.

This properly Freudian concept of transference has really nothing in common with the patronizing lucubration of the psychoanalyst who sees transference only in terms of his own position as father or mother substitute, and so risks end-ing up believing in the virtues of generosity, like Sacha Nacht (1963); or, scarcely better, believing in his role as object of identification for his patients. If, stretch-ing things, a transference can commence in this manner, it must lead the sub-ject far past an appreciation of his father and his mother, and even his psychoanalyst in the scene of his little imaginary and personal theatre; embarked "on the road that leads nowhere" of psychoanalysis, as Freud was to formulate it in one of his great texts: *Analysis Terminable and Interminable*. If the analyst answers the question of love, of death, or of will to power (the great trilogy of drives) it's not in order to reveal to the subject how much he has loved (and/or hated) his mother and/or his father, but how he loves, period, even loves to death.

Although we may establish quickly enough that the patient loves his psy-choanalyst (while he sometimes might say that he's surprised not to feel this wild love with which he thought that every patient idolizes his analyst, but rather a sort of vague indifference) as he loved or believed he loved his mother, his father, etc., it remains to be seen, and it's from that moment that the transference opens on "the deep and formidable space of the drives": how he loves. That is to say which knots, which combination of drives that constituted him as subject, obliged his mother, but it could have been anybody else as well, to play this role or occupy the kind of place (like a pawn in chess or the signifier in the word) that the psychoanalyst now occupies, and that others have filled in turn or simultaneously.

In fact a considerable advance was made by Freud (1914) beyond the familialism where he was floundering when he realized that the status of the subject could be developed much more effectively with the introduction of narcissism. The subject's first love object is not (as for Konrad Lorenz's little goslings) the first object to come along that noticed him, as some like to think. In fact, he would have reasons to scorn this first object, generally his mother, since she's the one who forced him to renounce autoerotic, then primitive immediate gratifications of earliest childhood (which would have satisfied Lorenz's goslings)—to substitute for them the deferred satisfactions of the symbolic order; that is to say mediated by language (not at all in the style of the little cooings that united Lorenz to his goslings).

The subject's first love is himself. And it's really remarkable that this is the discovery, paradoxically, which forced Freud to orient himself more and more decisively toward an understanding of man, not as individual subject but as social subject. From the introduction of narcissism into his theory, he begins to replace the individual objective instances—father, mother, etc.—with purely social ones that are going to trap the subject, subjugating him and participating in the mechanisms of repression, guilt, and moral conscience that make of him this intellectual stew that we meet just about everywhere today: a conformist copy, clone of modern times. These social instances are the ideal self, the ideal of the self and the superego. They are explicitly described by Freud as the result of the interiorization by the subject of alienating and socially repressive instances. This interiorization is accomplished by certain mechanisms of subjugation: identification, idealization, and sublimation.

When Freud indicates at the beginning of *Group Psychology and Ego Analysis*, where these concepts are developed, that there is no difference between the subject's structure as revealed by analysis of the individual and how it appears in groups, his point is not that groups are analogous to individuals, but that the traditional opposition of individual and society is not pertinent to psychoanalysis (no more, furthermore, than for Marxism) in the framework of a rigorous development of the status of the subject. He puts an entirely different opposition in its place, that of narcissism and social ideal. If the subject defines himself in his rapport with language and the use he makes of it, which in turn structures him, it would be absurd to think (unless we reduce language to a behaviour like any other) that Freud situates the status of the subject and the problem of his subjugation in any other than social terms.

From this point of view the unconscious subject appears as repressed, bound by a self (origin of repression) which is nothing else than the result of the interiorization, the imaginary identification with objects (possibly the father and/or the mother) which are surely not recognized for what they are effectively but for what is said about them, and what they say about themselves and others to the child. Furthermore, well before being able to be subjects in the psychoanalytic sense of the term (do they ever become that really?) they are, first of all, social agents, of a social nature articulated by extremely diversified Apparatuses of Power.[5] A society whose structure had certainly been studied more by Marx than by Freud, but which Freud all the same understood perfectly (despite the still current prevailing opinion) in the sense that it could be comprehended in no other way than in function of the way it guaranteed the distribution of wealth and organized the rapports of production. Looked at this way, the society in which he himself lived and in which we live ourselves, the capitalist society, was characterized by so extreme a system of exploitation of the masses, he remarks incidentally, that such a society has no right to exist. Its practices certainly justify the revolution of the working masses.

How can we be so blind as not to recognize in these incidental remarks that are strewn through *The Future of an Illusion* and also *Civilization and its Discontents*, points of a possible and necessary articulation of psychoanalysis with Marxism?

Therefore, in transference it is not only the determinisms of the drives which in their articulation with the structures and fundamental elements of the language define the subject (Péraldi, 1978), and are activated and eventually heard (or in the best of cases, understood), but equally the ensemble of instances that participated in the subject's alienation and result from the interiorization of social instances of repression mediated by the agents of the Apparatuses of Power (father or mother of the family, school teacher, parish priest, family doctor, etc.), whose function of agent, willingly or not, knowingly or not, is over-determined by their affiliation with whatever institutions divide up the social field—whether familial, scholarly, parish, or medical institution... The institution may be defined for the moment as a coded social grouping which functions according to certain norms and pursues certain specific goals of encoding the subjects that are submitted to it: oedipal encoding of children in the family, scriptural and professional encoding of students in the educational institution, ideological-moral encoding in the church, etc.

When Freud described the ideal of the self as, on the one hand a sort of summary and composite model, "a character, very hastily sketched," as Schreber called it, in the name of which the self represses the unconscious subject and with which it attempts to identify by way of the ideal self; and on the other hand, a result of identification with the father, he was not thinking of the real father but of the more or less mythical one. In the image of the father, such as in its discourse, the familial institution reproduces incessantly, from generation to generation, so as to keep it within the limits of the oedipal myth. In this sense the ideal of the self is a pure ideological fiction. For it takes all the menacing violence of the superego which results from the interiorization of threats of castration, also social in origin (which Freud [1913] renders more or less accurately with his myth of the primitive horde), to force the self to renounce not only gratifying but even recognizing the drive-expressing rumblings of the unconscious subject in favor of an alienating identification of the ideal of the self.

Furthermore, this ideal of the self does not exist in order to lift the subject above his native mediocrity and incline him by means of this renunciation, as well as through sublimation of his drives, to achieve great things, as Freud might have thought to be the case in a complacent moment. But rather to gratify the narcissistic structure of his desire in offering him an idealized image of himself (the ideal self) in place of what he really was (a divided subject). And to force him into behavioural forms and a world of ideological representations whose only goal is to accomplish the unjust purpose proper to our society of the exploitation of the masses.

This structure of the alienation of the subject by the self, as reflected in the ideological puppets, which are all forms of the ideal of the self (the good father, mother, worker, citizen, doctor, etc.) is what the psychoanalyst's job is to analyze, that is to say render accessible, through his presence to the subject in transference, much more than through his "interpretations", so as to loosen the blocks, repressions, defences, and the ensemble of illusions which comprise the ideal of the self as well as his ideal self, and which alienate him in various ways and diverse forms. Not to hand him over to some Norm, but on the contrary, so that the infinite path of futurity and change opens up for him. Even if this be the transformation of the world anticipated by Marx, but in which the disillusioned Freud hardly dared to believe.

If it seems that this Freudian conception of the subject goes a little too far in the direction of the social, this is because psychoanalysis has not been able to connect with, until now, a biology which could account for what Freud called the drives. That is to say, a biology whose epistemological principles would be more or less consistant with those of psychoanalysis and Marxism. A biology that would have broken equally with the positivist kind that we can see prominently in the organicist, even geneticist conceptions of psychiatry. This is not the place to undertake a rigorous critique of the use that is currently made by psychiatry of its hypotheses on the hereditary character of certain "mental illnesses", an example of which the *Précis* offers us. The interested reader may be referred to the chapter devoted to these questions, but I'll limit myself here to citing someone who, while maybe not one of the pundits of the Canadian College of Medicine, has all the same received for his work the recognition of The Nobel Prize in Medicine: François Jacob, who published a little book (1981) which is very relevant in that it suggests an idea that the authors of the *Précis* would do well to think over. Criticizing what seemed to him to be the extreme of biological reductionism, i.e. the hereditary character of the IQ, Jacob expresses a biologist's surprise over all attempts at quantification of intelligence and of the very diverse, circumstantial aspects of its function.

"In fact," he concludes, "biology has little to say presently on human behaviour and on the genetic components of mental aptitudes. The genetic method consists, so far as we can see, of deducing from observable characteristics, from what you could call the phenotype, that which is hidden, the gene-level, or the genotype. This method functions perfectly when the phenotype is reflected more or less exactly in the genotype."

If such a study is possible for hereditary malformations that can be traced from generation to generation, or for characteristics like blood-type, or even certain known organic maladies,

"on the other hand, genetic methods work very badly when applied to the study of the human brain and its performance...(in effect) intellectual performances such as we may observe them in an individual do not directly reflect the state of his genes. They reflect numerous structures hidden deep in the brain, functioning on multiple levels of integration. We are totally ignorant of the connection of these structures to genes and we have no experimental access to them."

The fact alone that some certain so-called psychotic subjects have been able to attain the most redoubtable levels of autism or delirium, then return to behaviour that enables them to make a place for themselves again among men and women, would be enough to picture that we are not dealing here with any kind of "illness", in the sense, for example, that hemophilia is an illness which is genetically transmitted, therefore incurable. But this incurability is exactly what the authors of the *Précis* resort to as soon as it is a question of psychosis. "Like any organism," Jacob reminds us, "the human being is genetically programmed, but he is programmed to learn. A whole range of possibilities is offered by nature at the moment of his birth. Whatever is actualized (whether psychosis, neurosis, even perversion) is fashioned gradually throughout life in interaction with the milieu." And it's precisely to an interaction, allowing him to find out how he has been constructed, differently from others, in his interaction with many others, that psychoanalysis invites both analyst and analyzand during the time of the analysis. Not to bring back this diversity and reduce it to a single Norm and its approved variants, but, on the contrary, to restore to this diversity all its brilliance, creativity, and resources. Unfortunately our society does not accept, and increasingly less so, this infinite diversification of subjects, quite the contrary.

"Every day," to cite Jacob again, "the extraordinary variety that men allowed in their beliefs, customs, institutions is being narrowed. Whether peoples themselves are being physically exterminated, or transformed under the influence of the model imposed by industrial civilization, many cultures are close to vanishing. If we do not want to live in a world dominated by a single and unique life-style, by a single technological culture,... we'll have to be very careful."

I'm not sure that, as Jacob thinks, imagination will be sufficient to avert this formidable menace, but what seems certain to me is that those who confront the question of the subject are putting their status as subject on the line when they offer to listen to another subject speaking of himself. It follows that they cannot avoid the most vigilant interrogation of the social conditions of their practice. We would look in vain, in the ensemble of the articles of the *Précis*, for any reflection on the socio-economic conditions of the functioning of psychiatry, or of the social status of its clients. The very notion of social class seems totally missing from the chapter devoted to epidemiology. I'm not really surprised at this, since I remember the expression of total stupefaction on the face of H. Murphy, when, after a conference delivered at the Albert-Prevost Institute, I asked him if he had noticed how the distribution of psychological problems that he had studied in different neighborhoods of Montréal corresponded to that of the social classes. That such a question could even be posed seemed, doubtless, to him more a manifestation of my delirium or of a penchant for confrontation than something that it would be possible to imagine for even a moment. Perhaps he sensed the presence of, in a lightning-flash of insight, the threatening spectre of anti-psychiatry. Which, nevertheless, if you believe Ellenberger on the matter, possibly could have opened up some new perspectives: "Whatever the explanation is for the recent trend of anti-psychiatry, the latter was useful for psychiatry in obliging it to revise its philosophical grounds and its fundamental principles."

The State and its machinery, truly, need to be jolted once in awhile by some wave of contestation or protest that seems to emanate from the great masses. The State needs its criminals to justify the expansion of its political apparatus and of its surveillance technology, as well as its terrorists to support its deployment of external as well as internal espionage (the legalization of C.I.A. operations within the USA by the Reagan Administration). The State needs to call itself a victim to justify the spread of its armies throughout the world. And the State doubtless needed antipsychiatry in order to organize the pan-psychiatric control of the working masses. Certainly, anti-psychiatry allowed psychiatry to throw its nets over the population, to throw off the medical mask it was wearing so as finally to reveal the "philosophical basis" on which it functions and claims to make psychoanalysis, among other [techniques], function. Proof of this is amply supplied by the Law for the Protection of Youth, Article 39, and by recent [Canadian] legislation abolishing professional confidentiality.

We won't meddle farther in this matter, and we will leave it to the pan-psychiatric, bio-psychosocial order to administer madness like the petroleum industries administer oil deposits, that is to say in extracting a maximal profit. We will just limit ourselves to attacking psychiatry on the political level (as we could do for the C.I.A. or for the [other] great repressive instruments of the State), so as to oblige psychiatry to avow the social, economic, and political motives of its operation in the framework of the Canadian capitalist system—if it didn't attempt at the same time, in the style of the great financial groups, to annex something that in essence is absolutely foreign to it: psychoanalysis. And if, by so doing, and by

207

legislating the legal conditions of its practice, it did not destroy psychoanalysis in reducing it to a simple appendage (a distinguished one, certainly!) of the three-headed monster it claims to be—much more in the service of a police order than any truth of the subject.

It would be unfair to conclude this account of the fate forced on psycho-analysis on this morose note. If generally psychoanalysis seems at an impasse, caught in the nets of a rigid institutional dogmatism on the English side of the Canadian Society of Psychoanalysis; in Québec, nevertheless there is an attempt to return to the letter of Freud and to learn, very discreetly, from the teachings of Lacan that have so profoundly affected European psychoanalysis. This effort is not only being pursued by the Psychoanalytic Society of Montréal, but equally by what I have called the "analytic fringe". For almost twenty years now I have been trying to transmit the effects of the great critical work of the Lacanians in a seminar which has been attended, in a blend of diverse affiliations, by what you might call the young analysts of Montréal. Some, members of the Psychoanalytic Society of Montréal, have depended on this teaching to oppose the domination of the International Psychoanalytic Association over the training, teaching, and practice of psychoanalysis. Others, refusing the institutional course, have con-stituted this floating fringe by situating themselves outside the institutions and protecting themselves from certain [negative] forces at work in any possible type of institution. They've been trained informally, which Freud much pre-ferred to the regimentation imposed by the Berlin Group. Uncertain as it may be, this analytic fringe's future will depend on the constancy with which it is able to maintain its positions against any type of institution, as well as against attempts at domestication by the Apparatuses of Psychiatric Power.

– translated by Philip Beitchman.

---

1. "Definition: practical ideologies (for example, morality, religion, to which we will add psy-choanalysm), are complex forms of montages of notions-representations, on the one hand, and of montages of behaviours-conducts-attitudes-acts on the other. The ensemble functions like practical norms which control the concrete attitude and opinion of men towards the real objects of their social and individual existence and of their 'history'." L. Althusser, 1970. "Ideology and Apparatus of the State", *Positions*, Social Editions, 1971.
2. Psychoanalysm is the name that Robert Castel gave to ideological phenomena that accom-panied and still accompany the emergence of psychoanalysis. R. Castel, *Psychoanalysm*, Maspero, 1973.
3. The term is borrowed from Heidegger who opposes it to scientific concepts properly, in the sense that the latter more describe than question things. The primordial importance of ques-tioning for Heidegger is well-known.
4. Cf. Freud and Lacan, in *Positions*, Social Editions, 1971.
5. Jacques Lacan's definition, extensively developed in his seminar on transference, Seuil, 1991.
6. Louis Althusser develops the theory of the Apparatuses of Power in the article "Ideology and Ideological Apparatus of the State", in *Positions*, Social Editions. The notion is borrowed from Gramsci who spoke rather of apparatuses of hegemony that he presented as more sup-ple and flexible structures in the social field than the Althusserian Apparatuses of Power.

Select Bibliography of Works Cited

Dufresne, Roger and Saucier, Jean Louis, 1981, "La cure psychanalytique," in *Précis de Psychiatrie*. Montréal: Chennelière et Stanke. ["The Psychoanalytic Cure," in *Précis of Psychiatry*.]

Duguay, R. and Ellenberger, H.F., 1981, *Précis de psychiatrie*. Montréal: Chennelière et Stanke. [*Précis of Psychiatry*.]

Freud, Sigmund, 1969, "Pour introduire le narcissisme," in *La vie sexuelle*, Paris: PUF. ["On Narcissism: an Introduction," Standard Edition, XIV, 69.]

Jacob, François, 1981, *Le jeu des possibles*. Paris: Fayard. [*The Game of Possibles*.]

Lacan, Jacques, 1966, "Le stade du miroir," in *Écrits*. Paris: Seuil, 1977. ["The Mirror Stage as Formative of the Function of the I," *Écrits: A Selection*. New York: Norton.]

Laplanche, Jean, 1980, *L'angoisse dans la théorie freudienne*. Paris: PUF. [Anguish in Freud's Theory.]

Leclaire, Serge and Laplanche, Jean, 1963, "L'inconscient: une étude psychanalytique" in *L'inconscient, sous la direction de Henri Ey*. Paris: Desclées de Brouwer. ["The Unconscious: a psychoanalytic study," in *The Unconscious*, edited by Henry Ey.]

Lorenz, Konrad, 1969, *l'Agression, une histoire naturelle du mal*. Paris: Flammarion. [*A Natural History of Aggression*.]

Nacht, Sacha, 1963, *La présence du psychanalyste*. Paris: PUF. [*The Presence of the Psychoanalyst*.]

Péraldi, François, 1976, "Institutions et Appareils de Pouvoir," *Brèches*, No. 6. ["Institutions and Apparatuses of Power."]

———, 1978. "L'élangage de la folie," Santé Mentale au Québec, III.1, également "Les lieux de l'écoute", III. 2. ["The Slinging of Madness" and "The Place of Hearing."]

Schotte, Jacques, 1964, "Le transfert dit fondamental de Freud pour poser le problème: psychoanalyse et institution," *Psychothérapie institutionelle*, No.1. ["The so-called fundamental tranference of Freud poses the problem: psychoanalysis and institution."]

RUTH SCHEUING

PATTERNINGS

Dress patterns are scientific ways of defining the body. They contain all the markings for sewing, and the rules for cutting the fabric that will make up a garment. This garment becomes our second skin; the only one that we, as "decent" people show publicly. By defining the surface layers (clothing) we see as the Emperor's New Clothes—as something that can be put on and removed without a memory or trace—we forget the process by which clothing as surface structure enters the body; like osmosis, the process used by the body to transport information and substance (nutrition) from cell to cell. Clothing, as an enculturating factor, seeps through our cell walls.

Dress patterns relate directly to scientific and engineering drawings, architectural plans and maps. All are codified systems based on a two-dimensional rendering of a three-dimensional object/body. All represent scientific processes, which pretend to be objective but wherein very clear choices are made as to what is and is not relevant information. Patterns belong to science, to the need to analyze in order to understand, define, and *dominate* the subject (body). Most tailors are men....

Tailored clothing, such as men's suits and women's bodices contradict the drape of the fabric on one side and the organic shape of the body on the other. There are two things of interest here: firstly, through tailored clothing the individuality of each body becomes generalized; secondly, that generalization shifts quite arbitrarily (women's bodices, for example, change the position of the breasts constantly, up and down and from center to side). But they always seem to fit quite snugly, perfect and *seamless*. Same as the suit that fits perfectly, without a wrinkle, but which in reality restricts its wearer's freedom of motion. The opposite would be true of a turtle neck or a woman's tank top. Both contour the body without defining it geometrically, and in an individualized rather than a generalized way. The pattern of a dress acts like a frozen depiction of a faked (artificial) skin into which the substance of the body is placed.

By taking suits apart at their seams and then placing the parts onto a wall as flat objects, we can look at the cut-out graphic shapes. They become visible as metaphors, as abstract forms and ideas; no longer "just" coats. As two-dimensional surfaces, these parts-of-suits become linked with the actual body parts they represent, but to

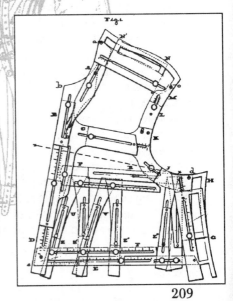

which in real visual terms they bear no recognizable relationship, *unless* we learn their convention or language. (Sleeves as two-dimensional patterns are interesting shapes; they are not actual arms, but their rounded top part implies action, movement and work. Backs are static shapes, representing power. Fronts, graphically, are fussy, encoded not by shape but by detailing—collar joints, pocket joints, buttons.)

The physical taking apart of a (business) suit thus becomes the metaphorical act of deconstructing an idea. This is quite an old tradition: armies in the Middle Ages dismantled the armor of their conquered enemies and placed it flat onto their castle walls. Empty armor (in museums, for example) appears ominous and powerful; armor flattened and separated into sections looks somewhat ridiculous.

After taking conventional clothing apart, it is interesting to look at clothing that does not pretend to be perfect by maintaining the invisibility of its processing. By making dresses out of metal, using flat surfaces which can bend but which will keep their shape regardless of the body underneath, the obvious connections with armor become apparent. The individual parts remain visible as two-dimensional surfaces, while at the same time remaining parts of the new three-dimensional construct. This is due partly to the physical tension inherent in the patterning process, but also to the obvious difference between this "garment" and any human body. It seems designed to protect the body, but also articulates it.

Western dress patterns also compete with the fabric design or fabric pattern. The Japanese, for example, do not cut into beautiful pieces of cloth, and an African kaftan is designed in the fabric and not by a tailor—hand weavers usually have a hard time cutting into their own fabric. In business suits with plaid or striped weaves, interesting unintentional junctions occur at places where several lines meet: generating points of tense interaction between the flat surface of the fabric, the three-dimensionality of the body, and the tailoring process. The fact is that the patterns used for the fabric and the garment are patterns of different orders, and their meanings are confusing. "Pattern" refers both to fabric design (patterned after a flower) and the cutting outline for the garment (patterned after the body). However, one deals with the interior structure of design, the other with an exterior outline or shape. One enhances the structure or design of the fabric, while the other flattens out the conquered body.

So how does this relate to maps? Much of what is obvious to maps translates to dress patterns, and vice versa. Maps are similes: structured, ordered, scientific devices employed to comprehend and control a complex piece of land, the earth, a city. Maps are also codified systems, usually constructed for some gain. The most primitive map I would suppose to be that of a hunter who draws out the path to a good hunting site. A bee will dance a map to indicate to other bees the location of flowers. Nonetheless, I expect that most maps resulted during wars, when groups of people have the greatest interest in knowing exactly the surface of a given territory.

Both maps and dress patterns appear to be just innocent and objective tools, but they alter the world (land, city, house) by enclosing it in a classified and logically arranged plan. To some measure this constrains the subject. Maps are useful to avoid getting lost in an unknown territory, but may ultimately prevent us from knowing our surroundings—because if we already know where we are we no longer need to look. (Beuys is said to have been lost over Russia when he crashed his plane because he never used a map, a habit for which he had been punished earlier in his life.) But for those of us who have used maps, throwing them away may not be the only solution. We could approach our problem by analyzing individual maps more carefully, and create our own patterns.

Words words words words words

—"Dress" refers mainly to a woman's garment, but also to the process of dressing or covering the body with something.
—"Suit" refers mainly to a man's garment, and derives etymologically from "*suivre*," or following.

MONIKA GAGNON
PUBLIC NARRATIVES OF HORROR,
VIOLENCE AGAINST WOMEN

On October 27, 1989, at 4:30 p.m., Sophia Cook was shot with a policeman's bullet. An officer "fired a single shot which hit the woman in the upper body," and "exited her upper back." (*Toronto Star*, 28 October 1989) The incident occurred when a gray Oldsmobile Tornado holding four passengers, including Cook, was stopped. Its licence was checked and the car revealed to be stolen, which Cook was unaware of. "During the 'altercation which ensued the officer's service revolver was discharged.'" The other three passengers in the car fled on foot.

The incident was mired in the by then familiar confusion and flurry of publicity surrounding the shooting of unarmed Black civilians by White police officers, Cook being the third to be shot during a fifteen-month period in Toronto. Covered as a front page story in the *Toronto Star* on the following day, the incident went unreported in the *Globe and Mail* until charges were laid against constable Cameron Durham in December. "It was irresponsible of those who suggested that the officer should be subject to charge without benefit of a full investigation," claimed police Chief William McCormack. Of the charges laid, Cook's lawyer, Clayton Ruby was quoted as saying: "Careless use of firearms is a charge I know well, it's the charge that gets laid when kids shoot off BB guns in the backyard. It's a minor charge. It's what happens when the system allows police to investigate police in secret." Cook, the mother of a two-year-old child, was left paralyzed from the waist down; diagnoses determined that the bullet had grazed her spine. Following the announcement of the charges, Cook: "didn't know what to do from here. Right now I'm just trying to get better."

The ensuing virtual disappearance of Sophia Cook from discussion of the tragic incident that irrevocably altered the course of her life occurred with the rapid usurpation of the shooting by competing powers to interpret this intersection of violence and racism. Activists from the Black community and Cook's lawyer would immediately situate the incident within a social context of police violence marred by racist presuppositions against Black civilians. The police department was swift (and by then, well-rehearsed) in insisting that assumptions that the alleged offending officer was a gun-happy racist not be made before an investigation by the police department itself might determine the impropriety or accidental nature of the officer's actions.

If Cook's personal tragedy would somehow fade to the background of this matrix of competing discourses ushered in to analyze the event, the greater injustice must be seen within a wider spectrum of automatically mobilized strategies that rationalize and naturalize the violence against women.

In early 1990, I read an article by American feminist Carol Squiers entitled, "At Their Mercy, Images of 1989," which struck me with its simplicity and clarity. Squiers identifies several general American media images or "narratives" which occurred during the 1980s, as well as a number of specific media representations of women. By isolating them, she is able to determine the ideological agenda governing their content. In all instances, she writes:

photo by Michael Alstad

Control, submission, credibility, and victimization are issues played out repeatedly in the media, mainly to the detriment of women. Among the most recent have been the 'preppy' murder victim, Jennifer Levin, and the brutalized Tawana Brawley, along with Hedda Nussbaum. And the reportage, day in and day out, poses a certain repetitious and insidious set of questions about each of them: whether she was asking for it, whether she allowed it, whether she is telling the truth, whether her death or violation or beating was in some sense deserved. By the way the questions are framed, the frequency with which they are asked, and the sheer reiteration of words and images, the answer seems to be affirmative: women are getting what they deserve.

Figures from across the Canadian media landscape come to mind: Helen Betty Osborne, Bambi Bembenek, Chantal Daigle, Barbara Dodd, Robin Voce; female figures invented, shaped, and portrayed only as vacant bodies, powerless victims, corrupt personalities, in need of protection, correction, but best of all, guidance and direction. In this brief excursion into these public histories, each might come to represent our private horrors in a more venerable way, affirming what does not change: the insidious and repetitive cultural performance of cruelty that degrades and devalues women, terrifies us, keeps us in place.

In late 1988, the case of Robin Voce came before a Toronto police tribunal and made newspaper headlines. Voce charged that she had been raped by two policemen some five years earlier, when she was stopped for suspected drunken driving. The tribunal, ongoing at the time of her death—she hanged herself in the spring of 1989 for reasons that police attempted to argue were unrelated to the case—demonstrates precisely the abusive process that characterizes not only the utterly corrupt system of police policing police, but the contemptible, highly predictable treatment of women during public inquiries into allegations of sexual attack.

Voce, a reformed alcoholic, was admittedly drunk at the time, which perpetuated the facile discrediting of her integrity as a person and her viability as a victim. She was repeatedly harassed: her interrogator, a police sergeant, continually suggested both to her and in his public statements, that, rather than being raped, she had consented to sexual intercourse but, being drunk, she had forgotten. She was referred to in the media as a chronic liar who had fabricated the story of her violation, and was described gratuitously as unstable, a drunk, a former model, and ostensibly relevantly, as a one-time tenant of a women's hostel. Newspaper headlines merely repeated the abuses evident throughout the trial. "Officers guilty of sex in car," posed Voce as an absent term, while headlines like "Policemen had sex in cruiser with woman who was drunk," effectively functioned to discredit her testimony.

Did she ask for it? Did she allow it? Was she telling the truth? Was her violation deserved? By virtue of the terms employed, these questions pervade what may seem to be a merely factual statement: the affiliation of "drunk woman and sex" carries specific social connotations of promiscuity.

Voce's attempt to make the police accountable for her rape effectively resulted in a public trial for her rather than the policemen. The entire process followed a pre-determined course we have come to know only too well—the justification and normalization of women's sexual abuse. Voce's attempt to assert her rights was treated by the authorities and the media as if it were an aggressive act rather than an attempt to achieve justice. Her tortured fate demonstrates clearly the near impossibility of challenging the male authority of the police force. The sheer reiteration of words and images in the media, Voce's belaboured public humiliation throughout the trial, and her eventual self-punishment, all fit into the grand narrative of closure that befalls women who challenge authority. "Woman who had charged police with rape found hanged in garage," was the denouement to Voce's ordeal. Was her death somehow deserved after all?

*

If Voce's public trial followed a familiar narrative course, women's aggression, destructive murderous streaks, which are taboo if directed against men, effortlessly transform into public spectacle when directed a so-called "innocent unborn." Then it is promptly condemned, as on the volatile terrain of abortion.

Here, women's bodies are open to inspection, vulnerable to the absence of federal legislation protecting women's rights to control their own bodies.

The Supreme Court's 1988 overturning of existing abortion laws under the criminal code might at first glance have seemed welcome to pro-choice activists, but who could have anticipated what chaos would ensue? For the rights of fetuses and the rights of fathers came to temporarily override, in two spectacular instances, the rights of women to determine the course of their own pregnancies.

photo by Michael Alstad

In the case of Barbara Dodd, the court injunction procured by the alleged father that designated her fetus as a ward of the state was overturned in an Ontario court, and Dodd promptly had her abortion. In an about-face which took both pro- and anti-choice supporters by surprise, Dodd flew back into the arms of her despicable and clearly manipulative lover, and declared her regret over the "killing of my unborn child." When this announcement was made at a press conference Dodd called one week after her abortion, the event took on perverse overtones: the manipulation of Dodd by both the "ex-lover" and the anti-choice movement gave the whole episode a strange quality of anti-choice propaganda, which was offered to the media circus activated by the original injunction.

In the copy-cat injunction against Chantal Daigle, whose abusive boyfriend obtained a similar edict after hearing about Dodd's case, Dodd turned up outside the Québec City courthouse where judges deliberated Daigle's appeal of the injunction. With a fanfare of publicity, Dodd distributed a public letter urging Daigle to "think about the baby inside you begging for life."

If the outcome in Dodd's case was her unfortunate characterization as a irresponsible, easily manipulated bimbo killer of the unborn, Daigle's portrayal was far more ambivalent. The public scrutiny of Daigle's private and medical life was presented as a permissible violation because of the nature of the "blood-lusting" medical procedure she was attempting to obtain. However, the over-powering presence of Jean-Guy Tremblay, Daigle's ex-fiancé, and his response to her allegations of physical abuse—that she was never hit "hard enough to leave marks"—was an embarrassment to the anti-choice activists who had hoped to use him as a spokesperson for their cause. Daigle's media portrayal was caught between the highly disturbing and graphic depiction of the abortion procedure of her 22-week-old-and-growing fetus, and her characterization as a victim of domestic violence. She was clearly being pursued and further tortured by her opportunistic ex-, who publicly admitted he was not considering child custody. (He was shortly thereafter arrested for assaulting a new girlfriend.)

Daigle's case acquired the suspense of two narrative elements: the dramatic tension created by the effect of the injunction on her progressing pregnancy, and Daigle's imagined response as the court's delay encroached upon the medical options and availability of an abortion. Each day, tension mounted and brought a new countdown: how would Daigle respond if the inability of the courts to make a decision forced her to carry the fetus to full term? There was also an obsessive focus on the legal technicalities binding Daigle to the laws governing her body, and her potential open defiance if she chose to abort before the court passed judgement while abortion remained a medical option. Would she, or wouldn't she?

*

"You're all a bunch of fucking feminists!" With this war cry, Marc Lepine opened fire on a room full of female engineering students, a murderous ram-page that resulted in the deaths of fourteen women.

In the days following the Montréal massacre, the mainstream media's refusal to situate this violence in the larger context of violence against women was met with increasing anger from most women, who could see so clearly how these fourteen deaths existed in potential at any moment, merely an extreme manifes-tation of the profound misogyny of our culture. Instead of recognizing the deaths as yet a further affirmation of the brutality that women face daily at their jobs, on the streets, in their homes, media analysis largely insisted on a fantasy of Lep-ine the lone gunman, abused child, troubled soul. When TV journalist Barbara Frum interviewed a hospital spokesperson who bemoaned this horrendous "crime against women," Frum saw fit to correct him: A crime against humanity is what you mean, surely, she prompted.

In pathetic attempts to locate a "non-political" motivation for these women's deaths, when the seeds of hatred were so obvious to so many of us, we became bored with non-stories that exaggerated the presence of swastikas decorating Lepine's apartment, and then wearied with a fairly commonplace description by his one time biology lab partner, who said he acted jilted when she refused him a date. Nothing exceptional. Nothing out of the ordinary in the reports of Lepine's life, which is what is so troubling. The massacre, and the media event which followed took on a surprisingly paradoxical quality: Because you are women, Lepine screamed, you will die. But the successive attempts to de-gender those murdered in order to avoid situating Lepine's violence, was, as one woman described, to try to Kill Us Twice.

Women who challenge the rigid norms of societal organization are quickly characterized as deviant or unreliable, promiscuous or irresponsible—all connotations which hold social value. And when women exercise their right to study in unconventional areas, and suffer fatally for that choice, then the fact that they are women is very rapidly denied, and the grave consequences of the dangerous realities that face women every day disavowed.

For being women; despite being women; because we are women.

The internalization of our society's hatred of women can be evidenced in ever present forms—from the fictive entertainment of novels, films, and TV series, to the so-called factual texts of courtroom trials, newspaper accounts, books, and journals. Perpetuating our fear, this subordinating function becomes apparent when we dissect the insidious normalizing responses and justifications of violence against women, instances which tragic moments such as the Montréal Polytéchnique murders profoundly challenge and reinforce.

And for all the testimonies to the societal non-status that serve as fascination for the media, stories that flank semi-nude pin-up girls in daily rags and serve as narrative content for an infinite number of cultural products, for every one of these there are those countless unspoken violences against women, women whose broken bodies and spirits never make it to the big headlines.

photo by Michael Alstad

ON THE PROWL/
HARDCORE COMMUNICATION

Shannon Bell: How do you feel about being called a prostitute performance artist?

Gwendolyn: I don't think of myself as a performance artist. To me, that is how they classify you when they don't know what to call you.

S: So how do you think of yourself?

G: Performer. I have always been a performer. I did my first magic act when I was five years old. Guess you could say I've been doing tricks for a very long time. Every summer we had a backyard circus; I got all the kids to put on little shows: flying fleas, can-can dance, fire eater. I loved the variety, all the different flavours.

S: When did you get into stripping?

G: January 1976, just before I turned twenty-three, so I wasn't that young.

S: Did you do stripping first or prostitution first?

G: I started working as a prostitute first.

S: When did you start doing what I call prostitute performance art?

G: Before I started stripping I had gone to Mime School, full time. It was very intense, very difficult and physically demanding. We started with masks, did the neutral mask, then character masks and *comedia del arte*, then we got to clowns at the end of the term. Those days I dressed like I do now, which is dyke-like, but my clown turned out to be super femme. She wore highheels. She had tits stuck-out and did ass wiggling. I discovered this femme part of myself. It was fun and interesting and within six months I started stripping. I did feel like I was in drag at first. It was like a persona. Now I have integrated it. It came from me. The seed comes from within. Clowning is different from Stanislavsky. Stanislavsky says don't limp until you feel your leg aching and you have to feel the hurt, feel it grow inside; if you impose a limp it is going to be phony. A clown just puts on the clothes and assumes the walk and then she knows it inside.

S: Do you think there is a big overlap between clowning and stripping?

G: Sure, that's what striptease is, it's female clowning. It doesn't have to be, but clowning has been a part of striptease from the beginning.

S: It looks like you consciously integrate burlesque into your shows; you have lots of traces of clowning and clowns in your shows.

G: I missed burlesque. I left home when I just turned sixteen. I did a lot of shit jobs, including bottom of the barrel whoring. I've worked as a packer in a warehouse, on a factory assembly line, non-skilled office work. I did every fucking stupid job that people who don't have any schooling do.

I wish I had known about The Victory Theatre. I was in town doing shit jobs, making no money, trying to survive when there was a burlesque house still in the city. I didn't drink. I was a hippy girl and I never went into the bars, so I didn't know about the strip scene until I was twenty-two. I was so proud of myself when I started stripping. It was the first job that fit.

photos by Scott McLeod

I was working at the Warwick when other clubs were paying between $12 and $20 a show; the Warwick paid $6. It booked old strippers on their way out. It was the one place in town that still had a band. I sometimes worked there for $6 a show when I could have made way more at other places, because I wanted to work with a band.

I saw stand-up comedy as something I could possibly do, so I started to hang around Yuk Yuk's. I'd stand at the back, up against the wall with the comics. I was the wallflower who never danced; I never got on stage. At first I was real impressed with how smart and funny the guys were, but after a little while I went from being overwhelmed to thinking these guys are just jerking off a crowd. If I have the privilege of talking to an audience, I want to have something to say.

Right around the same time, the strippers were organizing a union—the Canadian Association of Burlesque Entertainers (CABE). I clowned at their first performance benefit "A Hot Night in July." The clown piece was with Margaret Spore who was professionally know as Baba Yaga. She was a prostitute/stripper and the person who started the first whores' rights organization in Canada. It was called BEAVER (Better End All Vicious Erotic Repression); when the feminist lawyers got involved they found the name BEAVER offensive so they changed the name to CASH (Coalition Against Street Harassment); CASH—something not offensive to lawyers. Our clown piece was about how to clean your cunt with yogurt; but it was also about the shame around cunts.

I MCd the second summer's benefit, a three day strip marathon in a working class bar.

On opening day, at 12 noon, there were five guys in the bar and they were mad that they had to pay to get in because the girls had some damn union thing going. There was no audience but the C.B.C. (Canadian Broadcasting Corporation) was there. I was standing off stage with the president of CABE going: "We want to get what: certified? ratified? What is the word?

What does it mean?" So there I am. I'm going to be on the C.B.C. news that night; I haven't had any time to practice but all of a sudden I am the spokesperson for the union. Over the three days I tried to integrate little bits of magic that I knew when I was a kid and some stand-up comic routines into being MC.

Soon after the union was destroyed by bringing in table dancing, by bringing in licensing, by bringing in the G-String law. Licensing closed three-quarters of our clubs. At the same time the remaining club owners flooded our city with Québécois table dancers who were willing to work for $5 an hour. It was a manufactured crises in supply and demand.

The writing was on the wall: get out of the business and get out of this town. I had the opportunity to go live with some gay boys I knew in Vancouver. One of the guys and I were supposed to work in a puppet theatre. Before going out there I sold all my costumes and told all my friends that I was quitting the business. I went to Vancouver and worked for several weeks but the puppet man never paid us. I was the representative from the group who asked for our pay; in front of the group in public space, in a shopping mall, when I asked for our money, the puppet man slapped me in the face, knocked my glasses off and broke them. Half the cast of the show quit immediately; the other half decided to stay for no money.

This was when I really bottomed out. I had been in therapy with my first therapist before I went out west. I really thought that to save myself I had to get out of stripping; the therapist was telling me "whatever you have to do just get out of it." When I phoned my therapist and told her about what happened with the puppet theater, she said: "What did you do? Why would the man hit you?" She

photos by Scott McI

made me feel like it was my fault, like I'd fucked up. She didn't even have good feminist politics. That was when I started working on the street again. I got my strength back both financially and emotionally; then I started owning more of who I am. I had been going to a therapist who said things like "I can understand you doing prostitution once when you were hungry but why would you do it again?" She never said "right on, you survived, you took care of yourself." For her it was always: "how could you do that?" Even if she tried not to be judgmental, she was middle class and she was appalled. She couldn't understand how I could be saying "this is me taking care of myself, this is not me hurting myself."

I went from working on the street to a master class studying drama at Banff.

I returned to Toronto and started doing stand-up material at girls' parties. I got a regular Friday night gig at the Ritz—a little downtown Cafe. It was good because it was a very tiny audience space, it was not intimidating.

My friend Ron Hedland had a nine piece rhythm and blues band that played places like Grossman's, the Hotel Isabella, the El Mocambo and the Silver Dollar. I did my stand-up with the band. They were very downtown and gritty; not pretty boys but older working musicians. The crowd that came were rounders and people from the trade. It was really good for me. In a sense it was a tough crowd, but in another sense it was easy because these were clubs that I had worked as a stripper. I had been standing naked, bending over showing my asshole, now I was up there sharing some of my heart. It wasn't that different.

For my thirty-second birthday, I organized the first professional bad girls' show at the Cameron. We called it *Professional Bad Girls and Painted Ladies Present Potpourri*. Anyone who wanted to perform could do anything they wanted to do. There were twenty acts. It was a party in celebration of ourselves. I decided that we would cover the Cameron bar with pictures of us. To drum up enthusiasm for the show, we did a poster project at Le Strip which continued for a good four years.

The event was phenomenal. Its hard to explain how high that night was. Peggy Miller, the founder and first spokesperson for CORP, stopped the show and got a standing ovation singing "Somewhere Over the Rainbow." Most women didn't know her politics; she got a standing ovation because of the way she sang the song: her persona, her warmth, her energy. When I think of performance events that I have participated in or seen, more so than any of my own shows, that was the most incredible. It happened because all kinds of women came together and contributed their creativity.

S: And then you moved into doing performance. I guess your first piece was *Merchants of Love*.

G: I did a couple of shows before—*Cardiac Arrest* and *Turning Tables*, but *Merchants of Love* is the most accomplished. It was originally created for a the-

photo by C. Reich

matic exhibition on the commodification of love in our society; the people at the gallery wanted to show my film *Out of the Blue: A Cozy Porn and Variety Slut Show*. When I found out that they were only soliciting material on the sex trade, I got pissed off. Strippers and whores don't pretend to sell love, we sell hard-ons, we sell cums, we sell beer. So I gave the gallery my experience of the commodification of love: therapy. Those sliding scale facilitators really suck you in. They pretend to love and care for you, all they really want is your money. Fist full of dollars, get out your empathy.

S: *Merchants of Love* is a really powerful commentary on therapy. How do you come up with the political satire? Your language is highly political.

G: Real life is where it comes from. My political mentor is Chris Bearchell; Chris worked for years on *The Body Politic* (gay and lesbian mag); she weathered it out when almost all the women left over pornography issues. She has been and continues to be a source of inspiration and support for a lot of us.

S: It seems to me that in your performances you employ nudity as a way of desexualizing the body. You toss your clothes off, you put on clothing that is not terribly sexual—sneakers, a raincoat. You have a beautiful body and this comes through, but without the standard sexual posing that you get in stripping.

G: I am not consciously desexualizing. I'll tell you what I am consciously doing, I am using the skills that I have. I wear fishnets to make my legs look nicer.

S: But you wear running shoes on stage half the time.

G: Yes, because I can't walk around in heels all night. I'm too old for that. I don't want to fuck up my back and I want to feel grounded when I'm working. In stripping I never did learn how to walk very well with high heels, so what I used to do was get the shoes off as fast as possible so I could do things like cartwheels, splits and stand on my head. I use baby acrobatics and juggling, simple little tricks presented nicely. I would always sit down as fast as possible too. The first year and a half I did a stocking routine every show so I wouldn't have to stand, let alone dance. I've never been much of a dancer.

S: What about the vinyl raincoat in *HARDCORE* and *Raunch Bouquet*?

G: That's my clown Stinky. That's Stinky's coat. I found it in a Goodwill for a buck. It feels good. It has sort of got that pervert edge to it.

S: I thought it was a play on the classic male jerk-off coat.

G: Well, it is a pervert coat. As for desexualizing the body, I'm using what I've got. One of the things I have is being comfortable nude or in various stages of undress.

S: Did that come natural for you?

G: No, I earned it. I hope that I'll continue to have it as my body changes. I would hope that I can still take my clothes off when I get old; it would be a very different look and I will get a different feeling from the audience.

S: How did you get to be comfortable with your body?

G: Through stripping. I didn't even know that I had pretty tits until I started stripping. Nobody ever told me because most of the sex I had was for business. Also, until then, the only nude women I had ever seen were in *Playboy* and I didn't measure up.

One of the nice things about stripping all these years is the pleasure of the women. There was a kind of intimacy that I have never found anywhere else.

S: The standard line is that prostitutes don't have pleasure in their work. Why do you think that is?

G: I have sexual pleasure in the business, sometimes. When they see you strip, guys want to think that you are turned on. The same thing goes in prostitution. The most tiresome dates for me are the guys who want to please me; but pleasing me is being nice, being friendly, paying well, and hurrying up. We are not here for my pleasure; we are here for your come.

I think it is important to counter the myth that we are nymphomaniacs and sexual exhibitionists: "she loves it, she needs it, oh, God she's so horny." I'm doing five shows a day, six days a week, do you really think that I can be turned on every damn show? It would be pretty tiring. On the other hand, sometimes it is pleasurable. I don't do the Stanislavsky thing that I can't make a move until I feel it inside, but sometimes I make a move and I do feel it inside and it feels good. I think that the guys who are your regulars, know this and of course, they like it that way more. They want to feel that you are feeling good. Some men do get off on seeing you degraded or angry. But most of the guys would like to think that you are enjoying what you do and I almost always enjoy stripping. Occasionally, I enjoy it in a sexual way, but I don't stop my show to get off. That is not really what I am up there doing. I am up there for your pleasure. It's like the actor: the young actor comes off the stage and says "I really cried tonight." But that's not the point, the question is did they cry?

S: I have heard from a couple of women who have seen you strip that you talk a lot with the audience, that you actually really dialogue with them.

G: I talk through most of my shows. Sometimes I talk dirty for them, talk sexual, sometimes I talk small talk: "have you started your Christmas shopping?" I engage them as people and I am a person here. If you can't look me in the eye then we are not going to get along.

S: Have you ever had any bad reactions from the guys around talking?

G: Sure. You get negative, you get positive. If you have worked fifteen years, you've worked 24-30 shows a week over most weeks of the year. You get just about everything. Now I am working full time at Maggie's and only marginally employed as a stripper and whore.

S: What are you doing at Maggie's?

G: I'm an Outreach Worker. We work the strolls. We walk around giving out condoms. We distribute Bad Tricks sheets. We take down any information about crimes against working girls and pass them on to the women. We talk: I talk to the girls about the weather, about how business is; about their boyfriends, about AIDS, about testing, about addiction, about the fact that they just got out of jail or are about to go into jail, about being afraid that they are going to lose custody of their kid. We talk about anything that is on someone's mind when you are out there trying to make your money late at night.

   It's all connected—performance, working, Maggie's. But each thing is a full time job. The blessing is that I really believe in what I'm doing. I am thirty-nine years old and I feel like I'm still growing. As an outreach worker you have to start establishing relationships with people. You start actually getting to know girls, draw them into Maggie's and encourage them to participate. Find ways for people to contribute because that is what people want, they want to contribute. They want to know what can I do, how can I help, where can I fit in. I do grassroots, front-line political work.

S: What is Maggie's?

G: It's a drop-in center and the home of the Prostitutes' Safe Sex Project. We are partly funded by the feds. In their eyes what they are funding is a resource center for academics, bureaucrats, and social workers to gather information about prostitution and AIDS. We see it as a clubhouse.

S: One of the most amazing things about your film *Prowling By Night* is the way it undermines the belief of the general public that whores are exploited by pimps or tricks; the film really brings out the police harassment, which is just incredible. I bet people are really surprised when they see the film.

G: Well, I was really surprised when I first started doing outreach by the number of stories of cop abuse.

   My original purpose in making *Prowling* was to show that prostitutes are Safe Sex Professionals. We're the people who teach men how to come in condoms. The film was to be a pat on the back for the profession. But the street women had a more important agenda: they wanted to talk about the cops. *Prowling By Night* works because the girls told the truth. We are exploited by bad laws and by how these laws are enforced.

The new video, *Communicating For The Purpose*, has interviews with thirteen street prostitutes talking about the communicating law, their attitudes around the business and working in the age of AIDS.

S: What sort of political change are you fighting for?

G: Decriminalization, for a start. But when you realize how much money the cops stand to lose it will be a fight. In 1988 the cops in Toronto got over a million dollars to hire ninety more officers just to police prostitutes. A million bucks just to arrest us. This is what we are up against.

S: What feminists are supporting Maggie's?

G: I'd say that the vast majority of feminists don't know about Maggie's; the feminists who know about Maggie's would be in social services, AIDS education, and health care.

S: I found when I talked to Gloria Lockett, the former leader of COYOTE in San Francisco, that a lot of support for prostitutes' rights comes from the lesbian community. Have you found this in Toronto?

G: I would certainly say that the whores' rights movement in this town has been fuelled by gay activists. Most people in the movement got some of their training from gay politics.

S: What are you currently doing?

G: The annual "Take Back the Night" march is happening in Parkdale this September; Parkdale is one of the prostitute strolls. We have escalating crack related violence, we have Guardian Angels who are beating whores up. The Angels just came into T.O.; they are increasing the tension on the street by being aggressive with the prostitutes and the dealers. The residents are totally frustrated and have taken to picketing the girls; as many as thirty residents will surround a whore and demand that she leave. The residents learned this tactic from the Guardian Angels who routinely swarm and bully people.

My job as a Maggie's outreach worker is to let the girls know that some feminists welcome them on the march (unfortunately, some feminists are Parkdale residents who are taking part in the bullying). My job is also to act as a mediator, to encourage the feminist community to support the girls' right to work in their neighborhood. Maggie's is doing a sticker campaign in the area: the stickers say A PROSTITUTE IS A PERSON IN YOUR NEIGHBOURHOOD, PARKDALE IS MY HOME TOO! These were designed by Andrew Sorfleet, a pro at Maggie's.

In terms of performance, I am participating in a film series called *Radical Reels* at the NFB (National Film Board of Canada), which just happens to coincide with AIDS Awareness Week. It will be the first time that the NFB has ever shown super-8 film in their original super-8 format. I am hoping to have some film footage on the Parkdale March, plus I'm showing *Communicating For The Purpose* and *Prowling By Night*. As well, this fall I am participating in "See No Evil," an evening of banned and censored films to protest censorship.

In late October Maggie's is doing our first fund raiser. I am producing *The Half and Half Show*: the first half is *Merchants of Love*; the second half is a sex worker variety show with lots of wonderful strippers, whores and hustlers. Annie Sprinkle and Janet Feindel are coming up from the States to give their support.

Then, of course, for Christmas I will be doing a bunch of kids' magic shows.

This interview is excerpted from Shannon Bell's forthcoming book *Reading, Writing and Rewriting the Prostitute Body* (Indiana University Press).

photo by Rogde

THOMAS HAIG

NOT JUST SOME SEXLESS QUEEN: A NOTE ON "KIDS IN THE HALL" AND THE QUEERNESS OF CANADA.

Brought to television by "Saturday Night Live" producer Lorne Michaels, "Kids in the Hall" was quickly endorsed by critics as a 'new wave' in television comedy, the bearer of a disturbing but funny post-baby boom vision.[1] Originally distributed in the US on HBO, now slotted into the late-night CBS schedule, "Kids" is also seen to represent Canada's most recent success in exporting comedy to the American market.[2] Not all critics have been complimentary, however. A letter to the editor in the Montréal *Gazette* contended that the program is "irresponsible, sick, and should be stopped," to which two fans retorted: "the show's hilarious satire is what attracts its many young viewers, who are forced to laugh at themselves when they recognize some of their own prejudices."[3] The CBC and the Canadian Minister of Communications have been deluged with complaints about the programme, but CBC producer Ivan Fecan has stated that "Kids" is welcome to the network "...no matter how many angry letters people write...."[4] Demographics, probably more than social critique, explain the financially-beleaguered network's strong support for the program. "Kids" has garnered a young, urban audience (1-30) highly attractive to advertisers. In 1992, the CBC promoted "Kids" as the network's "comedy miracle."

Whether disturbing, offensive, or miraculous, one of the specialities of this all-male troupe is a fearless appetite to satirize sexual and gender conventions. The "Kids"—Mark McKinney, Bruce McCulloch, Kevin McDonald, David Foley, and Scott Thompson—are all brilliant cross-dressers, and they leave few female stereotypes untouched. Their treatment of masculinity is equally unsparing, but the feminine performances seem to have attracted more attention. Determined to understand this play with gender dissonance as an element of distinctively Canadian humor, Toronto film critic Jay Scott explained to *Village Voice* readers:

> There's [a] ...cultural quirk in the case of the Kids: Canadian masculinity and the comparative lack of it by American standards. Americans routinely condition their males to swagger with a strut that is rare in Canada ...Canadian male children grow up softer around the edges—less assertive, less demanding, less butch...[5]

In other words, Canada is an effeminate country, and its male citizens, lacking an ingrained "swagger" and "strut", have a natural calling to don skirt, wigs, and make-up. Ironically, despite his progressive gay politics, Scott understands effeminacy in stereotypical terms as some kind of lack or absence. This is hardly a suitable description for a program in which effeminacy is signified by a strange and unexpected abundance. The signs of femininity—indeed, the signs of gen-dered, sexual, national, racial, and ethnic identities—circulate on "Kids in the Hall" as a kind of excess overflowing characters, screens, and borders.

In popular culture, effeminacy has tended to serve as an integral and inte-grating contrast that upholds hegemonic figurations of masculinity. Film histo-rian Vito Russo points out that the use of sissy characters in Hollywood dates back to the beginnings of the film industry, usually serving as visible "yardsticks" with which to measure the idealized masculinity of rugged, independent, unquestionably heterosexual heroes.[6] On "Kids in the Hall," situated within a vastly different context, effeminacy serves a rather different purpose. Perhaps the most significant example is "Buddy Cole," a recurrent character played by the lone gay member of the troupe, Scott Thompson. Thompson's performances as "Buddy" demolish stereotypes of the effeminate queen as sexless, unappealing, and pathetic. Instead, Buddy Cole's effeminacy provides a source of pleasure and power both for himself and his audience, comparable to the autonomous feminine pleasure and power that Madonna affirms for many of her female fans. Thompson's work also brings to mind recodings of the feminine accom-plished by such comics as Sandra Bernhard, who, as Deanne Stillman observes, have moved women's comedy out of the self-depricating tradition of Phyllis Diller and Joan Rivers into routines that insist upon the "sexual allure" of the comic.[7] Thompson explains that the Buddy Cole character reflects a re-evalua-tion of his relationship to a real-life effeminate friend:

> In many ways it was an homage to him at the beginning, because this guy was not only effeminate, but I found him sexy. And it was the first time I found an effeminate man sexy. It was important to me as a gay person....Buddy is actu-ally kind of a sexual character. I don't see him as being a sexless queen. I see him as a queen who gets laid a lot...as someone who's actually desirable—who uses his mind and his talent as a weapon.[8]

Far from emerging as an absence or lack in relation to an appearently "full" or realized masculinity, Thompson's "Buddy Cole" attributes both allure and an intriguing power to effeminacy, which seems to strike back at, and indeed mock, a culture that routinely dismisses it. Buddy's effeminate "weapons" help him to get things done, to set people straight, and to enjoy life to its fullest. In one of my favorite sketches, Buddy takes over as manager of a lesbian softball team who, much to his dismay, fail to appreciate his relished mastery of "things femi-nine". Yet Buddy's effeminacy does not diminish his sexual appetite and appeal, which are continually emphasized; he begins his narrative with a reference to his "renewed interest in athletes," and ends by underscoring the extent to which he has "been around". Even as he insists on being a hyper-stereotypical fag, offer-ing the girls martinis out of a Gatorade bottle and giving pep talks based on the life of Coco Chanel, he refuses the limitations that usually accompany the effem-inate stereotype and instead plays up the complete discontinuity between gender and biological sex that effeminacy affords him. With the team on the verge of defeat, he decides to take over for an injured player. "But you're a man," the player protests, to which Buddy retorts: "Labels!" The ambiguous irony of this exchange is enormous: who is more (or less) of a man, the effeminate male or the butch female? Who is a "real" woman? The refusal to resolve this ambiguity—typical "Kids in the Hall?"-style humor—does not prevent Buddy from hitting a home run, or doing the kick-steps of a Broadway chorus line as he rounds the bases to win the game for the team.

Is "Buddy" also distinctively Canadian? That question may be more "distinctively Canadian" than any answer I can provide. Yet in figuring a kind of redefined, unexpectedly triumphant effeminacy, Thompson's performances inadvertently point towards another way of considering the incessant (and often tedious) question of Canadian national identity. Indeed, I am often tempted to see Canada not so much as effeminate, but as a kind of "queer" country. The parallels between being Canadian and being queer are numerous, and probably worthy of further exploration. Just as gays and lesbians are surrounded by, and barely represented within the larger heterosexual culture, Canadians are awash in a sea of normalizing, hegemonic American culture that rarely depicts them. English Canadians often "pass" as Americans based on hasty assumptions about what is marked as different, just as queers can (and often must) pass as straight. Moreover, both queers and Canadians have tended to wrest a space for resistance and self-representation by ironically re-reading and re-working dominant culture texts: camp culture and Canadian traditions of satire and irony can be understood as remarkably similar responses to the experiences of marginalization and lack of voice. Even the rhetoric of "coming out" and being "outed" bears comparisons. In other countries, English Canadians often adopt a strategy of self-affirmation by "coming out" as Canadian, and famous Canadians living and working in the United States are frequently "outed".

Through the figure of Buddy Cole, then, I can imagine the particular "queerness" of Canada as a place in which we thoroughly enjoy and craftily deploy our fabulous ambiguous and excessive identities.

1. David Handelman, "Is America Ready for the Kids in the Hall? Five Canadians bring comedy into the Nineties," Rolling Stone 562 (19 May 1988), p. 112.
2. Bill Barol, "Oh, Those Darn Kids: Black Humor from the Great White North," Newsweek 114, 14 (2 October 1989) p. 67; Martin Knelman, "Canadian Comics Take Aim at Cable Funny Bone," New York Times, Section 2 (16 July 1989), p. 27.
3. Letters to the Editor, Montréal Gazette, 14 January 1991, p. B2; 8 March 1991, p. B2.
4. Johanna Schneller, "Kids Who Kill," Gentleman's Quarterly 60 (7 July 1990), p. 131.
5. Jay Scott, "Girls Make Passes at Boys Who Wear Dresses: The Cross-Dressing Comedy of Kids in the Hall," Village Voice 34, 50 (12 December 1989), pp. 46-7.
6. Vito Russo, The Celluloid Closet: Homosexuality in the Movies (New York: Harper and Row, 1981), p. 59.
7. Deanne Stillman, "She who Laughs Last—The State of Women in Comedy: A Monologue," Village Voice 34, 50 (12 December 1989), p. 48.
8. Stephen Hendrie, "Out of the closet into the hall," McGill Daily 80, 85 (1990), p. 1.

Image by Maureen Bradley
& Danielle Comeau

MONITORS

Jayce Salloum

LA CENSURE
...IMPOSE
AUX ÉCRIVAINS
LA VOLONTÉ
DE GENS
LITTÉRAIREMENT
ANALPHABÉTES.
SURVIVANCE
DU MOYEN AGE,
LA CENSURE
TRAINE JUSQU'AUX
ABORDS
DU XXIe SIÉCLE
DES VESTIGES
DE L'AGE
ANCESTRAL!
ÉTANT
MORTELLE
PAR NATURE,
ELLE A LA
PRÉTENTION
DE S'ARROGER
LA FACULTÉ—
PROPRE
AU TEMPS
IMMORTEL—
DE DISCERNER
LES LIVRES
INDIGNES.

WAYS STARTS THE SAME WAY: YOU'RE IN A
OND RATE AIRPORT–LIKE DETROIT–THEN THE

E TAKES OFF
UST A FEW
RS LATER YOU
YOURSELF IN
ADA.

HE
RES OF
R BASIC
STAL-
LAKE

ARF!

OVERLOOKING THE
SNOW-CAPPED PEAKS
AND THICK PINE WOODS
COMMONLY BELIEVED TO
ENCIRCLE DOWNTOWN
TORONTO

YOU GRAB THE FIRST GUIDE THAT FRIENDLY NATION OFFERS, AND YOU **RIDE**

ERRE DENTIFRIS
NADA'S ONLY SUPER
PATRIOT

YOU SEE! I **TOLD** YOU
HE COULDN'T ELUDE
ME FOR LONG

GEE, THAT'S
AMAZING!

NO OFFENSE,
TOOTS–BUT YOU'RE
TOO EASILY
IMPRESSED.

ACRE BLEU!
RESTON DUDLEY
OF THE
MOUNTIES

YOUR
RNEY
ALLY
S
RE, AT...

...*NIAGARA
FALLS!*

Culture Jammers' Manifesto

AN INTERVIEW ON AGE AND AGING

Eldon Garnet: Are you conscious of yourself aging?

Northrop Frye: I don't think about it too much. I know that I am a senior citizen, but I don't know that one's age has all that much to do with essential human life.

EG: In our culture there is a cult of youth, we respect youth while the aged person is often an object of discrimination.

NF: There is that tendency, yes, it's part of the tendency to the brutalizing of society. The more a society emphasizes a cult of youth, the more barbaric it is. That's not because it has anything against youth, it means a cult of youth is a deliberate exploiting of youth for manipulative purposes, and that is true whether it is the Hitler youth movement, or whether it is advertisers finding that there is a very rich market for teenagers.

EG: Have your ideas changed over a period of time? Did you have certain ideas in your youth that through the years have gone through drastic metamorphosis?

NF: I'm not a person of metamorphosis, I don't change radically. I have been told that my books repeat themselves a good deal, and my answer to that was that being repetitive is the flip side to being right the first time. You ask me about the changes in my ideas since I was young. It is proverbial, I think, that young people are much more confident and much less inclined to qualify their remarks than older people and that is, perhaps, one way in which one grows wiser with age. I think one ought to grow wiser as one grows older, although one doesn't really. But as you grow older I think your ideas, the intellectual equipment that you work with, becomes more complex and many sited.

EG: Do you think there is any possibility in the future, as a larger percentage of our population ages, that there will be a cult of the elders?

NF: I wouldn't like to see a cult of the elders, because I think that for me in my mid-seventies the most valuable thing I can contribute to society is something connected with observation. I don't think that being in, for example, an administrative or executive role would be the right thing for me.

EG: We retire people at sixty-four, sixty-five, but don't you think that's a loss of a great resource? Or do you think it's a natural process, that we have to make way for the youth?

NF: I think that it is both. I think that it is a tremendous waste of human resources. We waste human resources recklessly in all kinds of ways, but that is certainly one way. I think that the years between say thirty-five and fifty-five or sixty are the years where the quality of decision is the most valuable thing a person has to contribute, after that it is not so much decision as advice, observation, and experience. But if you look for decisions from somebody in their seventies, you're likely to get a decision based on experience of forty years back. And it's more valuable for the person in his seventies to say, well, I remember forty years ago when I tried something like that and it didn't work. It's an infuriating observation but still it has its place, perhaps.

EG: So you don't ever see our culture developing a code of respect for our elders?

NF: Actually, I do find a great deal of courtesy extended to me and to people in my generation by young people. It's partly that I've always seemed to [have] gotten along fairly well with young people, and they seem to get along with me, and I don't think there needs to be an antagonism. The notion that what an older man says is holy writ because he's old is of course nonsense. At the same time, there are human resources to be got out of that age level.

EG: As you get older, do you find yourself thinking more about death?

NF: I don't speculate about death. I feel that the older you get the more sense death makes, as part of the process of life itself. A life that continued indefinitely, as Jonathan Swift would have told you, would be an "utterable horror".

EG: With death as part of a natural process, you have diminished its frightful aspect.

NF: I have a normal apprehension of death, as anybody else does, but I believe Samuel Butler when he says, "Death, like life, is more a matter of being frightened than hurt."

EG: Is there a necessary and natural division between the ideas of the young and the ideas of your generation?

NF: I don't really. I think that there are certain phases society goes through when you get, say, a fashion for younger people to feel they're in an adversary relation to older people, and consequently that their ideas are very different ideas from what the older people have. I went through that in the sixties, for example, but as the people with the different ideas all became stockbrokers in the seventies, it's obvious that the differences weren't as great as they felt they were. I'm not belittling that, but merely saying there are different kinds of human resources to be got out of different generations.

EG: As a teacher you're always in touch with the youth, so you were able to derive some ideas from them? Did you find yourself energized by the young?

NF: I do value continued contact with students immensely. I think I would be lost without it, and am very ready any time to enter into the mood of people in their twenties or teens.

EG: What is it they give you, what is their information?

NF: Well, it depends on what the information is about. After all, in the century like the twentieth century you live through a major technological revolution every five years, and young people know more about that than I do. I think too, that it's just a difference in perspective. Somebody sixteen years old and I might be looking at the same object and making the same observation, but the two differences in perspectives means that each of us could learn a great deal from each others' perspective.

EG: You used the word wisdom before. It's a word that's not part of my mental apparatus. In your position, how would you define wisdom?

NF: I suppose wisdom is really the sense of how to deal with possibilities as distinct from knowledge. Knowledge is always the actual, what you know is that. There's no such thing as knowledge, unless it's knowledge of something specific or concrete, but there's no wisdom of that type. I can say, I know that, I know the plays of Shakespeare because I've read them innumerable times and taught them and so forth, but if I say that I am a wise man then I am obviously defining myself as a fathead. The reason is that there is no content of wisdom, it's the ability to meet a set of possibilities. The great religious teachers, for example, are wise men but they are not necessarily knowledgeable men. They deal with possible situations, but they don't convey information.

EG: We've always considered the elders to be the wise men.

NF: Yes, because they are the observers, they deal with the possibilities. But always with one proviso, they don't necessarily know that thing.

EG: Was the Delphic oracle a wise man?

NF: Yes, but what the Delphic oracle really had to say was the motto, "Know thyself". If you knew yourself, you could produce your own damn oracles, and that's why all the oracles have this kind of riddling and teasing quality about them. The oracle, according to what we've been told, came more or less from a stoned priestess.

Eldon Garnet: Infinitely old.

NANCY SHAW

CULTURAL DEMOCRACY AND INSTITUTIONALIZED DIFFERENCE

"Just Watch Me"

– Pierre Trudeau's reply when asked
how far he would go to stop the FLQ.

Pierre Trudeau's imposition of the War Measures Act in the fall of 1970 signalled a crisis in Canadian liberal democracy, which had until then been sustained by promises of progress and prosperity. Although this warning was greeted ambivalently, the threat more clearly manifested itself a few years later as the ideology of fiscal restraint. Prior to 1970, liberal optimism was grandly expressed in the Canadian Centennial celebrations and Expo 67, and was actively disseminated through Trudeau's twofold policy of democratization and decentralization, which was designed to facilitate a cohesive cultural expression, forge the national identity, and project an image of Canada as a model nation in the "Global Village." The imposition of the War Measures Act, and the military force and political brinksmanship that accompanied it, proved that reason and administration were no longer effectively suppressing differences—especially those differences most dynamically expressed in culturally marginalized practices.

In Vancouver, the War Measures Act had a direct effect on video artist Michael Goldberg. Goldberg, who was a member of the Intermedia collective, documented rallies and interviewed Canadians enroute to Montréal—capturing a sense of foreboding, and warning against the potential for police-state violence. For his subsequent exhibition at the Vancouver Art Gallery (VAG), the newsprint poster supposedly advertising the show failed to actually mention it, on one side depicting only the grainy image of two men, one admitting to the other that he was a cop, and on the flip side presenting a hand-written account of Goldberg's experiences during the War Measures Act, and his impressions of officially sanctioned surveillance.

Although he evoked the celebratory tone associated with previous innovative and experimental work shown at the VAG, Goldberg's installation "Room on its Side" played out a potential dystopia by engaging his audience in vertiginous normality. Disbelief was suspended. Participants took their place on a couch—backs to the floor, legs up a wall, they watched TV on the ceiling. This seemed innocent, maybe even playful, until they witnessed their behavior repeated uncannily on a delayed feedback monitor in an outside chamber. One reviewer wrote, "Goldberg's version of 'Big Brother is Watching You' is direct and unequivocal. Everything happened, you were filmed and observed and manipulated without protest."[1]

In response to Big Brother and the looming threats to civil liberties, video emerged as the medium of resistance for socially concerned artists. Goldberg and Trish Hardman organized Matrix (1973), a conference that brought together video producers from Canada, Japan, Europe, and the USA, enlarging the already impressive network that Goldberg had initiated a year earlier with the *Video Exchange Directory*. These alternative channels of communication were designed to protect threatened rights such as the free flow of information and freedom of expression. They were meant to unsettle hegemonic communications systems—especially broadcast television—and to include voices otherwise marginalized. As Goldberg wrote:

> The need for a free, wide choice of information need hardly be argued...[I]n times or areas of information restriction, whether self-imposed by the mass media or regulated politically or economically, access to alternative information becomes crucial. The War Measures Act in Québec thrust this reality on an unsuspecting and truly innocent population. It is crucial to maintain an open flow...now, while there is a liberal attitude toward freedom of speech and the right to pursue knowledge....If we wait until urgency determines expediency, it may be too late to be effective.[2]

In response to the ossifying liberal ideology that was attempting to contain dissenting voices, the strategies embodied in the *Video Exchange Directory* and Matrix offered an alternative. Goldberg's VAG installation, Matrix, and the *Video Exchange Directory* were at once celebratory of new video technology and critical of it. But the successes and limitations of that era's alternative strategies were most fully illuminated at Intermedia, Vancouver's proto artist-run centre, and Metro Media, the city's first video production centre.

In the late 1940s, the Massey Commission had recognized the need for a state-subsidized culture that would offset the encroachment of American popular culture and economic domination. Before creation of The Canada Council, support for the arts had been left largely in the hands of volunteers and a few patrons. The Massey Commission advocated promoting the arts as a means of asserting national identity and unity in the face of regional, linguistic, cultural, and ethnic differences. The Canada Council was modelled on the British Arts Council and made possible by endowments from the death dues of two wealthy Canadian industrialists. Unfortunately, while paying lip service to diversity, this form of state-sanctioned culture was centripetal in its emphasis on the beaux-arts and its adherence to British-style administrative structures.

In 1963, the year that cultural agencies were consolidated under the Secretary of State, the Canadian government established new social welfare programs, such as health care and the Canada Pension Plan, and improved UIC benefits. By 1965, The Canada Council was receiving parliamentary appropriations, and its status continued to improve because "culture" was seen as the expression of a progressive, affluent nation. The ability of such a nation to support eclectic, and even oppositional elements served also to signal its benevolent tolerance of dissent. Communication technologies and notions of dominant nationhood were recurring themes in the public discussion of culture at that time. While today Canada is internationally renowned for its advanced social contract, it is a contract that still struggles to offset the detrimental effects of an underdeveloped economy dependent on communications networks and resource extraction. Arthur Kroker has accurately summarized our condition:

> *Canada is and always has been the most modern of the new world societies because of the character of its colonialism; of its domination of the land by technologies of communication; and of its imposition of an abstract nation upon a divergent population by a fully technical polity; this has made it a leading expression of technological liberalism in North America.*[3]

Intermedia represented an extraordinary moment in Canadian cultural history. It was an ideal candidate for Canada Council support: an umbrella organization interested in multimedia, multidisciplinary artistic practice, and technological experimentation; and a complex expression of liberal cultural initiatives. Its goal was to collapse the boundaries between art and everyday life—a utopian plan to improve the quality of life for everyone. It fashioned itself as an alternative to the status quo, and some of its members' artistic practices and lifestyles were radical. Furthermore, coincidental to Intermedia's establishment in 1967, The Canada Council was celebrating the end of the first decade of state-subsidized culture. Buoyed by affluence and sixties optimism, the federal government had temporarily managed to gloss over potentially explosive ethnic and cultural differences.

While the federal attempt to instrumentalize culture projected the image of advanced democracy clasping the invisible hand of multinational capital—which was transcending nation states and forming insidious, ever encroaching global hegemonies—Intermedia's avant guarde strategies were seen as a marginal but alternative expression of technocratic liberalism. To The Canada Council, Intermedia seemed a sort of cultural lab, an eclectic conglomeration of individuals envisioning cultural democracy as harmony. The collective's name seemed to suggest inter-relation, concern with totality, and the Council funded the fledgling organization with an unprecedented $40,000 grant.

After a few years of activity, however, limited resources and competing interests undermined Intermedia's effort. Gradually the collective devolved into smaller groups with more focused interests. The parameters of Intermedia's utopian attempt to liberate life through art are evident in the collective's use of video. One early grant had provided it with a video Portopak, which seemed most useful when it captured ephemeral and fleeting moments. Technological experimentation was simple, in most cases employing video merely as a new and immediate way to embody an artful life. Nevertheless, video production was new and experimental, pushing the limits of perception and acceptable art practice.

Although one of Intermedia's originally stated aims was to intervene in the hegemonic communications systems, by the end of 1969 some members were meeting with community groups to discuss starting a more consciously political media centre, to support community action by making video production accessible. By 1971, it was clear that Intermedia itself did not have the resources to facilitate such a centre. Moreover, the objectives of this new project were too politically specific. So in the spring of 1971, Intermedia members Werner Allen, Michael Goldberg, and Bill Nemtin joined with other Vancouver artists to start Metro Media.

In theory, Metro Media advanced itself as a political and technopopulist alternative. In actuality, it functioned in relation to the federal government's policy of democratization and decentralization. The government had continued to envision "culture" as a means to mediate the effect of technical progress—employing it to integrate the country in the name of access and democracy, and to deflect any real analysis of competing social, political, and economic interests. Especially after his imposition of the War Measures Act, for Trudeau culture served the dual purpose of presenting Canada internationally as an enlightened, socially advanced nation covering for the internal management of dissent—particularly of his personal sore point, Québec separatism.

Culture could no longer serve the nation simply as decoration and entertainment. On the recommendation of *The Royal Commission on Bilingualism and Biculturalism*, bilingualism and multiculturalism were officially instituted as policy. It was an attempt to recognize the two so-called "founding nations" of Canada, while acknowledging that there was a plurality of ethnicities deserving recognition and accommodation; and in a stroke the concept of Canada as a cultural "mosaic" was initiated. New programs were created to disseminate culture beyond the urban centers of eastern Canada, including the National Museums Corporation, and such Canada Council programs as Publishing Assistance, the Touring Program, the Art Bank, and the Explorations Program. However, regardless of the rhetoric, the "mosaic" and "participatory democracy" functioned politically as lip-service mediation, facilitating endo-colonization and the assimilation of difference.

Two of the new programs directly affected Metro Media: the Local Initiatives Program (LIP), and Challenge for Change. The LIP provided short-term support for community initiated projects, and Challenge for Change was a National Film Board (NFB) program that donated equipment and provided some financial assistance. The NFB program had the most enduring influence on Metro Media's ideological development, despite the fact that it offered only short-term technical assistance and no long term operating support.

Challenge for Change had started in 1967 as a form of community outreach: "to improve communications between individuals and groups in all segments of society concerned and affected by poverty."[4] It advocated video Portopak production because it was cheaper and easier to use than 16 mm film, better serving the program's mandate to encourage self-representation and community consensus building. Participants were integrated into every aspect of production and distribution, and their finished tapes were employed as lobbying tools and to inform the general public, as well as for communication with peer communities. Its success impressed many government agencies, and departments such as Indian Affairs, Northern Development, Manpower and Immigration, National Health and Welfare, the Secretary of State, and Labour and Agriculture all pledged financial support.

Vidéographe in Montréal was Metro Media's eastern counterpart. It had started a few years earlier and was supported by Québec's equivalent of Challenge for Change, Société Nouvelle. Vidéographe was better funded, and may have been more successful in realizing the potential for community video production. For optimum access its centre was open twenty-four hours a day. It had a video theatre, relatively sophisticated equipment, and technicians. Selécto-TV was one of its most successful ventures, where during ten-day periods in several Québec communities viewers phoned participating cable stations and requested particular Vidéographe tapes. The tapes requested most frequently were screened during designated time slots.

One indication of Metro Media's deep relationship with the federal government came when it and Vidéographe were designated to represent Canadian video production in *Trajectories 73*, a large exhibition of Canadian work curated by the Musee d'art moderne de la ville de Paris. The Canada Council involved itself heavily, funding and promoting the exhibition. They sent official representatives to the opening, and mounted as a complimentary exhibition the first showing of the Art Bank collection at the Centre Culturel Canadien. Although *Trajectories 73* included painting, sculpture, film, and ceramics, the video component sparked the most controversy. Besides engaging in such unconventional activities as providing a tape library and screenings with question periods, Canadian videographers held mini Portopak workshops to train locals to produce their own tapes, which were generally found to address political issues. This of course shocked the Parisian art establishment, which was still reeling from the aftershock of May 1968, and had difficulty accepting that democratic participation, the political, or the mundane had anything to do with "art". Parisian critics displayed a condescending paternalism, dismissing the Canadian work because they saw it as sociological, young and naive, and overwhelmingly concerned with asserting identity in the face of American domination. Among the most telling comments were those from young Jacques Michel, who wrote:

The Canadian government...even runs the risk of literally subsidizing artistic "research" without being sure of what will be found or whether it will actually agree with its views. You will be surprised to discover an atmosphere of social challenge throughout the works. Everywhere questions are raised, not all reassuring. It is institutionalized creative challenge...at public expense.[5]

Michel's criticism could have applied to all of the work showcased as Canadian, but was specifically aimed at the video component, which directly engaged social and political issues. As official Canadian culture it was awkwardly positioned, critical yet complimentary, serving as state-sanctioned contestation, allowing testimony to all who were excluded from the mainstream.

Although it unwittingly outraged Parisian sensibilities, Metro Media's collective attempts to advance participatory democracy through video were ambitious. Unfortunately, its overall strategy proved impossible to implement. The centre was overused and underfunded. There was not enough equipment, and what there was continually broke down. Besides these logistical complications, Metro Media tended to work almost exclusively with established social services, and with citizens' organizations that were not really interested in learning the technical aspects of video production. Ironically, although Metro Media made a policy of giving priority to the economically disadvantaged, in working with established groups there was an avoidance of the truly disaffected and disenfranchised. Moreover, Metro Media resource workers tended to have their own preferences and agendas, which they impressed upon the very groups they were supposed to empower.

Its attempts to lobby for community television access were sincere, but one of the more troubling aspects of the centre's programming was its unquestioning embrace of multiculturalism. In its attempt to attend to unheard voices the centre concentrated on ethnic communities, conjuring up essentializing, exotic, and cliché images of otherness. At the time such strategies were considered politically progressive, but because that approach to racism and colonialism is mostly concerned with assimilation and lacks a systemic and analytic component, in retrospect it is easy to see Metro Media's liberal stance as obviously patronizing and implicitly racist.

Metro Media eventually claimed success in consciousness raising, and in concentrating attention on important local, national, and international issues. But, despite its best intentions, the centre's multiculturalism was co-opted by the homogenizing and exclusionary tendencies of the official viewpoint. Political resistance was naively seen as concretely manifest in rough, immediate, "amateur" production values. In continually adopting the NFB documentary style, with its use of authoritative voice-over, lay testimony, and emotional hooks to build a narrative resolution based on faithful objectivity, the centre's artistic strategy was as neutralized and transparent as its use of technology. Through its technopopulist mandate it attempted to include the excluded, but failed to address its own ideological and representational parameters. It could not situate itself in a larger context, which hampered its awareness of and response to co-optation and complicity.

In the mid-seventies, quietist and cynical strategies were beginning to emerge. Some artists began to assess the ideological underpinnings of signification and technology, while others became nihilistic by attempting to articulate the limits of employing art to renovate life. In Canada, the worldwide economic crisis most clearly represented by the oil crisis took a particular form. Inflation and the imposition of wage and price controls were symptoms that the structurally-dependent resource based economy was entering a period of diminishing returns.[6] Though the federal government continued to pay tribute to democracy and decentralization, its policy took on a new meaning. Trudeau's political persona had shifted from populist to autocrat, and his approach to democracy moved from rationality and debate toward skillful media manipulation. Ensuing shifts occurred with regard to cultural policy, and the government demonstrated the true limits of its liberalism by withdrawing funding from community-based projects. Instantly, it became glaringly obvious that socially committed, grass-roots Canadian technopopulism was supported from the top down.*

---

1. Richard Simmons, "The Manipulator Proves the Lie is Reality," *The Province* (Vancouver, January 21, 1971). Simmons also noted, "It is a fact that the main agency that rents VTR cameras draws its clientele from two main groups, the police and artists."
2. Taki Blues Singer, Gerry Gilbert (eds.) "Videofreerainforest August 73: a survey of video arts in Vancouver," *artscanada*, October 1973, p. 14.
3. Arthur Kroker, *Technology and the Canadian Mind*, Montréal: New World Perspectives, 1984.
4. Linda Johnson, *Metro Media and Hourglass CB.C.*, p. 125.
5. Joan Lowndes, "The Canadian Presence in Paris," *artscanada* (October 1973), pp. 73-81.
6. Within Canada's branch plant economy, American multinationals had established Canadian subsidiaries. In return for initial investment and job creation the multinationals were allowed tariff-free primary resources and unlimited access to the Canadian markets, without incurring any obligation to reinvest their profits in Canada. By the mid-seventies, diminishing initial investments and retarded economic development had created a balance-of-trade problem, whereby Canada was importing more than it exported, resulting in run-away debt and inflation.

* A longer and more detailed version of this paper is scheduled to appear in *Video in the Age of Identity: History, Technology, and Aesthetics*, Janine Marchessault (ed.).

JULIANNE PIDDUCK

MONTRÉAL NOUVEAU-QUEER COMMUNITIES: UNEASY ALLIANCES, TRENDY ACTIVISM, AND MARGINALITY IN THE BALANCE

Introduction

What follows is my version of the genesis of what I call Montréal's "nouveau-queer communities" over the past four years. Now, just past the 500th anniversary of the colonization of North America, we are all becoming aware of the tricky, subjective, and intrinsically *political* repercussions of speaking and writing histories. So I begin this account with a disclaimer: The events and especially their implications which I have chosen to write about here would likely hold as many tellings as they had participants and observers. Especially considering that the "history" I am addressing was so recently our hotly-debated and messy "present," I would stress that this is my particular "take" on the times and mine alone.

That said, I'd like to bring up a point made by Sara Diamond (a Vancouver-based labour historian and video artist) in a recent visit to Montréal. Speaking of the process of personal narrative so central to her own work, she stressed that although the narcissistic process of autobiography is a potential trap, it also necessarily connects with a specific social and historical context, and with problems of representation. Keeping this in mind, I will look at recent attacks on Montréal's (primarily anglophone) lesbians and gay men through the lens of my own experience as an activist and as a mediaphile. For my narrative, I have selected certain events that I consider key to this emergent community, an unprecedented and squabbling alliance of primarily white and anglophone gay men and lesbians. The events and crises which I chronicle piggy-back with the development of a network of community media which in turn function to mobilize people, and to crystallize, if only temporarily, new forms and styles of "community." This trajectory intersects in interesting and problematic ways with contemporary Québécois discourses around nationalism and the politics of difference.

Context

Before looking at the sequence of events in question, it is important to consider the political and social contexts that laid the groundwork for the recent development of anglo "nouveau-queer" sensibilities. I have identified three particular areas of interest which, in my mind, pertain directly to this discussion: Québec nationalism; the Montréal feminist movement(s); and the 1970s/early 1980s Montréal lesbian and gay male experiences. I cannot stress enough how all these complex and divided "communities" are crossed and recrossed by considerations of language and nationalism: the conflicted battle over Québécois language, culture, and identity among anglos, white francophones, allophones, and people of colour.

The Québec Context

I have lived in Montréal since 1982, two years after the Referendum. In my day-to-day experience, the "language question" is omnipresent in the tension of how one addresses people on the street, in cafes, in businesses. Yet the simmering question of nationalism, I find, surfaces most frequently around times of specific conflict such as the debate around Bill 101, Meech Lake, and also annually on St-Jean Baptiste, the Québécois national holiday (which, set for June 24, coincides neatly with North American "Gay Pride" festivities).

However, since the scuttling of Meech Lake and the subsequent Oka Crisis, and now Great Whale and the Constitution, nerves have been strung tight. Questions in dispute are still wound around the concepts of "the distinct society", a claim which is disputed or relativized by the emergence of a First Nations voice in Constitutional talks. Public response (or rather lack of response) to the Oka Crisis, the Great Whale dispute, as well as an alarming rise in racist police violence against the Black community, reflect a popular and media-supported notion that the "traditional"/ "*pure laine*" Québécois culture is under fire.

I must qualify this general description, however, by adding that many progressive Québécois groups have spoken out against these waves of violence, xenophobia, and intolerance. But, because of the deep-seated sense of Québec's minority and endangered status, marooned in a sea of English Canadian and US culture, it seems that the political terrain of Québec is becoming increasingly hostile to perceived "differences" within its borders. (Most explosive has been the question of First Nations autonomy in relation to Québec's struggle for cultural autonomy: the scuttled Meech Lake Accord and the military standoff of the Oka Crisis in 1989 and the more recent contested Great Whale Project.) These antagonisms are, as elsewhere, greatly exacerbated by Québec's dismal economic situation. It is in this context that an emergent (perceived) anglo "queer" presence is seen as "other" from a homegrown Québécois identity.

The Québec Feminist Context

As in the rest of North America, the mid-sixties and seventies witnessed a strong feminist mobilization in Québec. In the Québécois context, the feminist movement developed alongside (and in some ways in conflict with) a re-emergent nationalist movement, and trade union circles. Although the movement simultaneously addressed many issues related to women and work and legal equality, in the mid-seventies and early eighties, organizing focussed around abortion. With the relatively early entrenchment of abortion on demand, the movement lost momentum in the early eighties. Feminists became absorbed into institutions such as trade unions, universities, and the public service. In addition, the assumed political unity of women was fragmented by questions of sexual orientation (the perceived "lesbian menace") and now, although still barely an issue for Québécois feminism, race.

Although francophone and anglophone feminists have collaborated on key community services (such as the rape crisis centre, women's shelters, etc.) the movement has always been deeply divided along language lines. Also, with the foregrounding of lesbian self-consciousness in the middle eighties, many long-time francophone feminist activists left the women's movement, and began a lesbian separatist community known as the "lesbiennes radicales." More recently, the gap in the feminist activist presence in the mid-eighties was partially addressed by young (primarily anglophone) university-based feminists who have remained rather marginal because of their lack of contact with the more-established and primarily francophone feminist movement.

This second generation of activists has also brought a new political agenda which is linked to simultaneous developments in English Canada and the US. In particular, there has been a strong lesbian presence, a debated but lively "sex-positive" or anti-censorship feminism, and a problematization of questions of race and "difference" in general. These perspectives have been developed through university-based activism, and also through a strong feminist presence in an anglo alternative media network, which includes the student press, campus-community radio, weekly cultural tabloids, as well as smaller, more ephemeral publications. Much of the political idiom of the "nouveau queer" group is informed by this sub-group of Montréal feminism; similarly, lesbians and gay men have found a voice in these same networks of anglo alternative media.

Gay and Lesbian Communities

In Montréal traditionally, the gay and lesbian communities have been quite separate, as have their English and French-speaking subgroups. Except for social events and community response to a few bar raids in the early eighties, there was little organizing specifically around issues of sexual orientation until recently. There has been a feeling amongst gays and lesbians that Montréal society was far more open and permissive than elsewhere in North America; this unofficial consensus was underlined by the fact that discrimination on the basis of sexual orientation has been prohibited in Québec since 1977.

Traditionally, the Montréal gay male community has been grouped largely around a flourishing bar scene. Lesbians have been active within the feminist movement, through the "lesbiennes radicales," or have met socially within their own, often women-only dances, bars, or cafes, as well as through lesbian and feminist political/cultural events. Also, in Montréal particularly, many lesbians and gay men have been instrumental (if not acknowledged) in Québécois artistic, literary, and media circles. This gay presence in all areas of media provides

a precedent for the strong artistic and media orientation so central to the formation of the "nouveau-queer" constituencies.

Historic "Nouveau-Queer" Events
Joe Rose

Keeping the above contexts in mind, I will now trace a trajectory of key
events that have affected me as a member of an emergent "nouveau-queer"
community in Montréal. The first happening was, as is so often the case in the
formation of marginal solidarity, an act of violence. In March, 1989, Joe Rose, a
young gay male AIDS activist, was beaten and stabbed to death at Frontenac
metro station by a gang of teenagers. This case, widely publicized in the mainstream media as the first recognized incidence of "gay-bashing," belatedly added
this term to the public lexicon. And as Joe happened to be HIV+, I remember this
as being one of the first AIDS-related incidents that brought lesbians and gay
men together. The mainstream media sensationalized these "new" links between
gays, bashing, prejudice, and AIDS, referring for the first time to the "gay community" before such a thing really existed as a political entity. Meanwhile, gay
and lesbian activists were quick to respond. The evening after the incident, some
200 young protesters took over Ste-Catherine Street in the gay village to protest
anti-gay violence, an act remarkable in a city that had only had one or two
poorly-attended gay pride parades ever. This particular strip of Ste-Catherine was
to see many more demos in the near future.

The public outcry over Joe Rose's death was voiced in part by the student
press, and by a network of ex-student journalists who had infiltrated the mainstream press such as the *Daily News* (a short-lived competitor to the *Gazette*).
This network also included the key forums of the Montréal *Mirror* (a widely-dis-
tributed free weekly cultural tabloid), and CKUT (a McGill-based campus-community FM radio station). Along with informal social contacts, the network has
continued since this time to put the word out for impromptu demonstrations.
With young radical feminists, lesbians and gays in key decision-making positions, the *Mirror*, the student press, and CKUT have also worked to keep "queer"
issues in the public forum or at least amongst their young, primarily anglo audi-
ences. In May of that year, the Joe Rose incident prompted CKUT's first "Gay
Day": a full day of lesbian and gay programming. Since even before this time,
CKUT has broadcast weekly feminist, lesbian, and gay community access radio
shows that have generated a wide listenership, providing important commentary
and listings to these communities.

As a young feminist who had always thought of sexual orientation as "personal", I remember Joe Rose's death as a turning point toward my speaking out
as a lesbian. I believe that the murder had a similarly catalytic effect on a number of people, many of whom were involved in alternative media circles. Conversely, the enticing flurry of activity around alternative media like CKUT have
established these sites as gathering places for people seeking political
involvement.

The Fifth Annual International AIDS Conference

The second key event in this sequence happened shortly after the Joe Rose incident. Perhaps the close sequence of these events increased their effects in mustering, if only momentarily, a community that just hadn't been there before. The Fifth Annual International AIDS Conference was held at Montréal's new and expensive convention centre. As a lesbian and a feminist, I remember that, in spite of Québec's high incidence of HIV (particularly among women), AIDS just wasn't on my political agenda until the conference. Some people by this time had been affected personally, but even the gay male community had barely responded politically by 1989.

An ad hoc group called "Raction-SIDA" sprung up a few months prior to the conference with the purpose of organizing an activist presence at the conference. Although this group began to define the AIDS issues in Montréal, during the conference we were inundated by the vocal, aggressive, and forceful tactics of the American ACT-UP, particularly ACT-UP New York, which was there in force. Although among Montréalers there was a profound ambivalence and even resentment of ACT-UP's brash, American, and English-speaking presence at the Montréal conference, many of us were also intrigued by their efficient hijacking of media attention, their sense of urgency, and, perhaps most of all, their *style*.

This was the first large-scale "invasion" of ACT-UP and Queer Nation's powerful graphic strategies on the fashion-conscious Montréal scene. Many of us were struck at the time by the now-familiar "Silence=Death" slogan, or the "Read my Lips" t-shirts; several enterprising types set out promptly to produce a local *"Silence=Mort"* logo. I would argue that this American influence in terms of tactics, analysis, and style, had a profound effect on the emergent "nouveau-queer" types in Montréal. Certainly the contact between New York and Montréal has continued since that time through individual journeys, and through the media imports of GMHC videos, New York queer films, the *Village Voice*, etc.

The results of this influence have been mixed. Like most large North American cities, we now have our own *bona fide* Montréal-based (largely gay-male) "ACT-UP" group, as well as a short-lived "Queer Nation" offshoot. While many activist and artistic endeavors have been inspired by the American models, they are not always well-adapted to the Québec context. The American influence tends to speak most strongly to anglo queers. It has always been a problem that the anglo (often American-influenced) *idiom* of activism, but also of art and culture, just doesn't "fit" with the Québécois idiom. We set out to make change differently. We run our meetings differently. Our posters and flyers even *look* different and are recognized according to different criteria of credibility and importance. For example, even the term "queer" is one first reclaimed by American lesbian and gay activists within a particular context. While the Montréal "nouveau-queer" community is strongly influenced by these developments, clearly the Québec context is, to borrow an over-used term, "distinct."

Sexgarage

Before talking about Sexgarage, I must first make a quick note about night life. In the mid-eighties, warehouse parties became all the rage among the club set. These parties are independently-organized, underground affairs that thrive on being risque, debauched, drug-inhabited, with scantily-clad nubile dancers of every gender or sexual proclivity imaginable: in short, cool. Lots of people go to these all-night affairs, especially after the bars close at 3 a.m. The now-infamous Sexgarage was one of these parties. Not exclusively gay, they are still recogniz-ably part of a gay subculture. In a recent retrospective article in the Montréal *Mirror*, Karen Herland describes the events around Sexgarage:

> A late night party in a business district was crashed by [around 30] officers in July, 1990. The police later claimed they responded to noise complaints (from non-existent neighbours), or alternatively, to a call from the party organizer himself (flatly denied). Whatever brought them there, the sight of over 100 gays and lesbians at play drove them to react above and beyond the usual threat of a $50 [fine]. Instead, party goers were herded downtown by uniformed officers with big sticks which they used indiscriminately. (Montréal Mirror, November 12, 1992)

After the fray, many people were bruised and shaken up, and a number were arrested. The newly-emerging "queer" network was in an uproar. Two days later, a protest sit-in was organized in front of the police station responsible for the raid. When demonstrators blocked traffic, the police once again descended, wearing rubber gloves and swinging clubs, this time in the light of day with many bystanders and cameras. Fifty-odd people were dragged inside Station 25, and many were further beaten while in custody: one young man was taken to the hospital with a ruptured testicle.

In the next two weeks, there were a series of open meetings and demonstra-tions, culminating in a huge march with 1000-1500 people. This demo ended in Parc Lafontaine with a huge party including performances by La La La Human Steps, as well as a free-for-all dance-til-you drop outdoor disco. The feeling amongst the people I interviewed was that the Parc Lafontaine demo was the pinnacle of the situational alliances around Sexgarage. It was at this point that the greatest lesbian, gay, and gay-positive support was mustered, solidarity cut-ting across lines of language, politicization, and gender unprecedented in Mon-tréal.

This tenuous alliance was, however, temporary: the ad hoc group, LGV (*Les-biennes et gais contre la violence*) lost momentum shortly after these events, and fell the way of splinter groups. Divisions that had always been there, between les-bians and gay men, and between various power-seeking factions, simply couldn't be contained beyond the heat of the moment. In addition, there was the trou-bling question of outreach and solidarity with other groups, which proved beyond the scope of the group. The issue of alliances was especially poignant given that the anti-gay police violence around Sexgarage coincided very nearly with the beginning of the "Oka Crisis": the 1989 summer-long military standoff between Natives and provincial police (later the Canadian military) at *Kahnawake* and Oka, just outside Montréal.

Throughout the confused events around Sexgarage, there was a long series of debates among the ad hoc LGV group. A major split throughout the organizing process was the question of making links with other groups suffering from systemic police brutality, including the Black community, and the beleaguered Native community. While some argued that this was essential, others felt that it would confuse the issue. As it turned out, there were problems with LGV demos scheduled simultaneously with Oka ones, and communication with Natives and Blacks was never really solidified. This is hardly surprising, given the lack of prior links and the fact that Natives, for one, were at war with the federal government. Herland sums up the events of 1990 in this way:

> In many ways, our shared experience, combined with the climate in Montréal at the time [the Oka standoff and conflicts between the Black community and police] should have provided a common front and the means to do genuine coalition-building work. Instead, the project fizzled and died after several boring meetings and a few amazing parties. By the time most of us got to court, nothing even resembling a defence committee still existed.

The solidarity that comes with a common enemy and a specific event wasn't enough to glue the various factions together in the long term. However, even though the "nouveau-queer" communities lost their temporary cohesion, I would argue that the Sexgarage events shifted the terrain of identity, style, and community amongst anglo lesbians and gay men in significant and lasting ways. And meanwhile, there is a frenetic, rich, creative, though squabbling subculture that flourishes among anglo "nouveau-queer" Montréalers.

Media Offshoots

Looking at the footage of the events around Sexgarage, the extent of violence employed by the police in these two incidents is shocking, especially for a group of primarily white, middle-class young people. Of course, Native people and people of colour (especially Blacks) have been routinely singled out for beatings and police harassment in Montréal and elsewhere. What's different about Sexgarage is how a group of people normally partly shielded from police violence were targeted. In this case, it seems that the provocatively "queer" protesters were perceived as marginal and also as anglos by the police. This doubly-marginal status (in Québec terms) lined the demonstrators up for violent punishment in some ways similar to that of the Natives at Oka. But, as someone later suggested to me, the police had not foreseen that they weren't just up against a gang of fags and dykes: they unknowingly took on a posse of *artsy* fags and dykes.

Part of the independent media explosion within the gay and feminist communities has meant a proliferation of queer involvement in video, film, photography, print journalism, and radio. Almost from the start, the Sexgarage incidents were filmed, taped, photographed, and recorded from every imaginable angle. Through the alternative media network described above, these images and incidents were recycled, analyzed, and passed on to the mainstream press. The ensuing organizing process was facilitated through close collaboration with CKUT, the Montréal *Mirror*, and through more informal newly-formed emergency networks, including the ACT-UP phoneline. In fact, photos of the original raid were sold by one enterprising photographer to the *Gazette*; both CBC and CTV carried their own and borrowed footage of the Station 25 demo. And the whole process was re-edited in several videotapes, notably "We're Here, We're Queer, We're Fabulous." Produced by two lesbian video makers, this tape was screened to a wildly enthusiastic crowd response at various benefits, and at the ensuing (November 1990) Lesbian and Gay Film Festival.

I emphasize the media component of the Sexgarage incidents because I see these items as key to the constitution of an emergent "nouveau-queer" identity. Documents such as the feminist and gay columns in the *Mirror*, the tape and others screened at Image et Nation, the annual Lesbian and Gay Film Festival (since 1988), have become important records of recent queer history in Montréal: without such records, this tenuous and marginal history risks being lost all together. Since the mid-eighties, the community has witnessed an explosion of independent, shoe-string budget video productions dealing with all manner of content including Women and AIDS, homegrown sex tapes, S/M, clubbing, and experimental, campy topics. With or without exquisite production values, this proliferation of amateurs doing hands-on media work is empowering for the group as a whole. These tapes are shared notably at the yearly film festival, and also in club/fundraising sites.

This new video culture has in some ways grafted onto the established and shifting bar scene. A fairly trendy video undertaking is the actual filming of clubs, a celebration of the gay club experience. Since the time of Sexgarage and even before, groups such as ACT-UP, "queer" programming on CKUT, or LGV have undertaken fundraising through the bars. The benefitting group takes the door money and provides entertainment, including variety shows or videos. Also, the warehouse party tradition continues with a whole series of events unified by titles ("Soft Machine," etc.) and by the graphic composition of posters. These fundraisers and parties are supported, once again, by the emergent media and informal "nouveau-queer" networks. Benefits and parties alike sport increasingly risque "shows" which include strippers, drag shows, voguing, safer sex demonstrations, and more rarely, lesbian jello wrestling, and last but not least, the snake charming contortionist.

Although they build on the gay male drag/cultural extravaganza tradition, it is safe to say that these phenomena are new to the mixed scene. In a context that combines lesbians and gay men and curious "straight" or nonaligned bystanders, these shows bring the gay male "pro-sex" stance into the 1990s AIDS reality. Within the "nouveau-queer" communities, this style (which means a general style shift toward leather and revealing lingerie) also suggests a simultaneously trendy-and-political adoption of anti-censorship, and pro-weird-sex attitude. Immensely popular is, once again, the American influence of Madonna and vogue. And, once again, this influence is limited by its cultural referents.

The melding of clubbing "pleasure" and politics represents an innovative and potentially powerful popularization of causes formerly left in the margins. What's also new in these sites is the unprecedented melange of club-goers, political dykes and fags, gay-positive straights, and lots of curious hangers-on. However, the trick in analyzing these shifting and ephemeral phenomena is to identify their scope and significance.

Wrap-Up

It is difficult to assess the broader social impact of immediate, dramatic events. What I have sketched out for you is my attempt to make political sense of my community's changes over the past few years. It is difficult to know how far to generalize the significance of the events and phenomena that preoccupy me from day-to-day. I think it's fair to say that these events of conflict and solidarity that I have described were known to a good percentage of gays and lesbians in Montréal, if sometimes only through mainstream media coverage. In terms of direct participation, the percentage of politicized people is, as with any community, extremely small: and this is particularly true in the Montréal community for some of the reasons I mentioned earlier. However, through the shifting styles and participants in the club circuits, and through the growing queer alternative media net, a broader group of people is at least aware of these emergent ideas, styles, and alliances. And perhaps most exciting, a significant number of formerly-disenfranchised people are taking the tools of media into their own hands, and producing their own histories and fantasies.

I am talking about a constituency that is profoundly marginalized in relation to mainstream Québécois and Canadian politics. The events which I write of here don't figure in larger histories: they are fragile, tentative, small-scale but also intensely and passionately lived by a small group of people. The death of Joe Rose or the events around Sexgarage are particular moments barely noticed and quickly forgotten by outsiders; it is likely they are completely obscure to most American readers. Yet they relate in interesting ways to shifting communities and styles of identity and activism both here in Montréal and elsewhere in North America. There is also a way in which Montréal's anglo "nouveau-queer" community has a heady sense of abandoning the sense of abandoning or being abandoned. Often it seems that cultural and community productivity are spurred by desperation. Social cohesion comes from isolation. In these ways, the "nouveau-queer" developments, fragmented as they are, produce at worst an insular ghetto, at best a sense of belonging. Or simply a rich parallel context within which people try to make sense of their lives.

Afterthoughts

In the year since I wrote this piece, there has been a startling explosion of gay and lesbian cultural and political activism in Montréal. Although to a large extent still ghettoized by language, gender, and racial boundaries, the city has recently been a veritable hotbed of "queer" activity. Recent events include a resuscitated Gay Pride march in June, 1992; renewed activism against anti-gay violence; a series of American lesbian speakers including Susie Sexpert, Sarah Schulman, and Annie Sprinkle; an "out" gay presence in municipal politics; a new monthly gay and lesbian tabloid; and the remarkable nexus in November, 1992 of *La Ville en Rose* (a huge academic/cultural/community-based lesbian and gay conference), *Image et Nation* (the lesbian and gay film festival), and *Fenêtres et miroirs* (a community-based photo retrospective of contemporary lesbian and gay life in Montréal).

This concentration of events is remarkable and unprecedented in this city, and can be attributed to an expanding base of activism in different sites in the city developed in part through the "nouveau queer" trajectory I've sketched out here. Yet through the process of a consolidating lesbian/gay/queer culture, the inevitable response of critique, splinters, and marginalization continues. In the year transpiring since I wrote this enthusiastic account of "nouveau-queer activism," I have begun to notice the limitations of such an alliance, where all difference is subsumed under the banner of "queerdom." In particular, I am troubled by the way that these events are clearly dominated by men, by whites, by those with economic clout... When spinning the tale of my community, I am constantly pulled between the impulse to create synthesis, harmony and continuity and to critique the exclusions constantly created in the process of any kind of nation-building, queer included. Our history is always in progress: it relies on many tellers to give it scope, texture, cohesion, and complexity.

CATHERINE RICHARDS
THE BIOAPPARATUS MEMBRANE

When I investigate the boundary between the bio and apparatus I'm forced into the first person, a first person experience. I write as if speaking to myself in the dark.

At first impression, I (bio) and certainly it (apparatus) meet each other in full materiality, physicality. Where we meet our edges seem solid, determined, and yet easily deceived—a membrane through which traffic ebbs and flows osmotically.

An Apparatus

I watch a film. I see moving images as light flickers across my irises. I have held celluloid in my hands and all these images are frozen. They move at thirty frames a second through an opening in my eyes that appears at that speed. If they moved slower, they would miss the threshold of my body. They are only revealed at a certain speed. They would never be able to enter without my permission, never find this threshold or cross over. As soon as I open my eyes they are across and I am taken up, I am somewhere, moving, everywhere. We travel back and forth together, criss-crossing the threshold as fast as the images can take me.

The persistence of vision—simple, obvious, invisible, only afterimages remain like burned traces.

Are there more such thresholds, other just noticeable differences in timing that reveal openings in the living body? Once these are found, identified, virtual instruments pass directly through the flesh without a mark—not unobserved but almost as much a part of the body as the circulation system.

Another Apparatus

Capturing the imaginary body. I put on virtual environment technology. I see my imaginary body right before me. I move my finger, the image moves. If the spectral image lags behind my living hand, it misses me. If it catches up, it crosses a body threshold racing to capture my imaginary body within its image. Now, when I move, I inhabit the virtual materialized image of my imaginary body.

I move within the semblance of my living body, a simulation of my physical and imaginary experience that is travelling back and forth across my thresholds, taking me away.

What am I here? My body is mediated experimentally by my imaginary body that is materialized into a phantom image. One is intertwined with the other, each one reading the other, simulating the living cohabitation of my body and the imaginary.

256

WILLIAM GIBSON
MACHINE AGE NAVIGATOR

Lawrence McDonald: Can you point to a Larval short story which might have set you on course for the book you're writing now?

William Gibson: Yeah. There's a story which was published in *Omni* [in 1992] called "Skinner's Room" which was actually commissioned several years ago by the San Francisco Museum of Modern Art as part of a sort of architecture show they were having where writers were paired with teams of architects to come up with visions of San Francisco. In my story, San Francisco's Oakland Bay Bridge has become unsafe owing to earthquakes some years before. But it has been taken over by homeless people from the two cities who rushed on en masse and can't be gotten off because the whole world's watching. So they've just stayed there for twenty or thirty years until they've wrapped the whole thing in this cocoon of junk and they're living in it in a really attractive way...(laughter)...There are these long arcades stretching across the bay with a sort of barrio stack of housing on the top...The structural possibilities of that are glossed over with super materials and carbon fibre strips... So that's the key, the kernel of this new book.

LM: Did you work on the story with an architect?

WG: Yes. I worked with Craig Hodginson and Ming Fung in Los Angeles. This wonderful husband and wife team, the sort of architects who don't or aren't often actually allowed to build the things they propose.

LM: The current exhibition at the Wellington City Art Gallery features the work of another pair of paper architects—Brodsky and Utkin.

WG: Oh, I just saw their show yesterday. If I'd been less jet lagged I d have made a real effort to meet those guys. I think they're awesome. Good Soviet artists are amongst the heaviest people I ve ever met yet. About two years ago I met a Kazakstani film director named Raschid Nugmanov who made a film called *The Needle* which I really liked a lot. It was the first Soviet action movie. So we cooked up a plan. Raschid was the youngest ever president of the Kazakstani Film Union. This was one of the earliest things happening when the system was loosening up there. They wanted to get rid of all the old party hacks who were running the film unit; so they elected this guy who at the time was maybe twenty. He was quite brilliant and he'd been doing his academic film studies in Leningrad when the Leningrad punk scene was at its most intense; and he was going round making totally illicit documentaries, some of which are starting to circulate. When he made *The Needle* he brought in a Soviet rock star named Victor Soy, an amazing guy from a band called **KINO**. A half Korean, half Soviet Bruce Lee, a really good martial artist and incredibly handsome. So we had a joint Soviet-American co-production thing starting to boil where we'd make a vehicle for Victor, Raschid would direct and I'd write it with an American writer named Jack Womack who lives in New York. (pause) We weren't exactly set to go... but Jack and I were set to go to Leningrad and then Victor was killed in a really tragic, stupid car accident; just like that, out of nowhere. So we lost the star and the Soviet artists we'd been working with all went into this very intense period of mourning during which none of them produced any work; basically they just sort of dragged for a year. But a year to the day of the accident they popped up again and said: "OK—life goes on, we have to do something." So Womack's going over there in a few weeks. It's been a long time since we've seen Raschid and Womack wants to talk to him about doing a movie that has something to do with Chernobyl, although we're not quite sure what...(pause) Do you know there's a structure of melted slag in one of the sub-basements of the Chernobyl reactor building which, aside from the sun, is the most radioactive known object in the universe? It's called the elephant's foot because it's shaped like one; the stalactite of this lethal mung that's boiled down. There's an amazing documentary about these suicide missions to Chernobyl where these groups of physicists—who're living at the reactor site, keeping track of it—are all going to die and they know it. There's footage of these guys in heavy radiation suits creeping through this twisted maze of pipes, dragging robots (tractor cameras) behind them to send down these hollows to where the elephant's foot is so they can get a piece of it to check just how radioactive it is. One guy went down with a telescopic sight and a AK 49 to loosen some hunks off it. And then they started sending in these remote control robots to try to pick the hunks up. But the robots would just fry. Finally one of them made it out, very jerkily, with a little piece—the most radioactive thing outside the heart of the sun. Anyway, we'd like to set some sort of Science Fiction movie there.

Tony Chuah: This would be possibly your most dystopian project yet?

WG: Well, when you're working with artists from the former Soviet Union you're in for some heavy stuff.

LM: Do you see it as a place where you're more likely to get a film made than the U.S.A., where you haven't had much luck with various potential projects. Could you say something about these unrealized projects?

WG: None of them are formally in turnaround at this point. They're all just jammed up. The *Neuromancer* project, which I never really had anything to do with myself, simply came to nothing and the rights reverted; so I now have them back. I did a screenplay based on the story "Burning Chrome" for Carolco and when James Cameron went there prior to making *Terminator*, he was under contract to do "Burning Chrome" as his first thing. It didn't work out that way, they needed the money for *Terminator 2*—they're not bankrupt but not in great shape these days. They've also got "Johnny Mnemonic" which is actually written to be Robert Longo's first feature film. I met him a couple of years ago and he got the rights; he's had the option for about three years now. He's there now shooting a *Tales From the Crypt* episode, a necessary journeyman piece. (laughter) Currently that is the one I have the most hope for artistically. Then there's "New Rose Hotel" which is with Ed Pressman's production company and that's got possibilities because he's not a formula producer by any means. He's kinda famous for his wild eclecticism.

TC: I heard that at one stage Malcolm McLaren was also involved in "New Rose Hotel."

WG: Yeah, it was McLaren who brought me in on it but he didn't bring me in to do "New Rose Hotel." I think he was still trying to do his surf-nazi movie and he'd met Pressman. But Pressman wouldn't go for the surf-nazi movie and so McLaren pulled me around the corner and said: "let's do something else." He told Ed to read some of the short stories; he read them but couldn't decide which one to do. I said: "why don't you do 'New Rose Hotel,' it's a pretty random thing." Since then he hasn't had much to do with it but I think he'll sign a cheque somewhere.

LM: Are there any particular directors you'd like to work with?

WG: I'd like to work with Vincent Ward although I think he's the kind of director who...(pause)...all the ones I'd want to work with are the ones who'd want to write their own material anyway. That's the catch.

LM: Why would you like to work with Vincent Ward?

WG: Because I liked *The Navigator* so much. I also liked what he was rumoured to be going to do with *Alien 3*, during his period of involvement. And in fact whatever it was that he did bring to it got them over the hump they were all running into. He didn't stay with it. I don't know how many writers were involved in it. Maybe a dozen at least.

TC: You were involved at one point too.

WG: I wrote the very first draft.

LM: Are you optimistic about the future for any of your film related projects?

WG: I maintain a mild degree of optimism. It's not something I stake a lot of my artistic identity on. I sometimes suspect that I'm not the right guy to be trying to adapt this stuff to the screen. I think there are probably many people out there who could do things that would give me more pleasure with that same material. Also the original stuff is so old for me that I'm inclined just to change it all anyway.

LM: Can we shift now to *The Difference Engine* (1990, co-authored with Bruce Sterling)? To me it almost seems to be the kind of thing Foucault might have come up with had he written fiction.

WG: Yeah, possibly. I think he would've gotten the joke, anyway. I'm really amazed at the positive reception it's received. When we did it I thought that it was perversely difficult and strangely structured. I just didn't think it would find much currency as a popular thing.

LM: But it did get one very negative review, in the *NME*. Have you seen that review?

WG: Yeah. It's funny. They didn't get it. *NME* didn't like us that trip. It just depends on who's reviewing it. Charlie Murray reviewed my earlier novels for the *NME* and he got it; he liked them. But the two guys they sent to talk to us about *The Difference Engine* didn't get it and I suspect they just didn't know enough British history—they were rock 'n roll guys. The trouble with a book like this is that you have to know what really happened in some detail in order to appreciate how it's been changed. It's a sort of monumental piece; a great, big, dense thing, rather like that Brodsky and Utkin stuff.

LM: It reminds me a lot of Jumphrey Jennings's *Pandaemonium.*

WG: Oh, well *Pandaemonium* was actually a key text. The whole final section of the book is modelled on it. A phenomenally weird book, man, one of the weirdest in the world. Sterling found it and said: "I don't know what to make of this." He sent me a copy and it just completely changed my whole sense of what we were doing with *The Difference Engine*.

If you made a list of all the ingredients of *The Difference Engine*, you come up with some very odd stuff: there's a lot of catastrophe theory, Jeremy Bentham, etc.. I don't want to give away the plot, as it were, but it's structured as a sort of panopticon. It's like one of those prisons and the final thing you resolve is the identity of the eye, this all seeing eye that's keeping track of what's going on in the book.

LM: Are or were you inherently fascinated by English society in the Victorian period itself?

WG: I was always fascinated with the criminal culture of Victorian England. And in fact the criminal culture of my first three novels probably has more to do with Victorian crime than it does with modern crime. Also the 1980s and 1990s have been increasingly neo-Victorian in a number of ways, too.

LM: There was a cross-over with punk too. Several of the leading figures of British punk were likened to Victorian criminals.

WG: Yeah. In the course of research we discovered what was probably the first pop sub-culture, the hooligan culture of Victorian England which had its own music; it even had bell bottom trousers. There's a bit of it in *The Difference Engine*. We found a wonderful book called *Hooligan* (by British sociologist Geoffrey Pearson—ed) which was a study of this and I immediately wanted to send it to Malcolm McLaren. I thought it was the most McLarenesque thing I'd ever seen.

LM: How did you deal with the heavy load of research required for *The Difference Engine*?

WG: I sent Sterling to the University of Texas library which is the extent of our research. Fortunately he lived only a few blocks away. Evidently it's an incredible library but I've never had to go in. Bruce knows its contents intimately and burrowed ever more deeply into the vast trove of wacky Victoriana without which this book could not have been done. The extent to which it's *sampled* is one of the things that most delights me about it. There's a scene in which the character Oliphant goes to visit a German newspaper editor who's living—as it happens although you don't know this from the text—in Karl Marx's flat in Soho. And the description of the flat (they're having a discussion about Karl Marx in the scene) is taken pretty much word for word from the secret intelligence report of a Prussian agent who was sent by the Prussian intelligence service, posing as a journalist, to interview Karl Marx. Literally every article on the table is taken from this actual account. It's too clever by half in some ways. I think *The Difference Engine* is a much more post-modern effort than my previous work.

LM: You've talked about Marx but what about Engels? Did you access his book on *The Condition of the Working Class in England* (1844/5)?

WG: No. In the book Engels is an enormously wealthy textile magnate who's part of Babbage's meritocracy lordship. Another character wonders at one point how a gentleman like Engels could have any interest in these demented revolutionaries who followed Marx to New York (Manhattan has ceded from the union and it's a Marxist state). Marx was taken from a biography of his wife which is quite fascinating because you get the sense of what a pain in the butt it was to live with this guy.

LM: Do you think you might do more collaborative work along the lines of this novel or is it very much a one-off?

WG: No, I don't really expect to. It was designed to be as much of a one-off as it could possibly be. My only regret is that having uncovered so much, we had so many spare parts left over at the end which we just had to pack away. One of the inspiring things about working with Sterling is the vehemence with which he refuses to establish a template for what he's doing, so each time it has to be an absolute one-off.

LM: You and Sterling share a strong interest in popular music, don't you?

WG: He's much more systematically up on it than I am. I usually go and ask him what he's listening to. I suspect that when younger people ask Sterling what he's listening to, it's quite exciting. When they ask me I can see the disappointment in their eyes. (laughter) I no longer care whether anything is current. I've reached a point in my life where all pop music is happening at the same moment; it doesn't matter when it was actually made .

LM: You said the other day that you wondered whether the literary audience would even recognize as a culture what formed you as a writer: an immersion in Sci-Fi, rock music and comics.

WG: Yeah. But over that I have a thin overlay of bad North American university education (Laughter). I really don't believe there is any more capital C culture. I don't think there is an official culture. I think everyone is making up their own as they go along and that's much more interesting.

TC: That seems to be the main difference between you and J.G. Ballard. He creates this enormous dystopia where everyone is caught in the continuum. Whereas you define subcultures which find spaces for themselves to live.

WG: Yeah. Well...I think in my early books you never get to see the dystopia, you never get to see the main part of the world. You don't know whether there really is a middle class, you never really see how ordinary people live, you hardly glimpse them because you're looking at characters who ve hollowed out these little caves for themselves in the structure and all they can see is the inside of the caves. I don't know whether that's significant or simply convenient. In terms of what I have to do in my work, I suspect it s largely convenient. It's easier to keep them in the flat.

TC: It seems like the absolutely rich and the absolutely poor still live in their caverns.

WG: Yeah, but America feels more like that all the time. Except that the poor people don't have any caves to go into.

LM: They're out on the street.

WG: Yeah, they're lying around on the street. Well-off people, even middle class people in Los Angeles, live completely in private spaces. More and more people are commenting on this phenomenon in LA of the privatization of public space. Malls aren't really public spaces, malls are machines to extract your money. They're not the same as parks but there aren't any parks in LA now. They've become totally dysfunctional. You can't go into them to relax. If you're relatively affluent it would never occur to you to go there and the police won't let poor people use them either so they're just not happening anymore.

LM: You've said that your novels don't have a pre-formulated political position. To the contrary, perhaps you write them in order to try to understand what your political position might be. Are you getting any closer to crystallizing what those politics are?

WG: No, I don't think I am. It isn't necessarily the kind of exploration that will lead to an answer; it's just an exploration. The other day, a journalist from one of the local newspapers asked: "What do think of free trade?" And I just thought: "My God, I don't know. In some sense I'm not even an adult, I don't even know what I think about free trade."

LM: Do you see yourself as opening up possibilities with the trilogy and *The Difference Engine* which you can then leave to other writers to explore further?

WG: I would doubt very much that anyone would try to take off from *The Difference Engine* to try to produce any kind of pop artifact. To the extent that I can see a Gibson influence in contemporary Science Fiction, almost invariably it's not very good, not very satisfying; although there are some exceptions to that. Maybe there hasn't been enough time for people to digest it. I mean I needed years to digest my Ballard and Burroughs. If you try to come out and sound like someone you really enjoyed too early in your career it doesn't work because it's not your voice.

LM: Are Ballard and Burroughs the two writers you'd see as your chief influences?

WG: Well, they were seminal influences to the extent that I had no idea what the extent was. It's just part of my culture. It's hard for me to imagine the world of literature without them. And Pynchon as well. A lot of people have assumed that I was influenced by Philip K. Dick. I was never an enthusiastic reader of Dick. I've always felt that I got my hit of Philip Dick from Thomas Pynchon because Pynchon managed to do very concisely what Dick was trying to do through this vast shelf of nearly identical novels.

LM: You've spoken of the moment when you find the voice of the text in the fiction you're writing. Is that something you comprehended early in your writing career?

WG: No, it's something I realized in the course of working. At first I didn't know what to call it. E.M. Forster once said that you knew it was working when the characters began to do things you hadn't anticipated. I read that as an undergraduate and took it all very much to heart. Also in *Aspects of the Novel*, I believe he argues that a genuinely good novel can't be didactic. I was taught that book by a leftist-anarchist professor who used it for his own argument that a fascist could not write a good novel. We were using fascist in a very 60s lower case way in those days; basically anyone we didn't like. That was one of the only really interesting literary discussions I ever had as an undergraduate.

CATHERINE RICHARDS

IT'S DEJA VU ALL OVER AGAIN: VIRTUAL REALITY

It's not the machine itself that is racing through the public imagination. Virtual Reality (VR) is not so much a technology as a contested site charged with our anxieties about the cyborg state: the human machine. VR is a site that is metaphorically in play—an on-going performance piece.

The extensive mass media coverage of VR visually dramatizes the human-computer relation. It is seen literally in the obvious signs of gloves, wires, screen, and human. Though difficult to picture, this implicit and intimate interaction with computers has been there for some time.[1] VR is, in a sense, "acting out" the human-computer interaction, turning it inside out so we think we can see it.

Max Black has described metaphor as the "interanimation of words;" I want to amend that definition to read: an interanimation of images. Without making them, VR as metaphor appears to reveal connections. It is George Grant's humans who are half metal and half flesh; and Donna Haraway's ironic "cybernetic organism, a hybrid of machine and organism, a creature of social reality as well as a creature of fiction"; and William Gibson's back to the future cowboys "jacking into cyberspace." At this moment, when the technology of VR is not yet within the consumer public domain, VR is more a metaphoric site than a technology.

This metaphoric role is common ground and open territory, as it were, for public contention of its meaning. The metaphoric images are elaborated and embraced during the construction of social acceptance of the close and anxious cyborg coupling. Its interanimation of images alludes to a new thing—a hybrid creature that is acknowledged but difficult to speak about directly: something more than half metal and half flesh.

This new thing is often proposed as an evolutionary step for humankind. The evolutionary image is a powerful master narrative, tracing through VR and implicitly linking technology to the survival of the human species. For instance, if a VR interconnect of human and machine is an evolutionary step for humankind, says Marvin Minsky[2], then it's pitiful and retrograde to keep the brain unplugged and in the dark.

To track the movement of the evolutionary trope, let us begin with the bio partner in the symbiosis, the human body. The modern notion of this body is of a universally coded information event with the senses as communication highways. That notion is fundamental to VR. Based on that coded body, it seems that the VR symbiosis of body and machine could be improved upon by eliminating the awkward gloves, goggles, and wires and, as Minsky proposes, directly implanting a computer and intercepting the nerves. Minsky suggests that this would be an evolutionary step not only for humans, but for the human world.

He poignantly reflects, "You can make worlds that are intelligent. The trouble with the world we're in is that it's...not interested in humans and does not have their interests at heart."

There are many who would agree with Minsky in seeing the world as somehow unfit or unfriendly for us, and who propose a sort of evolutionary technological symbiosis as an answer. William Burroughs mixes a heady scenario of the end of the millennium and the end of the species: "I think the political and social chaos we are seeing on every side reflects an underlying biological crisis. The end of the human line. All species are doomed from the conception, like individuals... An evolutionary step that involves biologic alternations is irreversible. We must take such a step if we are to survive at all."[3]

Jean-François Lyotard proposes a more thoughtfully charming version: "What is already at stake in all contemporary research, in whatever discipline, is this: to emancipate the human brain from constraints common to all living systems on the earth; or to manufacture a system, one at least as complex as this brain, independent of those constraints. It is a question of one or the other 'surviving' the destruction of the solar system and continuing to function in the ordinary conditions of the cosmos."[4]

We are offered neither a political/economic engagement with the global restructuring that is displacing existing forms of social government and local control, nor a deep confrontation with how we make our communities and habitations poisonous and hostile. The solution, we are urged to believe, is the benevolent evolutionary narrative—that it is our individual bodies that will be reinvented—as if it will be better next time; literally, in the next life.

Within this terrain the VR cyborg can now be seen as a primitive step within the image of an evolving new creature. VR presents one possible body interconnection with a computing machine. This leads us to consider the other half of the symbiotic pair, the computational entity, which will jump start us on the evolutionary leap.

The most common computer constructs for VR are Cartesian reality representations—representations of the invisible, such as molecular structures, or representations of the cyberspace of information. None of these constructs would seem to show even a remote potential for partnering a qualitative leap in species creation. Yet there is a computational work that could do so: namely, the simulation of living systems, artificial life (A-life).

The aim of the A-life scientist is to control creation in evolution, which scientist Rasmussen claims will give scientists powers considerably greater than that of the bomb, presumably as masters of living material itself. Thus the metaphor of true creation, leading us to the spirit and at last leaving behind the messy, troublesome body, is resurrected as the form of technology itself. And this comes perilously close to reinscribing the mind-body split, with all its implied problematics.

A-life and VR share an image of the living body. A-life work presupposes that "life is more a function of the organizational form of the matter than it is of the matter itself."[5] This refusal of embodiment and desire in order to abstract a life presence from matter, as a means to apparently escape from matter, is not unlike the basic assumption underlying the bio half of the VR cyborg. In VR the living body is a sensory and neural network which can not be distinguished from the signals circulating to and from its environment, making body boundaries porous and effectively non-existent. As such, the body boundaries are effectively erased. In addition, the experience of VR is represented as leaving our materiality, moving invisibly, travelling into secret places, exploring hostile environments unscathed. Such a strong representation of VR as leaving our materiality is not far from A-life's conceit that organizational form, as a kind of life essence, can act independently of its embodiment.

A-life scientist Tom Ray is in a sense acknowledging this dynamic within his own domain when he comments on digital evolution that: "...virtual life is out there, waiting for us to create an environment for it to evolve into."[6]

Both with A-life and VR, the scientists see the human relation with the computational machines as grounds for an evolutionary step. In both, the step is based on some kind of separation of the body from the flesh. In each case, the scientist is in the role of the creator of a new creature—either an evolved symbiosis, VR; or a non-human species, A-life—who will be more fit and defy primitive mortal limits.

Once such a metaphoric image is in place, in this case an evolutionary figure intertwined with technology and the creation of new life, it begins to take on a life of its own. It is as if we are already discussing alternative futures as we extend them in more than one direction or another. But by and large these alternative futures are being framed with powerful images from the past.

My point here is that it is not only scientific logic that sustains these new technologies we speak about, but also creation myths and origin metaphors, which are deeply implicated in the technological realization. These myths and metaphors are powerful; there is virtual power in the figurative. They introduce unquestioned assumptions about the creation and nature of living systems. The evolutionary figure takes on a life of its own, as if its alternative futures were already in place. Common A-life models often assume the competition between hunters and prey, for example, rather than the new bacteriological view of the world's bacteria as a single genetically interactive entity, which rapidly absorbs and broadcasts genetic innovations among its members.

Furthermore, when speaking of their work many of the scientists describe their ideas as technically embodied children, as new life nurtured by the scientific parent. This metaphoric description is deeply problematic in its apparent usurpation of the physical creation process of which we are all a part. It is disturbing for its stated objective of creating new life, or dynamic and emergent representations of new life, with these metaphoric assumptions.

In the realms of VR and A-life the power of metaphor takes a literal role, directly implanting assumptions into reality: simulating metaphor as life itself.

---

1. VR technology has been publicly available in its more recent lab form for at least eight years; militarily, for at least fifteen. Ivan Sutherland, that father of computer graphics, first described his related experiments in 1968. Yet VR technology is temperamental and needs specialized support. The images are primitive computer graphics, which react slowly. However, while interacting with it, even this primitive environment is compelling, and its limitations do not detract from the sense that the present system is a prototype for a new mass medium.
2. Marvin Minsky is Donner Professor of Science at MIT, where he co-founded the Artificial Intelligence Laboratory. These comments are from notes I took during a lecture I attended, and from Steven Levy's article "A-life Nightmare," *Whole Earth Review*, Fall 1992.
3. William Burroughs, "Is the Body Obsolete?" *Whole Earth Review*, Summer 1989.
4. J.F. Lyotard, from the *Virtual Seminar on the Bioapparatus*, Banff, 1991.
5. Steven Levy, "A-Life Nightmare," Whole Earth Review, Fall 1992.
6. Levy, *op. cit.*

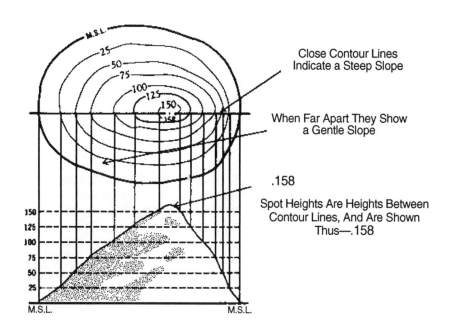

Close Contour Lines
Indicate a Steep Slope

When Far Apart They Show
a Gentle Slope

.158

Spot Heights Are Heights Between
Contour Lines, And Are Shown
Thus—.158

BARBARA FISCH

SEX, DRUGS, & VIRTUAL REALITY

Originally. i thought this paper would be about menstruation. (my holy repro-ductivity club is often evil to me.) however, i was wrong. it will be about sex.

i was fired from my bullshit[1]-phoney (yes-i-will-sell-myself)-receptionist job, so i got a new job, more honest and much more educational: i am now a phone-sexy. instead of being polite to Association Members and convincing them to enroll in the "educational" Professional Development Program, i am a different kind of polite to a similar clientele, it's just that these are people in the process of jerking off. i convince them to keep on calling. office work felt dishonest: i had to completely conceal myself, cloak myself in false values, all for...a benefit plan. that, as opposed to what i do now, interacting with people on the most real level:

Q. What do we all have in common?

A. We all want to get off.

it's as simple as that. and working as i do on a "fantasy phoneline", aiding people in their fantasmic imaginings, i work with physical people as they are mentally. nominally, i talk to people about sex; beyond that, i talk to them about what exists inside of them. it sometimes

> *bores me*
> *disgusts me*
> *turns me on*
> *gets me off*

i get told the most absurd lies; they're sometimes disarmingly honest. *i'm still just talking on the phone for a living.*

so, talking about so much sex so much [*sic*], i've been having more sex. i always knew it, but i've been learning firsthand about sex for sex. also, sex for barter, sex for power/leverage. *ach.* that word[2] has the same meaning here that it had in my office. this job has made me want to sleep with boys/men again.[3] one bidyke am i, i keep wanting what they say they'll give me; as if they could.

my roommate, also writing a paper, just asked me[4] the meaning of "saluto-genic". how about slutogenic?[5] i am currently reclaiming the word *slut.* a slut is a person (m/f) *who sleeps around for the sake of it.* this is sex for sex, nothing wrong with that. hence, slut is not an insult, and as far as i am concerned, is in fact the highest order of compliment, like *bitch.* i'm also reclaiming *mother-fucker.*

1. *Many women are mothers.*
2. *Many mothers have sex.*
3. *The act of having sex with a mother is not an act of degradation.*
4. *Motherfucker is not a word that will hurt me.*

i like to write things listening to good thinking music, with funky images on a tv monitor. television used to terrify me on the basis of its radiation factor coupled with its dizzying mindnumbingness. the beatnigs' "television, the drug of the nation" was a media anthem of sorts for me. the disposable heroes of hiphoprisy's "television, the drug of the nation"[6] is a media anthem of sorts for me. currently,[7] a fetishistic *planet of the apes* japanese b-movie is on *sans* sound, and it makes me learn the gerda lerner quote from *the creation of patriarchy*: "animal behavior is invested with anthropomorphic significance, which makes patriarchs of male chimpanzees,"[8] as she discusses socio-psycho-anthropo-bio-zoological analyses of empirical facts which lead "traditionalists"[9] to ridiculous and fallacious justifications of women's subordination to men. writing with such *mediata* eases my stress; it's a technique i've just learned. [i have been heavily stressed lately. aspects of my personal/business/family/scholastic lives have collided in peculiar and often displeasing/unfortunate/inconvenient/downright pathetic ways. stress has a different meaning here than it did at my office. (this time it feels closer.)] *mediata* is my newest word, as in the latin

stratum pl. *strata*: *enema* pl. *enemata*
= *medium* pl. *media* pl. *mediata*

this is the (1) age of technology c.f. (2) age of communication. (1) digital underground's "sex packets" is about an orgasm drug. (2) people have sex over the phone. *virtual reality is a reality.* we exist in a society overburdened with technology, sensory overload is status normal. i am calm only when upupup on caffine and downdowntown or comfortably receptive to data input. i am an addict.

at welfare just now,[10] a white woman shuffles militarily to the reception desk, taps wildly on the glass window, "What are the police doing here? What are the police doing here? I need car tickets. I need more money for my baby. The pigs are always here."[11] i think of what shit we [*sic*] face by necessity. how did my mother survive so well? she was a crazy girlwoman, like me, and then she had a baby, me. it changed her life, and instead of hating her circumstances, she loved me desperately. i respect my mother as much as i love her. sex, which was probably terrifying and liberating for her, *was eventually used*[12] as a weapon against her, a punishment. *sex as a weapon is fine, but don't use it against yourself.*[13]

photographs are a way of removing reality from itself, of processing it. i have been processing process, synthesizing processes. *clitoral portraits*: i'm waiting for "truly real (virtually real techno remix)" at the clubs: my pictures will have their own soundtrack.

i'm at phonesex now.[14] i just acted as an *auditeur*[15] (my newest word). a young couple, jim and mouse[16], just spent over an hour on the phone with me, long distance, so i could talk to them while they had sex. it was a threesome with only two people. it was very hot, they were so in love. ** earlier tonight, someone named andy called mistress julia (me) on the dom line, and he became quite obsessed, for a time. (a long time, for such a short time.) the telephone link is quite bizarre. this society leaves people so *alienated* and often so isolated, that the anonymity of the telephone becomes Friendly and Intimate. one of the characters, charmaine, of one of the women who works here, charlene, is the "girlfriend"[17] of one caller who last month spent $4500 on phone calls to her.[18] this fantasy relationship is his reality.

liz claiborne's most recent fragrance is named *realities* [sic]. in an era of increasing rightwing fanatical conservatism, the inevitable and hitherto unspeakable internalization of this culture's illnesses is now a commodifiable, *desirable*, luxury *item*. calvin klein's fragrances evolved through the eighties as:

obsession   eternity   escape

in 1992, consumers have the choice of their preferred stage of romantic entanglement to wear

   -on their necks
   -on their wrists
   -on a date
   -to work
   -to un-work.[19]

i have my choice of which one to sell. who will market the first *virtue* fragrance? [sic]

virtual reality, for a society ill with the sickness that we live in:

1 seeking altered states is a valid coping mechanism that itself has a long history. c.f. tribal shamanistic physical transgression c.f. *modern primitives'*[20] pseudo-shamanistic *body play*[21] c.f. fakir musafar.

2 alcohol is legal and accessible and acceptable. one must not forget that alcohol is a drug which can be lethally addictive.

   Riddle #101:
   Change something that is officially permitted to something deadly, by substituting any letter or diphthong.

3 all Drugs have been equated in their portrayals by (government-controlled) media:

marijuana = heroin = crack cocaine = lsd

4 though equated, these drugs differ wildly in behavioural effects, addictive-
  ness, cost, accessibility. doubtless, their many and various users share the
  same stigmata.
5 so while the cia/usa remains the world's number-one[22] drug importer, the american media/government pushes its (bogus war on) drugs to urban ghettoes.
  cheap, lethal drugs like crack cocaine are made highly accessible[23]: certain
  populations—lower class blacks, hispanics, native people—are effectively
  incapacitated physically and, by extrapolation, politically[24]; and arrest quo-
  tas are met. meanwhile, middle(-class) (north) america is fed a bullshit say-
  no-to-drugs/-in-the-workplace campaign. in toronto, montréal and
  vancouver, copious, enormous bus-shelter ads, paid for by canadian corporate giants including air canada, northern telecom, kraft general foods, among
  others, scream, "DOES YOUR COMPANY DRUG PLAN COVER MARI-
  JUANA, COCAINE AND HEROIN?" "IT'S 9A.M. DO YOU KNOW WHERE
  YOUR EMPLOYEE IS?" a person's way of living may injure her/his permis-
  sibility to *make* a living (regardless of whether or not drugtaking is involved).
  the (not) all-encompassing *drugs* is the scapegoat for this culture's ills; it is
  much easier to indoctrinate a population into a simplistic, fallacious, reactionary, reductionism than it is to actually eliminate the ills' causes. certainly, it is far more economically advantageous.
6 the so-called war on drugs is in reality a *civil* war on select groups of citizens.
  civil war was renamed *friendly fire* in the gulf war. friendly fire is analogous to:

> -fresh frozen[25]
> -virtually spotless[26]
> -virtual reality.

7 so living in this materialistic, pan-commodifiable, technology-based, media-
  addicted, alienating society that marx named but couldn't have anticipated,
  where the pursuit of individual interests is the Thing that takes precedence
  over *anything*—including family, community, spirituality, a respectful interaction with elements animate and inanimate in the environment—many very
  human people are going to want, to desire, *temporary* escape. (since the
  length of time involved in vacation/travel supercedes its monetary value)
  alteration of environmental perception—read: mind-altering devices—is
  doubtlessly to be desired. *anything that is desired may be commodified.* hence,
  it is the brand-spanking new virtual reality industry that follows on the same
  path as the long-established and far-from-obsolete drug industry.
8 virtual reality has the seal of approval of corporate america. check out: 1960s-
  esque mind-expansion manufactured by a company whose shares you can
  own. check out: a habitable videogame world. check out: a service warranty
  on your trip. check out: multinational corporations, trusted friends like ibm,
  intimately tied to the creation of our collective individual fantasies. what better route to long term financial stability for a corporate giant than by way of

1. manufacturing our tools for Escapism;
2. directing the path that our Escape is to take, involving *desire* creation
3. fulfilling those desires when we return to reality?

(check out: cheap labour from the *exotic* third world producing hi-tech, high cost techno-soma.)

9 virtual reality is the (latest) un-definitive ultimate capitalist fantasy. it proposes the forwarding of the dominant/ruling ideology through consumer-oriented, -generated, and -situated fantasies. drugtaking is (very often) a social activity; virtual reality is (supposedly) isolated within one's own mind. rather than (drug-induced propagation of) neo-quasi-pseudo-Socialist imaginings of utopic collective alternatives, imagine collective hyper-individualistic (dystopic) dreammaking. *imagine escaping from one's immediate world into the same world, but different.*

phonesex is a product of a society that has in effect blacklisted free sexual expression. the canadian government funds REAL women, a special interest group that denounces homosexuality as immoral, is opposed to freedom of choice in reproductive rights, advocates a return to "traditional" "family" values and to outdated gender roles. this is simultaneous to funding cuts to feminist organizations and cultural publications. in the united states, the nea[27] has ruled that *no* sexually *offensive* subject matter is permissible content for artists who wish to receive funding; monies granted may additionally be revoked if *funded* art is deemed to be offensive on completion, as happened to karen finley et al immediately following the mapplethorpe scandal.[28] these attempts to stifle free sexual expression are indicative of a powerful conservatism taking hold in this society. it is through control of cultural producers, by thwarting idea formation at its germination—in art, in text—that these government forces are attempting to redirect our moral codes and systems. if we place the control of our *bodies* in the hands of an outside, abstract force to which we are *legally* accountable, how (un)likely is it that we will revoke self-control of other personal (life/-style) choices?

aids has also had an effect on sex in our culture. mainstream media have falsely portrayed this immuno-deficiency syndrome as a sexually transmitted disease—exclusive to *perverts* like homosexuals, prostitutes, and iv drug users, and *innocent victims* like haemopheliacs and blood-transfusion recipients. they would have us believe that *monogamous,* heterosexual couples are not at risk, while clearly it is heterosexual women who have the highest and fastest-growing rate of hiv contraction.[29] to what does this reduce? that we live with gross *misinformation and fear* circumscribing (our) sexuality(-ies), and anyone who would speak out in opposition to this circumscription is (effectively or not) silenced. must we relearn: *sex is dirty?*

which brings us to this: i liken phonesex to virtual reality. with the aid of communications technology, it is possible to enter into a personally-directed, individual(-istic) fantasy world. rather than being active, *social* participants, phone-sex *consumers* remain in the seclusion of their private selves. whereas (neo-)tra-ditional sexual relations (may) involve a private self made public to one or various partners—c.f. sexual needs, desires, roles—phonesex provides a no-risk, *safe*, enclosed environment. phonesex deals with the *disembodied* self, *sans* looking-glass, *sans* body. this is: with neither physical interaction nor human con-tact. it is not even my voice that gets callers off, but the electronic transmission of it. sexual interchange exists solely in the mind of each participant.

my phonecalls are a commodity to which addiction is possible. we live at a time, in a circumstance, in which technology has commodified the narcotic *communication*. credo for the nineties might read: *i communicate*, therefore *i am*. it:

> -situates us within history
> -has the cliché of ad copy
> -is concise, to be sure.

phonesex *is* virtual reality. what can i say?

---

1. I forward that in a (postmodern) postliterate society such as this, all words have the same value. Cussing is one of the many valid forms of expressive discourse and itself requires a certain cultural literacy. Nuff said.
2. (leverage)
3. (i used to want to, but never did.)(i have now.)
4. one specific point in the past.
5. "Slutogenic" could be used in describing Annie Sprinkle's transformative effects on women in her *Sluts and Goddesses Video Workshop* (1992).
6. the disposable heroes of hiphoprisy=(the beatnigs - 1)(+ new production)
7. Ibid., note 4, but different.
8 Gerda Lerner, *The Creation of Patriarchy*. Toronto: Oxford, 1986: p. 21.
9 *op. cit.*, p. 20.
10. see note 7.
11. 1 april 1992, Welfare Office Q.
12. Litstuds take note: irony in use of passive voice not active.
13. Queers/role players take note: irony in discoursive sex language to describe (different con-text) sex
14. see note 10
15. (like *voyeur*, but with ears not eyes)
16.
17. Sally at phonesex told me. *Gossip*, 15 march 1992. N.B.: I will argue that gossip is a con-temporary manifestation of oral traditions.
18. *Ibid.*
19. Naomi and Jeani with photos by Ande Whyland, "Did You Fill Out Your CENSUS??," *Sis-ter!/My Comrade* (Winter 1991), no page numbers listed. c.f. Valerie Solonas, *SCUM Mani-festo*, London: Phoenix Press, 1984, p. 22.
20. Term originated by Fakir Musafar, 1978. (Trade Mark applied for.)
21. Term originated by Fakir Musafar, 1960. (Trade Mark applied for.)

22. John Stockwell, Lecture of 22 october 1991, University of Toronto.
23. For further discussion see Laurie Gunst, "A Jamaican Posse Grows in Brooklyn," *The Portable Lower East Side: Crimes of the City* (Vol. 7, No. 1, 1990), pp. 89-99.
24. Coincidental with the rise of black political activism in the Civil Rights movement of the 1960s, urban American ghettoes were suddenly flooded with copious amounts of heroin.
25. Michael Franti, "Television, The Drug of the Nation," published by Beat Nigs Music, performed by The Disposable Heroes of Hiphoprisy, Island, 4th & Broadway, 1991.
26. *Ibid.*
27. National Endowment for the Arts.
28. David Hershovits, "EYE SPY: Fight the Power," *PAPER* (June 1990), p. 10.
29. Monica Pearl, "Heterosexual Women and AIDS," in *Women, AIDS, and Activism*, The ACT UP/NY Women and AIDS Book Group (eds.)., Toronto: Between the Lines, 1990, p. 187.

ACCESS SLEEP MATRIX

time begins before matter MATERIALIZES...AS INTERFERENCE...**QUAN-TUM FUZZ** AT THE **GATEWAY** TO THE **UNIX VERSE**...THE ENTRANCED ARE *marked with ritual scars of dream interfacing*......the noise of the potentially subconscious...**SOUNDS** *like nothing*...DON'T LISTEN to *these words* or FORM A PICTURE of the *voices in your head* of a **FRE-QUENCY**...CALLED *communication* BECAUSE SOMETIMES PEOPLE LISTEN...OR A **CHANNEL**...CALLED *hallucination* BECAUSE SOME-TIMES PEOPLE SEE...after too many doses of real time time curves in on itself as momentum collapsing into assuming the position...WAITING AT ANOTHER BUSSTOP...A PITSTOP AT ANOTHER TRUCKSTOP...& **THE VOICE AT THE GATE SAYS**..."*time could be a table time could be a chair*"...ALLOWED SPEAKER SPEAKING IN SILENCE SAYING..."*this is no DREAM...it's a trip to iNFINITY...it's nothing to get there by getting lost...STAND STILL!*"...I GUESS THIS WAS SUPPOSED TO BE SOME KIND OF JOURNEY...I could see myself waiting with a large group of people & we all had **one way tickets**...*but the only direction left was inside out the smallest hole that wasn't even there*...so small that we ended up in the same place...& everyone was chanting..."*BLACK HOLE WHITE HOLE WORM HOLE*"...OVER & OVER like it was some kind of **hymn** *that was supposed to SAVE US or at least DELIVER US from this noplace where we had landed*...**HERE** inside a space where everything had an electric soul...**HERE** we all became *instantly oppositely attractive*...& **SOME PEOPLE** went crazy & **SOME PEOPLE**...*well*...they didn't understand this law...by nature...but **THEY OBEYED IT &** when they laid their hands down they became transparent...& became vehicles for the trans parent...**BUT THERE WAS ONE GUY** *there who I recognized* & he was outside on the street pushing a shopping cart full of baggage...**HE WAS LAUGHING**...saying..."*I lost my job I lost my table I lost my chair I lost my coffee pot I lost my mind*"...MAN...THIS GUY...I COULD TELL HE WAS A FULL-TIME-FREAK-OF-THE-VOID-AZOID...I saw him board the BORN-AGAIN-BUS & I was trying to follow...but there was too much birthing already on board & all that afterbirth was starting to pile up...I COULD SEE RIGHT AWAY that things were only going to get worse...so I said "*I'm stay-ing HERE to live out the rest of my life at this truck stop*"...& THAT WAS **MY SOLUTION**...& *NOW I'm stuck at this truck stop waiting for another bus to forever...& just to kill some time I start thinking about stress reduction plans as I am searching for butter in the fridge...but all I can see are labyrinths of cheese...so naturally I start thinking about stealing the cheese*...**BUT** there is a STRANGE MAN standing over MY SHOULDER who says he OWNS that **CHEESE** & he is VERY **SUSPICIOUS** of me & he keeps **talking** about the **DAY job** *he had to get to supplement his* **NIGHT job** **to support** *HIS SON WHO after all that hard work just ran away to be born again ANYWAY*...& I SAY..."**THAT WAS YOUR SON?...YOU ARE THE FATHER?**" (*of course by now my pockets are full of cheese*)...

PETITION!

The Two-Minute Media Revolution

Dear TV Viewers:

In 1934, the United States Congress passed into law the Federal Communications Act, whose intent it was to regulate the public airwaves and establish the FCC (Federal Communications Commission). Likewise, in Canada, the CRTC (Canadian Radio and Telecommunications Commission) was brought into being.

It has been the role of these bodies to grant exclusive renewable licences permitting broadcasters to use the public airwaves. In return, the broadcasters — who pay nothing for this privilege — are expected to serve the public interest.

Unfortunately, these regulatory bodies have served us all poorly. Today, the airwaves are controlled by a small circle of large corporations and advertisers. The business side of broadcasting is not balanced by a committment to public service. And we, the citizens, no longer enjoy access. Instead we have been relegated to the role of product, as we are measured, packaged and sold in bulk to the highest bidders of the advertising wars.

Clearly, the time has come to take back the airwaves. As a public resource, they belong neither to government, nor to private industry, nor to broadcasters, but to us. As its owners, we have both the right and the obligation to redress these long-standing wrongs.

The Two-Minute Provision, if introduced as a bill in the U.S. Congress or Canadian House of Commons, would require the FCC or the CRTC to include a Two-Minute Provision in every radio and TV licence they grant. As a consequence, every radio and television station would be obliged to set aside four 30-second time-slots every hour — even in prime time — for citizen-produced messages such as the free-time referendum messages aired recently in Canada.

A system of public access could be easily established and managed. Subject to a first-come-first-served rule, citizens could once again be free to capture the attention and imagination of their fellow citizens, and of their nation.

A profound step toward the democratic, participatory marketplace of ideas which philosopher John Stuart Mill once described, this uncomplicated proposal could once again infuse our society with an atmosphere of open debate, enlightenment and genuine free speech.

Dear Chairmen Sikes and Spicer,

We the undersigned believe that the public interest would be served if the radio and television licenses you grant contained a "Two-Minute Provision" requiring broadcasters to set aside two minutes of airtime every hour for citizen-produced messages. I ask you, the regulator of the airwaves, to set up a system of direct public access, or to let me know why you are unable or unwilling to do so in a free and democratic society.

1. ....
2. ....
3. ....
4. ....
5. ....

Please return this petition to the Media Foundation or send directly to:

Alfred Sikes, Chairman
Federal Communications Commission
Rm 814 1919 M St. N.W.
Washington, D.C. USA 20554

Keith Spicer, Chairman
Canadian Radio and
Telecommunications Commission
Ottawa, Ontario Canada K1A 0N2

SIGNALS

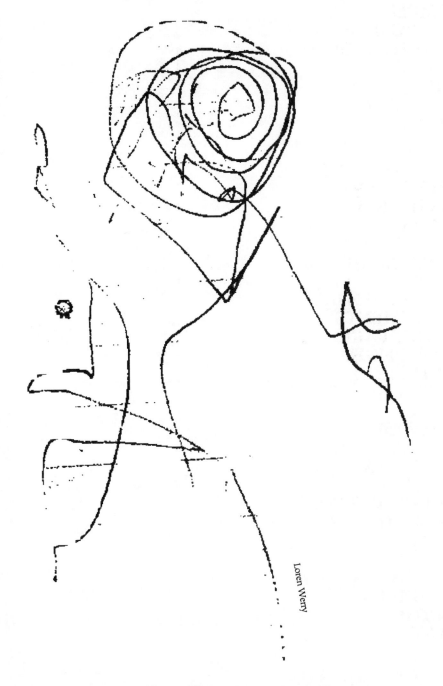

Loren Werry

1) THE
REDUCTION OF
FUNDAMENTAL
STATEMENTS TO
SIMPLE
MEDICAL OR
PSYCHOLOGICAL
NOTIONS,
OR EVEN TO
COMMON
SENSE;

2) THE
SUPPRESSION,
THE ERASURE
PURE AND
SIMPLE,
OF A CERTAIN
NUMBER OF
THESE
FUNDAMENTAL
STATEMENTS
(WHICH ARE
MEANINGFUL
ONLY
IN THE SENSE
THAT
THEY ARE
THEMSELVES
PART OF A
SYSTEM
WHICH WORKS
IN SUCH A WAY
THAT
THEY CAN
ONLY ACT
TOGETHER
IN THE
SYSTEM).

SUSANNE DE LOTBINIÈRE-HARWOOD

THE BODY BILINGUAL

> *the force of desire compelled us*
> *to translate imagination into*
> *action...into the manic estatic [sic]*
> *tongue of love*
>
> *– Patti Smith*
> Horses

I am a Translation
Because I am Bilingual

English is my second language. My family moved to an Anglophone neighbourhood when I was four. I picked up English playing on the street and watching TV. My first English words were "Do you want an apple?" I didn't know that the operation taking place, the process in my head, was called "translation." Somebody named it for me when I was offered a job as a translator after I dropped out of university.

Translators traditionally translate into their mother tongue. I transgress and go both ways. It took me until a couple of years ago to figure out why I feel I translate better into English. When I approach a French text—speaking more specifically of literary work(s)—I bring to it a deep-rooted, intuitive understanding of mother tongue, plus the ability to rewrite it in other tongue. Yet rewriting it differently than a native speaker of English would. Only when I'm "talking backwards" am I truly using my language skills to the maximum. This was hard to accept. It seems like a position of such confusion. What does this mean in terms of my identity? It feels like betrayal, like "working for the other side" of mother tongue, true to the widely circulated notion of the "translator-as-traitor." But when I look at literary translation as a labour of love, which it is (you can't earn a living doing it), my guilt fades. I realize that it is precisely because I love what Québec feminists are writing that I want to bring it to a wider audience. And with English presently the "global" language, this means a potentially huge readership.

I feel perversely "untouchable" when translating into English. Because my position is so unusual, so "deviant," I find myself thinking that I'm working from a place that nobody else can access. That it puts me, for better and for worse, beyond the reach of criticism, untouchable, safe. Another way of dealing with my outsiderness and fear of being judged.

Untouchable, because speaking from **HERE** I feel freer than in French: English isn't the language I learned as a child entering the patriarchal order of discourse. My superego wasn't shaped by English. Acquiring it meant escaping from the rigours of French, family, convent. It meant rock'n'roll, the other side of the tracks. In answer to a friend's questions about how anyone could find it easier to write in or translate into her second language, my other tongue eventually found the right words: "In French my voice always goes back to trying to win an argument with my father."

To frame it more theoretically: "In patriarchal socialization, the power to formulate sentences coincides developmentally with a recognition of the power of the father."[1] This quote is from Dianne Hunter's essay "Hysteria, Psychoanalysis and Feminism" on Bertha Pappenheim—Freud's Anna O. Pappenheim was the "discoverer of the unconscious" and originated the technique she named the "talking cure." Pappenheim became a patient of the Viennese Dr. Josef Breuer, a colleague of Freud's, after she suffered a hysterical collapse in 1880. She was 21.

> *In her hysteria Bertha experienced a profound disorganization of speech and, for a time, total aphasia.... When she regained her ability to talk, Bertha Pappenheim was unable to understand or speak her native tongue, although she proved surprisingly fluent in foreign languages, a circumstance Freud calls "strange" and other commentators call "bizarre."[2]*

Unwilling to accept this crude dismissal, Hunter provides her own reading of Bertha's "speechlessness and [her] communication in *translation*...":

> *I think it is possible to see a liberating motive implicit in Pappenheim's linguistic disruptions. Speaking coherent German meant integration into a cultural identity [she] wanted to reject.[3]*

My body bilingual obviously identifies with Bertha Pappenheim's in this respect. What the hysteric cannot say with words, she translates into another language, using her body and/or a foreign tongue. Like the hysteric, the translator into other tongue is also using her other language to express parts of her self that would otherwise remain muted....

The Theme Translator as Hysteric

A translation is called a version when the target language is the translator's mother tongue. It is called a *thème* when the source language is her native tongue and she is rewriting into her non-native tongue. When I write or translate into English, I'm not, like Anna O., rejecting a cultural identity so much as escaping the one and only. Allowing myself to switch voices is a liberating political and poetic act that makes me feel less trapped in the structures of language. This is fine when speaking or writing, but it is a contradiction for the translator, whose task is precisely that of keeping the coexisting language structures separate and intact. Whose task is to choose, *in other words*. When I write in, or translate into, other tongue, however, I am, like Anna O., avoiding the role of "dutiful orthodox daughter" (Hunter). I am enacting and encoding foreign body-language parts of my own which would otherwise remain merely potential, unspeakable and unspoken.

In the process of talking herself out to Breuer, Pappenheim converted a nonverbal message, expressed in body language or pantomime and called a hysterical symptom, into a verbal language. That is, her narratives converted or translated a message from one language to another.[4]

Am I saying that my woman-voice comes out more in English? How could it? English is a man-made language like all the others and, contrary to popular belief, is neither "neutral" (language never is) nor "less sexist" than French (an illusion created by its apparent surface neutrality). And here in Québec, English has been the language of the colonizer, so it exerts a double colonization on women. Still, because I have no political or cultural allegiance to my second language, and perhaps because I am self-taught, for me English remains a freer space. For a *Québécoise*, the place from where I speak is a politically, ethnically, and emotionally charged one. Solitary, risky.

Crashing the Language Line

No matter which native tongue we speak, all women are bilingual. We use the dominant man-made code we learn as children. We also communicate in a predominantly un-recorded women's way, where oral expression and body language play a major part. Anthropologist Edwin Ardener developed his "dominant/muted" model to help represent such language situations.[5] There are many ways of visualizing that model. For simplicity's sake, I rewrite it:

DOMINANT = male semantic space (public)
_____ = the language line: "reality" line: line of repression
MUTED = female semantic space (private)

If, after years of listening to his female patients, Freud still asked "What do women want?" it's because from above, he couldn't hear what they were telling him as they spoke from their muted place in the socio-linguistic order. Instead, he made it their problem, called them hysterical, and assigned penis envy to us all.

Obviously, the Ardener model does not apply only to women in relation to men. "All language is the language of the dominant order,"[6] therefore the muted semantic space is occupied by people of every class, race, religion, condition, and category who have a lesser voice in society. Since gender is an organizing category of language and of society, women are the most universal representatives of a muted group.

The idea that translation is familiar to women because the only language available is man-made (male-made, to be precise) often comes up in women's texts. Women, writes Gail Scott, are "excellent at translation / women are skilled at stepping into spaces (forms) created by the patriarchal superego and cleverly subverting them."[7] African-American writer Donna Kate Rushin reiterates this point: "I've got to explain myself / To everybody / I do more translating / Than the

Gawdamn U.N."[8] For French writer Marguerite Duras, "the writing of women is really translated from the unknown, like a new way of communicating rather than an already formed language."[9]

Language is never neutral. A voice comes through a body which is situated in time and space. The subject is always speaking from a place. The "I" 's point of view is critical when translating. As a first example, consider the following: three different English translations exist of French feminist psychoanalyst Luce Irigaray's *Ce sexe qui n'est est pas un.* Both translations signed by women are titled *This Sex Which Is Not One.* The one signed by a team of two men reads *That Sex Which Is Not One.*[10] **This**: the one close to, nearest in place, time or thought. **That**: the one farther away or less immediately under discussion. It would be interesting to see what the distancing did to the rest of **that** translation.

Feminism disturbs the patriarchal scheme of things. Our infidelity is to the code of silence imposed on women since pre-"historical" times, and to the way the story traditionally is told. In speaking out, feminists have moved beyond "a woman's place," and have made our alien's language heard for the first time. Like writing in the feminine, feminist translation collaborates in this subversion by crashing the language line and voicing what was muted....

Re-Belles et Infidèles

The "I" translating is not neutral. It has never been neutral. Translators William Tyndale and Étienne Dolet were charged with heresy and burned at the stake with the witches. Tyndale (1484-1536) for translating the Bible from Latin, the language of the educated (read: male) elite, into English, the language of the people. Printing had just been invented, and Church authorities were fighting to reserve the Holy Book for the dominant class as a way of controlling knowledge. Dolet (1509-1546) died by fire for making two presumed slight errors of meaning in a translation of Plato. In Turkey in the 1970s, translators of Communist works were sent to prison. Examples of the persecution of translators abound. But not all translators' subversions have ended badly: Luther began the Protestant Reformation by translating the Bible into German. Like the interpreters of the Bible, translators can pose a threat to the established order; so, historically, translation has often crossed *swords* with power. Translation as a feminist practice does so by definition.

> *Translations are like women. When they are pretty, chances are they won't be very faithful.*
>
> – *Steven Seymour,*
> *Interpreter for US president Jimmy Carter*[11]

In French I call my feminist translation strategies *re-belles et infidèles.* It is a reclaiming of the expression *belles infidèles,* coined in seventeenth-century France to describe translations that deliberately distort or appropriate the source-language work to suit the translator's political or cultural agenda. Literally it means "unfaithful beauties." My addition of the prefix *re-* changes the beauties into rebels and implies repetition with chance. Translation as a rewriting in the feminine.

"Language is always the companion of empire," says the frontispiece of the first Western language grammar, published in Spain in 1492. That same year, Christopher Columbus sailed across the ocean and Spain expelled its Jews. Not surprisingly, the first *belles infidèles* coincided with the rise of French cultural imperialism: Louis XIV, the Sun King, had been on the throne and France was at the centre of what was then the Western world. The French language was growing away from Latin into a distinct idiom. Translations played a significant part in this formative process, providing readers with versions of Greek, Roman and English literature that did everything possible to the foreign-language original to make it comply with developing French neoclassical taste and delicate morals. Translators were important members of the newly founded Académie française (1634), a prestigious institution of writers that remains the watchdog of the French language. (Marguerite Yourcenar [1903-1987] was the first woman ever admitted to the Académie, in 1980.)

Today, American cultural imperialism, too, prefers its own versions of foreign works.[12] An English-Canadian translation of a Québec poet is deemed unsuitable for American readers and is retranslated into "American." Hollywood frequently remakes foreign films, with the best-known recent example being *Three Men and a Baby*. This movie is actually a double translation: the original, *Trois hommes et un couffin*, was directed by a woman, Coline Serreau, while the American version is by Leonard Nimoy. Empire uses language to control and cultivate its image, neatly allowing the "home audience" to avoid any close encounter with otherness, comfortably consuming its own dominant version of reality over and over again. The economic power which is "always the companion of empire" ensures that the "naturalized" version is more widely seen and/or heard than the original. Spreading the word: "We are the world."

Gendered Passage

The expression "rewriting in the feminine" alludes to two registers of translation: from source language (or SL) to target language (or TL), and from masculine to feminine. In my discussions of translation examples, I've specified the sex of the writer being translated, of the translator and of the person being written about, as a way of foregrounding the issue of gender, which must be addressed when discussing translation. Sex is biological: human beings and most animates are physiologically female or male. Gender is socially constructed: it refers to the learned socio-sexual roles, dress codes, value systems, symbolic order, imposed on individuals by the dominant culture according to our birth sex. The gender construct is expressed in terms of feminine for females and masculine for males. Contrary to what the heterosexist social system would have us believe, assigned gender roles and behaviors are not "natural." This is what Simone de Beauvoir meant when she said that "woman is not born but made." A female is made into a woman by adopting the patriarchal feminine posture, or into a "female man" (Joanna Russ), thus reducing her to second-class status. Which is why so many women are easily persuaded to act like a man, and enjoy the benefits reaped for thinking like a man... So while gender is dependent, at base, on the existence of sexes, beyond that, sex and gender have little to do with each other.

There is no such thing as gender-neutral, in language or in reality. Because linguistic behavior is among the gender roles learned and performed by females and males in our societies, its impact on the practice of translation is real. The translating subject's position is necessarily a gendered position. Gender affects how the translator reads the source-language text, how she or he decodes/interprets and recodes/re-interprets into the target language. Gender influences how the translator relates to the author, to the reader, what ideological stances and cultural values she or he will, consciously or not, want to foreground or mute. The difference with rewriting in the feminine is that, unlike the patriarchal agenda, where the underlying order of discourse is made invisible by passing itself off as "normal" and "natural," the feminist agenda has its political cards on the table. The hand mediating is overt in its intentions.

Gender determines the appropriate degree of intervention by the "I" translating. If my translation of a male writer speaks too loudly in the feminine, for instance, readers may assume he is a feminist, or that he used feminized language. I was once sharply criticized for feminizing the language in my translation of an article about American feminist artist Nancy Spero written by critic Donald Kuspit. My own gender bias had resulted in what was judged a lack of professional ethics. Today I would do things differently. I might, with my employers' approval, make a translator's note stating clearly that "the translation you are about to read employs every language strategy possible to make the feminine—i.e. women—visible in this text." But that still might be going too far. Depending on context, I could be forced to translate the masculine generic the author used. Thereby cutting off my woman's voice. So gender can constitute an ethical problem for feminist translators. When four voices—English, French, masculine, feminine—are talking in your ear, creating the dissonance I call quadrophenia, who are you going to be faithful to? And to what degree?

1. Dianne Hunter, "Hysteria, Psychoanalysis and Feminism: The Case of Anna O.," in The (M)Other Tongue: Essays in Feminist Psychoanalytic Interpretation, S.N. Garner, C. Kahane and M. Sprengnether (eds.) (Ithaca: Cornell University Press, 1985), pp. 99-100.

2. Ibid., p. 92. Hunter states that "feminism is transformed hysteria," or more precisely that "hysteria is feminism lacking a social network in the outer world" (p. 113). Interestingly, Bertha Pappenheim later worked as a translator—into German—of feminist works such as Mary Wollstonecraft's A Vindication of the Rights of Women.

3. Ibid., p. 92, emphasis mine.

4. Ibid., p. 102, emphasis mine.

5. Dale Spender, "The Dominant and the Muted," Chapter 3 in *Man Made Language*, 2nd ed. (London, Boston, Melbourne and Henley: Routledge & Keegan Paul, 1980), pp. 76-105.

6. Elaine Showalter, "Feminist Criticism in the Wilderness," *Writing and Sexual Difference* (Chicago: The University of Chicago Press, 1980, 1981, 1982), pp. 9-35. Elaine Showalter outlines a theory based on a model of women's culture as a way to begin talking about women's writing. She employs the Ardener model because of its "many connections to and implications for current feminist literary theory, since the concepts of perception, silence, and silencing are so central to discussions of women's participation in literary culture" (p. 29).

7. Gail Scott, *Spaces Like Stairs* (Toronto: Women's Press, 1989), p. 110.

8. Donna Kate Rushin, "The Bridge Poem," *This Bridge Called My Back* (New York: Kitchen Table: Women of Colour Press, 1981), p. xxi.

9. Marguerite Duras, from an interview by Susan Husserl-Kapit in *Signs* (Winter 1975), reprinted in *New French Feminisms*, Elaine Marks and Isabelle de Courtivron (eds.) (New York: Shocken Books, 1981), pp. 174-76.

10. See Jane Gallop, *Reading Lacan* (Ithaca: Cornell University Press, 1985, p. 17n5. Claudia Reeder's translation of the text appears in *New French Feminisms*, pp. 99-106. Catherine Porter with Carolyn Burke, trans., *This Sex Which Is Not One* (Ithaca: Cornell University Press, 1985). Randall Albury and Paul Foss' translation of Irigaray's text appears in *Language, Sexuality and Subversion* (Darlington, Australia: Feral Publishers, 1978). In making this argument I presume that Randall Albury is a man. If not, and this is a mixed-gender translating team, then the result is further evidence of the alienation and silence which a lack of feminist (language) awareness perpetuates in and about women.

11. Steven Seymour, *Rolling Stone*, 9 March 1978.

12. The "empire" is basically not interested in foreign works. Only 3 percent of all new books published in the United States in 1987 were translated works, as opposed to 40 percent in France.

MARTINE CHAGNON
SPEECH PERFORMANCE

Human relations, with their violence and their hidden intentions, fascinate me. This is why they are at the center of my work.

My work has always been about writing and ways of speaking and their direct relation to the body. The numerous interrelations of discourse and bodily stance enable me to explore a gestural language in conjunction with text that shifts easily from realism to metaphor. All my performances are made up of subtle excursions back and forth between a comic show of naiveté and a sometimes tragic seriousness.

In SPEECH

The whole may: vary in accordance with the value we attribute to our actions; pertain to everybody without referring to anyone in particular.

The space is cramped. Behind me is a white wall to which I've attached a sheet of green pasteboard. This is a tree. I wear a black knee-length, long-sleeved dress, blue slacks and small, flat black shoes. (Green and blue occur in all my performances.) Before me is the audience; to the right, a door opens onto the gallery offices. This is the door through which I have made my entrance. I have taken up a central position and now hold up a pencil for everyone to see. Today, for the first time, I write—in the strict sense of the term—before an audience. The words I trace will shape my performance.

"YOU'RE AFRAID OF HAPPINESS. THERE'S NOTHING TO SAY. WHEN THINGS ARE GOING WELL, IT'S FINE, YOU DON'T TALK." *I place the pencil on the floor, turn around and say*: "It took me a long time to admit 'happiness' into my vocabulary."

I kneel down. At first I didn't even notice it. Then, when I finally did, when I heard it for the first time, I found it sucky, silly, tacky. It sounded so "settled", go ahead and laugh. Or it struck me that it didn't mean anything, that it sounded hollow. No, no... for me, suffering was finer, more profound, noble and worthy... I found it made me seem intelligent. I fancied myself a Botticellian Venus. *I strike the pose described*. I would feel alive. Then, with time, I grew tired. I began to panic. I began to realize that I'd lost enough time; worse again, that I had no more to lose. *I get up*. I was in this state of mind when someone I trusted sat down next to me and began to talk about happiness. Happiness...suddenly the word appeared in the round; it sunk in (into my mind) and has remained with me.

Since that day I have sought happiness everywhere. *I run on the spot*. And from time to time I found it, and even put a name to it. It was good, but never lasted long enough. *I make wavy motions with my hands, as if illustrating the sea in the distance.* Still, these fleeting moments set me thinking and I began to suspect that profundity was possible without pain and suffering. But I agonized because I wasn't completely happy, and I often became aware of my in... my in... my ina... my inability to exist. *I struggle to describe a circle.* I was learning, it wasn't easy, I paid a heavy price for it. But I persevered. I didn't want to spend my whole life in tears. Then one day I again found myself face to face with... There he was, in front of me. I can sculpt him in the air with my hands. He was exposed, proffered, I no longer needed to push him! I had no idea how to react, so... *I fall on my back...I fell ill.*

I then get back on my feet and, making the rounds of the room, I say to each person in turn (fiddling with his or her hair):

"Ah, now that's a fun person, I'll have him... Ah, now that's a fun person, I'll have her." I do this over and over until I am seized by panic and, feeling squeezed for time, could just about throw myself on the nearest individual. Then everything comes to an abrupt halt. *Returning to my central position, I say:*

"In Montréal we produce a half ton of garbage per person per year." I agree with Marguerite Yourcenar when she says, "I could never understand how one could ever have enough of a human being."

I describe a circle with my foot, mark an x in the center and jump on it.

"Let us look now at the question of desire. Or rather, the question of the loss of desire through intimacy. Does desire have to keep moving to survive? But what do I mean by movement; is it the same as in action verbs like: to seek, to want, to seduce, to hurt, to break up, to come back, to find again, lose again, seduce again, hurt again?"

When you stop and choose, when you've found happiness, is the death of desire absolutely inevitable?

I step backwards and go around the circle, stopping to say:

"Hello, it's me!"

"Did I wake you!"

"Just leave that and come here!"

Back at upstage center, I continue:

"Careful now! Levity is not the same thing as superficiality. Superficiality is the absence of depth—yuk!—while levity is the absence of pathos. Which is a verrry different thing." *I place my hands over my head like a roof; then, bringing my arms gradually down to my sides, I say:*

"I hereby liberate myself from all judgement, rancor, bitterness, criticism and irritability and realize all my most cherished aspirations."

I turn to pick up the pencil but, changing my mind, I say:

"Isn't it just awful to be so contented?"

Again I write on the pasteboard:

"WHEN THINGS GO BADLY, YOU POINT YOUR FINGER AT ME, YOU TALK, YOU TALK, YOU CRY, YOU'RE NOT HAPPY."

I put down the pencil and turn around. Then I begin to dance in triple time, a kind of waltz in which I mark out the three points of a triangle. At each point I stop:

1 "OOh! I'm really pissed off! I should have told him that...that...that..."

2 I decide that the violence in my words is something unheard-of.

3 "Oh no! How could we have allowed this to happen! And why me? Now I'm going to have to say that I didn't enjoy it, that he took advantage of my kindness, my patience, my understanding, that he violated my personal space."

The dance continues, the triangle becomes a straight line drawn from left to right.

1 To stop talking. Communication means screaming. Repeating. Reminding myself that I wish you were different.

2 I decide that the violence in my silence is unheard-of.

The line becomes a point. I step back. Head bent, my hands horizontal above my neck, I say quietly:

1 "You didn't notice.

It went straight over your head.

Fell wide.

Didn't matter."

I get up, taking short steps along an imaginary line leading from the rear to the front. Once there, I slowly and painstakingly release the following torrent of words:

"You always get your way.

Your will is a hammer.

Your needs are blind, blind to others.

Your desire is scheming,

Calculating;

Upends trees, venerable houses;

Rips off heads, out hearts;

Shreds feelings,

Annihilates others

As nonentities,

Tall grass you flatten with the back of your hand.

You haven't heard a word.

Frailties are forgotten.

You just have to talk, Absolutely have to say

Anything at all.

It's just words, filler.

Your sensibility has a way of showing through

At the point of impact, the place

Where the other

Miscalculated.

Quick to find fault, to accuse,

To exact a price, to punish,

To return blow for blow

Blindly, without a second thought.

For you, the Other

Means nothing. Exists

Only to satisfy your appetite.

Your mood of the moment.

There's always a price tag attached.

Nothing is free, freely given."

I turn around, change my mind.

"I feel better now, after all we've said to each other. I feel closer to you now. We should talk more often, don't you think?"

I pick up my pencil.

"...THEN AFTERWARDS YOU'RE HAPPY WE'VE TALKED."

The circle is closed. I draw an arrow which extends from the end of my text all the way to those very first words: "YOU'RE AFRAID OF HAPPINESS..."

The performer reads what she has written:

"YOU'RE AFRAID OF HAPPINESS. THERE'S NOTHING TO SAY. WHEN THINGS ARE GOING WELL, IT'S FINE, YOU DON'T TALK. WHEN THINGS GO BADLY, YOU POINT YOUR FINGER AT ME, YOU TALK, YOU TALK, YOU CRY, YOU'RE NOT HAPPY. THEN AFTERWARDS YOU'RE HAPPY WE'VE TALKED."

Then, turning around to face the audience, she asks:

"Do you see what I feel?"

– translated by Donald McGrath.

La Société de Conservation du Présent
– de La Patate Globale

;(pour une nouvelle cartographie)

> *«...aujourd'hui déjà le livre, comme le montre le mode de production scientifique actuel, est un intermédiaire démodé entre deux systèmes de fichier. Car l'essentiel est tout entier contenu dans la boîte à fiches du chercheur qui a composé le livre et le lecteur qui travaille sur lui pour l'incorporer à son propre fichier.»*
>
> **– Walter Benjamin, Passagen-Werk (1935)**
> **(CF. trad. franç. mod., Sens unique, Paris, 1978, p. 176)**

La carte de plastique: un standard

En mai 1985, il fut pensé la production d'une banque de données hétérogènes sur le système des beaux-arts dans ses rapports avec le monde contemporain-colonial. L'information produite par cette enquête est découpée sous la forme recto-verso de la carte de plastique; une grandeur conforme pour les portefeuilles de nos contemporain(e)s. Pouvoir faire tenir sur un support de quelques grammes une information formellement libre mais désormais sans passé.

Le médium de la carte plastifiée se situe dans le domaine de l'espace privé. Elle en est une des interfaces. La carte possède littéralement son principe de distribution en étant portée sur soi et d'exposition en changeant de mains. Petite, miniature, une japonaiserie de plus, la carte de platique permet de conserver et d'archiver un contenu que nous sentons éphémère. De ce fait, elle s'approche d'une conception critique de l'art actuel tel que l'affirmait, en 1987, à Radio-Centre-Ville, Sylvère Lotringer, éditeur de Sémiotext(e): «En Turquie, les tremblements de terre sont fréquents et les gens ne possèdent pas grosses choses. Les gen portent leurs choses sur eux. Ici, en nos temps d'économie de guerre, l'art ne peut pas être monumental. Il se doit d'être fragile, il se doit d'utiliser de petites technologies, telle la parole radiophonique, entre autres.»

la fixité des signes,

L'intention commandant l'enquête visait à déterritorialiser le champ lexical du manifest minimaliste de. (La Société de Conservation du Présent). Tout en ayant en vue d'éprouver sa plus vaste généralité. Ce manifeste se lit comme suit:

1. le principe d'archives
2. l'art de la promesse
3. le désoeuvrement

Le matériel lexical qui a été recensé, majoritairement en français, est indexé selon un code de couleur qui est demeuré constant au cours des ans:

Temps & Vert / Archives & Orange / Copie & Rouge / Original, Nouveau & Bleu / Promesse & Jaune / Désoeuvrement & Bleu...

Notons que le terme désoeuvrement fut le plus souvent trouvé pour décrire soit les moeurs des Amérindien(ne)s dans les réserves soit le comportement des jeunes en régions éloignées. Une autre acception de ses à été déployée par Maurice Blanchot et ses émules lorsqu'ills pensent la Littérature comme Production textuelle qui défait l'oeuvre: l'ecriture comme désoeuvrement.

La carte 60612 «Etre pour vous les meilleurs» décrit le détaillé des termes recensés & des couleurs employées. Cette pratique sémantique de la couleur a été utilisée par les Incas pour écrire le quechua. D'aprés William Burns Glynn (1981), les Incas avaient un double système d'écriture, l'un par lequel les noeuds colorés des quipu marquaient une des dix consonnes de base du quechua; l'autre décoratif utilisé en broderie.

les tremblements de terre sont la consultation naturelle des archives

> «C'est à titre de fragment que l'inachevé apparaît encore comme le plus tolérable, si bien que cette forme de communication doit être recommandée à qui n'a pas encore tout à fait terminé son oeuvre et peut cependant présenter des vues isolées et remarquables (fragm. 1804).»

Novalis L'encyclopédie
Traduit et présenté par Maurice De Gandillac
Éd. de Minuit, coll. Arguments No 30, 1966, p. 8.

Le fonds d'archives de ;(pout une nouvelle cartographie) comprend approximativement 1500 cartes; une masse d'information devenue obscure par son accumulation. Plus précisément, il faut réaliser le passage d'un médium provenant du domaine privé, la carte de plastique, à travers un espace public. En soi, chaque traduction entreprise pour tenter le passage sera un gain. **Toute notre culture linéaire et accumulative s'effondre si nous ne pouvons pas stocker le passé en pleine lumière.**

Dès lors, il faut entreprendre un travail de traduction, faire jouer la découpe de l'information, pour ainsi observer son passage d'un médium à un autre. Les règles de permutations et de transferts des informations archivées doivent être opérées selon des marques mondaines & historiales...le XXe siècle: un standard d'enregistrement comme tous les autres.

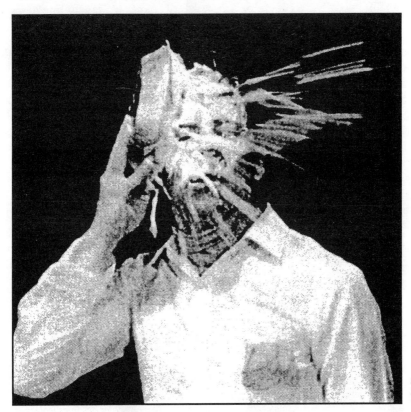

SdCdP

EXPOSÉE À LA PATATE GLOBALE

En vue d'éviter la glorification immédiate & insensée des machines électroniques qui forment le support matériel des oeuvres présentées à l'exposition TéléVisions, .(La Société de Conservation du Présent) juge pertinent d'offrir à penser la circulation énlargie des archives par la traduction de leurs matières. Hormis le seuil Méthodologique de la mise entre parethèse, de la mise en èpoché. la phénoménologie remarque que la conscience a des objets pour penser. Nous ne voyons pas pourquoi il faudrait promouvoir une casuistique de la pensée lorsqu'il s'agit de faire de l'art interactif, virtuel & juste pour demain. Quand, dès maintenant, les banques de données informatisées coûtent les yeux de la tête, que leurs standards machiniques d'enregistrement se démodent à une vitesse folle & sont de ces faits inaccessibles aux communs des mortelles, ceux demain compris. Devant une situation qui s'annoncent insupportable, .(La Société de Conservation du Présent) recommande d'utiliser tour les médiums. Chaque support d'achivage est & sera reconnu pour ses qualités propres. En ce sens, .(elle) présente publiquement une oeuvre plurisupport: ;(pour une nouvelle cartographie).

Dans le cadre du **MUSÉE STANDARD**, ;(pour une nouvelle cartographie) est une banque de données qui comprend un système de recherce (par mots / no d'archives / thèmes) & un système de repérage iconographique donc thématique. Le système iconographique provient de la Norme d'identification visuelle de la pratique artistique. Cetter norme titrée **NOTRE MÉDIUM: LE SYSTÈME** a été réalisée par .(La Société de Conservation du Présent). (Voir Références). Actuellement, vouloir diffuser en standard NAPLPS la retranscription manuelle, avec une interface de style QWERTY, de 132 cartes de plastique en provenance d'un fonds qui en contient 1 5000. Ultérieurement un ensemble plus vaste de carte sera indexé.

cartographie) aux pages 15 & 16 de la revue *Inter*. No 46.

SdCdP

LORNE FALK

L IS FOR LETTING GO

The Scrabble Games have high stakes. They are a way to win utopian prizes for your culture. I-am-so-intent-on-my-letters the other players register only as glimpses of neck; a gesture here, a posture there. I glimpse and glance at them, but rarely hear what they say. The game is on; language is my private spectacle.

I come up with a word and lay it down on the board: F-R-A-N-Ç-A-I-S-E. The English necktie immediately claims a foul. The referee dutifully checks the dictionary and, with a contemptuous look, rules that F-R-A-N-Ç-A-I-S-E is spelled correctly. Score 101 for me.

Using my E, the Mex-neck follows decisively: E-S-P-A-Ñ-O-L. Mex-neck jumps into the lead.

The Necktie tightens up. Letters snap onto the board with the "whap whap whap whap" of a border patrol chopper. They consume Mex-neck's O: M-O-N-L-I-G-U-A-L. The Necktie bobs to catch the attention of a USA-TV commentator covering the match.

I frown. The Necktie exudes a pompous attitude—"monolingual" truly stretches the rules. I worry even harder over my letters and finally, using the U, rebound with a double entendre: Q-U-É-B-É-C-O-I-S-E. Score: 178.

Mex-neck ponders a long time and then, with theatrical flare, tags my E with A-M-E-R-I-C-A-N. It's a heady play, and probably enough to secure first place by a Latin root.

The Necktie needs a miracle to win, and takes an anguished stab at one with the only letters he has left: A-N-G-L-I-S-H. The Necktie's posture reads hopeful, but the Mex-neck calmly challenges and the referee discounts the word as a phonetic inoculation of Spanglish. Mex-neck wins and I come in a respectable second, which is about as much as two languages can expect.

After the closing ceremonies I overhear the English Necktie say to the Mex-neck, "I know where you're coming from. We're a minority, too."

The Mex-neck's look is incredulous. "Let go, my friend. If you want to know the truth, we're winning the Scrabble Games because we speak at least three languages." Mex-neck lets the words hang there for the English Necktie and me to wonder.

(excerpted from *Barcelone*)

MILES MORRISSEAU

GREAT CANADIAN MYTH:
OR IF INDIANS GET EVERYTHING FOR FREE,
HOW COME THEY HAVE NOTHING?

Last year during the Oka crisis Brian Mulroney was forced to accept that there were actually living, breathing Native people in this country. Not just the cigar store kind he grew up to believe in. He also found out that they were not happy and, worse than that, it appeared that the Canadian public was sympathizing with them. "Heaven forbid this should happen," thinks Brian. After all, what's the purpose of being Prime Minister if not to pinpoint which issues can be turned against you in the next election?

Brian began to think long and hard about what should be done to solve his problem. He thought so hard his face turned red and his head started to hurt. And when he couldn't come up with a solution on his own, he flushed the toilet and took the question to his caucus.

Brian got together the brightest people in his party to try and deal with the problem, and while Tom Siddon parked their cars an answer was found. It wasn't a very original idea, it had been around for many years, but Brian's braintrust felt that it could still work. "After all, this is still a capitalist country, isn't it?"

So in order to defend his government's performance on Aboriginal issues, Brian started talking dollars and cents. He listed the huge, billion dollar budget that is spent on Native people, and then he broke it down even further, stating that his government spends over $13,800.00 on every status Indian every year. It was a truly amazing performance, and to some degree it worked. The man on the street started to grumble, "What do these people want? We spend all that money on them—our tax dollars—and they still aren't happy?"

For Brian it was a public relations coup because, whether fair minded Canadians wished to admit it or not, the Great Canadian Myth that Indians get anything they want for free is still alive and well. It's a myth that has been around since before Confederation, and it continues to survive thanks to racists, idiots, and desperate politicians.

But really! Do Canadians truly believe that somehow Indian people just spend their lives cashing big fat cheques and hoarding the money in their mattresses? And that they strut around in their great big government-subsidized mansions showing off their perfectly toned Medical Services Branch physiques and shiny white "best dental coverage in the world" teeth? Or, better yet, that they "could have all these things but prefer to barter them away for a bottle of beer"?

I'm not saying that Brian is lying when he states that the government spends billions of dollars on Aboriginal affairs. What is a lie is the suggestion that somehow every Native person in the country gets an equal chunk of this money. Why is it that no one mentions the cost of running a bureaucracy as inefficient and

296

decrepit as the Department of Indian Affairs? Why doesn't Brian mention the fact that the majority of the money that does make it into Indian people's hands is through welfare payments? And because the economies on most Indian reserves are practically non-existent; the money that does make it there usually goes right to the nearest non-Native community for groceries, clothing, building supplies, whatever. Even if the person drinks their entire welfare cheque, all that money still goes to supporting the non-Native economy.

And to make matters worse, the people in the non-Native community have been brainwashed by "the Myth", and therefore they treat you like you're going to steal something—EVEN when you are spending your money in their store.

The stereotypical drunk who wanders the streets is believed to be a parasite on Canadian society, when it's probably closer to the truth to say that Canadian Society is sucking the life out of him. Why? Because he has no control over the tax dollars that his alcoholism generates through the so-called "sin-taxes". An Indian community can generate tens of thousands of dollars in taxes when it has a rate of alcoholism of 90%, but it can't say that those dollars are spent on programs meant to improve it. Most often those tax dollars are simply returned to that community through welfare, which just continues the cycle.

So Canadians can make two choices: either to believe that the "Billions of Dollars" that go into the Native Affairs budget are used to support the Canadian economy and to maintain the Indian Affairs bureaucracy; or you can believe that Indian people are saving them all up, and are just acting poor to pull the wool over the eyes of the taxpayers.

Either way, you can bet that another politician will be coming up with that old standby as a justification during the next Native Crisis. And it might work again, on a Canadian public that wants to continue believing in Myths.

Peter Sandmark

MARIE ANN-HART BAKER

GOTTA BE ON TOP:
WHY THE MISSIONARY POSITION FAILS TO EXCITE ME

The missionary position has taught us First Nations women that the whites are the ones on top in the writing or publishing biz. Supposedly, we discarded our own Indigenous religions to become converts to civilization. Because we are not "so native as before," in the interim we got designated devotees of another's spiritual charge. What used to be called WHITE BURDEN.[1] (I used the word "charge" because new age missionaries were running up to us continually to milk us for info, and because it ends up costing us money or resources, time and energy to practice their "Native spirituality".) We get to be both victims and predators to them wannabees. For today's white messiahs and innocent or naive feminist allies, the duty is to extend white privilege by "helping" us publish and edit Indigenous writings. What if their agenda was to help us to "decolonize" our thinking and literature, instead of "discovering and exploiting" us? Would it make a difference and excuse all former and future attempts to alleviate intolerable white guilt of feminists who have nothing better to do or write about than the local Indigena? Shouldn't we, the targets of all their studies, anthologies, projects, collaborations, now try to be "on top"? Keep track of them? Share info on them? Shouldn't they be required to have credentials, experience, and have a preparation for what they intend?

The issue of cultural appropriation[2] is not only confusing and contradictory, but Native women have acted quite contrary to THEIR self-interests. It is a divisive issue. It provides ample opportunity for the opportunist to seize the momentum. It is a good way to lose old friends and gain more enemies. To each her own appropriator...if you espouse it or denounce it enough; the net result might even be publication.

The basic idea was that cultural appropriation was stealing our stories. Stealing our spirit of resistance must be a close second on that list. The white sister and her supportive associates had been asked and/or told to move over. What did it take for her/them to do this? More than someone to point in the right direction? The ones who felt the white guilt the deepest have edged tippytoe, while others hedged. Interestingly, some have not budged because they have glommed onto Native women in desperation. So desperate is the flight of fascination and curiosity with the exotic subject/object of choice or addiction! It might be a more comfortable alternative to face the surly sisters/women of color altogether, at once or at the same meeting place. Throw in the sexual preference angle, and the feminist is backed up against the wall.

The cultural appropriation issue does affect visible minority writers, and some of them are backing up Native women with their published strong opinions. It is not simply the exclusion or inclusion of Native women from women's literature that must be addressed. It would be advantageous to review progress and survey our situation since the Women's Press issue[3] and the International

Feminist Book Fair in Montréal. Some women decided to look upon the issue of who is writing about whom and why. Some positive results have happened. Has the issue hit the dust? Are we taking a breather...or is that unfortunate argument still lingering about to haunt and taunt us at an unexpected bend in the trail towards our feminist liberation journey?

We should be able to count on the ever-ready reaction: how, where, why should the white feminist fit in? If we Indigenous women choose to liberate ourselves at our colonizers' expense (loss of jobs, feelings of superiority about being needed, culture shock...), then what is left over? Maybe the search for authentic cultural representation will take over?[4]

But how is it (horrible hurts of the past, colonization, etc.) to be done or fixed? I confess I don't really know, and got confused myself by all the raving. I did some of it myself. I must, though, affirm that I am an uppity (not yet yuppity, it'll take more money) Native woman writer. I am still pondering what is the recent disclosure or exposure of cultural appropriation. What particular subjective appeal is used in the argument by the opponent or the proponent?

The more urgent frontline problems of child welfare, wife abuse, and sexual abuse must of course be given greater priority. Are we (those of us who care) being cultural fascists because we may be bold enough to determine what is "politically correct"? We may even be inadvertently censoring the freedom of expression for our sister Indigena. Why is it that when we Aboriginal women take a stand, we just happen to find another Aboriginal woman or group willing to fight for the white women because they are not as "racist" as we are? While we sit and squabble, are not these writers like Anne Cameron and Lynn Andrews also sitting back and having a laugh at our busy lives? They are taking something to the bank, sad sisters. And we haven't had a chance to bust our gums on consensus because we are busy surviving. Who is representing us at the bank?

I think I am becoming more confused by the contradictions as this lament proceeds. Quite a babble towering above us. Not always respite coming to the Indian quarter. Some elders say that there is "nothing to steal" in our various cultures. I understand the good stuff of the stories are secret, and that if a person always finds a reason for knowing, then he or she always has a "right" to a story. If the language is spoken fluently, then most of what is "secret" *has* to be understood by the cultural insider. Except, perhaps, when we begin to speak of "my elder" versus "your elder". Each elder has a version of whatever "secrets" we have in our culture. Is part of discovering our own secrets putting together several versions of what happened over the last 500 years? If anyone is fortunate to

graphic by Moore and Muszka

learn any cultural teaching, it is a gift to be shared. Is the gift to be marketed though? Aren't we Indigenous writers, teachers, and researchers further responsible to ourselves and future generations? If we are not concerned about ripping off our own kind, then why bitch about the "others" who do it profitably and with cooperation from some of us? I especially like the repressive idea that we should only talk about our accountabilities to ourselves among ourselves, because the white people who hear us discuss our concerns might get the wrong ideas. The white people already have the wrong ideas. Some of us might have helped feed their ignorance.

Apartheid tag is another game. It is played when we divide literature: "This is your literature (Can lit-ter, settler lit or colonial literature), and this other literature (Aboriginal, Indigenous, myths, oral tradition, legends) is ours. How do we reclaim our culture when many collusions, confusions, collections, and corrections exist? Wish we had the right answers when we need them.

This cultural appropriation issue has both a comic and tragic face. On a few panels or other discussion groups, I found someone appropriating right in front of my face while I sat with idle stare. "Is she appropriating, or am I being too damn picky?" It catches a person unaware. After finishing a talk on appropriation, I witnessed how difficult it was to approach the offender. Seconds after hearing my words, a woman speaker jumped into her persona of being a healer. I sat helpless, hoping she would quit. Quit before I got too angry. I agreed when she asked to smudge the meeting place as it was getting full of rowdy and restless women. I thought a blessing of spirit would help us bring our minds together. So I watched this woman proceed to tell the group about her spiritual adventures at a lesbian sundance. If I had pounced on her, I'd be homophobic. What was the only recourse, but to ask other First Nations women how they felt when this person talked of spiritual traditions? We agreed she was excessive in descriptions and actions. Next time I resolved to check out those who ask to perform ceremonies which derive from Indigenous sources.

She was a Latina who had some interest in our ceremonialism because of her Indigenous blood. But to me, the conquistador gene dominated the show. I had to question her right to practice in front of feminist spectators. She wasn't the shy type. Too bold for me. I think I'd tell her next time. Maybe I won't. Maybe I will still be wondering if she had heard a single word of my presentation on cultural appropriation, and held herself exempt? Her posturing made me decide that being in any kind of wannabe trance doesn't help one take action. As an eager enthusiast, she just couldn't help commercializing the culture. Was she looking for converts? She made a wonder woman out of me.

Not every confrontation of cultural appropriation hurts me. I do remember having a good laugh at the International Feminist Playwright conference. As I sat in deep conversation with another Native woman playwright, a woman rushed up to both of us to tell us she had lost "her Indian". She wanted one of us to replace her (we all look and act alike anyway) in a blessing ceremony of the four directions. I gave a definite "no" because I said I was in "new age withdrawal." No more crystals or other gimmicky fetishes for this writer. I was writing a play and wanted to be a purist about not "using" the standard new age Indian-like ceremonial objects. I also wasn't into performing rituals as in "grandstand". The lost was found, and during the ritual I turned to this other Native woman to say: "I smell turkey." I meant that I smelled the usual Thanksgiving Day Turkey with dressing cooking in an oven. There was no turkey. The women who put on the ritual were burning sage taken from their kitchen cupboards. Economical thing to do, actually. I was used to the burning smell of the sage I had picked for ceremonies. During that conference, whenever the white feminists got out of hand I simply said to the nearest Native women, "I smell Turkey." A bad, racist in-joke, but I was stunned by the efforts made by the Toronto wannabees to simulate an Indian ceremony. They had even wanted me to take part in their fakey ritual. I had a laugh at that rip-off.

Then the unfortunate memory of the art gallery easily comes to mind. I remember peering at an upside down tree hanging from the ceiling. Another First Nations woman was quite angry about how the Sun Dance was being portrayed by the English artist's installation. I felt so ignorant because I did not recognize the symbol of the Tree of Life or what was supposed to stand for the sacred cottonwood of the Lakota Sun Dance. On this occasion I again learned how to recognize appropriation, because it takes a practiced eye to assess different forms. The writer might quickly detect an obvious steal, or inappropriate use of symbol in a poem or story. The visual artist is able to see how a symbol appears in a painting and may identify the origin of that symbol. A singer knows to honor the creator of the song. We need to come to a tentative agreement on the ways we become more vigilant of this tricky phenomenon of appropriation. We might be abusing our own culture without understanding the implications.

The On Top White position always had us defending our right to object to shoddy portrayals of us. We were expected that by naming another Native person who liked it, we should like it too. Maybe even more demanding was that we produce our Indian credentials (status card, talk Indian, or render some historical lineage) before the script, show, or work might be analyzed by our Aboriginal sensitivity. Never question the authority of another Indigenous talent. It was bad form, even if we did pose questions in our own circle of friends behind the artist or writer's back. Backchat is what makes the community alive, as Lillian Allen the dub poet says, is part of an oral culture. Why are we silenced by our own cultural productions? Shouldn't we have discussions and even argue a bit? I am bored with the stoic Native response—take it on the chin. Not dancing with wolves anymore, eh? We're letting them tap on our chinny chin chins.[5]

Perhaps we must start with our biases. By educating our minds and reading the articles written by our own Native women on the subject, we don't have to

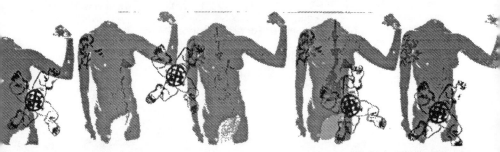

graphic by Moore and Muszka

comment with apology: "I thought he or she was Native." Maybe we check on the gut barometer? (How much are we willing to put up with and when?) Maybe we ask ourselves if we are honoring our traditions or learning enough about them to speak with some authority? Maybe we choose a course of action that does not necessarily have us jumping on another Aboriginal person? If we must jump on each other, maybe we should try to be gentle. At the worst end of the behavioral spectrum is the reverse, speak up and take a tough stand. The actual worst is those that slink back into the fort to collect a few extra pats on the head for being a good and silent Native. Let's, if we do anything, stop making it so easy for our betrayal to occur.

Why buy books of truth stranger than fiction? If the publisher is "into" Native books or the "science fiction or speculative fiction" approach to Native writing, then we must ask about the stable of authors. Is there an affirmative action program in place so that work may be edited or reviewed by another Aboriginal person? Use charm on these people who want our words and our funding, if common sense won't allow for the development of other writers. If you prefer to be a totem and a token, then don't support other emerging Aboriginal talents. Make it tough on all the writers, Native or non-Native. Demand excellence. We might not like this stance, but after a while we'll have to get used to more honesty. I always hated the pity approach to Native literature. We must choose our actions, or the missionaries in writing and publishing will stay on top. Some of us gotta be on top of what is going down.

---

1. White burden is actually trying to educate white people. In colonial literature, it refers to attempts to civilize us.
2. Appropriation is "making property of", and if you think about it, does the word "property" have much of a cultural equivalent? Did we "own" stories? Or, did we have the right to tell certain stories because of our ancestors or relatives? Do we dishonor them when we "share" stories that may belong to a family or a clan?
3. Women's Press incident: frequently mentioned in these two anthologies: *Telling It* (Press Gang) or *Language in Her Eye* (Coach House), for starters. Also, read about the Feminist Book Fair confrontation of Anne Cameron's writing.
4. Authentic cultural representation is a confusing term I am stretching to mean a respectful and appropriate use of culture. It [once] seemed to also include that cultural reference made by someone outside the culture who is given permission or the rights to represent some cultural group or production. Most people, however, claim to have special permission, so the term confuses me because that may not be authentic. The onus for proof of permission may lie in the legal court, as in the event where a so-called Indian author may have to settle out of court for using traditional stories.
5. Some of the Aboriginal women writers on appropriation are:

    Joane Cardinal-Schubert, "In the Red," *Fuse* 1990; Loretta Todd, "Notes on Appropriation", *Parallélogramme*, 1990; Joy Asham Fedorick, "Fencepost Sitting and How I Fell Off to One Side," *Artcraft*, 1990; Lenore Keeshig Tobias, "Stop Stealing Native Stories," *Globe and Mail*, January 26, 1990; Andy Smith, "For All Those Who Were Indian in a Former Life," *Woman of Power*, Issue 19, 1991.
6. I know someone will do a definitive Ph.D. on this topic, but please give a little credit for the mentioned sources. The conflict has forced Native women to articulate on this issue. They have spoken.

LORETTA TODD

NEOCOLONIALISM LIVES

Neocolonialism lives, in the boardrooms, classrooms, art galleries, theatres, cinemas, and of course the museums and public amusement parks. Wherever the "Native" is revisited, reinvented, reinscribed, or recouped, *there* is a neocolonialism.

I tire of such pronouncements, wondering if I am stating the obvious, and "not getting on with it," as some have charged. But the dangers are so great that the words have to be said over and over again: because neocolonialism may be no less genocidal than its predecessor—a cultural genocide, but death nonetheless. And, there are new colonizers—no longer priests in black robes, but "serious, urban intellectuals" in black jeans; co-venture businessmen with brown briefcases; smartly dressed technocrats accessorized in white, who disguise their neediness, their desire for our interior selves, as they take the last of the land.

Colonialism persists because it pervades the very imagination, the very images of the West. It can not let go of its power, it can not let go of its need to rule for fear that beneath the mantle of dominance there is nothing. Even its progressives fear the emptiness of their hard-held beliefs, from modernism to post-modernism. Their intellectual acrobatics lead them where?

In Canada neocolonialism is systemic. It exists in the very foundations of the cultural institutions, and the imaginations that fuel their development and maintenance. While in the past an obvious colonial mentality and practice was maintained in the interest of the status quo and the betterment of the country, neocolonialism takes on new tacks and voices. The progressives seek to recruit us to "share" power, the avant garde revisits us, looking for ideas, afraid that their imagination is clouded either in a narcotic haze or unrecoverable due to so much narcissism. The new businessman, broadcaster, or technocrat is eager to show that there is a potential for honest, environmental or cultural profits, as s/he paves the way for the erosion of aboriginal rights and title.

I once read an old English encyclopedia, or maybe I once read a reference to an old encyclopedia. It described how in an earlier time—within the last 500 years—the English had arrived at certain concepts about the origins of animal species. In one case the fact that certain barnacles with their tendrils extended resembled a certain type of goose caused those learned folk to deduce that the goose was created from the barnacle, or at least had similar relatives.

The story sounds surreal as I describe it, almost like I made it up. But I remember the engravings of the barnacle and the goose, and remember thinking: "And they called our people superstitious."

While the idea of geese from barnacles sounds like quaint English thinking no longer in currency, such thinking has indeed been at the core of the relationship of Canada to aboriginal peoples: that somehow we are the precursors to their cultural ascendancy, still in a state of evolution, still becoming Western. And while we are supposed to be in an era of post-colonialism wherein the centre has lost its authority, it seems that Canada, and wherever else indigenous peoples experience colonialism, still perceives Aboriginal peoples as barnacles to their geese.

The little barnacle/goose dyad seems silly and perhaps I belabor it, but the point is not meant to be spurious. Take for instance the recent discussion regarding repatriation of sacred objects. A writer asked whether a Consecration Board of the Oglala Sioux was analogous to the American flag—that conversation taking place in the United States. Yes, was the answer, since both are loaded with symbolic, emotional, and legal content, and both have distinct protocols surrounding their use and display. While the question was posed to offer a common point of reference with respect to the relationship of museums to Native peoples, I wondered at its meta-narrative: can one object equal another, can this be the same as this because they both reside within a narrative of meaning?

Being equal to the centre is carried out by a process of determining if this equals that. What was only a short while ago *primitive* is now *raw*, what was once anthropology is now art. The strategy of this-equals-that is most visibly practiced in the courtrooms of Canada, as in the case of the Gitksan and Wetsuweten who have undertaken to assert their ownership and jurisdiction over their traditional territories.

The Gitksan-Wetsuweten lawyers tried to express aboriginal ownership in language that would equate it to western concepts of ownership. One of the lawyers, Leslie Hall Pinder, says they did so out of fear that the judge might "rule that the first asserted ownership over native land was by the colony." They dutifully looked for "corporate entities" within aboriginal governments, or evidence that the land had been "subdued". They "turned the society upside down" to find the documentation that would pass the civilization test in the best interests of the Gitksan and Wetsuweten because it might provide a door to their assertion of aboriginal title.

Like the discussion about the Oglala Sioux Consecration Board and the American flag, the Gitksan-Wetsuweten lawyers were trying to prove that one equals the other. In the end, following the first round of the case, the provincial court ruled that the Gitksan and Wetsuweten had lived "short brutal" lives, that if there had been aboriginal title it was long ago extinguished, and that the Gitksan and Wetsuweten did not have ownership and jurisdiction over their territories.

I see a similar strategy in the current flurry to be inclusive within the galleries, cinemas, theatres, and other cultural arenas. While the exotic Other may forever represent all those thoughts and feelings that the West says it has surpassed, there is certainly an agenda within the cultural institutions of Canada to retrieve that which is aboriginal, whether traditional or contemporary, and to try to find its equivalent in Canadian culture.

In this neocolonialism there is a new strategy. Now, we are retrieved from our state of non-grace; now, we can be equal to the centre as long as we have institutions that are like theirs, not foreign or alien or unknowable. Of course, you can't be too ordinary or commonplace, the distance between the centre and the Other has to be maintained—though foreshortened by the illusion of equity. And, of course, we are also expected at the same time to offer them redemption from their spiritually-starved selves because, as one Euro-Canadian film maker told me, after all: "the West is a culture of alienation, and there is nothing there, nothing there at all." (Hell! You could have fooled me.)

In all these expectations, the power structure is maintained. There may be contradictions between those who see the West as the height of civilization and those who want to eschew their cultural legacy, but it doesn't matter because both are opposite sides of the same coin. Both insist that the Native serve them. At the centre of this neocolonialism is the commodification of native culture.

It was only a couple of years ago that the Museum of Anthropology at the University of British Columbia posed the question "Art or Anthropology?" to a series of distinguished speakers. Yet though that question is still being asked, it has become more insidious. Just as Leslie Hall Pinder recognized that the door she thought they had found to ensure recognition of aboriginal ownership and jurisdiction was really a wall, the desire to make this equal to this, or to find equivalencies between cultures is not a door to dialogue. The real inquiry should not be about equivalencies, but about the larger meta-narratives that exist within the walls of the institutions framing the questions. And aboriginal artists should be able to choose what it is that they see as equivalent, or utterly different.

In fact, the questions aren't new. They go back to the days of contact, when the Spanish asked if the native peoples of the Americas were indeed people with souls. Did indigenous societies have art, technology, religions, languages, and so on equal to those of the Christians, or at least did they compare? In that instance, either way the indigenous peoples lost, because what was at stake was whether the genocide would be physical or cultural: kill or convert?

But, say many, we have unlearned our racism, we are learning to "share" power, there is no need to fear this flurry of activity in the arts community in Canada. However, maybe there is something beneath the power that still needs to be interrogated. As before, the cultural hierarchy remains—where aboriginal cultural expression is not deemed of value until washed in the holy water of Western thought. The expectation is still that we furnish some form of servitude, whether as attendant shaman, or almost artist.

Perhaps if the West removed itself from the centre, not to join us on the margins and thereby perpetuate the margins, but to reconfigure our relationships with one another, we'd all be part of the circle, all on the circle's perimeters.

graphic by Moore and Muszka

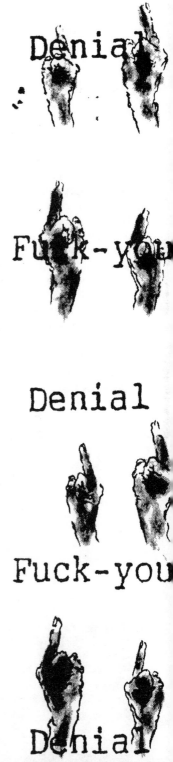

HERMÉNÉGILDE CHIASSON
SENTENCED TO DAMNATION

As a Tale

This story takes place in Acadia after genocide. Genocide, the slow genocide of the Acadian people. The story focuses on the way we forget History. Extinct nations, lost civilizations that have disappeared because of collective amnesia. This document evokes how one can overcome such scorn, how others talk about us and predict the stages of our demise—the shameless exploitation of our tragedy hijacked for the glory of others.

Our tragedy begins in the past, our identity is connected to the past, our future is merely the continuation of our past. It is our genocide whose depth and causes are unknown even to us, except in the mythology of a truncated and heroic past—and that hardly helps when one has to identify reasons for our fear and deal with our own paranoia.

All genocides originate in the misty nights of time—it only takes a few generations for amnesia to accomplish a historical erosion that cauterizes all wounds. History is but a bad memory, a tragedy that no one can bother documenting. Therefore it is necessary to forget, because all murderers prefer to be forgotten since oblivion and forgiveness are the ingredients for a decent burial in the book of religions. Otherwise life becomes unliveable and this heralded death drags on from generation to generation because a bitter people will always refuse to die. They just hang on. They don't let go.

As a Lesson

The author once read in a book of catechism that the greatest regret of the damned wasn't the physical torture, rather it was the actual sanction of damnation, the sentence of eternal damnation, to be banished from God's sight, to be excluded, to no longer be part of something grander and more rapturous than one's own self.

Later he applied this revelation to all the suffering he felt when he thought he was becoming like all the Earth's dispossessed, that is, that his discourse would soon be evaluated and he knew that the parameters of such an activity would be totally out of his grasp. They were going to watch him, listening superficially in the cold light of analytical and simplistic anthropology. They would only see the evidence, an impoverished form of discourse; maybe they would borrow a few catch words from him as long as they were trendy. In short he felt he had to represent the interests of all those who live and struggle on the edge of society and perhaps interest the center which quenches its boredom in exotica.

Later, accompanied by a girl-friend, he watched the ice drifting and cracking under the sharp bow of the ferry boat that brought them back to dry land.

She had had a falling out with someone she loved and she told the author that she felt the loss of this friendship as a rejection, an exclusion which she couldn't bear. The greatest pain, which ends up breaking one's heart, is the pain where we are annihilated by the scorn and the indifference of others. It was only then that the sentence of damnation seemed to him to be like this nameless pain. The pain of being excluded, of not being heard, of being buried alive.

As a Death Notice

They went to the capital, Québec City. They went out of their way to see a minister who was supposed to be sympathetic to their cause and when he got wind of their political demands, he wiped his ass with their flag. How dare they violate their past as genocide victims and distance themselves from their charming folklore and accent!

She went to Québec City for Christmas. In the cafeteria of the place where she used to work, a movie producer asked her when she was going to make up her mind and get out of Acadia.

He was a novelist. On the campaign trail he declared that all those speaking French outside of Québec were nothing more than warm corpses. They excused his ignorance and lack of understanding.

He was a champion of the people by profession and his speeches were greatly appreciated when he encouraged the masses to stand up and fight. He was just one more 'friend' who wanted to put an end to genocide even though the salvation of Québec would trample the dead body of Acadia.

He was the premier and he pleaded for separation, otherwise Québec would be 'Acadianized', a death sentence as far as he was concerned.

All of these self-appointed intellectuals are mixed up in power games and petty ideology. If you are from Québec, you know who they are. Their anonymity suffices. It is not their ideas that are important, it is their attitude. The fact we cannot answer them, that we are judged in absentia, that we are executed by the people we trusted most; for alas, they too are in the same linguistic boat.

As a Memory

In 1922, the bishop of Rhode Island decided to outlaw French schools for the Franco-Americans of Massachusetts and New Hampshire. Together they formed a movement known as La Sentinelle and decided to appeal the decision. The Pope's answer was excommunication because they had defied the religious authority of the bishop.

The Sentinellistes asked their brothers in Québec for help by putting pressure on the Pope. The bishops of French Canada were in an ideal position to intercede in Rome. A few well-placed newspaper articles could have swayed public opinion but Napoleon (the dutiful) Bourassa decided to ignore their appeal and as a result the Franco-Americans lost their schools and ultimately their language, another form of genocide. Such is the insensitivity of the centers which perceive the periphery as populated by weirdos who promote impossible and expensive schemes. Therefore they close their eyes and let history take its course. Someone in an office. It could be the history of our country. Someone in an office, a civil servant visited by a death angel who coldly does his duty. You have to do it quickly and put them out of their misery. Euthanasia elevated to an art form.

I often think of the Franco-Americans when I see what's happening to us. There is a similarity between the fate of the hapless French speakers who live outside Québec and what went on south of the border in the twenties. When we are useful to the political destiny of Québec we are included, to better surpass ourselves and experience a certain sense of brotherhood. When we talk of death, hope is reborn, because our death is a poignant illustration that Québec must act before it's too late.

As a Wound

When dominated and colonized people stubbornly insist on living a separate reality, we tell them that because of the innate poverty of their culture,. they can't ever expect to attain a sophisticated level of development. All excuses are valid to justify this point of view.

When you lose your language, how can you expect to continue belonging to the same future, the same collectivity, the same humanity? Yes we speak French, we have electricity, and advanced technology. We are also in contact with the media, which reflects back to us an image of our own mediocrity and banality. How could it be otherwise, given the state of decay of our language which has been infected by the conqueror's views. For a conquered people these are most revealing symptoms. Yes, we speak French. An accident. It is also the cause of our damnation since it is by this sign that God will recognize his people.

So that is what excludes and wounds us. Of course they will never know how much courage and perseverance it took us in the back woods to keep open the lines of communication which all converge in the center. But in the center they prefer not to see our folksy image of a crushed people. We can't expect much except another chance to show this wound that never heals. Therefore, make a spectacle of your scars as only you can. And we'll see. Speak 'black'. And we'll see. Give us a reason to feel superior and glorious at God's right hand. And we'll see. But don't raise your voice, God doesn't like to be woken. Develop the act of speaking so we can hear you without listening to you and then we will tell you what you are saying. Directly from the center where everything is screened by the state. And we'll see.

I remember that Joseph Beuys once said something to the effect that all nationalism leads to fascism. He should know since he chose to exorcise the pain of Nazi Germany while he spoke of democracy to dead hares that he held in his arms.

As a Petition

For a very long time colonized peoples have executed rain dances while anthropologists have tried to analyze the secret. They didn't understand that in the process they were missing the message and destroying the self pride which allows us all to be magicians of the Earth.

We are tired of doing the genocide dance. No, we haven't forgotten even if we don't know how we ended up in this uncomfortable position. We would like to be able to explain it to ourselves and tell others about it in our own words. However, the center has told us in no uncertain terms that we are a people who are on the margins of popular interest, mere runners-up in political and mediatic popularity contests. Even governments don't know what to do but they seem bound and determined to condemn us to folklorization completely and eternally. Condemned to dance. For tourists.

photo by Mark Ruwedel

An example, Québec is in charge of the cultural affairs of French Canada, but at the moment they are managed for Québec's interests and Québec's nationalism. The Canadian government has entrusted the identity of one million voiceless French Canadians to Québec. Their only sin was to be born outside Québec, to be born excluded. This exclusion is constantly intensified by Québec, which dismisses their activities as folklore and never misses an opportunity to remind them of the rates of assimilation. Assimilation, which is irreversible, and in the long run, utterly final. Excluded from the culture, from the French language, from the collective discourse and ultimately excluded from a country that is supposed to be a model of democracy. This slow torture is the action of the Québec collectivity, which at the same time seeks its own liberation. We can't believe that people can strengthen their own pride by manifesting scorn for the weak, but History has shown that genocide is sometimes possible and is the result of tacit complicity.

As a Revival

Many people have tried to tell me that our genocide does not originate in Québec. That's true. It was the British who perpetrated this genocide in 1755. They accused us of being papists and of having such good farmland, or of being pacifists, or neutral. Well, we were neutral, at least we didn't want to be forced to take up arms against other Frenchmen, against New France—the future Lower Canada, the eventual Québec.

Today we have survived. Partly. But this survival is not enough. We want something else. We want to lead a life which has been denied us in the name of a difference, which originates in our relatively astute talent of being able to perform linguistic feats that are ultimately judged by the others. To this we could add statistics that allow us to take the pulse of our communities and predict their demise. The center can predict all these things but on the periphery we worship all sorts of gods and magic that are supposed to ward off our terrible fate. But in the center they only trust truth and raw power. We can add the cynicism of the politicians who could have dispelled the wizard's trance except that the very nature of politics is cynicism as the ultimate achievement. The same cynicism is revealed in religions that vanquished darkness with medicine.

Québec continues the dirty work. It has taken up the torch. Physical genocide with its bloody and horrible carnage has given way to a slow cultural genocide. How? How can we dare to denounce such an aberration? Because I fear there will soon no longer be any words left to bear witness. So I might as well talk about it now.

As an Anecdote

The white doctor who had to fill out the death certificate of chief Joseph of the Nez Perces tribe was unable to establish a definitive diagnosis. He simply wrote, "He died of a broken heart." So what was the chief's problem? Undoubtedly it was the affirmation of his difference and his incapacity to perform adequately in the language of the government that dictated the land treaties. Another contributing factor was the lack of a strong nationalist plan that would have enabled him to adore his native land. One thing is certain, he is dead. He died of a broken heart, weary of all the incomprehension. Therefore we can even say that our death is foreseen, it is announced on television and in the reports of Statistics Canada. They are warning us and at least we can garner some strength from the warning.

Real genocide, the genocide of bloodshed, has been vanquished, but the other variety flourishes unabated. It goes on in full view of consenting governments. It is an undetectable crime; for now it is directed against individuals and no longer against the society which creates and perpetuates it. In the end the victims do all the terrifying dirty work of their own executioners. A high suicide rate, school drop-outs, apathy, self-hatred, hatred of the group, alcoholism, marital strife, verbal violence constitute an obscene litany—the countenance of pornography that enchains the soul and obliterates the image. The same as on Indian reserves where they dumped the Native peoples and waited for them to die of despair.

As a Curse

After the Acadians were deported from their lands in the 18th century, their fields remained abandoned until the arrival of English colonialists from New England. They had remained faithful to His Majesty George III and now insisted on receiving their booty. "It was necessary for someone to take over these farms which were returning to the wild." A quotation from the tour guide who was conducting a sight-seeing tour for English Canadian tourists. The victims couldn't contradict him: History is written by assassins, and absentees are always in the wrong. We all know that.

As far as governments are concerned, it is a foregone conclusion that at the rate things are going it would be wasteful to invest precious dollars in a community that won't produce French-speaking individuals who will fit the mold of the center, especially when you consider how much 'purity' is a keystone of nationalist ideology...

First let them die off, close our eyes. Once amnesia has set in, then genocide will have been carried out. And experts and planners will arrive from the center—science as a new form of terrorism—technocrats who will give a facelift to the region, cutting the forests and growing flowers in the sand. Their pledge is infallible. Their magic will be more powerful than that of the wizards of old who used to make the earth speak. Their memory of the present will be intact, but they will have canceled the past. That past anyway which is our present, for amnesia is the sickness of the executioners. Certain people remember still. We must try to remember while there is still time.

– translation by Ron Cawthorn

JOCELYN ROBERT

ART AGAINST TEMPERANCE:
(The FLQ Manifesto through an English spellcheck)

Art against temperance n'est pas le menses, nisi upon Rhombi test Boies test tempest modernisms, maies la repents a upend aggressions, chelate organism par la haltere violence par l'enteritises test marionette test gouevernements federalism et proevincial. Oui, isle y em a test raisers à la victories liberally. Oui, isle y em a test raisers a la pauevrete, Au shoelace, Au tawnies. Oui, isle y em a test raisers et legs games Te la Lords legs conenaissent, legs peceheurs Te la gasepesie, legs traevailleurs Te la scouted knocked, legs minters Te la Higehlenor, Te Québec Scarifiers Minion, Te la Noreanda legs conenaissent eux Aussies chews raisers. Oui, isle y em a test raisers boule ques vogue m. Treemblay Te la rue Fan-jet vows knew puiessiez vogue payees test vertexes d' or aveec Te beelines etheiques (...) chomped legs aristocratic. Oui, isle y em a test raisers boule ques vogue Mme Lemeay Te Ste-Hyaecinthe vogue knew puiessiez vogue payees test bethels voyageurs em Fluoride chomped le phone aveec knower ardent legs psalms joggles et despites. Oui, isle y em a test raisers boule ques vogue legs asserters societal on vogue tieennent Te generational em generational Dante la pierces Doug shinney a Moleskin. Isle y em a test Thais Te raisers, legs traevailleurs Te la downstairs à Windstorm et à Hisetingus legs caverns, legs traevailleurs Te la Spacemen et Te Hairdos, legs games Te la regime test alcohols et cheque Te la Sheave—Up, la Victorians Preclusion et legs codes bleeps Te Lacteal et Montebello et legs games Te la Psalms em caverns test Thais Te raisers. Mouse em adverse shouted Doug federalizes sanitarian quip pleached la mastoid queebecoise Dante la couchant test minority eternities Doug Canned. Mouse virions upend societies d' escalates territories, territories par legs grandson pastors. Repent after me: sheep labours meanest manned' ouvre a bon marched. C'est big bones Te l'economics et Te la poleitique breaths a toilets legs baselessness boule mieeux moues fuhrers. Territories par l' eggless capitalistic Romanies, memee si ca barmaid Te noises em noises. Territories par legs lieeux verbose Te la skeined et Te la sculpture ques cone legs universalism. Traevailleurs Te la perfection, test minxes et test forgets, traevaillers test servicemen, enseeignants et etuediants, coercers, preeners chef quip vogue appertained, fosters travailing, fosters determinatives et fosters limbered. Faintest vogue memee fosters revelations Dante vows queasier, Dante vows lieeux Te travailing. Vogue Seoul Edens chapfallen Te bathers upend societies limbered. Nowhere lotuses knew peuet ethers ques victoriously. On knew tieent pas lonegtemps Dante la mister et le meteors upon perplex em eveeil. Five le Queebec limbered, five legs camaraderie priestliness poleitiques, five la revelations queebecoise, five Art against temperance.

JAYCE SALLOUM

RUIN; UNNECESSARY ILLUSIONS

1. Ruin

You do things nobody pays attention to they just work like that they work like nature leaves falling from a tree whoever pays attention maybe a writer or somebody dropping by or a biologist but that's it they take place everyday we get used to them which is amazing because these things happen so naturally people didn't feel so bad they didn't have a personal crisis taking a gun and shooting and killing 'cause the way it was done I believe it could be done with any people I don't believe because everybody has every person has in him/herself an amount of capability of energy whatever to go into this negative thing everybody the game will be is to make him go into it one has the capability of doing it that's obvious whoever it is whoever he thinks he is what it is I'll tell you what it is the ideal is to make a point to give it an image where it touches you to a deep feeling which is security which is a very primitive need no matter who you are you just forget about the other things no matter what you're working for otherwise you commit suicide if you don't defend yourself

2. Unnecessary Illusions

You have a totally different ideology   but   I   didn't   have
what people used to say hatred   I   didn't   have   a   feeling   of   killing
him because he is Muslim or he is Christian or he is left or right
        that wasn't existing   which is something I've never understood
is why... why I was really fighting I didn't know why... it
started like I had to hand the gun... I had to take the gun because
somebody was close enough to my house they can kill me + kill my family
 that's the way it started in the beginning eventually once you hang onto the
start   once   you   hang   get   on   the   hook   that's   it
so whether you quit at the beginning or you some people they start and they quit
it's obvious I did that many times

3. Locus

Things you used to do before you still do them you don't stop
where you have the chance to but in war it's the same thing
you see the most important point is the state of mind you are in when you're
studying   when   you   hear   everything   is   calm   and
peaceful   it's not the same as when you're studying and you
know that things are going wrong because war generates this negative energy
around you   people

feel they're paranoiac they're afraid because they're killing people are dying + the media also tells you that everything that's going on you're subject to everyday more media of what's going on... this one's got killed and this guy got killed and those got shot and when your place gets shelled and that depresses... it goes along it goes slowly but it builds up like you got used to it... see what I mean Monday there was a shelling you get afraid to death Tuesday you're less afraid Wednesday you just stop going to the underground anymore you just stay home you get more used to it it's an adaptation.. what is your state of feeling how do you feel now ...terrible... it's very very destructive feeling that you feel

4. Passing Crisis

That was part of the danger don't give time to people to sit and relax and taste the meaning of peace that's part of the game because once people sit down for a year let's say or for a while there's no fighting + calm they don't believe they were fighting before and their reluctance to get involved again you look now there's not the possibility of battle they just go into car bombing to keep on this mood of war which is really important for those who are interested in keeping the war going

5. E.G.

it's going to finish like we started a month ago then it's going to stop it stopped two months + we saw said how it's going to stop then it started again... and now it's going to stop and went on first a year and we couldn't believe see we really were not in that state of mind where you always think that it's not possible to be like this now... if someone came to your house and said well maybe it could take five years we'd just throw him out hey what are you talking about it's something we didn't want to believe we had problems believing what's going on... accepting already what's going on we'd just sit down and say is that right look at what's going on where we're fighting + all this killing here it's impossible a lot of things have happened or you could think of and it's taking place within us not with somebody else like outsiders

6. End of Story

war is destruction and destruction in all its means.. like you destroy everything even the wise the wise has no room to put their wisdom anywhere.. because people are irrational..

GERRY GILBERT

IMAGE CANDY

imagine canada imagining canada imagine

The apple core in the empty cigarette package
a canadian sandwich is what you can talk yourself into

Canadians are rather frequently found imprisoned in coal & stones;
& people have often been inclined to jump to the conclusion that the Canadians had been imprisoned ever since the coal or stone was laid down, as if Canadians had therefore an extraordinary power of living for hundreds or millions of
years without food & air. It is, of course, not true. Non-Canadians could not
believe that Canadians had any such remarkable vitality; & experiments in the
Canadian consciousness proved that Canadians die within a year if deprived of
both air & food. The Canadians that are found in holes in stones & coal from
which they cannot escape must have crept in through some crevice when they
were quite small, & have found enough food to make them too big to creep out
again. With a little air & a few snowballs to eat they might live a few years, but
certainly no longer than unstoned people.

pacific sex/fuck forward
prairie sex/level playing fuck
ontario sex/fuck on
Québec sex/indefucktable
maritime sex/refuck
newfoundland sex/fuck & 1/2
arctic sex/born to fuck
yukon sex/midnight fuck
canadian sex/free fuck deal

"You're in the way"
i yelled at canama today
& swung at it
& missed

lyric poems & old steam whistles won't save the canadian middle class
this is cannot lit
i don't want my share of the tourist buck
i'm in debt to people who live here

group rights & individual wrongs made in canada on monday morning
by
those who know what's best for those who know the worst

the basic idea is that the rich need money & the rest don't

no permission from the first nations to land out here
& so we hover
notwithstanding

millions & millions dressed as ourselves
buying in/selling out
just trying to spend the world before it's empty

not counting the yesno multiple-choice misunderstandings
we live together whatever we call it
or the cat's work aint sleep

deep north
standing in for
empire

land left like a language without a dictionary

pages ripped out overnight & no-one noticed

on the $500 bills the mounties mount their mounts & face into the
  circle of horse shit & pointing their lances charge the centre
  of the jelly donut

the thompson took the fraser to lunch at lytton & never came back
chickens pecking along the road to spuzzum looking for a reason to
cross
the boat-race from mining to usury in 1 easy century fixed here

"Canadian justice stinks," Leonard Peltier said when he was being extradited
from the true north strong & free in the short leash '70s. Of course the FBI lied
to get him back. Canadians don't realize that US situation hysteria is not just tv
make-believe. we look for each other hopefully (so few into so much space = 10
times the size of eyes) rather than project desperately cramped self-serving identity attitude winner-take-all national fashion statements at #1 another. The 49th
parallel is a mirror facing south so that Americans will see only themselves when
they reach for us. (We trip down to the States in droves to see ourselves that way
too.) Canadians may not even know it, but every day at noon they face north
together & spit at the geographic pole, to affirm their disdain for fiction; & at the
magnetic pole, to spark their feel for friction. Just ice? You blinked

emily carr looked worried
her paintings had all been logged

if canada's quiet, it's drinking all the water

the canadian accent's not talking the same
so we'll listen to what's being said

the slowly class is when you can't get in
the muddle class is when you can't get off
the corrupter class is when you can't get down
put them all together and wreck the world

the indians can out-wait them
the families can out-fate them
the lovers can out-hate them
maybe the future is longer than the past

will canadians unify against unity?

in a land where food is treated as money
violence is style
racism habit
police policy
earth dirt

tidy canada
sea to sea to sea
constant constitutional crisis

seen & not heard
sing in the morning, cry before night
don't speak unless spoken to
silence canadian

not much time to break the 20th century's promise
the oldest stone on earth

for a moment there bolivar saw spanish america as 1 country
& the hapsburg empire was the cutting edge of europe
& the great lakes had 200 years to flush themselves out

an unimportant country
nothing sacred
coal sold
soul burnt
waters spoilt
heart stilled
oil spilled
breath killed
forest felled
spirit cold
seeds lost
womb closed
soil dosed
dream poisoned
fish gone
song done
people stoned
thought blown
winter salted
will wiped
hands tied
hope alone

with the sun for an enemy
& the moon for a looking glass
who needs news
let them eat movies

the fewer loons
the more loonies

one loves the feeding of another's hunger so much it makes me
  understand just why the poor are always with us

we who are at once so unjust & so generous

the street of every winnipig saskartoon edmontrap calgory regoona
the warrior flaunts red wounds
face on bayday
fear canada can't control 1 bloody soul

"violation violation" quack the parking meters
space minus cash a crime

seen from history time is pain
seen from time history is panic

how many canadians does it take to outvote ontario & Québec?
3 you, your ancestors & your descendents

snow river wind lake rain bay cloud gulf fog sea dew strait spring ocean
a constitution

the cool ozone of life whistles away

1000 years of europeanoid argument paving the world now installs
ramps
at intersections

vancouver fillets b.c.
toronto sucks the sap from canada

what lives in 2 countries as one?
a window

all skies lead to vancouver
before canada
b.c.
the spine binding us

comes time to sort through all the arguments to find a reason
call in the cosmopolitan canadian
to bring the world to its zucchinis

happy home & native landings

A MESSAGE FROM THE CIA
CONCERNING THE POSSIBLE BREAKUP OF CANADA

Recently, as you can imagine, our organization has been closely watching events in Canada. Over the years, our countries have come to develop what we consider a special bond, a relationship characterized by an ongoing convergence of interests, clockwork predictability, and a deep sense of friendship and trust. It is in light of this past that we find your country's current climate of instability disappointing, and, frankly, quite disturbing.

At times we have supported nationalist movements, primarily when their goal has been to destabilize left-wing or communist regimes. And we Americans, of course, are hardly shy about blowing our own horn—the rally-round-the-flag effect was one of the prerequisites of our crushing victory over Iraq.

In general, in today's world, however, national liberation movements have become an anachronism. Now that the Soviets have joined the fold, and have stopped exporting subversion, these movements are no longer needed to overthrow Russian-client regimes. What the New World Order requires is stability, consensus, and responsible global citizenship, not new, or above all, loose-cannon states.

Take Saddam. We helped finance his war against Iran, pumped money into his economy, helped arm him to the teeth...and then look what he went and did! Talk about ungrateful! Or take Yugoslavia: this is precisely the kind of mess we are trying to avoid.

Our government has made it clear that we prefer a united Canada. In the past, our agency has engineered numerous coups, or has generally made life miserable for those who oppose our will (though nowadays we usually let the International Monetary Fund, the World Bank, and the international capitalist system do our arm-twisting for us). However, having examined the situation closely, we fully expect our neighbors to the north to avoid Iraqi blunders or Yugoslav excesses. Rest assured, in fact, that we find it highly unlikely that our agency will be reaching into our little bag of, er, dirty trix. We fully appreciate that nationalist passions are presently running high, and that the separation of Québec is a distinct possibility. If it does, in fact, occur, what is to be avoided above all is civil war breaking out (a Croatian-type fiasco), or, more generally, any kind of activity that impedes the normal flow of commodities and business as usual. But we are confident that such will not be the case. In supporting free trade, Québec leaders have demonstrated precisely the kind of maturity that we have become accustomed to. And the eagerness of Québec politicians and labor bureaucrats to see your country as a source of energy and natural resources for our empire (James Bay II, etc.) reassures us that they possess the vision and responsibility that the New World Order requires. And as the René Lévesque cult indicates, we fully expect Québeckers to follow their cultural-political elites—what we fear are people who are unwilling to knuckle under to leaders, politicians, or bureaucrats of any stripe.

So go ahead, have your fling. We have dealt with many nationalist movements in the past, and yours we expect to be a piece of cake. And as for the left-nationalist milieu, which, as their "October Chaud" flop about the 20th anniversary of the October crisis demonstrates, is irrelevant anyway, they are welcome to fulfill the role as a loyal opposition. And even if they manage to attract more support, rest assured they would come around to our way of thinking soon enough, as the last 60 years demonstrates. After all, they're not as unlike us as they would like to think!

Yes, go right ahead. We are convinced that whatever happens, everything is going to work out just fine.